Tina Turnbow

DAPHNE MERKIN, a former staff writer for *The New Yorker*, is a regular contributor to *Elle*. Her writing frequently appears in *The New York Times*, *Bookforum*, *Departures*, *Travel + Leisure*, *W*, and *Vogue*, among other publications. Merkin has taught writing at the 92nd Street Y, Marymount, and Hunter College. Her previous books include *Enchantment*, a novel, and *Dreaming of Hitler*, a collection of essays. She lives in New York City.

To Kitty,
Best wishes,
Daphne Merkin

Additional Praise for *The Fame Lunches*

"Merkin has exhilarating insights into the men and women she profiles, from Michael Jackson to Cate Blanchett to Henry Roth. . . . [Her] essays are adventures, veering in unexpected and profound directions."
                                                                    —*Slate*

"Neither academic nor journalist, these essayists find their roots in a style, sometimes aphoristic, that goes back to Montaigne, in which everything high and low qualify as ingredients for a delicate recipe known as sensibility. . . . She reads both books and the world like no one else. . . . Don't miss [*The Fame Lunches*]."
                                                        —*The Huffington Post*

"Merkin displays a knack for what she calls 'shining sentences,' along with bracing perceptiveness. . . . She is the challenging, self-revealing, and down-to-earth friend you can't get enough of."
                                                            —*The Toronto Star*

"Outstanding . . . One of our best narrative nonfiction writers. Merkin's voice is secular and modern and yet filled with some sort of ancient wisdom, and coupled with intellectual and emotional honesty, while maintaining a pureness of heart. That is no easy feat."   —Elaine Margolin, *Jewish Journal*

"Merkin writes like an angel, whatever the subject. Pick almost any page at random and you find radiant felicities."
                                                —*The Buffalo News* (Editors' Choice)

"No matter what topic, readers will be treated to mesmerizing prose, lively wit, and penetrating analysis; the collection is a joy to read."   —*Publishers Weekly* (starred review)

"Like Montaigne, [Merkin] writes to figure something out, not because she's already figured it out. . . . Essays that go down like candy but nourish like health food."   —*Kirkus Reviews*

THE FAME LUNCHES

ON WOUNDED ICONS, MONEY, SEX, THE BRONTËS, AND THE IMPORTANCE OF HANDBAGS

DAPHNE MERKIN

PICADOR

FARRAR, STRAUS AND GIROUX

NEW YORK

www.picadorusa.com
www.twitter.com/picadorusa • www.facebook.com/picadorusa
picadorbookroom.tumblr.com

Picador® is a U.S. registered trademark and is used by Farrar, Straus and Giroux
under license from Pan Books Limited.

For book club information, please visit www.facebook.com/picadorbookclub or
e-mail marketing@picadorusa.com.

These essays originally appeared, in somewhat different form, in the
following publications: *Best Life, Bookforum, The Daily Beast, Elle,
Forward, The New Leader, The New York Times, The New York Times
Book Review, The New York Times Magazine, The New Yorker,
Reading Room, Slate, T Style, Tablet,* and *Vogue.*

Grateful acknowledgment is made for permission to reprint lyrics from
"Look at Me, I'm Sandra Dee," copyright © Jim Jacobs and
Warren Casey, courtesy of Hal Leonard Corporation.

Designed by Jonathan D. Lippincott

The Library of Congress has cataloged the Farrar, Straus and Giroux
edition as follows:

Merkin, Daphne.
   [Essays. Selections.]
   The fame lunches : on wounded icons, money, sex, the Brontës, and the
importance of handbags / Daphne Merkin.—1st ed.
      p. cm.
   Selected essays previously published in various periodicals and journals.
   ISBN 978-0-374-14037-3 (hardcover)
   ISBN 978-0-374-71192-4 (e-book)
   I. Title.
   PS3563.E7412 A6 2014
   814'.54—dc23

                                                            2013048986

Picador Paperback ISBN 978-1-250-07476-8

First published by Farrar, Straus and Giroux

First Picador Edition: September 2015

10 9 8 7 6 5 4 3 2 1

Certain shades of limelight wreck a girl's complexion.
—Truman Capote, *Breakfast at Tiffany's*

Don't tell me the moon is shining; show me the glint of light on broken glass.   —Anton Chekhov

CONTENTS

INTRODUCTION:
TRAVELS AT MY DESK

So here I am, sitting at my desk, more than fifteen years after the publication of my first essay collection, still prowling around the contemporary scene in the manner of an armchair sleuth, dusting for clues, weighing the evidence, and deducing the who, how, why—and, not least, the *what it all means*. Directly across from me is an apartment building filled with people who are unknown to me despite being part of my landscape, just as I must be an occasional *Rear Window*–like presence to them. Downstairs on the corner is a Williams-Sonoma store, selling burnished copper pots, heavy Le Creuset saucepans, and a myriad of clever gadgets for the culinary-minded. I am not any sort of cook to speak of, but sometimes I go into the store in search of distraction and wander around, if only to marvel at the sheer display of so much inducement to labor. I pick up packages of Himalayan pink salt crystals and sugar cubes imported from France, eye the whisks and the knives and the mandolines, and think of all that goes into mastering the arts of cooking and baking. I have often wondered if the act of writing would be less arduous than it is—less of a lonely conversation between the self and the self—if it came with a greater number of ingenious implements, something beyond the limited and austere armamentarium of screen and keyboard, pad and pen, pencil and eraser.

Of course, there is no getting away from the fact that even if writing did come with more doodads—had more in the way of physical equipment attached to it—it would remain a luxury, while the preparation of food is a necessity. If we don't eat, we eventually die; if we don't write (or read, for that matter), life more or less goes on. Which brings me to the subject of essays, in particular, an idiosyncratic breed that lights up the eyes of some readers but has never enjoyed a good rep among publishers. One might argue that since there has never been a welcome time for essays—at least not since Montaigne—now is no worse (although, arguably, no better) a moment for them than any other. Then again, there are so many reasons *not* to write at unhurried, reflective length in the age of the tweet and other Insta-outlets for people's attention that the imperative (if that's what it is) to do so might be said to be an ever more valuable one, in need of impassioned practitioners.

It occurred to me while putting this collection of essays together that I write, in whatever guise, largely out of emotional necessity. This is as true of me now as it was when I first began writing poetry as a young girl. I still remember my debut poem, which was about the unhappy life of a Victorian doll—who was, as I put it in my wordy ten-year-old way, "neglected, ignored, yes, even scorned." This poem was eventually thrown out along with a sheaf of others, but that phrase has stayed with me down the years, the insistent lament of the unloved child I took myself to be.

I suppose that one of the reasons the effort to make sense of things when I sit down to write feels so crucial is that I lead my life in an incurably unstructured fashion, bordering on the chaotic, with the specter of attendant meaninglessness never far off. Much as I might long to be a person of orderly routines, I have spent most of my adulthood wildly discarding rules and regulations, some of them dictated by my Orthodox Jewish upbringing and some imposed by the characters, parental and otherwise, who raised me. Despite this—or, as is more likely, because of it—I have always been interested in trying to create shapely narratives out of the unwieldy material the world offers up, unraveling surface incongruities the better to detect an underlying pattern. To echo Virginia Woolf, I write to "create wholes." It seems to me that if I only look long enough and think deeply enough, what appears at first glance to be beyond fathoming will prove intelligible.

Although I have come to be known for bold, almost reckless self-disclosure in my work—whether the topic happens to be the terrors of pregnancy, the erotics of spanking (a two-decade-old essay that will undoubtedly dog me for the rest of my days), or my habitations on various psychiatric wards—in my life I am a cautious and at times fearful person, the kind who has trouble leaving home. (This might be as good a place as any to mention that I've never learned to drive and that I live within a mile of where I grew up.) I'm also a champion brooder, someone who circles her psyche like one of those infinity scarves, knitting anxiety and obsession together in an inextricable loop. Writing, for all of its being an entirely cerebral activity, is a means of navigating beyond my own confines and challenging my native inertia; it gets me out of my head, forcing me into unpredictable encounters, whether I'm traveling halfway across the globe or no farther than my desk. In doing so, it appeases my intractable and utterly catholic curiosity—about the ravages of divorce, the global disappearance of girdles, the lives of the Brontës, and everything in between.

The truth is I've been something of a bifurcated, high/low girl from the very start, as you'll see from this compilation, someone as intrigued by the seemingly superficial as by the culturally momentous. Culled from a body of published work spanning four decades (and more than three hundred thousand words of literary journalism), this book encompasses profiles, book reviews, and what used to be called think pieces. In pulling together such a diverse group, I aspired to create something approaching a stylistic imprint—what Flaubert once referred to as "an absolute manner of seeing things." These essays, then, are bound together by the sensibility behind them, informed by all its deliberate habits of mind and unconscious blind spots. If I had to define this sensibility, I would say that it's characterized by a certain porousness—an unfiltered receptivity to the comings and goings of the zeitgeist—as well as a cultural egalitarianism, a willingness to examine the vagaries of fashion or the meaning of lip gloss with the same attentiveness I bring to the politics of reputation (as in the case of Bruno Bettelheim) or the poetry of Anne Carson. I proposed many of the subjects herein to receptive editors, although in some instances (Adam Phillips, Alice Munro, Margaret Drabble) I had to keep coming back to argue my case in the face of initial resistance. Others, such as Michael Jackson and Sandra Dee, were suggested to me, and turned out to have a surprising grip on my imagination. I've also included a selection of my literary criticism, the genre in which I began my writing life and to which I will always return.

So, too, I've always liked to talk about the unmentionable, whether it's our love-hate relationship with money, our demonization of fatness, or the brute reality of living alone. It is my belief that this bare-boned way of seeing things helps keep me intellectually honest. What I admire most about my favorite essayists, whether it be William Hazlitt, or Roland Barthes, or, ever and always, Virginia Woolf, is the way their voices seem to emanate from the corners of the writing self rather than its booming, position-taking center. I like to think I have achieved some approximation of that intimate, taking-you-into-its-confidence tone in my own work.

I suppose a word is in order about the title, which came to me in a flash when I was writing the essay to which it is appended and later decided would make an apt title for the collection as a whole. I never intended it as a literal description—as in having actual lunches with actual famous people, although I have had my share of those—so much as a metaphorical one, a comment upon our obsession with celebrity and the ways in which celebrity affects, for better or worse, those within its halo, as well as those outside it. Sometimes it seems to me that the private life no longer suffices for many of us, that if we are not observed by others doing glamorous things, we might as well not exist. This may be a too reductive—or, simply, general—way of putting it, but what I know for sure is that our consciousness of fame has changed the equation by which we measure our lives and validate our actions.

Finally, my hope is that these essays, wherever you choose to pick them up, will provide some inner nods of recognition, a reverberation of thoughts and feelings you might have had on your own. Perhaps you will even find something nurturing in them. I would be lying if I claimed they were always fun to write, what with hovering deadlines and the jitters-inducing pressure to pin down—"create wholes" from—half-formed thoughts and hazy impressions with some degree of grace and lucidity (while not, heaven forbid, coming up too short or too long vis-à-vis the prescribed word count). That said, there is invariably a liberating moment that arrives at the end of this process, when all the writing and rewriting, the arranging and rearranging of paragraphs, has made the story as good as I felt I could possibly make it. At that point there is nothing further to be done but to send the piece out into the world, for it to be discovered—or, perchance, neglected, like my long-ago Victorian doll. It's a chance we writers take over and over again, against all odds, half-wishful, half-willful, alone behind our desks, scribbling into the darkness.

I

STARDUST AND ASHES

THE FAME LUNCHES

2000

This is a story about sadness, writing, the promise of fame, my mother, and, oh yes. Woody Allen. Marilyn Monroe figures in it, too—as someone I've thought about enough to try and rescue from her own sadness, after the fact, in the form of writing about her—and somewhere over in the corner is Richard Burton, with his blazing light eyes and thrown-away gifts, whom I've also written about in a redemptive fashion. Elvis never spoke much to me—too Southern, too baroque—but if he had, you can be sure I'd have tried to save him, too. What this really is, then, is a story— its roots go back to adolescent fantasy, but it lingers with me even now—about trying to save myself through saving wounded icons. Famous people, in other words, but not just any famous people. These were fragile sorts who required my intervention on their behalf because only I understood the desolation that drove them. I imagined having long, intimate lunches with them, in which we shared ancient sorrows. These occasions would end on a tentative note of self-celebration that was all the more consoling for being so fleeting.

It begins, I guess, with my mother, because it begins with my sense of not having been loved—or, to put it more precisely, re-sponded to in a way that felt like love—as a child. This sense of emotional deprivation, of not having gotten what you needed when you should have, is a deeply subjective feeling. It's hard to prove, in any event, lacking any concrete evidence except your own impassioned testimony, which is why this conviction elicits its share of eye-rolling impatience from people who believe that this kind of retrospective interpretation is a self-indulgent, fairly recent phenomenon, brought on by too much therapy or too much navel-gazing. Still, it seems to me to be a feeling a lot of people share, and I think it has to be given its due, even if only as a negative trope—a context of origins that explains all later failures or shortfalls. It can lead to radically different outcomes; you can become a serial killer, or you can become an artist. Jeffrey Dahmer or Kurt Cobain. (Interesting, though, how both of them came to violent ends.) Most people, of course, land somewhere in the middle: they try to arrange themselves around this perceived loss and go on from there, hoping they'll do it better with their own kids or that they'll find what they need with a lover or spouse, the dream of grown-up romance covering over the scars of childhood.

What it led to in my case was an imaginary life as a serial killer and an ongoing real life as someone who was afraid of (not to mention furious at) her parents but who sought refuge in writing—who kept trying to establish herself, firmly and concretely in her own mind, as a writer. (It's hard to think of yourself as a professional writer: I still think of it as something I do on the side, even though by now I make something approaching a living at it. I think this has a lot to do with the fact that there's nowhere to go in the morning when you're a writer, even if you have an office, except inside your own head.) As for the serial killer business, what I mean by this is not that I was furtively luring people into my home, there to chop them up, and then sprinkling their remains with Chanel No. 5 so no one would suspect anything because of the unspeakably foul odor emanating from my apartment. It was a far more mediated kind of thing, in which for a rather sustained period during my twenties, I continually aired the possibility of killing my parents on my then therapist, a gifted guy with a red beard. He tried to defuse my very evident distress by giving me every antidepressant known to man—this was before the age of Prozac—and he also used to

suggest, only half humorously, that I walk up and down in front
of my parents' apartment building with a placard saying, "Mer-
kins unfair to children," as though I were an underpaid worker
on strike.

I read a lot of books about serial murderers, to help fuel my
wavering but quite genuine parricidal impulse and out of a sense
of identification with their rage. One, called *The Shoemaker*,
about a father-son homicidal duo, stuck out in my head, because
of the atrocity of the details, which included the use of a hammer
to keep the family in line. But I also wanted to figure out whether
any good could possibly come out of this course of action,
beyond an extended prison sentence. Perhaps, I mused, I'd grow
strong and well in my little cell, away from the impositions of
everyone I had known in my past life . . . It was in this light that
I envisioned myself becoming a sort of Birdwoman of Alcatraz,
an expert on the mating patterns of the hummingbird. What I
really wanted to know, though, was whether my shrink would
appear in court in my defense, the better to explain to the stony-
faced jurors that I had been mistreated from birth and hence
was simply exacting my due.

The shrink in question died abruptly, of a recurrent illness,
but to cut to the chase—which is a phrase a friend of mine always
uses whenever I go on in my loop-the-loop way, in which one
dangling thought leads to another—what I think I'm saying is
that I was a desperate character from way back. Even when I was
younger and thinner than I am now, I was desperate, although
it's hard for me to imagine from my present vantage point how I
could have been desperate then, when I was so young and thin.
But I was, and one of the ways I tried to rescue myself from my
own sense of desperation, aside from musing about murdering my
mother and father, was to imagine that other people—not just
any other people, but people who took up space in the public
imagination—were as desperate for validation as I appeared to
be. I was a nobody, but it seemed to me that even somebodies—
somebodies who hadn't been loved enough in the cradle, that
is—felt themselves to be misunderstood nobodies, deep down. I

knew this in my bones, just as I knew that I had never liked that
famous poem by Emily Dickinson, the one where she trills in her
mysterious hide-and-seek voice:

> *I'm Nobody! Who are you?*
> *Are you—Nobody—Too?*
> *Then there's a pair of us!*

The woman had it all wrong, but what would she know, stuck
in those New England snowdrifts all by herself? The trick was to
get out of being a nobody by harnessing yourself to a somebody
who was, deep down, a nobody, too. *The trick was to give status to
your own woundedness.*

So I went and wrote a letter to Woody Allen one day in my
early twenties. The early, achingly funny, pre-scandalous Woody
Allen. After watching *Take the Money and Run* and *Bananas* and
reading *Getting Even*, I had fixed on him as my alter ego, somebody who dared to take up space even as he pretended he wasn't
taking up any. He was the perfect non-celebrity for a non-groupie
like me. It wasn't a letter, really; it was a poem, one that I had
written in a college writing class. It was, I suppose, a fairly interesting poem as far as such things go, but what I remember about
it are the last two lines. "You are my funny man," I wrote. "You
know you can be sad with me." There it was: I was a nobody who
understood the hidden torment of a great comic mind.

What can I say? The hook took. He wrote me back, compli-
menting me on my poem and pointing out that if you X-rayed his
heart, it would come out black. I had been right all along, it
seemed. Desolation Row. I rushed in to show the letter to my
mother. I shared everything with her, even my plans to kill her.
Now, finally, she would realize who I was, hiding my light under
a bushel all these years, this savant whom she mistook for an
ordinary girl, one of three daughters. Now she'd see: I was me,
which was to say I was more than me. I was the wounded icon by
proxy.

Time passed. I went from publishing movie reviews in the
Barnard newspaper to publishing book reviews in various places,

such as *Commentary* and *The New Republic*, the sorts of magazines where you had to disguise your heart under your brain,
where the price of entry was that you sounded as if you had
always thought in polished sentences and never, ever sounded as if
you were the kind of person who stood in your kitchen staring at
the knife in your hand, wondering if you should use it on yourself. I was living near Columbia, on 106th Street between Broadway and West End Avenue, no less desperate than I had been
when I was living at home, on Park Avenue, when I got a fan
letter in the mail. It was the late 1970s, the period of elaborately
plebeian stationery. Woody Allen, his name printed in bold red
type at the top of a brown sheet of paper that looked as if it were
meant to wrap an egg-salad sandwich, had written to tell me that
he liked a book piece of mine in *The New Republic*, about another wounded creature, the writer Jane Bowles. He added that
he wondered why I was wasting my talent on book reviews, and
I answered, rather primly, that I considered book reviewing to be
an art form and well worth my while.

I did, and I still do, but I knew what he meant. *Dare to take
up space.* He wrote me back and I wrote him again, assuming
a correspondence was now in swing, and he replied, not un-
promptly. There were promises of getting together for drinks
that were always put off, and he continued to send encouraging
messages about my writing, but I suppose he never knew what
I really wanted from him. I mean, I couldn't come right out and
say *save me.* I must have come close enough, though, because
once there was a phone call from his secretary, offering me the
name of a psychiatrist. His psychiatrist, I think it was. But what
use was that to me? I had seen virtually every psychiatrist of any
repute in New York City, almost as many as I gathered he had.
They always threw you back on yourself, when what I wanted
was for someone to come and knock on my door and say, "You,
Daphne Merkin, are hereby invited to lean your head on my
shoulder for ever and ever. You are small and wounded, and I am
large and wounded, and together we will create an invulnerable
universe." Or something like that. Needless to say, it never
happened.

I did finally get to have a drink with Woody Allen. It came years later, after I had written a novel, gotten married, become a mother, gotten divorced, done many of the things that are supposed to make you realize life is not particularly amenable to gratifying the wishes of the unhappy child you once were but that there are substitute gratifications to be found. The two of us had never completely lost touch, although there was a long barren period after he had returned one of my more inchoately miserable letters, filled—in those long-ago Smith-Corona days— with x-ed-out typos and splashes of Wite-Out. He had gone and scrawled across it: "I don't understand what you're asking me to do . . . If there's any way I can help you, please let me know."

I guess we were able to meet on slightly more poised footing after I became a movie critic for *The New Yorker*, alternating a weekly column with Anthony Lane. We had one drink and then another and then lunches every so often. I can't say it's changed my life, or even that it's changed my habit of coming late to everything, although I wish it had. I'm still a desperate character; I'm probably destined to be one until a ripe old age. In fact, it wasn't so long ago—four or five months ago, to be exact—that I leaned over the table in the fancy Upper East Side restaurant where we were having lunch and told Woody that under my sprightly patter and carefully applied makeup I was feeling depressed. How depressed? he immediately wanted to know. Quite depressed, I said. Did I have trouble getting up in the morning? Lots, I answered. Did I ever stay in bed all day? No, I said, but it was often noon before I got out of my nightgown. But of course I continued to write, he said. I answered that I hadn't written a word in weeks. He looked quite serious and then gently asked me if I had ever thought about trying shock therapy. *Shock therapy?* Yes, he said, he knew a friend—a famous friend—for whom it had been quite helpful. Maybe I should try it.

Sure, I said. Thanks. I don't know what I had been hoping for—some version of *come with me and I will cuddle you until your sadness goes away*, not *go get yourself hooked up to electrodes, baby*—but I was slightly stunned. More than slightly. I understood that he was trying to be helpful in his way, but it fell so far short. We shook hands on Madison Avenue and then gave each other a polite peck, as we always did. It was sunny and cool as I made my way home, looking in at the windows full of bright summer dresses. *Shock therapy?* It wasn't as though I hadn't heard of it or didn't know people who had benefited from it. Still, how on earth did he conceive of me? As a chronic mental patient, someone who was meant to sit on a thin hospital mattress and stare grayly into space? Didn't he know I was a writer with a future, a person given to creative descriptions of her own moods? Shock therapy, indeed; I'd sooner try a spa.

It suddenly occurred to me, as I walked up Madison Avenue, that it might pay to be resilient, if this was all being vulnerable and skinless got you. People didn't stop and cluck over the damage done unless you made it worth their while. Indeed, maybe it was time to rethink this whole salvation business. Or maybe I was less desperate, less teetering on the edge, than I cared to admit. Now, *that* was a refreshing possibility.

PLATINUM PAIN

(MARILYN MONROE)

1999

Sometimes I think we respond to Marilyn Monroe as strongly as
we do not because of her beauty or her body but because of her
desperation, which was implacable in the face of fame, fortune,
and the love of celebrated men. Every few years, she comes
around again, the subject of yet another revelatory book (there
are more than a hundred to date) or of a newly discovered series
of photographs. Her films continue to be watched and reassessed,
her image pilfered by everyone from Madonna to Monica Lewin-
sky. We will never have enough of Monroe, in part because there
is never sufficient explanation for the commotions of her soul,
and in part because we will never tire of hearing about the native
sadness behind the construction of glamour. The damaged creature behind the pinup, the neglected foster child who became a
blond vision in sequins: her story has entered the realm of myth.
Its unhappy ending makes her less the exemplary heroine of a
fairy tale than its cautionary victim—a glittery example of female
entrapment in the male star-making machinery.

Monroe was, of course, the wiggling embodiment of male
fantasies at their most pubescent, all boobs and bottom and
wet-lipped receptivity. At the same time, there was something
wholesome and aboveboard about her image that invited mental
pawing without eliciting accompanying feelings of shame. It's
this unsoiled quality that made her a favorite of American troops
stationed in Korea and enabled Norman Mailer to describe her as

"the sweet angel of sex" in the opening lines of *Marilyn*, a biography in the form of a sustained masturbatory reverie. And yet, as we well know, she was regarded as a troublesome type, both personally and professionally—the sort of woman who would slip away to consort with her demons as soon as you turned your back, and who wasn't worth the high maintenance she required.

Monroe's short, spectacular time on this planet—she died on August 5, 1962, at the age of thirty-six, presumably by her own hand—has prompted greater and more literary examination than, say, the life of Jean Harlow or Carole Lombard. Along with Mailer, the snobbish Diana Trilling weighed in twice (once with a review of Gloria Steinem's book about the star); Roger Kahn, the author of *The Boys of Summer*, wrote a book about Joe DiMaggio's ten-year relationship with Monroe; she has inspired a rarefied academic volume, with footnotes from Foucault and Baudrillard, titled *American Monroe: The Making of a Body Politic*; and she made more than a passing dent on Saul Bellow, who, in a *Playboy* interview in 1997, described the actress as having "a kind of curious incandescence under the skin." (This is not to overlook the endless words contributed by those who had access to her, including her half sister, her personal maids, and former lovers such as Yves Montand.)

Monroe has been treated by writers like an anthropological find, a sort of Truffautian wild child. The tragic circumstances of her death help to account for this fascination, as does the evidence of her quick wit, which always endears populist icons to the intelligentsia. There is, too, the fact of her seeming to be intriguingly unauthored—a multilayered personality in search of a coherent self. She was constantly looking for guidance, whether from dead eminences, such as Dostoyevsky, Yeats, and Marx, or from real-life gurus, who included Lee Strasberg, the director of the Actors Studio, and her psychiatrist Ralph Greenson. One can't ignore a certain mutual-admiration aspect in this, either: Monroe was one of the few babes to be drawn to brainy men, specifically writers. When she was put in Payne Whitney Psychiatric Clinic for four days in 1961, she was reading Freud's letters (she had already read Ernest Jones's biography of him), and she

herself was a fluid letter writer who was given to jotting little
notes to herself about her mental state. It's hard to imagine whom
she might have taken up with if she had lived for any length of
time beyond her failed marriage to the playwright Arthur Miller,
but you can be sure it wouldn't have been Eddie Fisher.

The mysteries surrounding Marilyn Monroe's life are many,
beginning with the question of who her father was and ending
with the disputed events of her death. The central enigma, however, is whether she was an innocent victim or a calculating user.
Was she made of fluff or of steel? Two recent additions to the
Monroe canon infuse new life into the hydra-headed genre of
biography and conspiracy theory that arises around doomed
ur-figures such as Monroe and her most famous lover, Jack
Kennedy. Barbara Leaming's biography, *Marilyn Monroe*, takes
a more ambivalent approach to its subject than does *The Last Days
of Marilyn Monroe*, Donald H. Wolfe's account of the forces that
plotted to do Monroe in. Leaming, who has written biographies
of Orson Welles and Katharine Hepburn, portrays a woman who
both resisted and exploited her own commodification. Her Marilyn is less a sweetheart than a manipulator—someone who is
concerned with the effect of her actions on her public image
rather than with the personal fallout from those actions. "Though
Marilyn had initiated the divorce," Leaming writes of Monroe's
decision to leave DiMaggio, her second husband, "she must appear to be as devastated as Joe." She goes on to detail the cunning
scenario that Monroe orchestrated, together with her attorney,
for the benefit of journalists waiting outside her house after she
served the divorce papers: the actress, holding a pair of white
gloves in one hand and a handkerchief in the other, "seemed
disoriented as flashbulbs exploded en masse," "appeared to feel
faint," and "seemed on the verge of collapse."

Leaming provides a glimpse of Monroe's emotionally impoverished childhood, allotting it eight pages of a 464-page book;
although she throws the reader a bunch of social-workerish clichés, conceding that Monroe was a "sad, lonely little girl" filled
with a feeling of "utter worthlessness," she is less interested in

probing the vicissitudes that shaped Monroe's development than in condemning its outcome. The "poor, abused child" rapidly becomes a coy, shrewd young woman with a full-blown exhibitionist complex: "She was willing to pose in any and all circumstances." Leaming writes that the adult Monroe "affected a quality that Joe Mankiewicz once described as her 'pasted-on innocence'" and censoriously notes that Monroe's unhappy early years were immediately enlisted as material for her ongoing press campaign: "In interview after interview, Marilyn portrayed herself as a courageous little orphan girl, a sort of modern-day Cinderella, whose childhood has been spent being passed from one foster home to another."

But, in truth, it had, hadn't it? Leaming seems to suffer from a reflexively adverse reaction to her subject's story that afflicts some of the writers attracted to Monroe. It's as if the insistent neediness jangling beneath the surface of the actress's allure were too threatening to contemplate, except from a safe and slightly supercilious distance. Interestingly, it is Wolfe's account, concerned though it is with the logistical minutiae surrounding Monroe's death, that delivers the more complex picture of the lost little girl who became, as Nunnally Johnson, the screenwriter for *How to Marry a Millionaire* (1953), called her, "a lost lady."

Monroe was born and died in California, that state beloved of dreamers and drifters—people like Maria Wyeth, in Joan Didion's *Play It as It Lays*, who are not "prepared to take the long view." Monroe's plight was in essence that of misplacement: an absence of the locating vectors of identity. She started as an illegitimate child without a real home, in Hawthorne, a suburb of Los Angeles, and she ended up alone with her telephone in a newly acquired, barely furnished stucco bungalow on a secluded cul-de-sac in Brentwood. The specter of mental illness haunted Monroe throughout her life: both her maternal grandparents died in mental hospitals, and her mother, Gladys, who suffered from intermittent psychotic episodes, was in and out of state institutions from the time her daughter was very young. Her father was listed as Edward Mortenson, address unknown, but her actual father appears to have been a man named Stan Gifford, whom Monroe tried repeatedly over the years to make contact with, and was always rebuffed.

Within two weeks of her birth in a charity ward, the infant called Norma Jeane Baker was farmed out to a foster family. She spent the longest period—seven years—with Albert and Ida Bolender, a devout couple who boarded children to supplement Albert's income as a postman. Even those who cast a cool eye on the heart-wrenching version of Monroe's beginnings—as does Donald Spoto, whose 1993 biography of Monroe is exhaustively researched—concede that the atmosphere of the Bolender household was austere. Standards of discipline were high, the movies were never mentioned, and God hogged the spotlight. Norma Jeane's mother contrived to set up a home of her own when her daughter was seven; she rented the upstairs to the Kinnells, a British couple who worked in film. As Wolfe tells it, the adult Monroe recalled—first in an interview with Ben Hecht and again a few weeks before she died—that she was molested by Mr. Kinnell during this brief period, which ended with Gladys's being institutionalized again. (Other writers have dismissed or ignored this charge, but I'm inclined to believe it, since this was decades before the dawning of recovered memory syndrome.)

When Norma Jeane was not yet nine, her mother was declared legally incompetent, and Grace McKee, who had become friendly with Gladys when they worked together in a film-cutting laboratory, acted as her guardian. McKee was genuinely fond of her charge and was the first to see star potential in her. But within less than a year she, too, was unable to look after Norma Jeane, and so, on September 13, 1935, the quiet, pretty little girl with blue-green eyes entered the Los Angeles Orphans Home. McKee stayed in close touch with her, buying her presents (which she billed to Gladys), rhapsodizing over her appearance, and overseeing the family situations in which an adolescent Norma Jeane would be placed after she left the orphanage. Gladys emerged for occasional visits with her daughter, during which she acted dazed and cold, but Norma Jeane's most stable companions were her glossy daydreams, in which she envisioned "becoming so beautiful that people would turn to look at me when I passed."

Monroe herself took a fairly grim view of the forces that propelled her. "Yes, there was something special about me," she once wrote, "and I knew what it was. I was the kind of girl people expect to find dead in a hall bedroom with an empty bottle of sleeping pills in her hand." In the event, her scenario proved prescient, but it doesn't explain Norma Jeane's rapid and dazzling transformation into "the Monroe." What, then, does? One might deduce from even a minimal acquaintance with the literature that she was aided by casting couches, by mentors cum lovers (including Johnny Hyde, the William Morris agent; the Twentieth Century Fox executive Joe Schenck; and Spyros Skouras, the CFO of Fox), by cosmetic improvement (she had her nose bobbed and her chin rounded), and by sheer will. Did she sleep her way to the top? The answer seems to be yes and no. She slept with men who could help her, if she happened to like them, and she refused to sleep with men in power—among them Harry Cohn, the lecherous head of Columbia Pictures—whom she disliked. She seems, that is, to have been possessed of a situational sense of integrity. Thus she didn't agree to marry an ailing Hyde in order to inherit his money, as he suggested she do, not only because she didn't want to look like a gold digger, but because she wasn't in love with him.

The truth, of course, is that no matter how you contrive to get yourself noticed, you can't sleep your way to mass appeal— to making your presence indelibly felt by audiences sitting in the dark. Although Monroe insured her own life for a paltry three thousand dollars, and the jewelry and furs she left behind were worth less than fifteen hundred, her box-office value was in the millions. When she died, a frantic Cohn, whose expedient definition of good movies was "those that make money," is supposed to have yelled, "Get me another blonde!" (He was served up Kim Novak.)

Monroe's mutation from what the critic Richard Schickel calls a "pneumatic starlet" to a bulb-popping Movie Star has something of the epiphanous, dream-factory quality that adheres to the Lana Turner story. One minute you're just another pretty hopeful, sipping soda at a Schwab's counter, and in the next everyone wants a piece of you. Or as Cherie, the wannabe "chantoose" that Monroe played in *Bus Stop* (1956), hypothesized with exquisite simplicity, "You get discovered, you get options, and you get treated with a little respect, too." Except in real life it never quite happens that way; in Monroe's case, a good deal of energy was expended on trying to convince people that there was a serious contender inside the bimbo curves—a concept that continues to this day to be treated with a creeping note of disdain.

In *Intimate Strangers: The Culture of Celebrity*, Schickel refers to "her thin and unsingular autobiography" and argues that "confession was a vital part of her success." But it was Monroe's early life that gave a poignant edge to the bombshell trope—that, in effect, made her such a compelling mix of visible assets and invisible deficits. I'm also unconvinced that, especially when viewed in light of today's tell-all standards, she ever made much use of the confessional mode. She seems, rather, to have had a fairly well-developed sense of privacy. When she was asked to comment on the breakup of her marriage to Miller, she replied, "It would be indelicate of me to discuss this. I feel it would be trespassing."

What's clear is that Monroe believed in her rapport with the public more than she believed in her rapport with Hollywood. Indeed, there were always industry people on whom her charms were lost, who never saw her as anything but the trophy girlfriend she played in *All About Eve* (1950)—"a graduate of the Copacabana School of the Dramatic Arts." Darryl F. Zanuck, the production chief at Twentieth Century Fox, where Monroe was first signed to a studio contract, referred to her as "a strawhead." (According to Leaming, Fox dropped her in 1947, a year after she was signed, because Zanuck "thought she was unattractive.") John Huston, who directed her in *The Asphalt Jungle* (1950) and *The Misfits* (1961), observed with his cavalier style of non-endorsement that Monroe "impressed me more off the screen than on"; Donald Spoto notes that although Huston took credit in his autobiography for immediately spotting Monroe's talent, he had initially rejected her for the role of Angela in *The*

Asphalt Jungle and agreed to cast her only after Louis B. Mayer was impressed by a screen test.

Monroe bonded primarily with the camera; her professional conduct was richly unreliable almost from the start. Chronically late and often so flustered that she stammered her lines when she did show up on the set, she required the constant assistance of drama coaches. (Paula Strasberg was eventually paid a queenly salary of three thousand dollars a week for her services, which generally amounted to no more than nodding or shaking her head after a particular take.) Billy Wilder, who directed the actress in *The Seven Year Itch* (1955) and *Some Like It Hot* (1959), resisted what he termed the "cult" of sanctification that blossomed after her death, grouchily observing, "Marilyn Monroe was never on time, never knew her lines." But he admitted that "for what you finally got on the screen, she was worth it." Tony Curtis was less charitable: after suffering through retake after retake in *Some Like It Hot*, he made the notorious observation that kissing Monroe was like kissing Hitler. But Robert Mitchum, who appeared with Monroe in *River of No Return* (1954), directed by the bullying Otto Preminger, thought that her problems were rooted in a childlike sense of terror rather than in the narcissistic acting out of an indulged *nymphette terrible*: "Every time a director yelled 'Action!' she'd break out in a sweat . . . I mean it. She was scared."

There were those who perceived Monroe's peekaboo brand of magic early on. Groucho Marx was so taken with her signature, hip-wiggling walk when she came in for an interview at the age of twenty-one that he devised a tiny cameo for her in *Love Happy* (1950). "She's Mae West, Theda Bara, and Bo Peep all rolled into one," he enthused. Until that time, Monroe had uttered two words—"Hi, Rad!"—in a movie called *Scudda Hoo! Scudda Hay!* A few months later, she posed nude for a calendar manufacturer, who had seen a Pabst beer poster of her in a one-piece swimsuit. The photographer, Tom Kelley, nestled his entirely self-possessed model against a red velvet backdrop and proceeded to shoot her in dozens of positions. The most famous picture, titled *Golden Dreams*, reappeared several years later as *Playboy*'s first centerfold. By 1952, when the *Los Angeles Herald Examiner* got wind of this indiscretion, the actress who had seemed to be destined for nothing much was dating a baseball great and was receiving two or three thousand fan letters a week. Somewhere between *Love Happy* and *Don't Bother to Knock* (1952)—where she gave a subtle, nuanced performance in her first leading role, proving her ability to convey the tug of emotion as well as of sex—the ferocity of Monroe's ambition overcame the obstacles posed by her insecurities. At least for a time.

The contradictory versions of Monroe's ascension are matched only by the varied explanations of her free fall into personal chaos and professional disfavor. (She was fired from her last film, which was called, appropriately, *Something's Got to Give*.) Depending on whom one is inclined to believe, she was either destined for suicide all along (having made four previous attempts at it) or aided and abetted in her self-destruction by everyone around her. Neither view really satisfies: the former seems too briskly dismissive, the latter too puffy with melodrama. If Monroe were a fictional character, I would conjecture that what killed her was fatigue, brought on by extreme insomnia and a lack of resilience. "Life," as Samuel Butler once wearily remarked, "is one long process of getting tired," and in Monroe's case the process was accelerated. By the end, it took her so long to get going that during the shooting of *The Misfits* she often had to be made up while she was still lying in bed.

In *The Last Days of Marilyn Monroe*, Wolfe asserts that the actress was the victim of foul play—a "premeditated homicide." Such conspiracy theories are easy to laugh off, and they're hard to follow in the richness of their speculations unless one is a buff or a complete obsessive. But, except for the hairiest, visitor-from-Mars variety, they usually have valid issues attached to them, and in the instance of Monroe's passing there are some curiously dangling threads. These include time-line problems—an unexplained lag of several hours between the moment she died and the moment the police were called, during which period her house might have been ransacked—and several puzzling forensic phenomena, such as a number of bruises on her body and the stunning amount of drugs in her bloodstream, which have been attributed to a "hot shot."

Wolfe builds on the material that appeared in *Goddess: The Secret Lives of Marilyn Monroe* (1985), a spellbinding saga written by the journalist Anthony Summers, who concludes that Bobby Kennedy showed up at Monroe's residence on the day she died, though he isn't finally convinced that any malfeasance occurred. Wolfe adds some crucial interviews, particularly with Jack Clemmons, the first LAPD officer to arrive at the Monroe residence after her internist, Hyman Engelberg, called with the news of her suicide. Wolfe goes further than Summers, yet there's a steady purposiveness to his account; it feels like honorable work, not the effusions of a crackpot. The pivotal detail for Wolfe and other conspiracists is that Monroe, according to Robert Slatzer, a journalist who claimed to have been briefly married to her, was threatening to hold a press conference in order to rat on Jack and Bobby Kennedy after they dumped her. Whether you credit Slatzer's version or not (Spoto, for one, doesn't), the welter of incriminatingly replayed scenes and darkly knowing anecdotes begins to fuse together into a menacing set of possibilities.

Was a frightened Monroe invited to a Lake Tahoe lodge co-owned by Frank Sinatra and the mobster Sam Giancana the weekend before she died, drugged, and sexually assaulted on camera to ensure her silence about the Kennedys? Was she accidentally done in by Ralph Greenson, the overinvested and eerily controlling analyst, who, in an effort to revive her, injected her with adrenaline, accidentally hitting a rib instead of her heart? Or was it Bobby Kennedy's henchmen, brought in to deal with Monroe and to steal a red journal in which she had jotted down top-secret political information that she was privy to, who offed her? Or perhaps the housekeeper did it—Eunice Murray, a bizarre, loitering character whom Monroe had just given notice to. The amassing of documentation only confuses the reader, and yet, in Monroe's case, such theories have an emotional logic that goes beyond their literal substance: The Monroe that Wolfe portrays is an unclaimed yet invaluable object that everyone had a proprietary eye on. In the gap between her lack of self-regard and her charismatic dependency on others, there was ample space for the kind of exploitation that could shade imperceptibly into very real danger.

Finally, it's no accident that in Leaming's biography Elia Kazan is said to have "called her the gayest girl he had ever known," while in Wolfe's book Arthur Miller describes himself as being captivated by "the saddest girl I've ever seen." Monroe was both, and perhaps the greatest tragedy of her life is that the depressive swings in her personality weren't taken seriously enough—weren't treated, as the doctors at Payne Whitney apparently thought they should have been, as manifestations of a recurrent bipolar mood disorder. Instead, she was persistently categorized as an upper-middle-class neurotic, whose problems could be solved psycho-dynamically, with five-times-a-week therapy sessions and with endless tranquilizers and sleeping pills—Nembutal, Amytal, and chloral hydrate, among others. This seems regrettable, especially considering Monroe's unself-pitying attitude toward depression, which she expressed in a letter to Greenson about a doctor at Payne Whitney: "He asked me how I could possibly work when I was depressed . . . He actually stated it more than he questioned me, so I replied, 'Don't you think that perhaps Greta Garbo and Charlie Chaplin and Ingrid Bergman had been depressed when *they* worked sometimes?' It's like saying a ball player like DiMaggio couldn't hit a ball when he was depressed. Pretty silly."

One assumes that both Greenson and Marianne Kris, her New York City analyst, meant well by her; certainly Greenson, who consulted with Anna Freud on how best to deal with Monroe, was available to her by phone in the wee hours of the morning and in person, often at a moment's notice. But all those who came into Monroe's presence ended up ceding their boundaries, as if offering more of themselves would make Monroe think more of herself. It didn't work, didn't prevent her "night terrors" from taking big chunks out of her. "Last night I was awake all night again," she wrote to Greenson about a year before she died. "Sometimes I wonder what the nighttime is for. It almost doesn't exist for me—it all seems like one long, long horrible day."

Unlike other survivors of difficult childhoods, such as Joan Crawford, Monroe doesn't seem to have been toughened by experience, and remained intensely vulnerable to loss. (She never got over her breakup with Miller or the two miscarriages she suffered during her marriage to him.) Still, at times she understood herself better than the experts did. In a 1955 note to herself she wrote, "My problem of desperation in my work and life—I must begin to face it continually, making my work routine more continuous, and of more importance than my desperation." It's customary to say that Hollywood destroyed Monroe, but in fact she might have been happier if she had been able to embrace her career and comfortably inhabit her stardom, as Elizabeth Taylor did, instead of holding the costume of celebrity at arm's length and finding it full of holes. In her last interview, with the *Life* reporter Richard Meryman, she pointed out that fame, like caviar, "wasn't really for a daily diet, that's not what fulfills you."

In the end, Monroe retained the mind-set of a waif, looking for the sort of unconditional embrace from men that only a child comes by naturally, from his or her parents. What she needed was larger than sex, although she continually sought refuge in that easy place: it was a permanent fixing of things gone wrong, an undoing of her history. The stalwart DiMaggio, whom she nicknamed Slugger, loved her with the sort of potato love that might have made her strong if she had been able to take it in—and if he had been able to accept her with all her glamour-puss trappings instead of being enraged by them. "It's no fun being married to an electric light," he growled. Yet it strikes me that it was Arthur Miller—who comes off badly in many accounts of Monroe's life, and emerges least well in Leaming's biography, where he is painted as a pious, unself-aware careerist—who comprehended the desolation that drove her, the "relief" she sought from what he called her "detached and centerless and invaded life." Whether or not Miller wrote *The Misfits* out of a genuine artistic impulse or with an eye to creating a vehicle for his wife that would enhance his dwindling reputation, the role of Roslyn captures the bleakness that yawned beneath the lush persona, spreading emptiness. "The trouble is," Monroe says at the start of the movie to a sympathetic Thelma Ritter, "I always end up back where I started. I never had anybody much."

I can see why Monroe's genius—at least as far as men are concerned—is said to reside in stills, where she doesn't appear anxious and promises the kind of sexual fulfillment you don't need to buy but have only to ask for. She has also been widely acclaimed for her deft touch as a comedienne, in films like *The Seven Year Itch* and *How to Marry a Millionaire.* And there is indeed something innately humorous about the cognitive dissonance she inspires—the way her physical impact rubs up against her shy, self-effacing side, which is reflected in the Kewpie-doll voice and what one of her co-stars called "those famous liquid eyes." But I find her most interesting to watch in unfunny movies, like *Don't Bother to Knock*, *Bus Stop*, and *The Misfits*, where the dissonance is all but gone and, in its place, distress flickers around her like a penumbra, a halo of misery above her light hair. *Give me*, she says; *I need you.* Her eyes widen, her teeth glisten, her lips do that strange quivering thing which suggests, by some unconscious association of orifices, that she is yearning to take the male spectator inside her. And what about the female spectator? We sense her panic, and we wonder if anyone so beautiful— "gleaming there, so pale and white," as Don Murray gushes when he first spots her in *Bus Stop*—has ever conveyed so much loneliness. When she's not sending out that huge, delighted, and delight-inducing smile of hers, she looks inconsolable.

LOCKED IN THE PLAYGROUND

(MICHAEL JACKSON)

2003

It is a late Monday afternoon, the unseasonably benign weather has suddenly turned cold, winter jabbing us in the ribs, and I am sitting in my shrink's office, talking about Michael Jackson's recent arrest on child-molestation charges. All that raving pathology thrust once again into the glare of the headlines, his face caught in that creepy, deer-in-the-headlights mug shot, and everyone looking on, snickering and ogling, horrified and fascinated at the same time. That mixture of fame and fragility, which always seems to bring on the wolves.

I find myself feeling protective on his wounded, weird behalf—or, perhaps, on my own wounded, weird behalf. I am discussing how vulnerable he is, how skinless. I say that I don't believe—on the instinctive level, where we all make such assessments all the time—he is a pedophile and that he strikes me as presexual. Which is not to say that he's transcendently sane, like, say, Mr. Cleaver from *Leave It to Beaver* (although one might argue that Jackson is more like the Beaver himself, which is to say that if television were reality and Beaver Cleaver didn't have to grow up, things might never have gone so awry). When the shrink nods, I don't know whether to interpret his nod as a sign of assent or simply an indication that he is listening to me as I dedicate my fifty minutes to the analysis of Michael Jackson by proxy. I wonder aloud whether Jackson has ever sought psychiatric help: What exactly is wrong with him, in clinical terms?

I talk about him as though he were an invisible sidekick, representing the parts of me that I have learned to hide—the infantile wishes and regressive longings that swim under the surface of adult life. Only in Jackson's case, he has been hiding in plain sight for years, what with the wigs, the false lashes, the makeup, the shades, the Halloween getups, the parasol, the surgical masks. Peekaboo, I see you. He puts me in mind of a children's book my daughter used to love when she was very little, a book that began "Jesse Bear, what will you wear? What will you wear in the morning?" I always paused right before "morning," and she would always fill the word in, wobbling over the *r* in "morning" so that it came out "maw-ning." I think part of the allure of Jesse Bear was that it seemed as though he could begin all new again every day. Simply by deciding what kind of clothes he wanted to wear, he could decide who he wanted to be. If only it were that simple.

In watching Jackson's increasingly Houdini-like efforts to break out of the prison of who he inexorably is, we see the painful no-exit dilemma we are all stuck with as chronologically finished products—grown-ups by any other name. On the one hand, Jackson's increasingly bizarre efforts to crawl out of his own skin reveal what we have suspected all along—that personal identity is an imperfect construct, one that is wobbly and full of glitches. Its center is fragile and in psychological extremis often as not begins to show fissures. As we've watched Jackson's combination of self-destructive and self-fetishizing impulses play out, what has been no less vividly exposed are the limitations of a given identity—even in these cosmetically transformational, "anything is possible" times. The cultural zeitgeist of personal omnipotence—epitomized by Arnold Schwarzenegger's trajectory from a humble Austrian background to the governorship of California—makes it easy to forget that the delicate construction we call a "self" is not an infinitely malleable object.

For those of us who harbor a special fondness for the young Michael Jackson, who remember him as an impossibly animated little boy who made frequent guest appearances on *The Ed Sullivan Show*, performing as the pint-size lead singer in the perennially cheerful family musical group known as the Jackson 5, the distance he has so clearly wanted to put between himself and his origins is especially disconcerting. He was a human jumping bean with a well-behaved Afro, a heartbreakingly open smile, a huge voice, and a precocious ability to convey grown-up emotions. But what demons had we failed to pick up as we watched him, in black and white, from our living rooms, some of us already in pajamas—demons so extravagant that they required a desperate pilgrimage from one impersonation to the next? What legacy of family disrepair had been hidden behind the smooth television presentation of that remarkably polished young crooner who should, by all rights, have only recently graduated from listening to bedtime stories?

There is something about Michael Jackson that reminds me of those plastic replicas of the male and female body we all saw at some point during our formative years (as the Wonder bread commercials called them). These see-through models, in which the organs are on display—the brain, the heart, the kidneys— were meant to help us understand how humans worked from a biological perspective. Unmappable terrain like the emotions didn't show up, of course, which left us in the dark about something that was at least as important as where our gallbladders were located. In some sense, Jackson is a flesh-and-blood version of those models, only this time the area on display is the whole submerged terrain of the psyche. He represents in his one tortured and talented being every conflict of identity imaginable— beginning with race and gender—on the most astonishingly primordial level.

He is, in a way, a psychiatrist's diagnostic dream—or nightmare. If you were to throw the book at Jackson—the psychiatric bible known as the *DSM-IV*—most of it would stick. He is, one might conjecture, an Axis II borderline ("borderline" being one of those catchall terms that are used to describe people whose problems lie somewhere on the continuum between garden-variety neurosis and bloodcurdling psychosis) who suffers from body dysmorphic disorder (a relatively newly diagnosed psychic ailment that means that one is preoccupied with an imagined physical defect—that you continue, say, to experience a consuming hatred for your nose even after you've had it reshaped); gender-identity diffusion; and some variant of OCD (obsessive-compulsive disorder). And that's just for starters. One imagines he has sought therapeutic help, like the former Beach Boy Brian Wilson, who looked to a New Age therapist—a Svengali of sorts—to overhaul his psyche, one dominating father replacing another. Then again, Jackson's might well be the plight of the VIP therapy patient, essentially untouchable except through his handlers. "I doubt that therapy would have helped him," observes Glen Gabbard, a psychiatrist at Baylor College of Medicine and editor of *The International Journal of Psychoanalysis*, "because he created an environment with unremitting narcissistic mirroring so that he wouldn't be sufficiently motivated to explore his inner world in a therapeutic process."

In other words, welcome to Neverland. Given enough immunization in the form of wealth and celebrity, a person is free to relieve the tormenting pressures of his or her fantasy world in the sorts of floridly eccentric, boundary-violating ways that would never be tolerated from people in more ordinary circumstances, who are subject to more stringent societal constrictions (or, as may be the case, safeguards). Jackson's decades of freaky behavior with the gloves and the pet chimp and he dangled the baby over a balcony—not to mention the transformation of his face from that of a black man to a grotesque parody of a white woman's—speak to the near-absolute convergence of an individual symptomatology and a cultural pathology in which age and maturity are the enemy.

Would Michael Jackson be where he is today—would he be Wacko Jacko, as the Brit tabloids have nicknamed him—if someone had read aloud from *Goodnight Moon* or *The Runaway Bunny* as he drifted off to sleep instead of "training" him (Jackson has referred to his steelworker father, seemingly unironically, as a great trainer) to perform on command? Whether his father abused him or merely subjected him to harsh discipline, it is clear that Jackson was yanked out of his childhood well before he had finished growing up. Shades of the prison house—to borrow a phrase from one of the great poets of childhood, William Wordsworth—closed too early upon this particular growing boy from Gary, Indiana. If nostalgia is often bittersweet, nostalgia for what you didn't have must create enormous pain. And for people who have never had a childhood, being a grown-up isn't where the glamour is.

Now it appears that all Michael Jackson wants to do, at the age of forty-five, is to stop time and refind that vanished childhood, replay the trauma and make it turn out differently. I can't say I've ever believed he's much interested in anything other than having affectionate sleepover dates with these twelve-year-old boys, if only because he seems to be too confused on a core level of gender identity to be recognizably erotic in his functioning. "This is about pregenital longing," says Gabbard. "You can definitely have regressive longing without violating boundaries." On the documentary about him that was watched by twenty-seven million people when it appeared ten months ago, Jackson explained his feelings on the issue in his strangled, wispy voice, which made perfect sense from a nine-year-old's perspective: "Why can't you share your bed? The most loving thing to do is to share your bed with someone." Still, I'm not sure how much room our culture allows for a forty-five-year-old man to snuggle up with a twelve-year-old boy. Does our imagination of what love can consist of stretch far enough to include an admittedly exaggerated romance with the concept of childhood itself?

Meanwhile, what we have before us is a drama of damage, handed on down the generations, as it always is. Depending on whether you see Jackson as unjustly hounded or as a nutjob who's gotten away with pedophilia, he is either a little boy lost, preyed on by scheming and foul-minded adults—or a scheming, foul-minded adult preying on little boys lost. The truth is undoubtedly more ambiguous than either of those scenarios, as it usually is. For to the extent that we all live on primal as well as socialized levels, being an artist requires that one live on a more primal level than other people. That Jackson has greater access to the outlandish desires of his unconscious—and in the process to ours—can hardly be in doubt. That he has far greater license to flamboyantly act out these desires than we do—whether it be a wish to have alabaster skin, or to be feminine, or an eternal boy-child in a world of boy-children, or, again, some impossible mix-and-match incarnation of everything on the verge of becoming everything else—is what endangers him and, paradoxically, saves us.

"Mama, mama see me, I'm a pop star," Cat Stevens used to wail like a hyped-up kid back in the 1970s, when Michael still had his old nose and shade of skin, before Neverland clanged its gates shut around him. Not long after, Stevens saw the light, in a manner of speaking, and renounced the permanently juvenile pop-star life for one that adhered to Muslim traditions. Jackson, meanwhile, is still trapped in his lonely playground, unable (or unwilling) to put his childish ways behind him.

GIDGET DOESN'T LIVE HERE ANYMORE

(SANDRA DEE)

2005

At the height of her spectacularly short-lived fame, coverage of everything from her dietary habits to her taste in men was enormous, with approximately fifteen magazine articles appearing every month. The thing is, it all happened so fast, was over practically before it began, that we can almost be forgiven for misconstruing her as a cultural simulacrum: a blip on the monitor, a media invention, an adorable incarnation of a feminine ideal of the reluctant or unwitting nymphet, rather than a flesh-and-blood creature with needs and wishes (not to mention raging demons) of her own.

The lightning speed with which Sandra Dee was first heralded and then discarded may have been just another example of the "now you see her, now you don't" phenomenon endemic to the fever dream of Hollywood, but it also suggests the dark *Miss Lonelyhearts* side of the American manufacture of celebrity—the ruthlessness that drives it and the despair it feeds off of. She went from being discovered in 1956, at twelve, to winning a Golden Globe Award in 1958, to being hailed by the *Motion Picture Herald* in 1959 as the "Number One Star of Tomorrow," based on her promising pigtailed debut in the sterling weepie *Until They Sail* as well as her performance in *The Reluctant Debutante*. Less than a decade later, her career all but ended when she was dropped by Universal after her divorce, at age twenty-two, from

the crooner Bobby Darin. "Sometimes I feel like a has-been who
never was," Dee told the *Newark Evening News* in 1967.

In truth, she never entirely disappeared from the collective
imagination, and therein lies one of many painful paradoxes (she
was, for instance, among the last actors to be dropped as a contract player before the studio system expired) in what turns out
to be a story too full of them. Her moment as "a junior Doris
Day," as she once put it, or "a Tinkertoy," as an underwhelmed
journalist once put it—although she early on demonstrated a
far greater range of acting talent than she would later be remembered for—may have been vastly abbreviated, but there's no forgetting that fluffy neon concoction of a name, or what it stood
for. Even if you never caught her in her glory days as Gidget or
Tammy, Dee's legacy as an eclipsed and parodied icon, a cinematic reference that signifies everything blond and unviolated
about the 1950s, was assured by her immortalization in a catchy
song from *Grease*. Its broadly winking lyrics are declaimed by
Rizzo, the designated high-school Bad Girl, at a pajama party
and are aimed at converting the goody-two-shoes newcomer
Sandy to a life of carnal sin: "Look at me, I'm Sandra Dee /
Lousy with virginity / Won't go to bed till I'm legally wed, / I
can't, I'm Sandra Dee."

Precisely because of the mythic stature she's been endowed
with, it's hard to believe that the wisp of a girl who cavorted
decorously on-screen with John Saxon and Troy Donahue, in a
time before teenagers of either sex thought to have their tongues
pierced, lacked the grace to fade out, had the temerity to live
on—and so unfetchingly, her life marred by chronic anorexia,
alcoholism, and depression—after we were no longer paying her
any mind. Dee's death last February at age sixty, or, as is more
likely, sixty-two (her official age was obscured from early childhood, when her mother added two years to it; many obituaries
listed her age at the time of her death as sixty-two), of complications from kidney disease, impels us to retrieve her from
her vacuum-packed, nostalgia-inducing state as an idealized
adolescent prototype. This in turn raises a possibility almost
too disturbing to contemplate: how to envision Sandra Dee as

middle-aged—as anything other than a bubbling and bikinied beach babe, the candied yin to Annette Funicello's sultry yang, the sweet and genteelly chaperoned box-office ingenue whose popularity once rivaled Elizabeth Taylor's and whose elopement at sixteen with the scrappy Bronx-bred Darin, after a one-month courtship on the set of a forgettable movie (*Come September*), spoke to a girlishly starry-eyed fantasy of romance.

Then again, the "darling, pink world," as she herself characterized it, that Sandra Dee was thought to inhabit by her fans had always been a grotesque mockery, plagued not by an overripened case of virginity but by childhood molestation. The girl with brimming brown eyes and a fizzy lilt to her voice was born Alexandra Zuck in Bayonne, New Jersey. Her parents divorced when she was five; her father, a bus driver, disappeared from her life shortly thereafter, and her mother, Mary, married a much older real estate entrepreneur named Eugene Douvan within a few years. According to Dee's own account, as relayed by her son, Dodd Darin, in his touching and unglamorized memoir of his parents, *Dream Lovers*, her lifelong battle with anorexia—which would lead to three hospitalizations in her mid-teens, cardiac distress, and multiple miscarriages—began with Mary's bizarre approach to her daughter's meals: "My mother fed me with a spoon until I was six years old. She would make me a bowl of oatmeal . . . She'd crack an egg into it, raw, and . . . cold and lumps and streaks, I had to eat it all." Worse yet, Dee's devoted but manipulative mother turned a conveniently blind eye to the defiled sexual appetites of her new husband. Douvan, who liked to tease his wife that he married her "just to get Sandy," started having sex with his beautiful stepdaughter when she was eight and continued doing so almost until his death when she was twelve.

After her divorce from Darin, Dee never remarried. The former teenage sweetheart who had once received more fan mail than Rock Hudson became an anxious recluse whose primary connections were with her mother and her son. A cover profile in *People* magazine in 1991 depicted her as a damaged and isolated survivor—Dee poignantly expressed a wish to do a TV series, "because I want a family. I can have that if I'm part of a show"—and her son's portrait of her in his book only deepened the shadows. Dee had plans to write an autobiography and in 1996 did a brief stint as an infomercial spokeswoman for an antiaging cream. Last year she was played by Kate Bosworth in Kevin Spacey's movie about Bobby Darin, *Beyond the Sea*.

Sandra Dee's dazzling wreck of a life—the implausibly mete-oric ascent followed by the long fall—would, I suppose, make for a perfect Lifetime special. Or, better yet, a searing biopic all its own, underscoring the gap between the glossy image and the nightmarish reality. It would, that is, if the truth weren't so un-bearably sad, revealing a tale of ravaged innocence under cover of familial enmeshment, which led, in turn, to a wasteland of self-destruction. The problem with a story like this one, at least from a filmmaker's point of view, is that it isn't even a cathartic tear-jerker. There is no fortifying moral to be drawn from it, no re-demptive *Oprah* ending hovering in the wings. Look at her, she's Sandra Dee, lousy with debility. Tickets, anyone?

THE MYSTERY OF DR. B.

(BRUNO BETTELHEIM)

What becomes a legend most? Was Bruno Bettelheim a mounte-bank swathed in a thick Austrian accent and false credentials? Or was he a compassionate teacher and therapist who had penetrat-ing insight into the unconscious processes of emotionally trau-matized children, and whose time in Dachau and Buchenwald shaped an iconoclastic but humane vision?

Bettelheim's legend is eerily bifurcated—as though a snapshot of the man, round-faced and benign looking behind thick glasses, had been torn down the middle. In the 1960s and '70s Bettel-heim was an intellectual celebrity, with multitudes of believers reading his books and flocking to his lectures; in 1983, at what was perhaps the height of his incarnation as a wise paterfamilias, he appeared as a psychoanalyst in Woody Allen's *Zelig*. But in the seven years that have passed since his suicide, a figure who was once revered for his commitment to healing psychological wounds in the young has come to be reviled for his single-minded dedi-cation to the nurturing of his own myth and for his apparent brutalization of a number of the children under his care. As two recent biographies of Bettelheim demonstrate—*The Creation of Dr. B*, by Richard Pollak, and *Bettelheim: A Life and a Legacy*, by Nina Sutton—his life sets before us a fascinating study of the pol-itics of reputation and the curious mixture of pathology and re-nown that contributes to it. Although Sutton's book takes a more sympathetic view than Pollak's zealously debunking account,

there is some agreement on the basic facts, as well as on the notion of a troubling fault line in Bettelheim's character.

Bettelheim sailed into New York on May 11, 1939, on the SS
Gerolstein—along with more than a hundred other refugees
from the Third Reich—with three dollars in his pocket, a doc-
toral dissertation on the aesthetics of nature, and some experience running his family's lumber company. In Vienna, Bettelheim
had attended the opera, collected the lithographs of Käthe Koll-
witz and Egon Schiele, frequented the coffeehouses, and even
undergone analysis for a brief period. This cultivated upper-
middle-class life came to an abrupt end when he was arrested by
the Austrians on orders from Berlin in 1938. He was incarcerated
in concentration camps for nearly a year before he managed to
bribe his way out and escape to America.

Bettelheim had hoped to be reunited with Gina, his wife of
nine years, who had fled Vienna for America immediately after
the Anschluss, but these hopes were dashed at their first meeting in New York. Although he had ardently courted her, the
marriage had never been a happy one. (Even on their honeymoon,
the bridegroom, who was twenty-six, preferred to sit in a beach
chair and read a biography of Frederick II, while his bride rode
up into the Sicilian hills on a donkey.) After his wife's blunt rejection, Bettelheim turned to an old flame—Trude Weinfeld, a
nature-loving, Montessori-trained teacher whom he had known
in Vienna and who had since left for Australia. He had sent her
a cable informing her that he was free, and she joined him in
America some months later. (The two were married in May 1941
and eventually had three children.)

Helped by some official letters from a relief committee, Bettelheim set out to find work, but none materialized. Then, in the
fall of 1939, on a tip from a fellow émigré, Bettelheim arrived in
Hyde Park—a gemütlich academic community in Chicago's South
Side—to take an unpaid position on an ambitious secondary-
school-reform project under the leadership of Ralph Tyler, the
chairman of the University of Chicago's Department of Education. In spite of his tentative English and bouts of depression
punctuated by nightmares about the camps, Bettelheim proved

to be a quick study, and Tyler offered him a salaried post before the year was out. He also recommended Bettelheim for a job at Rockford, a small college for women near Chicago, where he taught a panoply of courses (including art history, philosophy, psychology, and German) and became something of a campus celebrity—"an intellectual Pied Piper"—known for a brilliant but scorching teaching style and for mercurial behavior with his young students: half "kindly Viennese uncle" and half "Erich von Stroheim."

Ironically, it was during this period of genuine accomplishment that Bettelheim, perhaps in response to the anxiety of exile, "reinvented his past," as Sutton says—or, as Pollak puts it, began to "dress up his vita"—to impress his colleagues. Among other dazzling Old World achievements, Bettelheim claimed summa cum laude in three disciplines, music studies with Arnold Schoenberg, extensive psychological training, firsthand experience with autistics, and an encounter with none other than Freud himself. He also began to circulate stories exaggerating his bravery in the concentration camps, and went as far as to suggest that Eleanor Roosevelt and Governor Herbert Lehman of New York had played a part in his release.

For all these elaborations, however, when Bettelheim wrote a paper about the camps, "Individual and Mass Behavior in Extreme Situations," his description of the experience was not only unadorned but, to some, disconcertingly clinical. This article, which was first published in a scholarly journal, was excerpted by Dwight Macdonald in an early issue of *Politics*, in 1944, and won the attention of an admiring intellectual coterie. It attempted to investigate the adaptation of Bettelheim's fellow prisoners in psychoanalytic terms and proposed that the extreme nature of concentration camp life (this was before the existence of extermination camps per se) led to regressive, childlike behavior in a majority of them. The authoritative tone and the provocative, unsentimental stance of the article were characteristic of Bettelheim's evolving public persona; the tension between this keen and disabused observer and the insecure refugee who felt compelled to glamorize his autobiography would mark him throughout his life. (Pollak, in a rare, grudging concession that his subject was given to an occasional honest impulse, notes that Bettelheim wrote Macdonald a letter correcting a mistake in his author's bio: "I am *not* a psychiatrist, I am only a psychologist. I just feel that one should not make claim to a professional standing which one does not have.")

Bettelheim's great claim to fame—and, more recently, to infamy—rests on the fact that in 1944 he became the director of the Orthogenic School, an institution for disturbed children under the auspices of the University of Chicago's Department of Education. The children's diagnoses included epilepsy and mental retardation as well as emotional problems, and its former director, a specialist in the electrical activity of the brain, was rumored to be a sadist. Bettelheim's own impression of the place, according to Pollak, was that it was "dirty and stank of urine," and his advice to Tyler, as he later told the story, was to burn it down.

Over the next thirty years, Bettelheim was to transform the Orthogenic School from a neglectful holding pen into a much-admired residential center practicing "milieu therapy," a form of treatment advocated by the Viennese psychoanalyst August Aichhorn, who specialized in the treatment of delinquent adolescents. In place of a stark, prison-like setting where the children were treated as small captives in need of bed-wetting supervision and neurological study, Bettelheim created a flexible dormitory environment. Counselors interacted with the children around the clock: shampooing their hair, reading them bedtime stories, and interpreting their every thought and deed. Bettelheim's reforms were as revolutionary as they were ambitious, coming at a time when, as a former counselor at the school put it, "mad children were seen as bad children." Milieu therapy aimed at curing rather than simply containing; the hope was that by creating a vigilantly responsive atmosphere, in which feelings from the past were observed as they emerged in the daily life of the school, children thought to be irredeemable would learn to stand on their own two feet.

And, indeed, some of the school's students must have felt that they had died and gone to heaven. The new director insisted on enhancing what Pollak refers to as a "sense of refuge," with aesthetically pleasing, even luxurious surroundings. Thanks to his skills as a fund-raiser, the school featured ample food, fine china, and red crystal drinking glasses, as well as bedrooms whose decoration was chosen by the children themselves. Candy was freely dispensed from a supply kept next to Bettelheim's office. Pollak reports, "Any child could raid this trove whenever she wished and was free to carry off as many Hershey bars, Chuckles, Baby Ruths, cookies, and assorted other confections as she liked, no questions asked." The director's own office door was mostly open, and he kept a pink pig-shaped cookie jar on his desk. Bettelheim also had an aversion to what he saw as a middle-class obsession with hygiene and bathroom habits, and instructed his staff accordingly: even regular bed wetters were not to be woken during the night, and he put an immediate stop to record keeping of the children's bowel movements.

But there was another side to Bettelheim—one that conflicted with his progressive anti-institutional instincts. He was often openly hostile to the parents of the children in his care, and strongly discouraged too much contact. This was at odds with Bettelheim's public views on the maternal role, which were sufficiently middle-of-the-road and reassuring to make him a popular child-rearing instructor for young mothers. (His 1962 book, *Dialogues with Mothers*, was based on these discussions, and for ten years beginning in the mid-1960s he also wrote an advice column in the *Ladies' Home Journal*.) Yet Pollak reports that as early as 1948 a confidential memo stated that Bettelheim was "incapable of appropriate parent orientation, or not interested in it," and it is clear that he treated many parents of the children in his care dismissively. It was as though he needed to inflate his already considerable power by diminishing the influence of other adults.

Then there was the question of discipline. Many of the children were difficult to control, and some were violent. Although the staff was not supposed to resort to corporal punishment, Bettelheim exempted himself from this prohibition, slapping the children when he saw fit. He was unwilling to comment in print on this aspect of the school; he feared, he said, being misunderstood by the average mother. But this reticence also served to ensure that the public's fantasy of the school, which he had carefully shaped in books such as *Love Is Not Enough* and *Truants from Life*, remained untarnished by its more demanding realities. The situation was further complicated by the fact that Bettelheim saw everything through a psychoanalytic prism. He would become especially incensed over seemingly routine accidents—a dish being broken or a stray rubber ball hitting someone in the head—which he regarded as being filled with unconscious aggressive intent. (He also treated adolescence, with all its swagger and rebellion, as a failure of moral development.) And who was to question his interpretations? Within "Bruno's Castle," as a colleague mockingly referred to the school, his authority was troublingly absolute.

As the years passed, along with effecting a magical transformation in the Orthogenic School, Bettelheim made an outsize name for himself as a maverick psychoanalyst and cultural critic. He was regularly tapped to pronounce upon controversial issues—racism, collective child rearing (in 1964 he visited Israel to do research on the kibbutz system), the Vietnam War—and he delighted in embroiling himself in intellectual debate. In his books, which were distinguished by catchy titles and a cogent, accessible style, he aired his views on subjects ranging from infantile autism to the true meaning of Freud. *The Uses of Enchantment*, his best-known work—an excerpt appeared in *The New Yorker*—explored the meaning of fairy tales. (Both Sutton and Pollak take up the charges of plagiarism recently brought against this book, which borrowed from an obscure psychiatric study published more than a decade earlier.)

In 1973, Bettelheim retired from the Orthogenic School and moved, with his wife, to Portola Valley, in Northern California. There he taught seminars at nearby Stanford and continued to pit himself in lectures and in writing against the reigning pieties of the day. Beginning with the death of his wife in 1984, however, Bettelheim suffered a series of blows—including a variety of debilitating ailments and a rift with his older daughter, Ruth—which led to a deepening of his chronic depression. In February 1990, he reluctantly moved into a retirement residence in Silver Spring, Maryland. Then, on March 13—the same day on which, half a century earlier, the Wehrmacht tanks had rolled into Vienna—the eighty-six-year-old Bettelheim committed suicide by downing some pills with liquor and then putting a plastic bag over his head, securing it at the throat with elastic bands. The news shocked and even angered many; the idea that this combative humanist had decided to take his own life seemed to undercut his feisty assertions about the need to overcome early damage and persevere in the face of the destructiveness loose in the universe.

The creation of an "anti-myth"—of a narrative designed to subvert the ordained text, in which Bettelheim featured as an impish icon, a godlike healer bringing joy and chocolates to youngsters who had formerly known only misery—began within what seemed only minutes of his death. The man whose oft-stated conviction was that "our job is to help the patient to feel anger" seems to have done all too good a job: several of his former patients stepped forward with charges that Bettelheim had not only psychologically tyrannized but physically abused them. A former patient at the school published an article in *Commentary* which suggested that Bettelheim had recklessly misdiagnosed some of the children under his care and had systematically destroyed their self-confidence. (The author of the article, a graduate student in international affairs at George Washington University, had been labeled autistic when he was placed in the school at the age of seven.) Suddenly, there were rumors on top of stories on top of reports, all conspiring to make a mockery of the regard and affection in which Bettelheim had once been held. The picture that emerged was of a ruthless, power-mad careerist and impostor.

Richard Pollak, a journalist and former literary editor of *The Nation*, is situated firmly in the enemy camp. Pollak's brother fatally fractured his skull in a barn accident at the age of eleven while he was on vacation from the Orthogenic School, and he makes no secret of the fact that he is fueled by personal animus: he explains in a prologue that he went to see Bettelheim in 1969, twenty-odd years after his brother's death, in an effort to better understand the circumstances surrounding it, and was horrified by the person he met. Bettelheim dismissed Pollak's parents—the father as a "schlemiel" and the mother as a villain—and went on to assert that the death of Pollak's brother had been a suicide. Pollak came away from the encounter thinking of Bettelheim in cartoonishly sinister terms, as "the evil Doctor Sivana, arch-nemesis of Captain Marvel."

This ominous image does not appear to be entirely a projection of the author's, but there is no way a reader can avoid the impression that Pollak is committed to putting the worst possible face on Bettelheim at every juncture. He recounts every deception, minor as well as major, in an exhaustive welter of details. (How much does it matter, for example, that Bettelheim embellished his stories of life in the camps with fanciful tributes to his own stoicism? If he wasn't quite the dashing hero he made himself out to be, he assuredly wasn't vacationing in Bermuda.) The result is a carping and distorted account in which Pollak strikes an accusatory tone even when it is not called for, and races past poignant moments or warm recollections for fear of being deflected from his mission.

Nina Sutton's more judiciously balanced—and more convincing—account zooms in on the small, embattled figure of Bruno Bettelheim from the opposite angle: she began as an ardent admirer, uncovered many of the same discomfiting facts as Pollak, and ends with a tempered respect for a person beset by demons yet capable of rising above them to help others overcome traumatic experiences. Among those demons, according to Sutton, seems to have been an almost Nixonian sense of shame and self-hatred; this endured throughout Bettelheim's life, in spite of his being "feted, respected and thanked," and gradually engulfed him after Trude, with her "reassuring and constructive gaze," died. (He wrote to a friend in Israel, "We had been loving each other for the last fifty years . . . I owe to her all I am.") Sutton points out that the man who committed himself to, as he put it, "working with children whose lives have been destroyed because their mothers hated them" had a difficult childhood himself. He never got over witnessing his father's tortured decline from syphilis and carried with him an unshakable conviction of his own homeliness. One of Bettelheim's favorite anecdotes involved his mother's alarmed reaction when she was first shown her newborn son: "Thank God it's a boy!" He was also profoundly conflicted about his Jewishness, which resulted in some misguided views of anti-Semitism; he saw in his religion a mirror for both the repellent—"I'm nothing but an ugly old Jew," he told his former editor as his depression deepened in his last months—and the admirable aspects of himself. This attitude, together with the feelings of guilt about his own successful escape from the camps, led him to condemn what he called compliant "ghetto thinking" and to take a censorious attitude toward the victims of Nazism that obscured his more nuanced insights into individual responses to aggression.

A central clue to who the legendary Dr. B. really was rests, as Sutton implies, with the drastic paradigmatic use Bettelheim made of his survival in Dachau and Buchenwald. He spoke of that period in boldly contrarian terms, as having been in some way cathartic; he wrote that the "impact of the concentration camp . . . within a few weeks, did for me what years of a useful and quite successful analysis had not done." Although the statement is, on the face of it, startling, if not outright distasteful, it makes sense in the light of Bettelheim's remark to a French journalist that his year in the camps was the only time in his life when he did not have thoughts of suicide. The harsh conditions there—and, horrifying as they were, Dachau and Buchenwald were set up as concentration camps rather than death camps—allowed him to extrude his inner conflicts, to come down unambivalently on the side of life.

His later application of the mechanism of survivorhood to the more subtle inflections of childhood damage set up a bizarre analogy. Just as the brutal intervention of the Nazis had shaken Bettelheim into psychological health, so he, in the form of the Big Bad Wolf (which is how he sometimes referred to himself), could direct the children's aggression away from themselves and onto a more suitable object: namely, him. This method, albeit neither fully conscious nor fully integrated, amounted to an energetic realpolitik approach to the tenuous mental processes described by Freud. "Here," Bettelheim told the counselors at the Orthogenic School, "the children are the id, you are the ego, and I'm the superego."

The emotional heat that circles around Bettelheim's memory suggests a continuing enthrallment, a primordial ambivalence of the kind a young child feels toward its parents. We are always looking for consistency in other people, especially in our psychological mentors, so it is hardly surprising that the earlier impulse to idealize Bettelheim has been displaced by an almost parricidal compulsion to break him down into his various—and often conflicting—parts. But if it is relatively easy to see how the man once thought of as "some sort of a secular saint," as Sutton puts it, could be referred to in the pages of Pollak's biography as "a fucking fraud" by one of his many detractors, it is more difficult to ascertain his genuine accomplishment in the blizzard of charges and incriminations that has covered him.

This is especially true in the area of his leadership of the Orthogenic School, where the portrait of Bettelheim as evil guru has obscured the less sensational but more accurate one of Bettelheim as empathetic visionary. Through his work there, he succeeded in demystifying the shameful subject of mental illness for a naive and resistant public, both at home and abroad. His beguiling writings about the students, which were filled with pithy descriptions of esoteric psychological processes, helped to establish an attitude of interest in and respect for children who were once seen as not only different but defective. He humanized those "hopeless cases" he had inherited so they came to be understood through their suffering rather than scorned for their symptoms.

It is important, too, to remember when considering Bettelheim's approach to antisocial behavior that in the 1950s and '60s corporal punishment was the order of the day, even for normal children. However questionable some of his tactics may appear to us now, they were less extreme than the standard institutional practices then in use: psychotropic medication, isolation rooms, and straitjackets. The real tragedy is not that Bettelheim resorted to force on occasion but that he felt compelled to perpetuate an idyllic version of the school, much as he had prettied up his personal trajectory. If these deceptions served to protect him from potential censure in the short run, they made him all the more vulnerable to attack later on.

As for autism, there is no doubt that he was mistaken, insisting on a psychological pathogenesis for the disease and also on a heady cure rate (85 percent) for the autistic children who were admitted to his school before the age of seven or eight. Even here, though, we would do well to recall that autism is still poorly understood and that the treatment for the condition in those days was more often than not to throw up one's hands and leave the afflicted to stare at their shoelaces. While his grandiose conviction that autistic children could be successfully psychoanalyzed undoubtedly caused a lot of needless pain to their parents (who were led to believe that they had "caused" the disease), it also demonstrated Bettelheim's passionate investment in the possibility of coaxing such children out of their frozen states. His dream was to "bridge the gap" between the crazy and the sane through comprehending the workings of the unconscious, no matter how dark and roiling they might be. It was a dream of inclusion, in which no child was to be abandoned.

Bettelheim's notorious antipathy to parents was, paradoxically, integrally connected to his advocacy for children. Despite his Dr. Spock–like interaction with mothers, he scoffed at the notion of a maternal instinct: "Of course there is none, otherwise there would not have been the many children who needed my professional services." His belief that parents could, wittingly or not, do enormous harm led him to view the parent-child relationship as suspect until proved otherwise. "I cannot accept that psychoanalytic writings have created parental guilt," he wrote. "Sure, they have added to it and given it substance. But guilt comes from way back when, way back deep down." Viewed in this light, Bettelheim's hostility has something paradoxically admirable about it: it is an undiplomatic manifesto meant to indicate whose side he was on, and he stuck to it well after the 1950s, when parent blaming was newly chic.

Fashions in therapy come and go, and the age of Prozac is unlikely to be receptive to a man whose emphasis was on psychosocial forces rather than on biological ones. The fluctuations of the zeitgeist, then, are partly to blame for the turn against Bettelheim and his colorful, time-consuming—not to mention costly—form of Freudianism. (The prescient Bettelheim saw the writing on the wall, noting in 1980 that "all is drug-related research and treatment and nothing longer than the ninety days the insurance pays for.") But there was also the weaknesses of the man himself, beginning with his own crippling sense of fraudulence. In the end, no single explanation can account for a figure so deeply divided within himself as Bruno Bettelheim was. Immensely commanding, yet personally wounded to such an extent that he never believed his own press, fabricated or earned, he would always be split between the therapist who could intuitively respond to the angry child and the self-promoter who tried to pull the wool over everyone's eyes.

Bettelheim's imperfections—in particular, the fact of his suicide—seem to have inspired a state of collective negative transference among those who once looked upon him as Father Knows Best. Finally, though, there is no minimizing his presence on the American scene. Many recriminations and counterstatements later (a third biography is in the works), it seems to me that he will be remembered, down the long curve of history, for his pioneering uses—rather than abuses—of power. As the world moves on to other agendas—to the cloning of sheep and the fine-tuning of neurotransmitters—the sort of dynamic and sustained treatment that Bettelheim advocated seems less and less likely to serve as a clinical model. And more's the pity: he paid a supremely lucid form of attention to children who were once considered unreadable, and fought ferociously to bring them out of emotional exile and back into the world.

HUNTING DIANA

(PRINCESS DIANA)

2007

There are stories that grip our adult imaginations with the same unrelenting moral force that fairy tales have for young children; they take hold in that place in our brains where we are still unsealed, still open to a feeling of wide-eyed wonder at the vicissitudes of being human. Such collective narratives speak to abidingly primitive wishes and needs, providing vital lessons in the creation of a durable identity in a fearsome and unreasonable world.

The life and times—and, perhaps most significantly, the untimely end—of Princess Diana is one of those stories. Its sway over us goes beyond its particulars into that imaginative space wherein we dream dreams of ourselves writ large: locked in passionate embraces that last forever and embarked on grand adventures that never go awry. At its heart lies an essential mystery, which is the conundrum of personality: why someone is unavailingly the way he or she is, charismatic (Princess Diana) rather than stodgy (Prince Charles), say, or endearingly lovelorn (Di) rather than merely pathetic (Charles). It touches as well on the unpredictability of that unyielding element known as fate, which enters by the gate when we aren't looking. Why her and him together, we wonder; why that pair of legs (hers) and why that pair of ears (his); why couldn't he, why didn't she; and again, why did he, how could she. Most of all, we wonder—as though they were our siblings or friends—why they didn't think to ask our advice, even if it wasn't ours to give.

The young woman at the center of this saga was, as one biographer described her, "a Gordian knot of contradictions: impossibly glamorous yet disarmingly self-effacing, bold yet riddled with self-doubt, worldly yet naive." Diana called herself "thick as a plank," and there have always been sniggering disbelievers who doubt that her brain ever stretched to accommodate anything other than the blandishments of pop psychology and the chicest, least politically aware sort of do-goodism. (These detractors are mostly of the smart-ass Brit variety, like Christopher Hitchens and Martin Amis. In his name-dropping memoir, *Experience*, Amis claims that Diana's favorite poem was a piece of "harmonial Victorian rubbish," when in fact she seems to have frequently dipped into Wordsworth and Yeats for inspiration. Hitchens, meanwhile, has ventured to call her a "bimbo" and make fun of her friendship with Mother Teresa.)

For others of us who looked on, however, it became clear soon enough that although she originally came across as a shopaholic lacking in book smarts (she didn't attend university and was a fan of her step-grandmother Barbara Cartland's dime-a-dozen romances), Diana was a person of considerable complexity equipped with outsize emotional intelligence and native wit, examples of which abound in any biography of her one happens to pick up. She described Charles's love of hunting expeditions—a passion he passed on to his boys—as "the glorious Windsor pastime of killing things." Similarly, showing more than a smidgen of self-awareness, she mocked her own mercurial character by warning her staff, "Stand by for a mood swing, boys." And she could turn rapier mean when crossed; after she maneuvered the resignation of Charles's trusted valet three months into their marriage, she dismissed the man with a withering rejoinder when he tried to discuss his future employment prospects: "Why don't you read the weather? It takes only two minutes a day."

As the tenth anniversary of her death approaches (she would have been forty-six had she lived), Dianamania has resurfaced with greater force than ever. This pandemic of affection for the vulnerable blond beauty with the spectacular figure and the showstopping violet-blue eyes has never entirely subsided, of course, as is evident by the appetite for conspiracy theories that continue to arise about her death. (Why did her driver take the more circuitous route from the Ritz hotel, one that snaked through an accident-prone tunnel? What about her eerily prescient description of her death—"My husband is planning an 'accident' in my car, brake failure and serious head injury"— ten months before the crash?) In the most gothically detailed of these accounts, *The Murder of Princess Diana*, Noel Botham argues that Diana was a potent combination of globe-trotting humanitarian and mentally unstable ex-royal, who threatened both the powerful arms lobbies with her anti-land-mine crusade and the throne with her press cachet and crackpot romances. (A woman scorned is one thing; a princess scorned, it appears, is another. Paul Burrell, Diana's doting butler, noted in his best-selling memoir, *The Way We Were*, that he saw his newly divorced "boss," as he somewhat irritatingly calls Diana, "put a collection of china that bore the Prince of Wales feathers into a garbage bag, then smash it with a hammer.") Although investigations by the French and British governments found no foul play, a documentary titled *Diana: The Witnesses in the Tunnel* ran on English television in June, and a full jury inquest into the accident will begin in October.

Such dark murmurings aside, this summer brings a boom in all things celebrating Diana: Her sons, William, twenty-five, and Harry, twenty-two, planned a star-studded concert for July in honor of her birthday and a memorial service in August. Her image is gracing magazine covers once again, and several new books will be weighing in, adding to the groaning shelf load of memoirs, anti-memoirs, hagiographic portraits, and exposés already in existence. Far and away the most serious of these offerings— and the most buzzed about—is the former *New Yorker* editor Tina Brown's kaleidoscopic *The Diana Chronicles*. Superbly researched and artfully structured, the book is also compulsively readable, thanks in no small part to its cliff-hanging chapter endings. This in-depth examination of one Anglo blond icon by another Anglo blond (demi-)icon largely succeeds in elevating the narrative of "shy Di" into the nuanced stuff of Shakespearean tragedy rather than the bold-type headlines of tabloid fodder. That it does so despite its flaws—its occasionally hissy asides (on, say, Charles's lackluster performance in the sack or Camilla's nursery advice to her mother-deprived lover to "pretend I am a rocking horse") and its somewhat wearying imputation of the importance of money to a woman worth about thirty-five million dollars when she died (Brown insists that what Diana was seeking as she entered her thirty-seventh year wasn't love so much as a "guy with a Gulfstream")—is a tribute to the author's firm hold on her subject. It speaks as well to her engagement with the various subtexts of class snobbery, psychological damage (both Charles and Diana had bleak childhoods), and Machiavellian machinations that swirled around the unfolding drama.

As one of those caught up in the Diana saga from its heady beginnings—I wasn't much older than she, which made it all the easier to project myself onto her tabula rasa—I remember exactly where I was when she got married in a blaze of televised glory. I was staying at Yaddo, an artists' colony in upstate New York, or, more precisely, squatting in an empty house nearby, equipped with a TV, that belonged to a friend of the late essayist Barbara Grizzuti Harrison—the only other inhabitant of the colony besides me remotely interested in watching the nuptials. The two of us looked on raptly as Lady Diana Spencer, a blushingly gawky and purportedly virginal—or, as Brown puts it in *The Diana Chronicles*, "plausibly *intact*"—girl of twenty was swept up in majestic, historical events and in the enormous twenty-five-foot train of her bridal gown. Brown, who was editor of Britain's prestigious and smart-alecky *Tatler* magazine at the time and had been hired by the *Today* show as its "on-air royalty expert," points out in her book that the Emanuels, the husband-and-wife team Diana chose to create "The Dress," so miscalculated the size of the train that there wasn't enough room to lay it out in the eighteenth-century glass coach that Diana rode in with her father, Earl Spencer. This oversight created a disastrous visual when the future Princess of Wales alighted. "The first glimpse," Brown writes, "made it look like a bundle of old washing until the two designers leapt forward and unfurled it like a billowing, creamy flag."

I recall with equally pointillistic detail where I was when the news broke that Diana had been in a violent car crash: at my parents' beach house, enjoying a peaceful end-of-summer weekend. My seventeen-year-old daughter still remembers that I burst into tears upon hearing that she'd died. The astonishing outpouring of public grief that followed—which was condemned by Queen Elizabeth (or "Mama," as her daughter-in-law incongruously called her) as an unseemly show of touchy-feely behavior in the film *The Queen*—didn't come as a surprise to me. I too had begun to feel protective of Diana, who always seemed to be looking for a port in a storm, first seeking to cuddle up to the robotic, shut-down family she'd married into, and then looking for love in all the wrong places.

I met Tina Brown (who was my "boss" at *The New Yorker* for five years) for lunch on a sunny Friday afternoon in May to discuss *The Diana Chronicles*. In the hope of stirring up a storm cloud of interest, the book's publishers had "embargoed" it, and *Elle* had to sign a confidentiality agreement before I received my bound manuscript. I raced through the mountain of pages the moment it arrived, propelled by the deftness with which the main plot, interspersed with absorbing digressions, was laid out.

Along the way to tracking Diana's ascent, hollow triumph, rude fall, and gradual reincarnation as a figurehead in her own right, Brown fills us in on the intricacy of the palace rituals, the convolutions of the pedigreed mating game that led to the choice of Diana as a suitable consort and "breeder" for Charles, and the hitherto-undissected allure of Camilla. ("Hers is one of those direct, country-house personalities that specialize in instant candor.") Brown gives a trenchant analysis of the fading aristocratic Sloane Ranger class from which Diana sprang: "Lady Diana Spencer came from the last batch of privileged British girls boarded out in agreeable, undemanding schools and allowed to leave qualified for nothing beyond the quest for a suitable husband . . . It's not cool anymore for upper-class girls to be as directionless as Diana was in the 1970s."

The book begins moments before the crash, with Diana emerging from the back of the Ritz in Paris wearing a "tight expression" of displeasure; the paparazzi, Brown notes, had stalked her with greater impunity after the divorce "transformed her from protected royal princess into free-floating global celebrity." It circles back, almost five hundred pages later, to the aftermath of the crash, when Diana's corpse lies waiting to be reclaimed under a sheet in a room at Pitié-Salpêtrière hospital. "Her eyes were closed," Brown writes, "but her unblemished face was so beautiful. Just as in life, she had sustained injuries that showed nothing on the surface." I'd finished reading the book early in the morning of the day Tina and I were to meet, reluctant to let it go, tears in my eyes.

Although Tina and I had bumped into each other during the years since she'd left *The New Yorker*, I was restruck upon seeing her by the aura of brisk, focused energy she exuded. She was wearing Chanel sunglasses and a leather jacket and had just returned from what she called a "Zen week" at the Golden Door spa. Newly adhering to the strict pre-book-tour diet she had been put on by one of the city's "tough love" diet coaches (who, like everyone in New York, is partly known for being known, having successfully terrorized the already-thin publicist Peggy Siegal and several other of the chattering glitterati class into dropping pounds), Tina ordered carefully and picked judiciously at her food; in a mere two weeks she'd already lost eight pounds, she explained, and was intent on shedding twelve more.

As Tina and I caught up on our lives, I could see why she and Princess Diana had often been compared in the press, yoked together as two charismatic and profoundly flirtatious British products. (Brown adroitly captures Diana's famous conquering look, her way of fetchingly "smiling under fluttery lashes," which she apparently employed on her father while still a little girl riding around on a tricycle.) There are, of course, more differences than similarities, beginning with their intellectual assets and going on from there to their psychological profiles. Tina has an Oxford-trained, rapid-firing mind; she is capable of being intrigued by almost any subject if it is presented seductively enough. Diana, as

Brown somewhat Waspishly reminds us, had "an aversion to books" and was drawn to the consolations offered by the healing arts and lowbrow troubadours such as Michael Jackson. Then, too, while Diana's charms seemed to be directed equally at both sexes, I'd always found Tina's warmth to be beamed primarily at men.

On a deeper level, Diana's character was marked by traces of the tentativeness created in her by her largely unparented childhood. "Acutely attuned to the radar of disaster," as Brown describes her, Diana had listened in on her parents' shouting matches since the age of five from her hiding place behind the door of the drawing room at Park House in posh Norfolk. "During her marriage to Prince Charles," Brown notes of this resilient habit, "she was always listening at doors, as she had as a child, seeking confirmation of the worst." Park House, a gray stone mansion that had been leased to Diana's father by his scheming mother-in-law, Lady Fermoy, happens to be a guesthouse on one of the Queen's estates. (In the exhaustingly intertwined fashion of British blue bloods, Lady Fermoy also was a lady-in-waiting to the Queen Mother and would eventually be one of the prime movers behind Diana's marriage.) Diana's mother, Frances Fermoy, from whom Diana inherited her looks, especially her mesmerizing eyes, "bolted" with another man from her resoundingly bad marriage to Johnnie Spencer when Diana was six, taking with her whatever gaiety had existed and losing custody of her four children to their father.

Tina, on the other hand, has the confident manner and feisty style of someone who was encouraged and loved in her youth. Despite her own Diana-like fascination with celebrities and skill at the media game (at which she pronounces Diana "the most artful practitioner"), there is an aspect of Brown that owes more to the British upper-class women of the prewar generation—whom she characterizes as having been "tough as old boots"—than to Diana's troubled and very contemporary personality, which sought to find salvation in bromides of self-transformation and believed in the power of the heart over the mind. Sympathetic and nuanced as Brown's account is, one can also detect an

undertone of exasperation on her part with the insecurities of a
young woman who inexplicably failed to realize the impact of her
own allure on Charles, notwithstanding his attachment to (as it
turns out) two mistresses: Lady "Kanga" Tryon and Camilla
Parker Bowles. "A more self-assured girl than Diana," Brown
writes, "might have perceived that it was she who held all the
cards in this contest. She could have seen Camilla off if she had
chosen wiles instead of tears, sexual artfulness instead of sexual
jealousy, but sadly, she was too young to know how." One
might argue that she was not only too young but also made of
different, more fragile material than either her biographer or
her competition.

"She was never good," Tina tells me, "with women who
threatened her—unless they could offer her maternal advice." As
a waiter hovers, Tina and I avidly analyze Diana as if she were
still alive, as though, indeed, she were a friend who might still be
deciphered and rescued from her own destiny, if only she were
less "thoroughbredish," less "damaged." "You've got to be in-
credibly tough to have that job," Brown says. "You've got to have
the hide of a pachyderm." We go on to discuss her untreated
postpartum depressions ("She was undermedicated," Brown suggests. "She would have been fine on Lexapro") and her "crazy
oscillations," the way she veered between "reckless courage" and
an abiding sense of narcissistic injury. "When Charles pushed
her," Brown muses, "she read it as belittlement. She always ended
up abject. We all know women like that," she adds. "When it
comes to men in their lives . . ." The sentence trails off. Brown
has no reason to clarify any further because Diana is a recognizable type, one of those girls lost in a great yawning loneliness
whom we think we understand from novels like *Madame Bovary*.
Not to mention our own secret identification with them.

Brown readily admits to being "ambivalent" about her subject:
"She was easy to ridicule—she could be ridiculous—but she was
also more important than that. And she was getting more disciplined. Her visit to Angola [where she toured minefields] is a
snapshot of who she might have become."

We linger over the many personalities involved in the tale, the "cavalcade of bizarre, second-rate" courtiers and hangers-on. Although so much went wrong, it is curiously difficult to assign blame (which is, I suppose, why I'm tempted to believe in the conspiracy theories), or even to divide the cast of characters into Good and Bad. Diana's mother, Frances, who was probably the most interesting of the bunch—Brown calls her "funny, tough, romantic, and selfish"—was only intermittently close to her daughter. Lady Fermoy, Diana's maternal grandmother—whose loyalty to both her daughter (she testified against Frances in her custody trial) and granddaughter (after conspiring to marry off Diana to the highest-placed bachelor in the country, she dropped her the minute she began flailing) was nonexistent—is the closest to a malign backstage presence. Diana's relatives on the other side, it seems, were no better. "The Spencers are a dyspeptic lot," Brown remarks. "They're a family always on the outs with each other." Diana's father, who cut a touching figure accompanying her down the aisle, turns out to have been something of a "sad sack," an Evelyn Waugh character barking at the gamekeeper.

Brown's most mischievous suggestion, in the book and to me personally, is that Prince Philip might have been Diana's savior— both romantically and sexually—if only he hadn't been her father-in-law. "Philip," she announces, "was the lover she needed. He was authentic. He has a kind of decency." (It's hard for me to see him as the "great guy" Tina makes him out to be, but then again, she herself has always had a taste for older, powerful men.)

As our meeting comes to an end, Tina and I ponder what Diana's psychiatric diagnosis might have been. She asks me if I think she'd be classified as a "borderline," but then we both wander off from this line of thinking, mostly because it doesn't seem useful in addressing the void left by Diana's fatal trajectory. "It was such a banal way to go," Brown says. "No one can bear the idea of something as wasteful, crass, and silly as a car crash."

What I am left with, after my former editor rushes into a waiting car that will take her to her weekend house in the Hamptons and I step out into the beautiful pre-summer weather, is a feeling of indescribable sadness. I'm still not persuaded that what Diana needed was, as Tina put it, "what Gwyneth Paltrow

needed—a gated community with a driveway and electronic in-
tercom which she could bark into and the gate would swing
open." She was, as Tina also conceded, someone who was "quite
capable of living in a cottage. She wasn't grandiose or pretentious.
She was a girl with no background." Although enough money
might have helped in moating her, in keeping the paparazzi at
bay, I can't imagine any amount would have shielded her from
what she needed shielding from most, which were her own intransigent furies. In that sense, the whole Dodi Fayed–as–Aristotle
Onassis scenario, which seems to speak to Brown, doesn't convince me. It might have been a solution if Diana had been a regal,
self-sufficient Jackie O. sort; in the event, she was a mother-starved
girl looking for affection anywhere she could find it.

The truth is that *The Diana Chronicles* has only provoked
more questions and left me searching for more answers—or,
lacking them, more speculations. For a moment, as I walk along
Fifty-Seventh Street, I find myself wondering how Diana's life
might have turned out if she and Charles had bonded over their
shared lack of mothering, their virtual abandonment as children.
Both came into the marriage with "transitional objects" from
their childhood, especially beloved stuffed animals: he with his
patched-up teddy bear and she with a small gang of well-worn
companions. What would have happened if they had had the
patience (on his side) and endurance (on hers) to address their
mutual longings for love and nurturance in each other? And then
it occurs to me that I am spinning fairy tales of my own, trying
to shift the script away from tragedy the better to give the spellbinding narrative of the princess with the golden hair and a com-
moner's touch a longer shelf life than fate would have it.

THE PEACEFUL PUGILIST

(MIKE TYSON)

2011

The gold caps on his teeth are gone, as are the frenzied trappings of celebrity: the nonstop partying filled with drugs and women, the cars, the jewelry, the pet tiger, the liters of Cristal. Mike Tyson—who was once addicted, by his own account, "to everything"—now lives in what might be described as a controlled environment of his own making, a clean, well-lit, but very clearly demarcated place.

These days, the forty-four-year-old ex–heavyweight champion is in bed by eight and often up as early as two in the morning, at which point he takes a solitary walk around the suburban Las Vegas neighborhood where he lives while listening to R&B on his iPod. Tyson then occupies himself with reading (he's an avid student of history, philosophy, and psychology), watching karate movies, or taking care of his homing pigeons, who live in a coop in the garage, until six, when his wife, Lakiha (known as Kiki), gets up. The two of them go to a spa nearby where they work out and often get massages before settling into the daily routine of caring for a two-year-old daughter, Milan, and a newborn son, Morocco; they also run Tyrannic, the production company they own. It is a willfully low-key life, one in which Tyson's wilder impulses are held in check by his inner solid citizen.

The astonishing discipline and drive Tyson once put into "the stern business of pugilism," to quote the boxer Jack Johnson, is now being channeled into the business of leading an ordinary, even humdrum existence. Tyson insists that quitting boxing is the best thing he's ever done, that he doesn't regret it, "not even a little bit. I don't like the person it allows you to become." Still, while it is impossible not to wonder whether this effort can be sustained indefinitely—whether, that is, you can reshape the contours of a personality by a sheer act of will—there is no doubt that Tyson has committed himself to a wholesale renovation. He spends some of his time involved in domestic activities, accompanying Kiki and Milan to classes at Gymboree and doctors' appointments or running errands, and some of his time furthering his post-boxing career, doing autograph signings, conferring with his agent and publicist about new opportunities. Although he no longer gets lucrative endorsement deals, Tyson earns fees for personal appearances in America and "meet and greet" dinner tours in Europe. He made a brief but memorable cameo in the blockbuster film *The Hangover* and will play a bit part in *The Hangover Part II*. He's hoping to nab more acting roles—genuine ones, in which he gets to play someone other than himself. "I want to entertain people," he tells me, smiling broadly. "I want a Tony Award."

As part of his cleaning-up campaign, he has been adhering to a strict vegan diet for nearly two years, explaining that he doesn't want anything in him "that's going to enrage me—no processed food, no meat." He says that he can no longer abide the smell of meat even on someone's breath and has dropped 150 pounds since he weighed in at 330 in 2009. "I've learned to live a boring life and love it," he declares, sounding more determined than certain. "I let too much in, and look what happened . . . I used to have a bunch of girls and some drugs on the table. A bunch of people running around doing whatever."

The life that he has created almost from scratch over the last two years has been defined at least as much by what Tyson wants to avoid—old haunts, old habits, old temptations, and old hangers-on—as by what he wants to embrace. One of the few links between his tumultuous past and his more tranquil present are his homing pigeons. He has been raising them since he was a picked-on fat little kid with glasses growing up in some of Brooklyn's poorest neighborhoods—first Bedford-Stuyvesant, then

Brownsville—with an alcoholic, promiscuous mother given to violent outbursts, which included scalding a boyfriend with boiling water. ("He had a tough mother," recalls David Malone, a childhood friend. "We knew to stay away from her.") Although he has turned down requests to do a reality show, Tyson agreed to participate in a six-part docudrama about his pigeons called *Taking On Tyson* that began airing on Animal Planet on March 6.

The young Tyson turned to birds as both a hobby and an escape; it was in defense of his pigeons that the timid kid who was called "sissy" and "faggy boy" got into his first fistfight. When he was released from prison in 1995 after serving three years for the rape of Desiree Washington, he went immediately to visit his coops in the Catskills. "The birds were there before boxing," says Mario Costa, who owns the Ringside Gym in Jersey City and has known Tyson since the early 1980s. "He feels peaceful around them." Tyson keeps coops in Las Vegas, Jersey City, and Bushwick, and to this day he seeks out the birds when one of his "bad spells," as Kiki calls them, strikes and his mood turns dark and agitated. "The first thing I ever loved in my life was a pigeon," Tyson says. "It's a constant with my sanity in a weird way."

I have never been particularly drawn to boxing, but there was something about the younger Mike Tyson—his way of seeming larger than the sport itself, of playing out impulses that seemed all the more authentic for being so unmediated, whether it was his desperate bid for Robin Givens's heart or his desperate biting of Evander Holyfield's ear—that caught my attention. He seemed like a man in huge conflict with himself as well as with the forces around him—the media, the celebrity machine with its perks and dangers—in a way that suggested that he was both vulnerable to manipulation and leery of being manipulated.

In preparation for my visit to Las Vegas at the beginning of March, I communicated through e-mail with Kiki, who manages Tyson's affairs, and the plan was kept loose: we were to meet at his house for several days of conversation, with no definite times fixed. I called the film director James Toback, who made an acclaimed 2008 documentary about Tyson and has known him since they met on the set of Toback's *Pick-Up Artist* in 1986, to find out what I could about a man who came across in the film as both very present and elusive, weepy one minute and matter-of-fact the next, capable of self-insight but also hidden to himself. Toback told me that Tyson was unpredictable, given to sudden psychological disconnections that Toback referred to as "click-outs." It was entirely possible, Toback said, that Tyson would back out of the interviews altogether. "Everything is contingent on the state of mind he's in at the moment," the director observed. According to Toback, he and Tyson shared experiences of temporary insanity—of "losing the I"—and "people who don't understand madness can't understand him. He's quicker, smarter, sharper than almost anyone he's talking to."

Toback went on to say that making the movie had been an "exhilarating" experience for both of them and that he senses that Tyson is happier now, that he doesn't have "the same degree of doom" he had before he met Kiki. He recalled their "late-night conversations about sex, love, madness, and death," and then, lest I think I might intuit something about the ex-fighter that had escaped others, Toback suddenly issued a pronouncement: "No one gets him. You can't get him if you haven't been where he's been."

The first object that caught my eye in Tyson's double-storied, sparely furnished living room was a plush, purple Disney child's car seat, perched on a chair near the screen doors that led out to a swimming pool. There was also a child-size table and chairs, and a cluster of Mylar balloons tied to a bar stool in celebration of the birth of the Tysons' week-old son, Morocco, who has a touch of jaundice as well as his father's narrow eyes. The white stucco house is in a gated community called Seven Hills, which has the hushed, slightly vacant aura of gated communities everywhere. The entranceway features a koi pond under Plexiglas, and the expansive, open interior is decorated in a style that could be described as utilitarian (the color scheme is plum, beige, and brown) with rococo touches: there is a huge contemporary chan-

delier as well as two gilded brass mirrors over a glassed-in fireplace that match the ironwork frieze on the front doors.

Tyson bought the place from a friend, the NBA player Jalen
Rose, in the down market of early 2007. (The property was originally valued at $3 million; Tyson paid around $1.7 million for
it.) It was built, he says, as a "party house," but he and Kiki have
been pushing it in the direction of a more traditional family
home, with clearly defined living areas and childproof touches,
like the Plexiglas panels on the stair railing. Tyson mentioned
that he bought the house because it reminded him of a New York
loft, even though he also says there's little he misses about his
hometown aside from the pigeon competitions and seeing people
from his old stomping grounds. "I have a big affinity with the
guys in my neighborhood . . . the guys with the broken English
and stuff . . . and then the pigeon world, it's not like there's a
glass ceiling, the pigeon world keeps evolving with time. There
are new diseases; there have to be serums for the new diseases,"
he said, sounding momentarily like a biochemist, albeit one with
an endearing lisp. "Antibodies."

Tyson and I sat diagonally across from each other on black
leather couches; in front of us was a glass coffee table on a Persian
rug. He took sips from a cup of tea with honey and snacked on a
banana. Kiki and her mother, who lives down the street and does
a lot of babysitting, were upstairs with the children. Tyson's assistant, Farid (also known, inexplicably, as David), had picked me
up at my hotel and driven me to the house in a maroon Cadillac
Escalade; Farid is a genial former IT consultant whom Tyson met
in jail, although Tyson was at pains to point out that Farid was
never a criminal type, just a geek trying to make some extra
money on the sly. In person, Tyson's voice was deeper and raspier
than it sounds in TV interviews, and he cut a much slighter, trim-
mer figure than you would expect. He wore a T-shirt that said
"TYSON" on the back and very white running shoes. His head
was shaved, and the left side of his face bore the dramatic tattoo
of the New Zealand Maori warrior that he got in the beginning of 2003. All the same, he seemed more shy than ferocious,
more of an introvert than someone out to create a stir.

As the hours passed, Tyson grew less wary and more at ease about saying what was on his mind. An autodidact, he likes to discuss characters he's read about, ranging from Alexander the Great to Constantine to Tom Sawyer, and he harbors a special fondness for Machiavelli. He knows the history of boxing inside out, watches films of Muhammad Ali and other boxers (including himself) most every evening, returning again and again to *Raging Bull*. He's also something of a homegrown philosopher, peppering our conversation with hard-knock truths. "The biggest tough guy wants to be likable," he observed. But there are also whole areas of his life he keeps firmly cordoned off, especially the raging Kid Dynamite days: "I think I was insane for a great period of my life. I think I was really insane . . . It was just too quick. I didn't understand the dynamics then. I just knew how to get on top; I didn't know what to do once I got there." He seemed to be edging closer to a deeper revelation, so I asked him if he had any regrets. He answered with rare snappishness: "I'm too young for regrets. I'm not in the grave yet."

The first big change in Tyson's convulsive life came when he went from being a ghetto kid whose world consisted of "a reformatory and welfare and rats and roaches" to being a rising boxing star living in a fourteen-room, antiques-filled Victorian mansion on fifteen acres in the Catskills as one of the charges of Cus D'Amato, the legendary boxing trainer cum life coach. D'Amato, who was seventy then, was known for his stern credo of excellence, his ability to mold young talent, and his eccentric, somewhat paranoid views; his protégés included Floyd Patterson and José Torres. The adolescent Tyson was introduced to "this old white guy" who didn't know him "from a can of paint" by Bobby Stewart, a counselor at the Tryon School for Boys, the juvenile detention center where Tyson was sent after racking up a police record of street crimes. D'Amato saw Olympic potential in the surly, antisocial boy who could barely read or write. "He said, 'Can you handle the job that's at hand?' And I say, 'Sure I can, I can do it,'" Tyson recalled. "But I really didn't know if I could do anything. I didn't want to be a punk or a pussy . . ."

The young Tyson began training with D'Amato and his staff at the Catskill Boxing Club on passes from Tryon; in 1980, while still a ward of the state, he moved into what was a kind of boardinghouse run by D'Amato and his companion, Camille Ewald. Camille served as materfamilias to the group of troubled boys—there were no more than four to six fighters in residence at any one time—teaching them manners and how to do laundry. (Tyson remained in touch with Ewald, helping to support her and sending her flowers on her birthday, until her death in 2001.)

D'Amato, meanwhile, devised a master plan whereby Tyson would be reprogrammed from being a street thug to being a warrior in the ring. "Cus was an amazing influence," says Tom Patti, another D'Amato protégé, who lived with Tyson at the boardinghouse and played the role of big brother in his life, although he was only two years older, teaching him how to drive and palling around. "He engineered his fighters and their success." To hone Tyson's physical skills, D'Amato taught him the two boxing techniques that he himself had developed and that were now his signatures—holding the gloves in a tight defensive position at ear level and maintaining a consistent head motion before and after punching.

As for mental conditioning, Tyson's ego was inflated nonstop. "They were telling me how great I am, telling me how I can do this if I really try," Tyson explained, sounding decidedly of mixed minds when looking back on this approach. "They kept it in my head. It had me form a different psychological opinion of myself. No one could say anything negative about me. I always had to have the supreme confidence that I'm a god and superior to everybody else, which is just sick and crazy. But it had its uses." After Tyson's mother, Lorna, died of cancer in the fall of 1982, D'Amato became his legal guardian and continued to oversee Tyson's training until his death in 1985. On November 22, 1986, D'Amato's tireless mentoring paid off big-time when Mike Tyson defeated Trevor Berbick and became the new world heavyweight champion (and, at age twenty, the youngest in history), exactly as D'Amato had predicted he would.

Tyson lives less than half an hour from the raucous, twenty-four-hour universe of the Las Vegas Strip, but it was preternaturally quiet in his house. The phone didn't ring, and the silence during conversational pauses was broken only by an occasional crying bout of Morocco's or some chatter of Milan's that trickled down from the second floor. "It's like a funeral home here," Tyson said softly, as if he were thinking my thoughts aloud. It was one of the few times he alluded to what appears to be the deliberate curtailment of his life—the lengths he and Kiki have gone to in order to keep his habitat free from too much stimuli or pressure, the better to preserve his somewhat fragile equanimity. At one point, Milan came into the living room and reached for a tiny handful of pretzels from a bowl. He picked up the toddler and hugged her tightly, then put his face in her hair. When he put her down, she stood against the couch across from him, and he kept his eye on her as she ate her pretzels. "Chew," he said gently. "Milan, you've got to chew."

Tyson has six biological children, who range in age from newborn to twenty, born of three different women. A seventh child, a daughter named Exodus, died at age four in May 2009 in a tragic accident at her mother's home in Phoenix; she was strangled when her neck was caught in a cord hanging from a treadmill. Tyson caught a plane immediately upon receiving a call from Sol Xochitl, Exodus's mother, but by the time he arrived at the hospital, the little girl was already brain-dead. The loss of his daughter critically altered his once-tentative grasp on his own accountability. To this day, he blames himself for not being there. "It made me feel very irresponsible," he says simply. "I wish she were here to hang out with Milan." The effects of the tragedy reverberated throughout Tyson's extended family. "The kids were very close to Exodus, and when she died, we were all devastated," says Monica Turner, his second wife. "I think that changed Mike forever." Tyson refers to Exodus repeatedly during our conversations with evident sadness and insists on keeping her memory alive by counting her among his living children.

Tyson has been married three times; the first marriage was to the TV actress Robin Givens when he was twenty-one, after a fevered courtship. The yearlong union proved disastrous, culminating in an infamous 1988 interview with Barbara Walters, in which Givens described the marriage as "pure hell"—while Tyson sat passively beside her, drugged on manic-depression medication. ("I'm tripolar," he tells me, laughing, when I ask him how he'd diagnose his condition today.) He went on to have two children with Monica Turner; he also considers himself a father to Turner's daughter Gena. Turner, who is on friendly terms with Tyson, filed for divorce in 2002, citing adultery. Along the way, Tyson, a notorious womanizer, sired two more children—eight-year-old Miguel and Exodus—with Xochitl. Tyson keeps in touch with all of his brood, speaking especially proudly of his oldest son, thirteen-year-old Amir, who is six feet tall. "He's just nervous and afraid of life," he says, sounding an apprehensive note. "But he's doing so well . . . There are no bad influences. I have so many hopes for him."

Tyson knows from bad influences, if only because he has been susceptible to so many of them since the death of D'Amato and his own emergence as a sports superstar. Following a brief glory period in the late 1980s, when he was arguably the most popular athlete in the world—he was asked to do endorsements for Pepsi, Nintendo, and Kodak, and hired by the New York City Police Department to boost recruitment as well as by the FBI to do public service announcements to keep kids off drugs—Tyson began spiraling out of control. His self-destructive patterns, which had been refocused by D'Amato, came to the surface once again, aided and abetted by the boxing promoter Don King, who successfully wooed Tyson in the wake of his split from Robin Givens. (Tyson filed a lawsuit against King in 1998, claiming that the promoter stole millions from him.) Once a moneymaking machine worth $400 million at the height of his fame, Tyson was reduced to filing for personal bankruptcy in 2003; he was $27 million in debt.

In late December 2006 he was arrested in Arizona on charges

of drug possession and drunken driving, and in February 2007
he checked himself into the Wonderland Center, a rehab facility
in the Hollywood Hills, for the treatment of various addictions.
Carole Raymond, a warm-sounding woman with a thick Yorkshire accent who worked as a staff member at Wonderland during
Tyson's stay, remembers that he had trouble finding a facility that
would take him and that he came to them a "beaten down" man.
Still, she remembers him as funny, "very humble," and eager to
embrace the program's ethos. "People who come from fame or
money have a hard time grasping the idea of recovery. He wanted
to be emotionally better than the Mike Tyson who was always
boxing." Tyson, in turn, credits the "life skills" he learned in rehab with coming to his rescue when a crisis hits: "You don't know
where they came from, but you're on the top of your game. You're
suited up and ready to work." When I asked him why he stayed at
Wonderland for as long as he did—more than a year—he leaned
over as if to emphasize what he was about to say. "I felt safe."

As befits someone who has been alternately idolized and demonized by the press, Tyson is wary of the public's continuing
interest in his saga. He says he believes that celebrity made him
"delusional" and that it has taken nothing less than a "paradigm
shift" for him to come down to earth: "We have to stick to what
we are. I always stay in my slot. I know my place." He asked me
outright, "Why do you want to know about me as a person?" and
at one point, anxious that he might be boring me, he got up to
show me photographs from the glory days in which he is posing
with other boxers (Ali, Rocky Graziano, Jake LaMotta) and with
big names like Frank Sinatra, Tom Cruise, and Barbra Streisand.
Underneath his deliberate calmness and considerable charm, there
is something bewildered and lost seeming about Tyson. Indeed,
he refers to himself as a "little boy" who "never had a chance to
develop," and it is in part this conception of himself as missing
out on a crucial period of maturation that fuels his present focus. "This is what the deal is," he said. "People just wait for you
to grow up and do the right thing. They're just waiting for
you to participate in the improvement of your life as a human
being. When are you going to do it?"

The most important and sustaining influence in Tyson's current incarnation as an introspective mensch rather than the Bad-
dest Man on the Planet is the presence of his wife, Kiki, whom
he has known since she was about sixteen (they met through her
father, who did some boxing promotions); they exchanged their
first kiss when she was nineteen and had an on-and-off romance
for more than a decade. They tried living together in Kiki's apartment in Manhattan in 2002 after Tyson's defeat at the hands of
Lennox Lewis, but it was, she says, "a disaster." "He was used to
juggling a lot of women." They remained friends, even though
the relationship didn't work out, had another fling in 2004, lost
touch again when Tyson was in rehab, and then reconnected
when Tyson called her after he got out. Their daughter, Milan,
was born on Christmas 2008, and they married on June 6, 2009.
"We know all of each other's secret stuff," she says. "He told me
everything, and I told him everything. We fight hard, but I'm
very much in love with him."

Kiki, who is thirty-four, is a well-spoken, down-to-earth
woman who seems pleasantly oblivious to her own exotically
good looks and celebrity status by virtue of being Mike Tyson's
wife. Making a viable life with the complicated, demon-haunted
man she has married requires patience. "It's a struggle," she says,
speaking about his relapses post-rehab. "You're always an addict
and have to work at it. It's easy for him to fall back in his own
life. He surrounds himself with people who are sober and doesn't
go out to clubs. If his pattern shifts, you know something's
wrong." Perhaps because she has known Tyson for so long, she's
clear-eyed about his failings. "He slept with every kind of woman
you can think of," she says. "Now he wants someone who knows
him and can be good to him. We're rebuilding our lives together
on a positive note." Tyson, meanwhile, seems continually struck
by his good fortune in having Kiki, whom he addresses as "my
love," by his side. "I never thought we'd be together," he told
me. "I thought we'd be sex partners. I told her not to marry me."
A few seconds later he adds: "I want to die with her."

Despite their cushy lifestyle, there isn't the kind of money
to throw around that there once was. But Kiki, for one, seems

indifferent to the sort of lavish expenditures that Tyson's former
fortune once enabled him to make: "Mike always says he's broke,
but it's relative. That type of stuff isn't important to us. We want
to build a nest egg for our kids' accounts. I'm not impressed with
money like that." Meanwhile, although Tyson still owes a sub-
stantial amount—"a few million" is how Kiki puts it—in back
taxes, he is adhering to a payment plan. He has a financial plan-
ner who negotiated a deal with the IRS regarding the purchase
of his house, which was paid for in full. If Tyson misses his high-
rolling days, he isn't letting on. "If you make a lot of money, you
end up being around people you don't want to be around," he
says. "Guys on allowance. It takes years to gather the audacity
to get rid of them."

On the Saturday before the premiere of *Taking On Tyson*, Mike
Tyson was in New York with Kiki and their two children, doing
publicity for the show. I met him in Bushwick, in front of the
run-down row house where he had gone to see his birds; Kiki,
meanwhile, had taken Milan to the American Girl store to meet
a friend. Tyson was with Farid and his friend Dave Malone, who
tends to the Brooklyn coops. On the drive back to the Ritz-Carlton
in Battery Park, where he was staying, I found the ex-boxer to be
in a contemplative mood. Or maybe he was feeling remorseful; he
had just come through one of his bad spells—what Toback alluded to as his "click-outs"—in which he feels alternately so low
that he wants to jump out the window and so angry that he
wants to crack someone's head open with a pipe. "They come on
you," he told me, "out of the blue." The birds helped him regain
his footing, as they always do, but these bouts must take a toll on
him (not to mention Kiki), opening up the floodgates of the past.
Driving through Brooklyn, we passed a bunch of kids playing
handball, and he reminisced: "When I was poor, I used to play
handball. That's how we all start." He called Kiki to check how
the playdate was going, sounding sweetly affectionate, and then
on the way into the hotel posed patiently for a photographer with
an excited bride and groom who spotted him coming in.

In his hotel suite, Tyson was eager to tell me about a book he was reading—*A Natural History of Human Emotions*, by Stuart Walton—and asked me to read aloud a chapter on jealousy. We discussed the difference between jealousy and envy, and when I asked whether he ever envies his children getting the sort of parental love he never had, he said, "How did you know that?" I inquired whether he misses the glamour of his old life, and he answered, "That's not who I am anymore." Around 5:30, Kiki returned with Milan, who triumphantly marched in, carrying a new American Girl doll aloft. Tyson and his wife kissed each other, and he said, "I'm sorry if I upset you." She answered serenely, "That's okay, honey," as she went to get ready for their night out.

A cynic might wonder whether the kinder, gentler Tyson is merely another act, a construction every bit as deliberate as he claims his invincible Iron Mike persona was—"a vicious tiger," as he describes it, "out there to kill somebody." And there is indeed something of the actor about Tyson, warming to his new role as a humbled rogue, a gentle giant with his delicate birds. But there is also a kind of heroism in his effort to construct a more accountable self, a reaching across the decades of excess back to the more disciplined days in the Catskills with Cus D'Amato. Now, however, the focus is not on invincibility or greatness but on the perhaps more elusive goal of keeping his furies at bay and trying to master his unrulier impulses rather than letting them control him. It's sure to be one hell of a match.

IN WARM BLOOD

(TRUMAN CAPOTE)

Long before I ever read Truman Capote's *In Cold Blood*—with its "immaculately factual" (according to Capote) descriptions of the lead-up to and aftermath of four random murders that occurred in the very early morning of November 15, 1959, in an isolated farmhouse in the tiny hamlet (population 270) of Holcomb, Kansas—bloodied images of the Clutter family used to color my adolescent dreams. Thanks to my mother's transfixed reading of Capote's account as it appeared in four consecutive installments in *The New Yorker* in the fall of 1965, when I was eleven, I was aware of the book well before it was published, and had pestered my mother for all the ghoulish details. I would lie in bed at night, envisioning Nancy Clutter, only five years older at the time of her death than I was then—kind, journal-keeping Nancy Clutter, sixteen and rarely been kissed—lying with her hands and feet bound in her pink and white bed, listening in the dark to the ominous sound of Perry Smith and Dick Hickock coming up the stairs in their boots. Nancy was dispatched with one shotgun blast to her head, like her younger brother and her parents (Mr. Clutter's throat had first been slit). I don't know when it was exactly that I learned of Perry's limp, acquired in a motorcycle wreck that was one of the innumerable mishaps that marked his own desolate growing up, but I do remember being intrigued enough by the detail to incorporate it into my re-creation of Nancy's last minutes.

For this was the thing about *In Cold Blood*—and about Capote's trumpeting of his "nonfiction novel" as an innovative narrative form that drew on both the persuasiveness of fact and the poetic altitude of fiction: it decisively upped the literary ante. Every detail about the Clutter case, from the idyllic-seeming family with conservative heartland values who were the victims, to the two punks who had little in common but a sense of derring-do, a collection of tattoos, and a chewing-gum habit, seemed thrilling and potentially life transforming. It was as though the more details you had firmly in hand—the killers' final pathetic haul of forty-three dollars, a pair of binoculars, and a transistor radio (a far cry from the ten thousand dollars they'd been told by a former cell mate of Hickock's that they'd find in Herb Clutter's safe); the lingering postpartum depressions of Mrs. Clutter; Perry Smith's love of esoteric, triple-inning words—the closer you might come to comprehending not only the age-old question of good versus evil but the haphazard workings of fate itself. It was as if the details could explain why one moment the small-town assumption that it is safe to sleep with unlocked doors still holds up, and the next moment the worst has happened and your neighbors suddenly strike you as potentially homicidal.

In Cold Blood made the largely passive acts of observing and writing seem freshly potent, as though the movies hadn't yet gobbled up all the cultural oxygen. The book made Capote, as he put it, "the most famous author in America"; George Plimpton described the newly lionized writer as becoming "so extraordinarily famous that he was recognized by the average person in the street." Whatever you chose to make of Capote's puffy claims about himself or the artistic ground he insisted he was breaking (he was at pains to separate himself from the pack of New Journalists, like Tom Wolfe and Jimmy Breslin, whom he considered to lack "the proper fictional equipment"), there is no doubt that he helped create a more intimate and artfully crafted kind of journalism. His anthropological method lent the aimless, misspent lives of Hickock and Smith a reality every bit as textured as the God-fearing, cherry-pie-baking lives of their victims. With only the sustained quality of his attention and his prodigious memory to call on, Capote succeeded in making the eventual collision of these two worlds a paradigmatic (and, as it turned out, psychologically plausible) tragedy that reverberated long after it actually occurred. In doing so, he brought to the literary landscape an energy and allure—a sense of high-stakes drama— that it hadn't seen since the days when Victorian readers awaited the death of Dickens's Little Nell.

Capote, the film, which opened last week, has been justly praised on many fronts, from its subtle, literate script (based on Gerald Clarke's biography, *Capote*) and quietly memorable cinematography (Adam Kimmel), to the unobtrusively effective score and the remarkable work of its cast. Perhaps the most striking aspect of the movie is how assured it is for a novice effort. It is the first feature for both the director, Bennett Miller (his previous credits include more than two hundred commercials and a one-man digital documentary, *The Cruise*), and the screenwriter, Dan Futterman (this is his first produced screenplay), and it is noticeably lacking, with one or two exceptions (such as the oddly mistuned, avuncular portrait of William Shawn), in wrong turns or amateurish moves. Almost from the moment the camera pans across the flat wheat fields and wide swath of Midwestern sky, the film establishes a sense of parallel universes, deftly cutting from a scene "out there" in unpopulous Kansas in which Nancy Clutter's best friend knocks at the door of the silent farmhouse where her friend lies dead, to a throbbing, smoke-filled Manhattan gathering where Capote, a cigarette in one hand and a drink in the other, holds an audience of literati spellbound with his glittering, frequently heartless anecdotes. The versatile Philip Seymour Hoffman inhabits Capote as though they were brothers under the skin, with a degree of empathy that circumvents caricature (unlike Robert Morse's portrayal of Capote in Broadway's *Tru*) and adds a note of poignancy to even his character's less endearing traits.

Most of us know Truman Capote only by way of the sensationalistic images he cultivated on his way up (*The New Yorker*'s Brendan Gill once described the young Capote as a "gorgeous apparition, fluttering, flitting up and down the corridors") or the scandalous gossip that circulated around the five-foot-three-inch "Tiny Terror," as he was dubbed, on his way down, after his muse had largely abandoned him. In those latter years, the perennially baby-faced creature, whose gargantuan charm and savage opinions wore less and less well, wobbled on and off talk shows in an alcohol- and drug-induced haze, still childlike of mien and sibilantly nasal of tone (Capote's voice was once compared to that of a baby seal), before he died at the age of fifty-nine. But right from the beginning, even before he moved into the social epicenter on the arms of the rich and beautiful women he called his "swans," there was something both ephemeral and larger than life about him. You can see it in the early, faun-like jacket photograph on the back of *Other Voices, Other Rooms*, where the twenty-three-year-old writer is posed lolling on a sofa for maximal winsome effect, like a beautiful boy who got lost on the way to reform school.

Capote is focused almost entirely on the six years during which *In Cold Blood* was being researched and written, and this deliberate sense of containment is a mostly inspired artistic decision. (I wish that the filmmakers had stuck entirely to their decision to keep the movie's scope small and not tried for a run at a fuller biopic treatment by telescoping the facts of Capote's eventual decline at the end.) Capote's exhibitionism and narcissism are very much in evidence, and lest we somehow fail to recognize these traits, his pal Nelle (the writer Harper Lee, played with great pliancy and an unexpected softness by Catherine Keener) is always on hand to help underline them. Nelle, who accompanied Capote on his first trip to Kansas and helped ease his dialogue with the solid-citizen types who were initially put off by his flippant humor and sashaying ephebe manners, is especially impatient with her friend's professions of having done everything he could to help the killers appeal the death penalty. (He did intervene on their behalf but eventually backed off.) When, for instance, we see Capote on the phone with Nelle toward the end of the film, trying to rustle up some sympathy after the long ordeal of writing the book and the more recent ordeal of having witnessed Perry's and Dick's execution, six years after their conviction, she crisply cuts into his self-absorbed reverie. "They're dead, Truman," she points out. "You're alive." (In Clarke's biography, it is actually Truman's lover, Jack Dunphy, who says this.)

Although some reviewers have charged the film with soft-pedaling Capote's more egregious sides—his betrayal, for instance, of the bonds he forged with the killers, or his eagerness to see them hang so he could have a conclusion for his book—the filmmakers strike me as more than keen to highlight Capote's moral compromises and deceitful journalistic methods. We see him telling Perry (played by Clifton Collins, Jr.) that he hasn't written much of the book (when in fact it is practically finished) and insisting that the title, which rubs Perry's aesthetic sensibilities and noble-misfit sense of himself the wrong way, won't be *In Cold Blood*. But the dark and unscrupulous strands running through Capote's character—the persistent suggestion that he cut his loyalties to suit his deadlines—strike me as much the least interesting part of the story. Capote could have been beset by these same flaws, the same powers of seduction and ambiguous affections, and not gone off and written a masterpiece in prose that Norman Mailer once judged to be "word for word, rhythm for rhythm" the best of his generation. Capote might have written a mediocre thriller, or a piece of competent journalism, instead of a book that transformed the workmanlike genre of true crime into a starkly realistic yet lyrical work of art that changed the way literary journalism was done, for better and for worse.

We surely all know by now that journalists are a bad bunch—a "morally indefensible" species of con artist always looking to *sell someone out*—if only because the best of them (Janet Malcolm and Joan Didion) are always ratting on themselves. The truth is that by today's scoop-obsessed and elasticized journalistic standards, Capote comes off looking better than most. At least he had the decency to be sufficiently conflicted about the devil's bargain he struck in pursuit of his story to still be summoning up the ghost of Perry Smith in an essay called "Self-Portrait," which he wrote six years after *In Cold Blood* appeared: "A young man with black cowlicked hair. He is wearing a leather harness that keeps his arms strapped to his sides. He is trembling; but he is speaking to me, smiling. All I can hear is the roar of blood in my ears. Twenty minutes later he is dead, hanging from the end of a rope."

In *Conversations with Capote*, a series of talks Lawrence Grobel recorded with the writer during the last two years of his life, Capote refers to the writing of *In Cold Blood* as "the most emotional experience of my creative life" and discusses his opposition to the death penalty. To say that he wasn't genuinely attached to the killers (and deeply sympathetic toward, if not erotically attracted to, Perry Smith) or exercised over capital punishment, as Kenneth Tynan and others have, seems to me blatantly unfair. I am convinced that the case haunted him—and ultimately derailed him—until his death.

Indeed, the insights of *Capote* have little to do with the cautionary tale aspect of the film. It seems to me that the film would have made a more compelling statement about the soul-scorching cost of the obsessionalism that fuels creative endeavor had it not, in fact, italicized the trade-offs and compromises that eased Capote's path, making it easy for viewers to write him off as a manipulative egomaniac. The real revelation of Hoffman's performance is that it shows Capote at the height of his astonishing powers, conscientiously plying his trade, looking, talking, brooding, wandering in his head, entering other people's heads, brooding some more, imagining his way into an alien world. Something flits across Hoffman's eyes early in the film, when he suddenly realizes he has made the wrong insouciant remark to Alvin Dewey, the lawman on the case, who was a close friend of Herb Clutter's. Then, in a matter of seconds, internal adjustments are made, decisions are taken, and the two men forge an alliance.

Film has tended to present the unkinetic profession of writing in one of two stereotyped ways: as a precarious occupation that takes place in garreted isolation—think of a red-eyed, holed-up Jane Fonda wildly puffing at her cigarettes in *Julia*—or as a cushy desk job that resembles a less energetic form of interior decoration, which is what it looks like whenever Diane Keaton sits down at her laptop in *Something's Gotta Give*. *Capote* enables us to grasp, more than any movie on the subject I have seen, what it is exactly that a writer does when he or she writes, how observation leads to perception leads to the crafting of sentences. In so doing, it gets far closer to the complicated, elusive heart of this strange calling—the way it is both an explicitly private and an implicitly public act, a means of rendezvousing with the self but also of showcasing the self—than any cinematic depiction until now.

During the film, Capote observes, almost as an aside, that he feels as though he and Perry had grown up in the same house, except that one left by the front door and one by the back. After paying a visit to Perry in his cell, Capote lies on his bed and watches bars of light move across the ceiling of his room, like a free-floating image of incarceration. That scene helps to establish the synaptic trick at the heart of great writing—the way it can cross over, on a dime, from envisioning unspeakable acts to recapturing a moment of unviolated innocence, from a restaurant in Great Bend where two drifters chow down on a steak dinner in preparation for their mayhem-producing scheme to a neat farmhouse a hundred miles away where the Clutters are sleeping unawares, under a full and impervious moon.

ENDLESS LOVE

(COURTNEY LOVE)

1998

Every age, or so it has been said, gets the icons it deserves. It's an observation as cynical as it is astute, and this seems as good a time as any to ask whether we deserve the bundle of raw ambition and astonishing resilience known as Courtney Love. Less than ten years ago, she was still gyrating in a G-string and pasties at Jumbo's Clown Room, a mini-mall strip joint on Hollywood Boulevard. Much like Madonna, whom she rivals in her attention seeking and whom she credits with paving the way for her dissy, fuck-all style, Love says she has always wanted to be famous, and now that she's made it out of the shadows, she shows every sign of hanging on to the spotlight for longer than her allotted fifteen minutes.

But before we can even pose the question of whether she's the right incarnation for our cultural moment, we have to define our terms—as in which Courtney Love, exactly, are we talking about? Is it the cleaned-up, surgically enhanced Hollywood celebrity, surrounded by a phalanx of lawyers, publicists, and assistants, who in the last two years has posed for *Vogue*, the cover of *Harper's Bazaar* (as one of "America's Most Stylish Women"), and a ten-page Versace spread shot by Richard Avedon that appeared in *The New Yorker*? Or are we referring to the bad, pre-1995 Courtney, whose degraded antics we thrilled to: the "riot grrrl" who specialized in rage, strutting around when she performed with her band, Hole, in decrepit party-girl schmattes that she referred to as "kinderwhore" clothing, and fearlessly diving into the mosh pit, there to be pawed by the crowd? This Courtney openly took drugs, punched out people, harassed journalists she didn't like with menacing phone calls, and stalked the Internet with graphic depictions of her inner state.

Love, who has been demonized as passionately as she has been embraced—and is in for a fresh round of name-calling with the release, this week, of Nick Broomfield's chilling documentary *Kurt & Courtney*—has described herself as "a cockroach." She survived a harrowing, unconventional background: a childhood spent in hippie communes while her heiress mother tried to find herself, followed by brief periods in foster homes and boarding schools; and an adolescence spent first in reform school and then as a stripper in Alaska, Taiwan, and parts in between. Love has said that her mother, who became a therapist, was "detached"; she had an even more sporadic relationship with her father, who calls himself "the Jane Goodall of rock and roll" (he has self-published a three-volume history of the Grateful Dead) and whom she calls "insane," claiming that he beat her and that he gave her LSD when she was a toddler. At thirty-two, Love has been an erotic dancer, a druggie, a groupie, a bit actress (*Sid and Nancy*), a punk rocker, a wife, a mother, a widow, and a movie star (*The People vs. Larry Flynt*), all in the amount of time it takes other young people to decide what they want to be—doctor, lawyer, Indian chief—let alone get there. She seems to be precisely the sort of person for whom the quintessentially 1990s term "morphing" was coined.

Some might argue that Love's most infamous transformation occurred on the day in early April 1994 when Kurt Cobain, her husband of two years, committed suicide, at the age of twenty-seven, by injecting himself with enough heroin to kill three people and then shooting himself in the mouth. Cobain, of course, was the lead singer of Nirvana, the enormously successful grunge group out of Seattle; he also wrote the group's songs, with their oblique lyrics, gigantic beat, and unexpectedly melodic hooks. The spectacular sales (eventually totaling ten million copies) of Nirvana's second album, *Nevermind*, turned the band into superstars overnight and their songs—especially "Smells Like Teen Spirit"—into slacker anthems. But, for the perennially disconsolate Cobain, success brought more anguish than happiness; he disdained the "yuppies in their BMWs" among his fans and escaped further into his heroin habit. Marriage to Love—Cobain once described their relationship as a mixture of "Evian water and battery acid," while she quipped that "we bonded over pharmaceuticals"—and fatherhood seemed for a while to calm his demons. (Their daughter, Frances Bean, was born less than six months after the couple got hitched in Hawaii, with Kurt wearing green pajamas and Courtney wearing a dress that had once belonged to Frances Farmer, the Seattle-born actress with whom Cobain was obsessed.) But at the time of his suicide Kurt was rumored to be deeply unhappy in the marriage and talking of divorce.

If Cobain's image—the unkempt-choirboy good looks and moody, antimaterialist style—had lent itself to idealization during his lifetime, it was ripe for sanctification once he was gone. The fact that Cobain, as several of his biographers have pointed out, had a youthful reputation as a bully—and, his disclaimers notwithstanding, was as driven to succeed as any other young rock hopeful—had been conveniently ignored while he was alive; in death, he was canonized as the noble prince of the streets. Courtney, brash and outspoken, became the vilified widow, the one who had dragged him out of his purist daydreams into the sewer of money and stardom: she was seen as the craven Yoko to his artistic John.

Love, whose acclaimed second album (titled, with retroactive irony, *Live Through This*) came out within days of Cobain's death, raucously mourned her husband and, some said, brilliantly exploited the tragedy. She didn't help matters by granting an interview to MTV the day after the suicide. She continued to talk about him every chance she got—when she wasn't going on shopping sprees (Love and her daughter were the sole heirs to Cobain's estate), checking into health spas with ex-flames (Billy Corgan of Smashing Pumpkins), attending the MTV Movie Awards with Michael Stipe of R.E.M., or having her image reupholstered by the publicity firm PMK, which she had hired at fifteen thousand dollars a month, and through cosmetic surgery. Love's original feelings about her physical appearance were summed up in the half-forlorn, half-sardonic title of Hole's first album, *Pretty on the Inside*. Over the years she has had her nose bobbed and rebobbed, her teeth done, and her breasts enlarged and lifted; she has dropped forty pounds and redesigned her once chunky body with the help of trainers and liposuction. The one thing that hasn't changed is her striking green eyes, which remain her best feature.

Along with this protracted physical makeover has come—or so we've been led to believe—a kinder, gentler Courtney Love. The woman who just nanoseconds ago cultivated a snarling, bad-girl persona both in her lyrics ("I don't do the dishes / I throw them in the crib") and in her life gradually began to reshape the public's perception of her. A writer for the London *Independent* noted last year that Love, in the presence of a publicist who was there to see that she didn't run off at the mouth as in days of yore, "looked fantastically attractive" and wasn't at all bothered by the prospect of becoming "mainstream." "How long do you have to be cool?" she asked. "How long do you want not to be married and not have kids and not have a family and not be grounded?" Four months before that, she had told a *Los Angeles Times* reporter that she thought of herself as "very conservative, a real traditionalist."

It's hard to reconcile these Tipper Gore–like sentiments with Love's thuggish endorsement of acting as a profession just a year and a half earlier—she described it as "a whole new way to kick ass," according to Melissa Rossi in her unauthorized biography, *Courtney Love: Queen of Noise*—or with her general reputation as a bully. "I punched some bitch in the mouth and her teeth got in the way," was how she explained a bandaged hand to a crowd in the summer of 1995, when she was playing Lollapalooza, the roving musical tour. Even if you grant that people can change, there's something unconvincing about the way Love has gone from pugilism to politesse—from the kind of person who gets booked on *Jerry Springer* to the kind you see on *Charlie Rose*.

Although Love, who once described her persona as "ugly and gross and psychotic," has been able to shed baggage from her past the way other people discard worn-out running shoes, she has had trouble outdistancing some rumors of seriously disturbed behavior. A 1992 *Vanity Fair* profile of her suggested that Love had continued to take heroin while she was pregnant; this not only enraged Kurt and Courtney but attracted the attention of the Los Angeles child services, who put the two-week-old Frances Bean in the custody of Courtney's half sister for two months. Love responded by railing against the writer, who, she said, had taken remarks of hers out of context. She also issued threats to any other reporters who might follow suit ("Remember, if you write anything nasty about me, I'll come round and blow up your toilet"), and she tightened her control over journalistic access. "With Pat [Kingsley] as her publicist, she was more than media-savvy," Rossi writes. "She was the press princess, able to place, kill, or at least tone down stories more effectively than the government or the mob."

There is one story that persists in dogging Love—and has now surfaced again, just when she's arrived at the glistening, neon-lit place she dreamed about as an unhappy, angry child. It sprang up a month after Cobain's death, as the result of an article in *The Seattle Times*, and it has been floating around the Internet and various outlets of the alternative media ever since. According to this account, the circumstances of Cobain's end were murky enough to suggest that it might have been a murder rather than a suicide. In case you haven't already guessed, it stars Courtney Love as a diabolical Black Widow—a tackily dishabille version of Barbara Stanwyck in *Double Indemnity* or Lana Turner in *The Postman Always Rings Twice*—scheming to dispose of the hubby and grab the dough.

It sounds like the stuff of die-hard conspiracy theorists—the kind of exotic, vaguely plausible scenario that the schizoid types who haunt the Internet entertain themselves with. And these speculations would probably have remained out there on the fringes, if it weren't for Broomfield's documentary, which follows the recent publication of *Who Killed Kurt Cobain? The Mysterious Death of an Icon*, by Ian Halperin and Max Wallace. The book is a mostly judicious presentation of explosive material and, as its title implies, the authors' four years of research has led to more questions than answers. They point to a number of unresolved issues concerning Cobain's death: the lack of fingerprints on the gun and the high level of heroin in his blood, which some say would have incapacitated him from using a gun; the fact that the singer's credit card (which Love had canceled) was used after his death; the alleged existence of an unfinished will excluding Love; and the evidence that there were two sets of handwriting on Cobain's so-called suicide note, indicating that it might have been a statement of his wish to resign from the music industry rather than a declaration of his intent to kill himself.

The most vocal proponents of the Courtney-as-murderer-by-proxy theory are Hank Harrison, her estranged father, and Tom Grant, a private investigator whom Courtney hired to help find Cobain after he escaped from a detox facility in Los Angeles, four days before he died. Grant, a former undercover agent for the L.A. County Sheriff's Department, has stubbornly pursued his suspicions ever since Love first found his name in the Yellow Pages. Although Halperin and Wallace are convinced that Grant "is sincere in his crusade," they also note that he has failed to produce tangible proof of Love's guilt. They draw a wider margin around Harrison, observing that many of his arguments are not only flaky but "subjective." They nonetheless use him as a source, citing his incendiary remarks about his daughter in a way that could only lead a jury. ("Face it," he gleefully tells them, "she's a psychopath. It runs in the family. She's entirely capable of doing something like this.") The writers insist that their agenda is to have the police case reopened, rather than to point a finger at Love, and they concede that Cobain's intensely symbiotic relationship with his wife, which he characterized in a lyric as an "umbilical noose," is hard to disentangle: she not only gave him the mothering he needed but arguably expressed, in her grabbing for power, his own masked wish to control those around him. It's clear that Halperin and Wallace have pursued this project (in spite of Love's alternating attempts, through her lawyers, to intimidate them and bribe them out of it) because of their affection for Cobain, whom they describe, as many have done before them and no doubt many will do after them, as "the voice of a generation."

If there are people out there who feel affection for Courtney Love—and there must be some—Nick Broomfield hasn't found them. The British director gravitates toward unsavory subjects— earlier films of his have examined the serial killer Aileen Wuornos and the Hollywood madam Heidi Fleiss—and *Kurt & Courtney* gives off such a stench that Love's lawyers succeeded in having it banned from the Sundance Film Festival earlier this year. (They claimed that Broomfield didn't have the legal clearance to use two songs.) Although the film covers basically the same terrain as Halperin and Wallace's book, its final effect is more unnerving: we begin in a sleepy Washington town, with a blond little boy who likes to sing Beatles songs, and we end up lost in the woods with no way out.

Broomfield is a skilled, if somewhat stagy, interviewer, wearing goofily large earphones and carrying his own sound equipment. The movie has its sweet moments: Cobain's aunt Mary, who gave him his first guitar, plays tapes of him singing at the age of two. "He was a pretty loud little guy," she says. Broomfield talks to former friends and girlfriends of Kurt's, who portray him as unremittingly sensitive and modest (one young woman remembers his arguing with Courtney over the purchase of a Lexus, which he made her return). But with the entrance of Courtney's father the mood of the film shifts. Harrison, a beefy man with thick features who resembles the old, untouched-up Courtney, seems harmless at first, albeit aggressively self-promoting. He stands on a sunny street next to Broomfield's car, trying to cut in on a piece of his daughter's action, angling a copy of his book (which is called *Kurt Cobain, Beyond Nirvana*) so that it will best catch the light and show up clearly on film. He chats about Love's "almost deranged thinking process," her "compulsion to succeed no matter what," her "well-documented violent-outburst pattern." Harrison at first seems paternal in an eerie kind of way, conversant with his daughter's less attractive sides as only a father could be, although you wonder why he's so ready to indict her.

After that, however, the negative pattern of the film is set, especially since Love refused to talk to the director and tried to block the film at every pass. (In the course of the documentary, it's revealed that Showtime, which is owned by Viacom, canceled its sponsorship, possibly because of pressure from Love through MTV, another subsidiary of Viacom.) The film cuts between anti-Courtney revelations and a taped interview with Cobain himself, in which he looks and sounds unusually self-possessed. "I really was a lot more negative and angry," he says of his stop-the-world-I-want-to-get-off attitude. "But that had a lot to do with not having a mate." Meanwhile, we encounter a former punk rocker and boyfriend of Courtney's, Rozz Rezabek, who reveals an amusingly acidic side of Courtney when he describes how she offered a "scathing review" of his performance upon meeting him, yelling at him in an English accent to "lose the green checkered pants and cut out the Rod Stewart poses." Broomfield follows Rezabek down into his basement, where he keeps boxes of Courtney memorabilia—journals and letters and papers, including some crumpled lists she wrote detailing "how Courtney will make it," from which he quotes: "Stop working at jobs; be financed; get a deal using the new connections and old ones; become friends with Michael Stipe." Rezabek, who seems more perceptive in his bitterness than many of the people who drifted around Love, says that she "would find out what your kink was or your peccadilloes and expound on it." Then, in a damning finale, he directly addresses the camera: "I would've ended up like Kurt . . . fucking shoving a gun down my throat!"

At the end of the documentary, the director finally meets Love—the new, shimmering, silk-sheathed Love—when she arrives at an

ACLU reception to present an award on behalf of freedom of the press. Broomfield is so galled by the irony of it, having just devoted a film to recording Love's manipulation of her image and suppression of anyone who tries to counter it, that he takes the microphone after Love and attempts to expose her, only to be hustled off the stage by Danny Goldberg of Mercury Records, who is the president of the ACLU Foundation of Southern California. Perhaps the most touching testimony comes from Frances Bean's nanny, a gentle, frightened girl with lank hair, who quit a week before Cobain's suicide. She says that she "couldn't stand it up there," because there was "just way too much . . . talk" about Kurt's will, that Courtney "totally controlled" him, and that she thinks he wanted "to get away" from her. "If he wasn't murdered," she almost whispers, "he was driven to murdering himself."

Nick Broomfield says he doesn't believe in the murder theory. "There's plenty in Courtney's behavior to suggest she's capable of doing it—she hasn't shrunk from physical violence—but it's still a step to blowing someone's head off," he tells me. When I ask him whom he believes, if anyone, he says he believes the nanny. Broomfield has been accused of skewed tactics, interviewing too many losers and loonies and not getting anyone to speak up for Love. He insists that he set out not to trash her but, rather, to honor Cobain, whose music he has admired ever since his ten-year-old son gave him a copy of *Nevermind*, and that "if she had wanted to use it positively, it could've been a different film. I was quite open to her persuading me that all that stuff was incorrect." So how is it that everyone he talked to either hates or fears Love? "I didn't find anyone who had anything wonderful to say about her," he replies.

Hank Harrison—or Biodad, as he calls himself online—is the scariest character in the bizarre lineup of figures in *Kurt & Courtney*. If the pure products of America go crazy, as William Carlos Williams once wrote, then the impure products end up worse than crazy. They inhabit a shadow world with a disorienting logic all its own; it's a world that is ultimately impenetrable to those who live in well-lit rooms. The true circumstances of Cobain's death seem unknowable, buried in a haze of heroin and weirdness. But none of the testaments to the sick ballad of Kurt and Courtney, not even the conflicting insinuations of foul play, makes as lasting an impression as Courtney Love's parasitic capo of a father. Broomfield interviews Harrison three times, and by the end he is out in full malignant bloom, explaining that he got pit bulls in order to discipline his adolescent daughter. Describing their relationship as "a great war," he elaborates, "I got her number . . . I got her nailed." Then, growing louder with each breath, he declares, "It's still tough love and I'm still the father . . . Keep on bad-rapping me, I'll keep kicking your ass." By now, he's really into the terrorism of it, and he points a finger at his head. "I know how she works inside," he chants. "I know what her next thought's going to be."

For all the garbage that is pelted at her in Broomfield's movie, one comes away feeling sympathy for the girl who grew up in the black orbit of this man and inherited his genes—sympathy for the hurt she must have endured, and sadness about the carapace of toughness she seems to have made for herself. But one feels a keen sense of dread as well. For if this is where Courtney Love began, and this is what she's running from, it's also what she seems destined to become.

Iconhood is a strange business. Who could have predicted that Elvis, fat and long past crooning when he died sitting on the toilet, would take up permanent residence in the imaginations of fans not yet born? (Cobain, according to a former girlfriend, was fascinated by "the whole idea of Elvis and Graceland.") Until recently, however, most of the women who were considered worthy of our sustained interest were imbued with beauty, character, or some sort of tragic dignity. You know the list: Greta Garbo, Eleanor Roosevelt, Indira Gandhi, Marilyn Monroe, Mother Teresa. It's true that there have always been screen vamps, tough-talking gals like Theda Bara and Jean Harlow, but no one mistook them as prototypes for emulation. Sometime in the past decade or two, however, beginning with the rise of the ballsy Catholic girl from Michigan known as Madonna, our taste in female icons has changed: we want them less exalted and more sullied—more tossed around by life. We have moved from a hierarchical form of voyeurism, based on idealization and the envy that goes with it, to a more democratic (or merely debased) form of voyeurism, in which everyone is pulled down to the same level by the dirty secrets—the appalling history of addictions, tantrums, weight problems, and messy relationships—that it's assumed we share.

One of Courtney Love's claims on our attention is the way she turned an atmosphere of real-life squalor into bad-girl atmospherics, which other women—more cautious or conventional, or simply less desperate—could inhale when they were tired of being good girls. She never even pretended to mind her manners, to defer to others, to contain her huge appetites. "I want to be the girl with the most cake," she sang, in that husky, compelling voice of hers. But it's also the pain, discernible under all the defiant stuff, that draws women to Love—just as it was the pain, discernible under all the glamorous stuff, that drew them to Princess Di. "Someday," Love wails, "you will ache like I ache."

It is fair to say, I suppose, that from such hopelessness and sorrow the avenging self rises, imposing its sense of injury on others. But it is also fair to say that the transformation of a personal hell into an artistic stance requires talent as well as force of personality: Love has clearly charmed some people with her swaggering charisma, just as she has antagonized others. Indeed, in her constant morphing she may be a genuine millennial type: forever self-inventing, carelessly straddling image and reality. Still, whatever harm she has done, it seems a pity that Love has gone the way of gloss, that she has tamed the wild child who beat her fists against the straight world and given us what we surely don't need—another movie star who's pretty on the outside.

DAYS OF BRILLIANT CLARITY

(RICHARD BURTON)

2012

Before Brangelina, TomKat, and—God help us!—Kimye, before the culture of celebrity became the instant windup machine it now unmistakably is, with supermarket sightings, up close tweetings, and a glut of red-carpet appearances, there was one acting couple whose name was synonymous with the ineffable magic dust of star power. They were Richard Burton and Elizabeth Taylor, better known as LizandDick, preferably said in one breath the better to underline their ensorcelled liaison and combined wattage.

From the early 1960s, when Burton and Taylor fell scandalously in love (breaking up both their marriages) while co-starring in the movie *Cleopatra*, on through their ten-year marriage and eventual divorce in 1974, short-lived remarriage and second divorce in 1976, they were the pair to watch. Their every move was dogged by paparazzi and crowds eager to catch a glimpse of them. They were unapologetically high living and perennially tan, dashing between yachts and luxury hotels, socializing with the likes of Grace Kelly and Bobby Kennedy, buying up jewels and planes, art and houses. In the hands of another couple, their existence might have seemed fulsomely vainglorious, but there was something about their combined magnetism—and, no small thing, their always evident senses of humor about themselves—that kept their glamour and intrigue intact.

The real source of their hold on us undoubtedly lies in the fact that underneath the extravagant surface of their union lay their extravagant passion for each other, clearly visible in photo-graphs and documented in the haunting letters Burton wrote to Taylor, a sampling of which were included in the 2010 biography of the couple, *Furious Love*. Those letters, as well as snippets from his diaries, revealed a Burton who was word struck as much as he was love struck, equally passionate about language as he was about Taylor, whose breasts he called "apocalyptic" and whose beauty he termed "pornographic." The recent publication of Burton's diaries—still incomplete but weighing in at over six hundred pages—furthers the impression of a man with considerable liter-ary talent as well as an incisive and relentlessly curious mind. In a television interview with Barbara Walters, done some years after Burton's death, Taylor referred to Burton as a "genius," which, I would wager, will not strike anyone who immerses him- or her-self in these intoxicating journals as much of an overstatement.

The diaries have been scrupulously edited by Chris Williams, who also provides an excellent introduction and footnotes that are sometimes helpful but too often clarify the obvious. (Do we really need an explanation of who Christopher Columbus was? Or what Kleenex are?) They officially begin with some forty-odd pages of cursory jottings made by the young Burton in 1939 and 1940, when he was a chapel-going, exam-"swotting" schoolboy, and then jump to 1960. Here we get some intriguing if brief entries—"I hate myself and my face in particular" and a descrip-tion of skiing as "an exotic, romantic and snobby sport"—but the real excitement begins with the more sustained entries that start in 1965, when Burton is married to Taylor and swanning around with famous people in luxe settings, like Gstaad and St. Tropez. On Sunday, January 3, for instance, he dines with Nat-alie Wood and David Niven, Jr.: "She emaciated and looks riddled with TB. Pekinese eyes. Sad case." And on June 8, Burton muses, "It is odd, too, that I almost always think—no condescension intended—of Americans as being gifted and brave but almost always child-like." The voice is intimate in the way of the best diarists, crackling with vigorous observation and writerly nota-tions: "(Memo write about reaction to fame or lack of it)." We very quickly get a sense of listening in on someone of exceptional attunement who happens to have had access to people and places of uncommon interest, many of whom and much of which he finds wanting. John Huston is dismissed as a "simpleton" and a "self aggrandizing liar," Frank Sinatra is no more than "a petulant little sod," and a fancy, "handsomely appointed" hotel in Puerto Vallarta is keenly sized up as showing signs of wear: "Oddly enough the clientele didn't look as if they could afford the place, and the barmen were slow and all their white jackets were soiled and sweat-marked under the arms." The only two showbiz people who escape his generally deflating attitude to his peers are Noël Coward and Mike Nichols, both of whom he deems "instinctively and without effort and un-maliciously witty."

Burton marks out his terrain early on: booze (at one point he refers to his diaries as "confessions of an alcoholic"), food, the allure of Jews, money, politics, celebrity and its hazards (he characterizes paparazzi as "these butterflies of the gutter"), bouts of boredom, melancholy ("black as a dirge"), and harsh self-evaluation ("I am as dispassionate as it is possible for a human being to be and not be a machine"). The charms and occasional drawbacks of his beloved "old fatty" (one of his many, many nicknames for Taylor) are interwoven throughout. He and Taylor seem to have enjoyed a certain kind of edgy passion, consisting of huge rows in which they hurled insults at each other ("I said that she was not 'a woman but a man' and . . . she called me 'little girl'"), followed by make-up sex. It must be said, for those who might be hoping otherwise, that there is not much of specifically erotic disclosure here; for such a randy and articulate character, Burton is touchingly shy about bedroom details.

We hear about actors and acting, as one would expect— "Warren Beatty seems very self-conscious and actory . . . He doesn't give that feeling of vibrant power as Rex does or the lethargic dynamism of Marlon"—but what one hadn't anticipated is the ongoing literary seminar. Burton, it turns out, is a demon reader, as avid as he is discerning, and speedy to boot: "I have just finished a very readable Life of Mussolini, which depressed me so much that I hurriedly re-read Waugh's *Vile Bodies* to put me in a good frame of mind for sleep last night." He thinks nothing of going to a bookstore on the Via Veneto and buying twenty or thirty paperbacks at a time (including "½ dozen detective stories" and a biography of Harry Truman) or of reading Auden's "latest collection of verse" while waiting on his wife's hairdresser, Alexandre, to get her ready for a scene. It was a habit inculcated in him as a boy in fairly desolate circumstances: "all the books I read, all the things I learned, all my early furtive shame in one little room by candlelight." (The twelfth of thirteen children born to a Welsh mining family, Burton was two when his mother died and was sent to live with an older sister and her husband, the latter whom he came to despise.)

Reading remained a constant pastime throughout his life, whether he was lolling in the sun on a yacht off Portofino or shooting a biopic of Tito in Yugoslavia. "I stayed in the bedroom all day yesterday," he writes on December 31, 1968, holed up with Taylor and her children in a Swiss chalet, "and read or rather re-read Schlesinger's massive tome on JFK. I must have read without interruption including mealtimes and visits to the lavatory for about 16 hours." While stopping at the Plaza Athénée in Paris in January 1969, he builds "a small library . . . of about 200 books excluding reference books," and his comparison of Ian Fleming's *You Only Live Twice* and Nathanael West's *Miss Lonelyhearts* is worthy of someone who writes reviews for a living: "West's book is taut, spare and agonized while the other is diffuse, urbane and empty. West hates himself and postulates a theory that you are always killed by the thing you love, while Fleming loves only himself, his attraction to women, his sexual prowess, 'the-hint-of-cruelty-in-the-mouth'-sadistic bit, his absurd and comically pompous attitude to food and cocktails."

One cannot help but wonder while reading these intricate, deft musings what would have happened if Burton had lived long enough—and had the necessary focus—to make use of these diaries as the basis for a proper memoir, as he considered doing. Certainly the urge to write was with him well before he met Taylor, and although he protests more than once that his journal keeping is purely personal, a hedge against his habitual laziness, it is clear that he also flirted seriously with finding a book project.

Convivial as he could be when the occasion called for it—when dining with the Duke and Duchess of Windsor, for instance (Burton's affection for this displaced pair makes me wonder whether there was more to them than I had previously thought) or the Rothschilds—his native temperament was essentially that of a misanthropic loner, perfectly suited to the solitary occupation of a scribe. Then again, it's all too tempting to regard Burton as a man of enormous and unfulfilled promise, whether as a writer or an actor; it was a view he was utterly familiar with, and dismissive of: "The press have been sounding the same note for many years—ever since I went to Hollywood in the early fifties, in fact—that I am or was potentially the greatest actor in the world and the successor to Gielgud Olivier etc. but that I had dissipated my genius etc. and 'sold out' to films and booze and women. An interesting reputation to have and by no means dull but by all means untrue."

Did he believe this, or was it the version—virile and unselfpitying, as suited the son of a miner—he chose to tell himself? Perhaps it's fairer, indeed kinder, to assume that in many ways he lived the life he intended to live. "But don't let's be stoned all the time," he wrote in January 1969. "Let's have days and days of brilliant clarity, etched and limpid, cool and surgical." On the evidence of these diaries, between the drinking and the idling, there were more than a few of those days, and he their eloquent conjurer.

II

SKIN-DEEP

AGAINST LIP GLOSS
OR, NEW NOTES ON CAMP

2006

Let us now deplore the present moment and lament all that has been lost on the way to becoming overstimulated and spiritually starved inhabitants of an imperiled social order. First we must ask: Where did we go wrong? Where did we go so terribly wrong? I know many of you would blame it on the usual suspects, on the insatiable maw of the media or on large, amorphous forces run amok—our having started up in Iraq, say, or our having ravaged the planet in the name of progress and capitalist gain—but I blame it all on lip gloss. I believe there is something irrevocably ruinous about a culture in which women are expected to go around with their lips in a permanent state of shiny readiness, a perennial Marilyn Monroe moue of glistening sexual receptivity, hinting at the possibility that they, like Monroe, sleep fetchingly in the nude. Just after this thought occurred to me on a recent Saturday night while I was waiting for the subway, I found myself sitting next to two college-age women who were discussing—I kid you not, this is either synchronicity or Sartre's idea of hell—the merits of various glosses, Kiehl's as compared with Lancôme's as compared with Trish McEvoy's, which one lasted longer and why.

I eavesdropped raptly, being myself the dissatisfied owner of many tubes and pots of said product—from the lowly Blistex and ChapStick versions to the designer jobs that can go for as much as fifty dollars—as well as of a mouth that always insists on

returning to type, which is a recalcitrant state of parched dry-
ness. The potential staying power of cosmetics is an inherently
unsettling concept, suggestive as it is of a kind of Viagra principle
of female enhancement—indeed, of a core confusion between
the messy imperatives of reality and the contrivances of theater,
which is, when you come to think of it, at the heart of everything
that is problematic, if not unbearable, about the way we live now.
It is, all the same, a concept that has been picked up with alacrity
by gay male commentators on the E! channel who espouse the
need for cosmetic "fixatives."

The E! channel, for those of you who have succeeded in hovering above the fray rather than flailing in it, exists to beam out
programs about red-carpet sightings of celebrities as well as the
inside scoop on their clothes, jewelry, and accessories for viewers
who wish to look like celebrities or, at the very least, long to be
mistaken for Jessica Alba. (There is, in fact, a brand-new E! program called *Style Her Famous.*) If you want to resemble a person
who is worthy of red-carpet treatment, it is crucial, apparently,
that your makeup not wear out and begin to show glimpses of the
unvarnished face beneath. As one of the Western world's leading
aficionados of beauty products, I am naturally familiar with the
existing range of complexion beautifiers—indeed, I own a batch
of barely touched tubes and bottles of primers, luminizers, cor-
rectors, and concealers—but fixatives were a new one on me, conjuring faces trapped beneath thick white coatings of Elmer's glue.

Still, if one is looking to condemn the zeitgeist wholesale—
which, to be perfectly clear about it, I am, since there is no place
to live but in the present moment, and I trust that I am not alone
in finding so much of it a trial—one has to begin somewhere and
trace the all-important dramatic arc from better to worse. Points
of origin are always hard to agree on, of course, and have become
even slipperier since the term "paradigm shift" started being
thrown around, but let me try. Once upon a time—not all that
long ago, really, yet inconceivably long ago if you are under
twenty-five and can't believe that typewriters once roamed the
earth, that anyone ever managed to get by without iTunes, that
colors like gray and navy were only, forlornly, themselves and not

yet harbingers of the new black—an essay appeared in a now-defunct highbrow journal called *Partisan Review*. The year was 1964, and the essay was by Susan Sontag, who was, I feel quite safe in saying, both the first and the last intellectual celebrity America has produced. (In France, where they believe in the glamour of the mind and where Sontag chose to be buried, but not before accepting an offer from UCLA to buy her papers and library for $1.1 million, intellectual celebrities are not all that uncommon, especially if you boast a good head of hair, as Sontag did, and as Bernard-Henri Lévy still does.)

The essay was called "Notes on 'Camp,'" and it attempted to define an emerging, homosexually derived cultural attitude—one that was, as Sontag characterized it, "something of a private code, a badge of identity even, among small urban cliques." Camp, according to Sontag, "converts the serious into the frivolous"; it sets itself resolutely against the hierarchical universe of value judgments—those tiresome "high culture" legacies of "truth, beauty, and seriousness"—and posits instead "the equivalence of all objects."

Camp, in other words, does away with the nuanced discrimination between High (complexly mediated) and Low (simplistically projected) levels of cultural expression—between the depressive ruminations of a writer like Robert Musil or W. G. Sebald and the air-spun sagas of Jacqueline Susann or Danielle Steel—that are the bread and butter of critical discourse and that helped establish Sontag's reputation as a discerning observer in the first place. None of which deterred her from championing it in her crisp and haughty "are you with me, you morons" manner. The camp sensibility, once deemed "esoteric" by Sontag, has since become so much a part of the air we breathe (like Brangelina or Bush bashing) that it is hard to imagine people used to walk around living their lives without an acute consciousness that they were "living" their "lives." Hard to imagine, that is, that a sense of radical disjunction between one's interior experience of self and one's stylized (or, as the academic jargon would have it, "performative") self hadn't yet become standard, permeating every other overheard conversation at Starbucks across the

land. It is a disjunction best evoked by those ubiquitous, irritating "air quotes," which is lingo for the act of bracketing every
declarative remark in invisible quotation marks, as though we were
all characters in a *Will & Grace* episode, referencing opinions and
convictions, searching for the reassuringly tinny sound of a laugh
track. Camp, Sontag noted, "is the consistently aesthetic experience of the world. It incarnates a victory of 'style' over 'content,'
'aesthetics' over 'morality.' " Goodbye, Matthew Arnold. Hello,
Andy Warhol. Goodbye, heavy-handed German metaphysicians
like Immanuel Kant, with their anxieties about the *Ding an sich*,
the unknowable essence beyond appearances. Hello, nihilistic
French theorists like Jean Baudrillard, with their blithe sanctification of inauthenticity. Welcome to our world of borrowed auras
and copycat identities, one in which we have successfully overcome
the response that Sontag describes as "the nausea of the replica."

The victory of the simulacrum—the pleasure we seem to take
in an infinite regress of reproductive images, in visual seriality for
its own sake—is, of course, nothing less than the triumph of
camp. Although as a state of mind it feels as if it's been here
forever—as if we've been cozy with its wink-wink approach to
traditional values for so long that the latest iteration of homophobia might be said to be heterophobia (a suspicion of unhip
straight people)—in truth the ascendance of the camp sensibility has been a while in coming.

It began in the early nineteenth century, with the technical
advances that the historian Daniel J. Boorstin, in his proleptically
anti-camp manifesto, *The Image: A Guide to Pseudo-Events in
America* (published in 1961), termed the Graphic Revolution;
sped up in the late nineteenth century with the invention of dry-
plate photography and then the camera; and acquired a plangent
but heartless mood of its own with Christopher Isherwood's Sally
Bowles as well as a bit of philosophical heft after Walter Benjamin
wrote his 1936 essay "The Work of Art in the Age of Mechanical
Reproduction." From there it was a hop, skip, and jump to the
club scene on the Rive Gauche, where the competing egos of
the young Yves Saint Laurent and Karl Lagerfeld used to hang out,
as evoked by Alicia Drake in her fascinating account of the two

designers' rivalry, *The Beautiful Fall*: "There were pockets of homosexual life and men cruising all over Paris, but Saint Germain in the 1950s was known for its *folles*, the name used to describe camp gays of the moment who were recognised by their bottom-swivelling walk and deliberately effeminate ways, including a habit of high-drama shrieking."

By the late 1980s and early '90s, *Spy* magazine, ever alert to the taxonomy of the risible—and newly available for scrutiny in what is itself a swishy form of homage, a book titled *Spy: The Funny Years*—was busy attending to the climate change, teasing out the fine line between "Camp Lite" (attending the Warhol auction) and "True Camp" (attending the Warhol funeral) in one issue, and again, almost three years later, charting a graph of camp icons with the aid of categories that included the "Health-ily Campy" (Robert Goulet), the "Forgiveably Campy" (Henry Kissinger), the "Rather Sad" (Priscilla Presley), and the "Just Pathetic" (Sukhreet Gabel). True to Sontag's dictum that the ethos does not allow for the possibility of tragedy, *Spy* allowed for none, either.

It seems hard to believe now that there was ever an age before ironic appropriation, before John Currin and Vik Muniz. Did Rembrandt think of himself in quotes, as "Rembrandt"? And is there any chance that we will ever know, buried as we are be-neath the rubble of postmodern rhetoric, attuned to the chip-munk chirps of vituperative bloggers and smug talk show hosts (I say this without ever having had the patience to watch more than five minutes of Jon Stewart)? How has the world become so fluidly post-gender and so unregeneratively boys' clubbish at one and the same time? And is the JonBenét story a tragedy, a piece of (witting) camp, or an example of (unwitting) kitsch?

Then again, there are so many questions I would like definite answers to. I am starved, truth be told, for a hint of the old directionality, the old imperialist verities that have ceded pride of place to provisional suppositions and apologetic stances. These days, those of us who don't wish to cast our lot with the intoler-ant or the ignorant have been collectively tyrannized by the doc-trine of equal validity that underlies the social construction of knowledge—by the belief, as Paul Boghossian, a professor of philosophy at New York University, describes it in *Fear of Knowledge: Against Relativism and Constructivism*, "that there is no such thing as superior knowledge, only different knowledges, each appropriate to its own particular setting." This might help explain why everyone I know feels marginalized in his or her "lifestyle," at risk of being exposed for not being sufficiently novel or, simply, aspirational enough in his or her aspirations. It might even help explain why I am frightened by the specter of mass customization so ingeniously exploited by Warhol—by the profusion of design choices in everything from typeface fonts (thirty thousand of them) to drawer pulls (fifteen hundred of them). Virginia Postrel, in *The Substance of Style*, her defense of our design-obsessed society, assures me that all this focus on "impractical decoration and meaningless fashion" is actually a good thing, an indication of our desire and ability to create "an enticing, stimulating, diverse, and beautiful world." We want, she crows, "our vacuum cleaners and mobile phones to sparkle, our bathroom faucets and desk accessories to express our personalities . . . We demand trees in our parking lots, peaked roofs and decorative façades on our supermarkets, auto dealerships as swoopy and stylish as the cars they sell." We do?

Then again, one might argue that the anxiety of artifice—an underlying uncertainty about the solidity of the perceptible—is as old as the hills or Plato's cave. The problem with camp is that it valorizes ambiguity by insisting on framing the narrative of real life as a series of celluloid outtakes. In doing so, it leaves us no place to look for confirmation but in the mirror, allowing for no rush but in the pseudo-image, the hyper-seen, and the reseen. These days, the threat of the artificial has been converted to an enticement: life as a Warhol silk screen. With a retrospective now on at the Gagosian Gallery and several new books, Andy himself is back in a big way this fall, although one might reasonably argue that he has never gone away—unlike so many of his hangers-on who died badly or lived on into pallid obscurity. In Ric Burns's recently aired hagiographic documentary about Warhol and his influence, we are treated to four hours of interviews with a cast of observers who vie with each other in ascribing ever more far-reaching transformational importance to this "most colossal creep," as one lone dissenter calls him, this cultivatedly affectless voyeur whose two gods were fame and beauty. If you pay close attention, you can spot a young, black-haired Sontag, early in Burns's film, smiling at Warhol's camera, her teeth photogenically white. As Warhol closes in on her, there is something unsettling about her smile, something snarling, almost feral. Maybe what she needs is lip gloss.

IN MY HEAD
I'M ALWAYS THIN

Here's the odd part: In my head, I am always thin. The persistence of this mental picture, given the alarming number on the scale, is such that I have intermittently wondered whether I suffer from an as-yet-unrecognized psychiatric condition that is the opposite of body dysmorphic disorder, the main symptom of which is an overly *positive* view of one's appearance. Or it might well be that this unchanging (and, let's face it, warped) perspective goes back to beginnings, to the first image of oneself in the mirror.

I had been naturally thin as a girl and then grew into a relatively thin young woman. Narrow hipped and tight of butt, with long, slender legs and full breasts—the sort of body that men reflexively eye, with enough shapeliness to cause a photographer to stop me one spring day on West Seventy-Second Street, many years ago, and ask if I was interested in posing for *Playboy.* Not skeletally, tormentedly, time-consumingly thin, mind you—a size 8 or 10 as opposed to a 2 or 4. I wasn't overwhelmingly careful about what I ate, and I worked out erratically, except for those times when I felt my weight inching upward and I'd get more serious about running or hitting the gym or going off to a spa to rev things up a bit.

This state of affairs remained more or less true, take or leave ten to fifteen pounds, throughout my twenties and until my midthirties, when I got married, became pregnant shortly thereafter, and put on a whopping fifty pounds. I eventually trimmed the weight off, although not with nearly the alacrity of a Jessica Alba, and returned to my previous size. At some point in my late thirties, I decided to have the breast reduction I'd been debating ever since pregnancy had expanded my already big breasts, after which I looked more proportionate and less matronly on top. There is a photograph of me with a boyfriend (I was divorced by then), taken at a friend's house one summer in my early forties, in which I look impressively lean in a polo shirt and shorts—my arms and legs taut and my face at its angular, high-cheekboned best. I remember this boyfriend as being both an avid flirt and conspicuously weight conscious, and while I was with him, I became ever so slightly more vigilant than I had been. I didn't count calories, precisely, because the very thought of doing so bored me, and I would have felt as if I were doing so only to please a man, like the most submissive of geishas, but I did try harder to deny some of my fattier cravings.

And then, somewhere, somehow—abetted no doubt by the inevitable slowing of metabolism that comes with age, by a raft of antidepressants, some of which are known to sling on the pounds, and, most incriminatingly, by a new habit of high-calorie snacking at 3:00 a.m.—I became inarguably overweight. Heavy, in other words. Or, in yet other words—oh dear God, do I dare try on the shameful term, unleashing all manner of self-hatred in its wake: FAT. Yes, I'll try it on again, this time in less-anguished lowercase: fat. Not, to the naked eye, obese, if only because my still-slender legs and still-trim butt saved me from an overall impression of amplitude. But I'd certainly sized myself out of Barneys and most of the clothes I coveted, which assumed the presence of a waist, a narrow back, and thin upper arms. Both waist and back had widened to such an extent that I never wore anything tucked in and sought out pants with elastic waistbands. My upper arms, while not enormous—certainly not "as big as those maroon-skinned bolognas that hang from butchers' ceilings," which is how Judith Moore describes her arms in her poignant memoir, *Fat Girl*—had lost their natural definition to the point that I rarely went sleeveless anymore. Not to mention that I felt like an out-of-breath caboose whenever I ventured outside, especially during the summer.

I must admit it makes me uneasy to write about all this, to render my predicament in crisp black and white for anyone to read and assess. There are, I believe, many reasons for this discomfort, but two in particular stand out. First, like many women who with age put on more weight than is culturally acceptable or than they themselves accept, I walk around with a self-protective veil—worn so unconsciously as to be almost second nature. I don't see myself, that is, with quite the same piercing clarity, the same objectifying gaze, as I imagine others do, because it would be too painful and, at its most extreme, lead to my never leaving the house for fear of public scrutiny.

Second, the stigma that fatness carries in the Western world at this moment is truly impossible to underplay. As not a few experts have observed, we've pathologized the problem of obesity beyond any corroborating medical reality. "The bulk of the epidemiological evidence," notes Paul Campos in *The Diet Myth*, "suggests that it is more dangerous to be 5 pounds 'underweight' than 75 pounds 'overweight.'" No less significantly, we've attached a reflexive moral judgment to the issue. J. Eric Oliver in *Fat Politics: The Real Story Behind America's Obesity Epidemic* argues that fatness has become "a scapegoat for all our ills" and that, against our "own chronic feelings of helplessness," the body "remain[s] one of the last areas where we feel that we should be able to exercise some autonomy." Being thin is viewed as a reflection of sterling character, while being fat suggests internal disorder and a lack of self-respect. In admitting to being overweight, I feel as if I were admitting to something truly heinous—something that overrides the more positive aspects of my character.

I am, it goes without saying, unhappy about my size. I am unhappy enough to have tried in the last two years alone a number of different approaches to weight loss. There were my five days at the Pritikin center in Miami, where I walked around in a ceaseless state of craving—a "yearning in the mouth," as one writer puts it—for something other than fruits and vegetables. My beloved carbs were off the menu, with the result that all I could think about as I went from an aerobics class to a class on deciphering food labels was pasta and rice, great heaping bowls of them. It was at Pritikin that I learned that no one has ever gotten fat from eating bananas, even several at one sitting (small comfort, this). It was also at Pritikin that I finally came to realize that what I thought of affectionately as my sweet tooth had morphed in recent times—ever since I'd basically given up on becoming thin again—into nothing less than a full-blown sugar addiction. I hate the overuse of addiction paradigms, but how else to characterize the thinking of someone who lives for dessert, as I do, stops off at Dean & DeLuca in the afternoon to buy glazed apple fritters, and has scarfed down an entire box of pillowy, chocolate-enrobed Mallomars within ten minutes of purchasing them?

I've also briefly availed myself of the services of the celebrity diet guru David Kirsch, who is known for getting the last stalled pounds off types like Heidi Klum. My problem here was that although I gave my all during the one-on-one training sessions and listened raptly as David laid out the draconian principles of weight loss (basically: eat nothing and keep on the move), I promptly went into high-resistance mode when it came time to actually apply these principles. I lasted, if I remember correctly, exactly one day on his prescribed three-day initial cleanse (which he then magnanimously decided I could skip) and less than two days on his regimen of protein shakes (the taste of which I couldn't warm up to) and itty-bitty meals (whose scantiness left my stomach growling, a sound that may make other women feel triumphant but makes me feel furiously deprived) before I sailed off into the comforting embrace of a buttery grilled ham-and-cheese sandwich.

The problem, truth be told, is even bigger, as I discovered when I went back and read an e-mail I wrote to myself as a kind of virtual food journal, on the weekend before my first appointment with Kirsch:

I am relieved there are a few days between me and the dreaded date. I commence to eat with ever greater abandon, convinced that every morsel of everything is my last. Two nights in a row I get out of bed, go into the kitchen, and

make myself a glass of chocolate milk with three or four
heaping tablespoons of Nestlé Nesquik, the one with less sugar.
I love Nesquik, even though generally I have more selective
taste when it comes to chocolate. I drink one glass and then a
second. I am happily sloshing down a third when I remind
myself that nothing goes better with Nesquik than Skippy
peanut butter (Super Chunk, reduced fat). So I start eating
peanut butter by the tablespoon and end up taking it to bed
with me. I forget my spoon in the kitchen, so I finish off the
jar first with my finger and then with a nail file. I feel glut-
tonous and gratified both. I feel as if this is better than the
best sex, just me and my taste buds and the Skippy going
down.

It seemed that without realizing it, I'd become one of those
pathetic creatures out of a Geneen Roth book about emotional
eating, one of those self-destructive women who goes to the garbage to retrieve the cookies she has just thrown out in the effort
to put temptation out of reach. I'm everything that Roth's
women are: I mistake food for love, feel desperate when faced
with a landscape of restricted (or, as some might see it, healthy)
choices, need my favorite foods now. There is no future filled
with guilt and self-flagellation coming down the pike when I'm
in the zone, my Skippy and me. Or, if I do glimpse it, I choose to
pay no attention.

Nonetheless, I don't give up on trying to rustle myself into
shape, because when it comes right down to it—to getting up in
the morning, facing my closet of increasingly limited sartorial
choices, and heading out into the cruel, anorexic world of upper-
end Manhattan—I feel imprisoned in my inflated body. Much as
I try to disguise it with narrow pants and oversize tops, much
as I try to disguise it from *myself*, there is never a time when I'm
not aware of being overweight. From there, it is only a matter—
depending on whether I'm in the presence of people who know
me well or whether I'm about to step into a first-time situation,
such as a dinner party or an interview with someone I've never
met before—of being more or less aware. It is in these latter in-

stances, especially when I'm dashing around at the penultimate moment, trying to conjure up the best presentation for my incommodious self (do I go with the black leggings? or the black pants? the black sweater? or the long-sleeved black T-shirt under a black cardigan?) and come head-on with my face in the mirror, a face that has lost its once appealing boniness, that I feel closest to falling apart, swept by a pervasive sense of sorrow for all that I've lost by piling on so much extraneous flesh.

If this feeling stayed with me, if I didn't whisk it away, perhaps I'd be willing to do what is necessary to regain my body. I'd be willing, that is, to give up the immediate, tangible gratification of calorie-rich edibles for the more complex and amorphous gratification of being slender. As it is, I make commitments to righteous eating that I immediately undo, overcome by a feeling of deprivation so profound it makes me dizzy—a feeling that goes back to childhood, when my siblings and I argued over who would get seconds (there was never enough to go around, despite our Park Avenue address) and were given bag lunches composed of white bread slathered with butter and chocolate sprinkles to take to school.

I fly, for instance, across the country to spend six days at a gem-like spa called the Pearl Laguna, in Laguna Beach, California. I huff and puff up and down mountains, always the slowest and most unfit in a group of uniformly fit women; try yoga once again, only to reconfirm that I actively dislike it; and eat tiny, tasty, exquisite-looking meals that, amazingly, fill me up. By the end of my stay I've taken off nine pounds and many inches. This should be inducement enough to make me feel that I've begun the journey toward reaching a goal in which I profess to be interested, but instead of carrying a sense of mission with me back to New York, I discard any sense of renewed dedication on the flight home, diving into the hot-fudge sundae topped with real whipped cream that comes with my business-class meal. Despite its tasting like nirvana after my chaste spa menu of nuts, egg whites, and berries, my faltering resolution both appalls and confounds me. It's not as though I lack self-discipline in all areas of life (although I'd be lying if I said it was my strong suit), and yet when it comes to exerting some control over what I put into my mouth, I give up at the first opportunity without a whimper. Why should this be?

"C-c-c-c-ookies, you love those c-c-c-c-ookies, don't you?" says a man I've known for decades, deliberately stuttering to make his point, a man with whom I once had an affair, a man who was once ferociously attracted to me. This man knows how much he comes in at on the scale to within half a pound on a daily basis and keeps careful track of the weights of the women he's involved with. These are habits I find odious, proof of his inveterate narcissism, but even so, his opinion means something to me. He has watched me blow up over the years with an air of puzzlement and slight disbelief verging on hostility. When he first met me, I weighed about 120 pounds (I was going to write 118, but that kind of crazy precision reminds me of him), and I worked out three times a week at the same gym he belonged to. He was focused on getting me into bed from the start, and, as I said, we eventually ended up there, years later. These days he still greets me with long kisses, but he isn't one to stand on ceremony about what he really thinks. Several years ago, in the middle of a conversation in my living room, he told me, right out, that I had become "unfuckable" at my present weight. I'd never thought of myself in such either-or terms—as inherently fuckable or not— and the fact that I could be categorized so brutally froze me in my tracks. I was enraged at my friend's effrontery but also weakened by searing humiliation, as though I'd been slapped hard across the face. I've never forgotten (or forgiven) his remark, and although it has not proven literally to be true, it has a whiff of bottom-line, sexist truth.

I look back, trying to recall a tipping point, a moment when I ceased obsessing over food and weight and dieting and just carried on as I am. "Letting herself go, as happens when one withdraws from the field of love." This is a sentence that has stayed with me, from J. M. Coetzee's novel *Disgrace*, haunting my nights when I've turned off the light and cannot fall asleep. In the mix of factors that have brought me to a present in which I am heavier than when I was pregnant, there is surely something to be said about men—or the current lack of them—in my life. On the one hand, I miss them, I do miss them, but on the other I can't help but wonder if my weight is in part an obstacle I place in the path to heterosexual intimacy, a way to ensure that I won't have to engage in a dance I've always found as problematic as it is pleasurable. Could I be attached to my weight, the frayed obduracy of it, the way one can get attached to a worn-out nightgown? I wonder if I'd care so much if I were a lesbian, if I lived in a small town, if I weren't interested in fashion, if, if, if . . .

In my head I am always thin, because—but can it be this simple?—for most of my life I was. One day, when I'm ready, maybe I'll go back to my old, svelte self. Meanwhile, I've been making plans to start exercising again, scheduling and breaking appointments with a trainer I once worked out with—who, in the way of all ambitious trainers, has embarked on plans for starting his own gym in the time I have been doing nothing for the greater good of my body beyond strolling to and from the crosstown bus. Meanwhile, I continue to buy junk food, c-c-c-c-ookies, and sometimes ice cream, and yes, hot-fudge sauce (ordered from the website of Stonewall Kitchen), and sometimes even chemical-ridden Cool Whip to snack on at night, as though I were throwing my ten-year-old self a series of birthday parties for no reason other than that I can. My daughter is worried that if I don't take better care of myself, I'll keel over soon. I see her point but can't figure out how to please both of us. I can't think of a woman even vaguely in my own age group who does not watch her caloric input like a hawk. And that, pure and simple, is not how I want to live.

Here's another odd part: what no one seems to realize is that even at my present weight I'm controlling myself. If I weren't, I'd already be Edie Middlestein, the doomed 332-pound heroine of Jami Attenberg's wise and funny novel *The Middlesteins*. Edie, needless to say, loves to eat, to the dismay of everyone around her. When she takes her daughter, Robin, a former fat girl, to a Chinese restaurant, there is no stopping her:

Edie seemed to be ignoring the fact that her daughter was across the table from her, or at least she did an excellent job of pretending she was alone. She ate everything on every plate, each bite accompanied with a thick forkful of white rice. Edie came and she conquered, laying waste to every morsel. Robin wondered what her mother felt like when she was done. Was it a triumph? Eleven seafood dumplings, six scallion pancakes, five pork buns, the pounds of noodles and shrimp and clams and broccoli and chicken. Not that anyone was counting. Was there any guilt? Or did she hope to simply pass out and forget what had just happened?

I'm not going to tell you what happens to Edie, but somewhere along the way she finds acceptance, and somewhere else along the way her ex-husband, Richard, believes he has "a glimmer of an understanding" into her self-destructive romance with eating. "Because food," Richard thinks, "was a wonderful place to hide." The minute I read that sentence, I hear a click in my head; I know I've just found a piece to the puzzle of overeating. It has something to do with the ordeal of visibility, something to do with the desire—mine as well as Edie's—to disappear. And something, as long as we're getting all existential about it, to do with the burden of consciousness and the wish to tune out, to blur the edges of things. Not to overlook that eating, for many of us, is an immensely satisfying way of nurturing the self, and I'm referring here not to wanton midnight foraging but to the deep pleasure of connecting to another person, man or woman, during a long, delicious meal at some intimate boîte where the lights cast a flattering glow. Any way you look at it, food has a lot to answer for.

THE YOM KIPPUR PEDICURE

2005

How can it be, you might ask, that such a travesty came to pass? How is it, I mean, that a woman like me, born and bred of preening Orthodox German-Jewish stock, came one evening two years ago to usher in Yom Kippur, the Holiest of Holy Days, in the most faithless way imaginable: by having a manicure and pedicure at Iris Nails on the Upper East Side?

You might ask, that is, if this were the beginning of an old-fashioned story by, say, Sholem Aleichem, one that had never been exposed to those newfangled and profane literary influences that do away with all meaning, much less a divine purpose. The kind of story that always includes a busybody or two—professional meddlers in the detritus of other people's lives—whose ordained narrative purpose is to stand around the town square, alive with the sound of peddlers hawking and chickens squawking, the better to discuss the latest *shanda*, a piece of news that would set your mother's ears on fire. Such sorrows shouldn't happen to a dog, they would undoubtedly cluck—if they happened, that is, to get wind of the tale I am about to recount—much less to a family of noble standing such as hers. To fall from such heights to such depths, all in a moment's undoing! Better you should excuse yourself than read on.

My own sordid little story is set in a traffic-ridden twenty-first-century city where anonymity is assured, rather than in a tiny nineteenth-century shtetl where village gossips held sway.

No one would chance to know of my brazen flouting of basic religious etiquette except for the fact that I feel compelled to reveal it now as another Yom Kippur approaches. Think of it as a form of belated penance, disguised as a shameless confessional performance. *S'lach loh-nu, m'chal loh-nu, kahper loh-nu.* Forgive us, pardon us, grant us atonement.

It was, I suppose, a piece of exquisite, fashionably postmodernist irony waiting to happen, the unforeseen and inconclusive resolution of years of wondering about how, or even whether, I fit into the larger Jewish picture, such as it is, now that the czars have been overthrown and girls walk around with their navels showing.

Then again, you could conclude that my having decided to opt for a set of shiny toenails over the chance to burnish my soul demonstrated just how hopelessly tarnished a soul I was stuck with. Or, even worse, it attested to nothing more profound than my inability to pace myself accurately, to ever be on time for anything—even Kol Nidre. I mean, it is theoretically possible to see to the needs of both the body and the soul without overlooking either, if one schedules these things accordingly. It's not as if every *frume* Sarah wears whiskers on her chin or soiled cuffs on her blouses. But I am always running late, always wildly cramming three plans into two, and why should this night, if I may mix my *yontiv* metaphors and borrow from the Passover Haggadah, be different from all other nights? Why, indeed, even if Erev Yom Kippur happened to be the ur-night of soul wrestling, the calendrical moment designated for coaxing and flattering and altogether finagling your way into good standing in God's annual ledger?

So there I sat in Iris Nails on that Friday evening in September, as the hands on the oversize wall clock moved inexorably forward and the shadows lengthened outside, paging through a month-old copy of *Vogue*, waiting for my toes—freshly polished in some subtle shade with a coy name like Allure or Delicacy, some imperceptible variation on the same basic pale-pink theme—to dry.

All around me for the past two hours the salon had been emptying out of its devoutly assimilated Jewish clientele, women with toned bodies and cosmetically altered faces who had just minutes earlier been on their cell phones busily discussing their various plans for breaking the forthcoming fast. One coiffed woman was expecting forty for dinner the next night and worried whether she had enough dessert plates; another described a less ambitious scheme to order takeout for her family. I sat there and eavesdropped disapprovingly, a spy in the House of Iris, wondering whether any of these women were real Jews—educated Jews like me—and knew enough not to wear their Louboutins or Manolos to shul (the wearing of leather being one of the holiday's prohibitions), or whether they had only recently jumped on the newly fashionable ethnic bandwagon and viewed Yom Kippur as just another pretext for a dinner party.

Did they understand, for instance, that it was crucial to be on *time* for Kol Nidre, that only the religiously ignorant and the compulsively unpunctual sashayed into synagogue after the service had begun? This lesson had been conveyed to me in my girlhood, and I, in my turn, had repeatedly impressed its importance on my adolescent daughter for the past two days, reminding her to be ready to leave in her sneakers and shul clothes by 6:10, 6:10 *sharp*. I'm not coming late to Kol Nidre, I warned her. If you're not ready, I'm going without you.

It was now eleven minutes past six. Twenty blocks away the same *chazzan* who had serenaded me fifteen years earlier as I stood under the chuppah (how was he to know that the marriage would be over in a few years, a minor blot on the golden record of family ceremonies at which he has continued to officiate?) was about to commence with the solemn prayer that announces the start of the twenty-four-hour fast. What on earth was I thinking? Here I had been alerting my daughter to this defining Jewish moment as though it meant something to me and by extension should to her, and now I was keeping her cooling her sneaker-shod heels while I sat in admiring contemplation of my toes.

I had to get out of there, fast. I gestured wildly to the shy young woman who had plied her fine-tuned, underpaid skills for the past two hours, trying to communicate some sense of urgency in spite of the fact that I appeared to have all the time in

the world. My faith was on the line, but how was she to understand my predicament if I myself couldn't? More important, how
had I managed to arrange my life in such a fashion that more
than four decades of roiling conflict about Jewishness had come
to a head right here in Iris Nails? On the one side were the hallowed claims of a patriarchal religion presided over by a grim and
reclusive (and, needless to say, male) God, who couldn't be expected to understand the significance of socioeconomic factors
in the formation of one's approach to shul-going: What did He
care if I associated Yom Kippur with the Upper East Side synagogue of my childhood, where the often newly Judaicized wives
of the synagogue's multiple tycoons showed up in the front row of
the middle section of the women's balcony in their designer duds
only for the High Holy Days and then disappeared into their glamorously secular lives?

On the other side, there was my feminine instinct to compete—
or, at least, not to be entirely outshone—by these buffed and
lacquered women, whom I had been eyeing in some form or other
ever since I was a girl. The fact that I still attended this same
synagogue (although, truth be told, I was a rare visitor) did not
speak to a deep conviction about its suitability as a place of worship
or even a commendable sense of loyalty on my part (I disliked it as
much as an adult as I had as a child) but to an inability to figure
out where else I might go.

I may as well admit, for the record, that, back at the nail salon, I didn't make much real effort at speeding things up. I had
seen customers in a hurry get their freshly done toes Saran-wrapped
for extra protection before putting on their footwear, but I wasn't
willing to risk messing up my own polish. Besides which, even I
could calculate that there was no way I could get home, dress,
and be at shul all within the next fifteen minutes. And who was
He (if He, indeed, existed) to me, when it came right down to it,
that I should be rushing myself for Him? Hadn't I tried to find
a religious footing for myself all these years, with a degree of
good faith that had included my briefly taking private Talmud
lessons in the hope that I might settle on some sort of locution
for myself in its disputatious language? At the Jewish high school

I attended, I had always warmed to the abstract reasoning of the Talmud, while the picturesque but pedantic tales that we studied in my Bible classes left me cold. The cerebral sparks given off by the various Talmudic commentators with their differing interpretations of a particular phrase reminded me of the splitting of semantic hairs that I found so intriguing about the analysis of literary texts. But none of this was anchor enough to keep me from scrambling around wildly in my head, hurling accusations at myself for failing to provide a proper role model for my daughter, failing to provide a role model for myself—failing, failing, failing at the Jewish thing.

Iris Nails is a prettier salon than many, mind you, and priced accordingly. It's not one of those fly-by-night affairs that tend to dot the urban landscape, put together with spit and a coat of quick-dry polish, a freebie wall calendar with photographs of kittens adorning the cheaply painted walls in lieu of interior decor. No, this is a plush oasis of a nail salon, replete with a crystal chandelier. The manicurists' stations are set luxuriously far apart, and there is a sparkling, peach-toned Italianate landscape painted quite convincingly on the walls so that if you half close your eyes and shut your ears to the indecipherable chatter of the Korean staff, you can imagine yourself on a sun-splashed *terrazzo*.

These incidental details matter, if you are ever to get the setting for this tale of divided loyalties and split identities more or less straight in your mind. If Iris Nails had been a less appealing place, for instance, instead of representing a sanctuary of sorts— a haven in a heartless world—perhaps I would have been less likely to linger among the shy manicurists, the soft lighting, and the trompe l'oeil Mediterranean backdrop. But as it was, I couldn't bring myself to leave this refuge in the midst of the gleamingly impersonal city I had grown up in, a city in which I had always felt spiritually homeless. And so I sat on, in my padded chair with the buttons that enabled you to get a heated back massage while reclining, immobilized by the comforting atmosphere of the salon and by my consuming ambivalence over Judaism—an ambivalence that led me to judge other Jews by my own lapsed Orthodox standards, as though I were a *rebbetzin* in disguise,

even as I indulged in pork-filled Szechuan dumplings. It drove my
daughter mad, the way I kept a foot guiltily in both camps, and
tonight's behavior would only further the crazy-making confusion.

Perhaps, too, if I had ever succeeded in finding a shul that
spoke the language of a welcoming home to me, instead of returning, lemming-like, year after year, to the same congregation
that had made me feel acutely uncomfortable ever since I first
stood in my hand-smocked Shabbos dress and black patent leather
Shabbos shoes, gazing down at the men's section where everything worth watching was taking place, things might have worked
out differently. Would I have felt the pressing need to paint my
toenails at just this pre–Kol Nidre moment, for crying out loud, as
though I were going to be inspected for trophy-wife-level grooming standards before being allowed into the women's section?

Perhaps, but then again, perhaps not. As you can see, my Jewishness and I are a vexed pair from way back. It's as though we
got soldered together when I was still young and impressionable,
and now I'm doomed to drag this ancient, sober-minded belief
system around for the rest of my life, like a giant ball and chain
clanking behind me, dogging my every move. Like Ruth and
Naomi, wherever I goeth, my cumbersome Jewish shadow will go.

The problem with this kind of tortured relationship, as with
all tortured relationships, is that at some point it is no longer
possible to conceive of having any choice in the matter. Letting
go seems no more of a resolution than holding on. My Jewishness is further complicated by my blue-chip credentials—otherwise
known as *yichus*, also known as lineage. Although I have rarely
met a Jewish person, of however attenuated an identity, who
didn't in some flimsy fashion try to link him- or herself up to an
ancient towering sage like the Baal Shem Tov or Maimonides, I
can lay claim to the Jewish equivalent of being able to connect
your Wasp ancestry directly to the *Mayflower*. My family history has produced generations of great scholars and influential
community leaders. This foamy bloodline comes to me on my
mother's side, which featured various founding fathers of modern Orthodox Judaism, including my great-great-grandfather Sam-
son Raphael Hirsch, who paved the way for the unique approach

to living in two competing worlds—the secular German one and the ritualized Jewish one (*torah im derekh eretz*)—that characterized German Orthodoxy. Then there was Hirsch's grandson Isaac Breuer, my grandfather, who, alone among his celebrated family, embraced the Zionist ideal when Israel was still only a gleam in the eye of Theodor Herzl, and emigrated to Palestine from Frankfurt in 1935.

My mother, meanwhile, had been the only one of her immediate family, which included four siblings and their collective twenty-four children (the obligation to breed and multiply being one that the entire Breuer clan took to heart), to abandon a life of high principles and scant material comforts in the fledgling State of Israel for a life of less obvious principles and visible affluence on Park Avenue, with no sign of a camel or a kibbutznik in sight. And yet I wonder, do one's origins ever explain as much as they obfuscate?

At an age when I was still too young to comprehend the historical evil of Nazism in any but the vaguest terms, I had a clear grasp of the way Hitler's web had disrupted the natural course of my mother's life, leading to two emigrations, one forced and one voluntary. It was because of the Nazis that in 1935 she had to leave behind her beloved Frankfurt with its famous zoo, which she had regularly visited on Shabbos afternoons, and immigrate to what was then Palestine, together with her family. A decade later, in the wake of her father's death, in her late twenties but not yet married, she left Israel for what was to have been a year abroad in New York to teach at a religious day school that was part of the thriving Washington Heights German-Jewish community, established by her uncle Joseph Breuer (as fervent in his anti-Zionism as her father had been in his religious Zionism) after he had fled Frankfurt.

Early in her stay, at one of those dinner parties expressly designed for matchmaking purposes that people used to be in the habit of giving, my mother was introduced to my father, an Orthodox bachelor of long standing and fellow *yekke* (as Eastern European Jews referred to their haughty German counterparts with an uneasy mixture of admiration and disdain). After a stop-and-start courtship befitting a man and woman who had resisted the lure of matrimony until the ripe ages of forty-two and thirty, respectively, they married on the roof of the St. Regis hotel and produced six children in rapid succession. My parents spoke to each other mostly in German, a language that always makes me think of swastikas, and gave off a general air of living in New York only under sufferance since it was all too obvious that America and its Orthodox Jews with their casual ways couldn't hold a candle to the Old World restraint and formality of their lost communities.

What all this percolated down to was a childhood bombarded by more mixed messages about what it meant to be an authentically Jewish person than you could juggle with three hands. For one thing, I was given the sort of predictably schizophrenic amalgam of social mores and moral guidelines that modern Orthodox Jewish girls are heir to, stemming from the vast and uncrossable gulf between traditional ideals of modesty, purity, and imminent wifeliness/helpmateness, on the one hand, and the brutal realities of the contemporary dating marketplace and current expectations of female self-definition, on the other. To get a sense of the confused atmosphere, you have only to stand outside a Jewish day school like the one I went to and watch the girls emerge in clothes that are maximally revealing while being at the same time appropriately unscanty—an aesthetic approach typified by long, tight denim skirts slit up the back or side that look difficult to navigate in without resorting to the kinds of mincing steps characteristic of Chinese women with bound feet.

But the messages we received in my immediate family about being properly Jewish went well beyond this in scope, covering every aspect of our presentation to a watchful world. This externalized aspect, bewilderingly enough, was what seemed to count most both for my mother and for the shul with the lacquered ladies that my father had helped found and over which he had presided for four decades. Although religious belief was presumably a manifestation of your inner life, Judaism struck me as a resolutely social institution, more about group behavior than private wranglings with God or faith. No one, it seemed, gave a damn whether or not you sinned in your soul, or hated in your heart, or fantasized about group sex right in the middle of the rabbi's sermon. Primitive convictions about the transparency of your spiritual failings were fine for Southern born-again types like Jimmy Carter, who confessed to *Playboy* that he had lusted in his heart. Jews—Jews like us—were more sophisticated than that.

This meant that in my family there was barely any mention of God and none at all regarding the vicissitudes of belief. The German approach emphasized rules and more rules—as well as the solemn aesthetic context surrounding their observance, the beautification of ritual that is referred to as *hidur mitzvah*. My mother was particularly proud of this aspect of her upbringing, and it undoubtedly added something to our Friday evenings: the table was beautifully set, flowers abounded, and we got dressed in Shabbos clothes, no lounging about in robes or sweatpants as I saw my friends do. But with so much stress on form, I began to lose sight of the priorities—whether it was more important that I look good (which meant Wasp good, as in understated: not too much makeup, certainly no red nail polish) or pay attention to the davening, or whether the most important thing of all was that I arrived in shul on time and didn't meander in when services were almost over.

I came home close to seven that evening. My pedicure had dried, Kol Nidre was well under way, and I immediately broke into tears. I insisted to my somewhat bewildered daughter that it was now irrevocably too late to go to shul—too late for Jews like us, who knew better. Mine was the emotionally dissonant (and perhaps unfathomable) logic of a lapsed Orthodox Jew. Confronted by the gap between my adult disregard for the unbending religious approach of my childhood and the powerful nostalgia invoked in me by memories of rituals scrupulously observed, I froze in my tracks. Even if I no longer believed in the letter of the law, I just as strongly believed that there was only one right way to observe the law—if, that is, you were going to bother at all.

My daughter is a wise soul, and I like to think she understands that my abiding sense of conflict speaks to some sort of passion, a connection rather than a severance. How else to explain my perplexing behavior that evening or on the following day, when I attended shul from late morning until the end of the fast, barely lifting my head from the *machzor*, like a person in a trance.

I wish I could end on an epiphany, on a note of true faith, as if I were a character in an old-fashioned story by Sholem Aleichem. For now, though, it will have to suffice to say that I am a woman haunted by a complicated past who is, ready or not, required to live in the turbulent present. And that nothing in my experience of religious life, then or now, has clarified for me in what, exactly, the essence of Jewishness—its meat as opposed to its husk— resides. But perhaps that is the point of so devotional and demanding a religion: one arrives at its larger meaning only through the petit point of observance. Or perhaps I will come upon the enigmatic heart of the matter one evening when the light is fading and everything seems momentarily serene, somewhere on the road between a pedicure and a prayer.

THE UNBEARABLE
OBSOLESCENCE OF GIRDLES

2008

Where are the girdles of yesteryear? The ones women of all ages once wore as a matter of course, huffing and puffing as they tugged at the reinforced elastic and lace, the better to encase their bodies to trimmest effect. The ones that were so pivotal that the sexologist Havelock Ellis felt compelled to weigh in, insisting that girdles were "morphologically essential" because the evolution from "horizontality to verticality" was more difficult for women than for men. (Without them, Ellis grandly theorized, "woman might be physiologically truer to herself if she went always on all fours" rather than try to imitate men by "standing erect.") How is it, as I discovered when I went in quest of a girdle, that this once culturally mandated undie has disappeared from the sartorial landscape like so much melted snow?

I remember the fascination girdles used to hold for me as a child growing up in the 1950s and '60s, the unvarying feminine ritual of them, taken on—or so it seemed to me—as a burdensome birthright. It might have been catching a glimpse of the pinkish rubbery garment with hooks and eyes up the front, custom-made by a European corsetiere, that my grandmother used to wear under her button-down shirtdresses when she came for her annual visit from Tel Aviv. Or watching as my mother prepared to go out for an evening, stuffing herself into a less sweat-inducing but still body-transforming version before she bent down to fasten her stockings to the garters and then, looking like an apparition out of *The Blue Angel*, walked into her bathroom to apply makeup. Where had my mother's mercurial ungirdled self gone to? I wondered. Did her inner dimensions change along with the outer, becoming more streamlined and compact? In my mind there was something immutably glamorous and grown-up about the very confinement of a girdle, demonstrating that you were no longer an indecorous girl but a woman, willing to suffer extreme discomfort in aid of—let's strip to the bare truth of it—capturing and keeping the male gaze.

So there I was, in search of such an undergarment, determined to appear thinner by external means rather than through an inner girdle of steely abs acquired by force of will and endless hours at the gym. Let other women pretend that they ate lemon rinds and endured the boredom of exercising to benefit their physical well-being. I was having none of it, despite the fact, as I soon discovered, that it had become politically incorrect to mention—much less wear—a girdle, as though the nomenclature itself had become suspect.

"I know what the original girdle looked like. I see it as something with four garters from years ago," said Susan Ornstein, owner of Livi's Lingerie on Third Avenue at Eighty-Third Street in Manhattan, a store she inherited from her mother and that's been in business since 1948. "The girdle as such is obsolete. There are senior citizens who are wearing it, but you couldn't live on that. I sell body shapers and control garments, more modern foundations, all the time. Women need help. Nobody looks like a mannequin."

Or a model, as we say these days. Well, I can report back that Ms. Ornstein, with her hair dyed a Lana Turner shade of blond, is absolutely correct. A proper, old-fashioned, breath-shortening girdle is nearly impossible to find. No retailer, it seems, wants to have anything to do with this once most essential and now most demonized aspect of a woman's wardrobe. In the course of my investigation, I came to understand that for a lingerie store owner to link herself to girdles would be to suggest that some of her customers might not be young or, a worse fate yet, not in control of their bedtime snacking. When I called the proprietor of a fancy little shop specializing in imported European lingerie on Madison Avenue in the Seventies and inquired as to his available stock, he could barely hide the note of horror in his voice, insisting that he no longer carried anything of this antiquated ilk. His clientele, I was politely but firmly given to understand, didn't go in for such measures (being, presumably, in prime neo-anorexic shape), and he suggested that I try Orchard Street or Brighton Beach. I attempted to coax him into greater receptivity by coming out in the open with my dual identity as a private customer with a professional interest in the field, but not even the possibility of getting his name in print stirred his interest. "Try Brighton Beach," he repeated. "They still cater to zaftig women."

Newly aware of my marginalized status, I decided to focus on stores renowned more for their fitting expertise than for their assortment of cashmere bed jackets or exorbitantly priced Swiss underwear. I went to a lingerie shop not far from where I live, one of a national chain that has gotten lots of ink—as well as an Oprah endorsement—for its skill at sizing bras. The place was bustling with saleswomen carrying rows of bras on their arms like so many stacked bangles. There were tempting gossamer pieces everywhere I turned, from itty-bitty white cotton briefs to lacy black push-ups priced in the three figures. For a moment it looked hopeful: How could a place specializing in shaping and modifying breasts not also pay attention to such readily expandable areas of the female corpus as the midriff, waist, and stomach?

As it turned out, the store staked its reputation on Spanx products in varying grades of holding power; it carried nothing beyond this limited range, no merry widows or hourglass corsets. I snaked myself into a long-legged number that was billed as the firmest of the bunch and discovered what I already knew, which was that Spanx had come into existence precisely in recognition of the fact that the era of zaftig was over, except in the subordinate boroughs. Spanx tights, briefs, and slips are great, that is, if you are already in possession of a body toned and firmed from hours in the gym; they add a last bit of smoothing gloss, a kind of gilding of the corporeal lily. But if you are in need of real help, if you are looking for body armor to shield your extra rolls from scrutiny, forget it.

It was incontrovertible: where girdles had once reigned, rowing machines, ab crunches, personal trainers, and plastic surgeons now held uncontested sway. With a few exceptions, girdles had gone resoundingly off the radar. These last outposts include fashion museums, histories of lingerie, and sex emporiums like Kiki de Montparnasse, where girdles have been reconceived as fetish objects. (Freud thought such fetishes spoke to castration shock.) Or they have been appropriated by aficionados of irony, like the fashion designers Jean Paul Gaultier (whose gold corset set the theme for Madonna's Blond Ambition tour), Vivienne Westwood, and Thierry Mugler. Just to utter the word "girdle," like the word "corset," which preceded it, is to hark back to fleshier, gaslit times—before the advent of pantyhose and before the diet and fitness industries had balkanized women's imaginations—and thus stigmatize oneself by implication as not only unfit but passé.

Of course, corsets—whether fitted with stays (later called boning), busks (long, rigid strips inserted down the middle, made of wood or steel or more elaborate materials like ivory or silver), gussets, or metal eyelets—were a byword of the female lexicon beginning in the late sixteenth century and lasting through the 1920s. The more flexible girdle, anachronistic though it may seem, is in fact a twentieth-century innovation, indicating that whalebones and the sort of drastic lacing that enabled Scarlett O'Hara to whittle her already-wee waist down to seventeen inches had been replaced by more pliant materials and devices. In 1829, back-laced corsets, which had presumed the presence of a servant, attesting to aristocratic or bourgeois status, were joined by a two-piece steel busk—the first corset a woman could fasten herself, thereby democratizing it. Still, the canons of gender, class, and fashion were, with a few remissions, upheld rigorously. "During the nineteenth century," Jill Fields notes in her fascinating account *An Intimate Affair*, "virtually all freeborn women in the United States wore corsets." (Indeed, most women still wore open-crotch drawers—to differentiate them from men's closed drawers and to demonstrate women's essential lack of sexual interest—until about 1910, when underpants were first introduced.)

As the twentieth century brought with it the rise of athleticism and the lure of the flapper, concepts of comfort, mobility, and bodily display began to offset the tenets of stoicism, sedateness, and modesty that had required cumbrous layers of clothing. This shift was met by immediate resistance, from both men and women; what was seen as the "fad" of corsetlessness was identified with radical feminist and utopian movements and was also seen as threateningly foreign, possibly even Bolshevik. Articles appeared like "Fighting the Corsetless Evil" and "Flappers Are Responsible for Corsetless Craze." The embrace of waist cinching returned with Dior's New Look in 1947, which posited a chastely feminine stylishness calling for longer skirts and tiny waistlines. Two decades later, though, the girdle was left for dead.

I finally found some semblance of support at Livi's, where Susan Ornstein fitted me with a panty girdle that she suggested I wear every day and an all-in-one by a line called Va Bien that she praised for its crisscross paneling and ability to hold the wearer in "beautifully." I tried out the panty girdle first, feeling the need to step gingerly into these new waters; within minutes it rolled over my waist, adding to instead of subtracting from my girth, and I spent the rest of the day surreptitiously rolling it up again. I fared better with the one-piece, which really did kind of lift me up. But I hit pay dirt with one of the items I had ordered from a sixty-four-year-old company called Rago, whose slogan is "Shapewear for Today's Woman" and whose control undergarments are apparently worn by Brunei royalty. Although I had high hopes for No. 6210, an "extra firm" high-waisted article that came equipped with a zipper backed with hooks and eyes and several different kinds of control panels (as well as four concealed garter tabs), I fell hard for No. 9057, a black lace all-in-one that I had ordered in two sizes just to be safe and that gave me a fetching *Belle de Jour* look, as though I were the older but still sexy sister of Catherine Deneuve—or a Pigalle streetwalker.

I would be less than honest, however, if I said that it restored me to my twenty-year-old body, and I've since passed the smaller of the two items on to my nineteen-year-old daughter, who had been eyeing it for its erotic potential. Which leaves me more or less where I began, in my comfortable but untransformative cotton underpants, seeking cover in untyrannical clothes from Eskandar, Shirin Guild, and the supremely talented Ronaldo Shamask. Have I surrendered my waist for good? Not quite. One of these days I'll sign up at my neighborhood gym and start working my way back to a waistline worth cinching.

BRACE YOURSELF

2006

My long-standing obsession with my teeth is not something I'm particularly proud of—the way I take pride, say, in my encyclopedic knowledge of the Bloomsbury group. It is, however, one of the few ways in which I consider myself to have been ahead of the cultural curve—an unwitting trendsetter, if you will—because, as is abundantly apparent these days, the search for whiter, straighter teeth has become a multibillion-dollar national pastime. The evidence is everywhere you look: at the proliferation of BriteSmile spas, the vaulting sales of tooth-enhancing products like Crest Whitestrips, and the blizzard of advertisements for "smile makeovers" in newspapers and magazines.

Teeth matter not because they are windows to your soul (that's your eyes) but because in our image-driven culture they are windows to something much more ascertainable than a soul, something that you can flash into the night like a diamond watch or a platinum credit card, conveying everything from economic standing to moral worthiness. Think of Marlon Brando in *On the Waterfront* observing with gruff tenderness to Eva Marie Saint, who has blossomed into young womanhood since he's last seen her, "You had wires on your teeth. You was really a mess." His admiration for her lovely smile (not to mention her unbracketed teeth) is a tribute not only to her comeliness but to her character. All of which probably helps to explain why I, a person who steadfastly refuses to floss and has never invested in basic homeowner's insurance, ended up with an armamentarium of bridgework and porcelain in my mouth when, several years ago, at the ripe old age of forty-eight, I embarked on a second set of braces.

My tragicomic thirty-some-year search for a fetching set of pearly whites began when I was a teenager, at the tail end of the 1960s. I wrote away for a tiny bottle of tooth-whitening liquid I had seen advertised in the back of the movie magazines one of my sisters and I used to devour. I can still remember the excitement with which I painstakingly applied the liquid (which looked exactly like typewriter correcting fluid) to my front teeth. I went to bed convinced I would wake up with a megawatt Ali McGraw grin, only to discover the next morning that my off-white teeth were now mortifyingly streaked with what looked like graying bits of Elmer's glue. If I had known the cornucopia of elective procedures that the combined forces of a free-market economy and the unflagging ingenuity of an international cast of worker bees (Swiss lab technicians as well as Korean and Italian ceramicists) would have in store for me over the next few decades, I might have gone off to school that morning in a less dark mood.

In that backwater of an era—a dental wasteland by comparison with today—perfect smiles were still a rarity, glimpsed mostly on movie and television stars; toothpaste was still being touted for its cavity-fighting rather than whitening powers; and grown-ups didn't wear braces. But just because no one had heard of Invisalign didn't mean that everyone walked around with chipmunk teeth. Braces—the old-fashioned "railroad tracks" kind—were the norm among urban, upper-middle-class kids, and I, like most of my friends and my five siblings, benefited from orthodontic intervention. Unlike them, however, I continued to agitate about the deficient luster of my teeth after the orthodontic work was completed—a fixation helped along by my innate and inordinate self-consciousness. I was in the habit, for instance, of trying on smiles in front of the mirror, assessing their varied effects, which is how I fell for that ridiculous tooth-whitening offer in the first place.

In the mid-1970s, just as I was turning twenty-one, a new technique for improving the color, size, and shape of teeth called bonding was introduced, and you can be sure I signed on at the first opportunity. In those pioneering days the bonding process was a more tenuous, touch-and-go affair than it is now, with the result that the resin had a tendency to break off at inopportune moments. I remember one particularly ill-timed incident when the bonding on a tooth cracked just as I was preparing to go to dinner with a somewhat imperious man I wanted to make a good impression on. I called him and tried to beg off, referring mysteriously to something urgent that had come up. When he pressed me further, I caved and mumbled something about a broken tooth. Instead of finding this bit of female vanity endearing, he snapped at me to get out of my "narcissistic jungle." Chastened, I rushed out to meet him and spent the entire evening trying not to reveal the flaw in my expensively touched-up smile.

As with so many costly habits, once you start, there's no looking back. Over the last decade, I have seen several dentists and tried an ever-evolving array of procedures, eventually arriving at the most extravagant phase of my obsession: braces. I had never liked the slightly flared effect my capped front teeth had, nor the slight thrust forward of my jaw when I smiled. These defects weren't something other people noticed (except for my teenage daughter, who is in the habit of scrutinizing my appearance and deemed everything about me, including my teeth, subpar). Yet, while some people are fated to be content with their looks, no matter what the prevailing ideal of beauty happens to be, others (me, for instance) will never live up to their own internal standards. And so I recently ended up in the office of Caroline Grasso, DDS, a young prosthodontist with perfectionist instincts and the enthusiasm to match. Grasso studied my mouth as though it were a valuable fossil and then reported that not only was my entire bite off but my bottom teeth had never been properly aligned. Orthodontic intervention was strongly recommended to prevent further migration of my teeth and damage to my gums. I was assured that the aesthetic gain, although secondary to the functional improvement, would be visible somewhere down the line.

The decision to wear braces should not be assumed lightly. Take it from me, who hesitated and then plunged into a sea of wires, brackets, and rubber bands from which I thought I'd never emerge. Braces are unsightly, uncomfortable, and inhibiting. Think cracked lips, persistent gum sores, and humongous, rivetingly painful blisters on the inside of your cheek. And that's just the beginning. There's a reason they're typically worn by children—who aren't called upon to attend business lunches or meet with editors—rather than adults. Think endless apologies before, during, and after meals about the bits of food that will cling unbecomingly to your braces, adding insult to injury. Think, too, of the slightly puzzling impression you and your braces will make upon people who had once relied upon your judgment and maturity only to now view you as a walking testament to misplaced chronology and arrested visual development.

You'll notice I haven't even begun to touch upon the delicate matter of the effect braces can have on one's love life. Remember Dorothy Parker's famous quip about men seldom making passes at girls who wear glasses? Well, just try being a grown woman wearing braces. Someone should compose a song about women wearing braces and call it "Unkissable You." As a divorced mother who went out on the occasional date and always liked canoodling, I would swear that braces put a damper on my already less-than-hectic romantic life.

Then again, perhaps I wasn't the right candidate in the first place, given the time-consuming care and maintenance involved. Put it this way: I've always had trouble with follow-through, and I've always had trouble projecting into the future—envisioning how an apartment might look after it's renovated, how a haircut might grow out, whether next week will really come to pass. The kind of person who's suited to braces should be either dazzlingly self-involved and unremittingly vain or a punctilious and goal-oriented type—like the writer I bumped into on my very first visit to the orthodontist. I could see that he was applying himself to braces with the same mole-like zeal he put into writing and playing tennis. As he smugly showed me how cleverly hidden his braces were—although my bite required the regular obtrusive kind of hardware, he had been fitted out with Invisalign—I was struck by the piercing realization that I didn't want to be in orthodontic cahoots with him (or anyone else, for that matter). I could just imagine his dropping our chance meeting into dinner-party chatter, indelibly linking the two of us as earnest seekers of self-improvement.

When my braces finally came off, two months ago, no one noticed but my daughter and my mother. Thousands of dollars and ceaseless humiliations later, I can say that had I known then what I know now, I probably would have settled for a clinically askew bite—a class III malocclusion, to be exact—and an aesthetically winning smile, skipped the braces, and gone straight to caps and veneers. Meanwhile, the demand for blindingly white, perfectly straight teeth continues apace (one out of five orthodontic patients today is an adult, and tooth whitening is the most requested cosmetic procedure), leading dentists to devise new whiter-than-white shades with the addition of custom-blended porcelain powders.

One might wonder whether the fixation on teeth is a symptom or a cause of what ails our culture in general, an indication of the zero-sum game of treating ourselves as objects in an exhibition, competing for face time with an invisible but harshly assessing public. "In the 1980s," observes Marc Lowenberg, DDS, a New York dentist who has created many of the elite smiles that grace the pages of magazines, "American women wanted big hair. In the 1990s, it was large breasts. The turn of the twenty-first century has brought an obsession with gorgeous white teeth." And although it may behoove dentists to emphasize the importance of healthy teeth, just as it behooves orthodontists to emphasize the structural importance of a corrected bite, I would guess that few of us are thinking about the welfare of our teeth when we decide to spring for laminates or braces; we are thinking about looking younger and more desirable.

As for me, I'm not entirely sure even now what I was thinking when I started on this journey, or what I hoped for when I splurged on braces three years ago. Maybe I believed I'd finally accept myself as I am, that with the prospect of prettier teeth would come a glimmer of inner peace. As you may already have surmised, dentition and happiness are indirectly connected at best. But sometimes when I'm feeling particularly downcast right before bed, in the midst of my nightly ablutions, I'll flash a smile at myself in the mirror just as I used to in the old days. Only now I kind of like what I see: that's me in the spotlight, losing my religion of self-doubt, if only for a moment, smiling to beat the band, secure in the knowledge that my teeth, at least, won't let me down.

ANDROID BEAUTY

2007

We have always been slightly uneasy—notwithstanding our growing cultural obsession with youth and physical perfection—about
the enormous value we assign to female physiognomy, based as it
is on nothing more substantive than an undemocratic rolling of
the genetic dice. Clearly, although we have all been bequeathed
a more or less similar arrangement of facial features (eyes, nose,
mouth, neck, skin), there are some women who emerge, either by
way of felicitous lineage or a hazard of good fortune, with mugs
to die for. Audrey Hepburn. Vivien Leigh. Grace Kelly. Julie
Christie. Julia Roberts. Halle Berry. Penélope Cruz. The varia-
tions may range from the gamine to the sultry, the classic to the
exotic—stopping along the way for the slightly more Slavic (or
these days, Slavic) look that often goes with blond lovelies—but
the theme is the same. *They* are undeniably beautiful; we, by and
large, however attractive or striking, are not.

This undeniable and unearned differential (one that is becoming ever more absolutist in a "lookist" society) has led us to devise
ways of minimizing beauty's importance with dispassionate abstractions or consoling, somewhat grandmotherly mantras. If you
want to get high-minded about it, you can clutch for solace at the
conjecture of the eighteenth-century philosopher David Hume
that beauty "exists merely in the mind . . . and each mind per-
ceives a different beauty" and hope that no one will notice that
this observation, if it ever held up, preceded the invention of

photography. Closer at hand is the adage "Beauty is as beauty does," which is the kind of snippy comment Mary Poppins might have made if she came upon one of her young charges preening before his or her reflection. Then there is the old platitude, "Beauty is in the eye of the beholder," which attempts a similar leveling of the playing field.

I suspect these reassurances never fooled any woman anxiously eyeing herself in the mirror before going out for the evening, and as we get older, this lifelong negotiation with the looking glass becomes only more fraught. (Many of us, I imagine, will eventually feel in sympathy with Bette Davis, who, as Queen Elizabeth I in *The Private Lives of Elizabeth and Essex*, becomes apoplectic at the very thought of catching a glimpse of her ruined face, screaming, "Break every mirror in the palace! I never want to see one in Whitehall again!") The really noteworthy fact, however, is not that these ploys ever much worked but how singularly irrelevant they have become over the last decade— almost like maxims from another planet. For one thing, the promise and gradual destigmatization of cosmetic surgery has led less-than-stunning women to believe that a gorgeous countenance is there for the paying. Another, more significant reason is that the contemporary archetype of beauty, as seen on the runways and in fashion magazines, is no longer applicable or even familiar. For that matter, it's barely recognizable.

The faces I'm referring to seem to have arrived here by spaceship from some silent lunar landscape, rather than by the bawling and bloody process by which ordinary mortals enter the world. The Platonic ideal of beauty is now as it never was: more humanoid than human, more the product of an art director's digitized pastiche of desirable features than a naturally occurring phenomenon. The reasons for this include our increasingly sophisticated techniques for airbrushing flaws or imperfections out of the picture; our fascination with self-invention and technosexuality (also referred to as robot fetishism); our ever more phobic attitude toward aging and dying; and our worship of young, blank, unlived-in faces that resemble the baby-faced characters in Japanese animated films. Thanks to these influences, our aesthetic

standards have mutated into an eerie image of female attractive-
ness that, if not unprecedented, has been relatively uncommon
until now.

I think of this new typology as Android Beauty: part inter-
galactic and part neonatal; part Tilda Swinton and part Miley
Cyrus; part *2001: A Space Odyssey* and part Bratz dolls (the post-
Barbie fashion doll with exaggerated eyes and lips that looks, as
Margaret Talbot wrote in *The New Yorker*, "as if the doll had
undergone successive rounds of plastic surgery"), with a little bit
of Bambi and those kitschy Keane portraits of lollipop-eyed waifs
thrown into the mix. You can, of course, coin any term you like,
but I'm sure you know what I mean.

The identifying signs of this change—a radical reconception
of what makes for feminine pulchritude—can be readily enumer-
ated. They include a high, rounded forehead; a giraffe neck;
enormous eyes that are usually spaced low on the head and wide
apart; an imperceptible nose; a pillowy or pouty mouth, but one
with the lips always everted, as if ready to be kissed. Because the
body on which this face is set is, needless to say, thin to thinner
to twig-like, the head looks proportionally larger, even other-
worldly. Think Mary-Kate and Ashley Olsen. Victoria Beckham.
Think, in a nutshell, Nicole Kidman at this year's Oscars, whose
weirdly vacant mien (especially unsettling in light of her native
comeliness) had everyone (who managed to stay up) talking.

The New York plastic surgeon Yael Halaas, who notes that
the laws of beauty have been "amped up," attributes Kidman's
cyboresque look to the "Vulcan eyebrows" that can result from too
much or wrongly placed Botox. It might also have to do with the
silicone-smooth surface of Kidman's skin, from which all traces of
emotional expressiveness—of having laughed or cried, struggled
or aspired—have been erased, leaving a blank slate onto which
we can read our own scripts. In this sense, Kidman functions
both as herself and as a "sim"—a simulated version of herself,
much like the Daryl Hannah character in *Blade Runner*. Where
once we tried to understand the fractured nature of identity by
way of psychological concepts that pointed to an interior life,
these days we appear to have traded in that somewhat demanding

approach for an exteriorized, sci-fi dramatization of the seemingly inexplicable divisions within ourselves. Goodbye, doppelgänger; hello, avatar. Goodbye, therapist's couch; hello, *Star Trek*.

But while the ubiquity of computer-manipulated movies, photographs, and other visual media may account for the extra-terrestrial, "Beam me up, Scotty" aspect of Android Beauty, old-fashioned terrestrial science may help explain its equally disturbing, arrested-in-time quality. You might wonder, given the feminist legacy of self-determination and the long-ago (or what seems like long-ago) vision of power dressing, why women have suddenly been pushed back to, if not quite the cradle, then certainly a state of prepubescence. Which is where evolutionary biology and the theory of neoteny—the persistence of larval or fetal features into adult life—enter the picture. Zoologists like Desmond Morris, in his book *The Naked Woman: A Study of the Female Body*, have proposed that our species'—and especially men's—apparent preference for juvenile features can be traced back to (or, if you like, blamed on) neoteny.

This theory, which can be seen as a conceptual breakthrough or a bit of nonsensical speculation, depending on your view of evolutionary biology, is in truth no more than an extension of Darwin's principle of sexual selection, which he developed to account for what appeared to be cumbersome and nonfunctional characteristics. (Until he figured out that gender-specific traits—like attention-grabbing fans on male peacocks—informed the dynamics of the mating game, which in turn trumped worka-day survival needs, Darwin was in a state of despair about the validity of his revolutionary ideas. "The sight of a feather in a peacock's tail, whenever I gaze at it, makes me sick!" he once admitted before finally embarking on *The Origin of Species*.) Accordingly, Morris points out that women have more neotenic physical traits—twice as much baby fat, smoother skin, larger eyes, and puffier lips—the better to arouse a protective instinct in males. The zoologist Clive Bromhall, in his book *The Eternal Child*, goes even further, suggesting that neoteny has been mis-understood. In a hubris-smashing moment, Bromhall claims that the entire human species has become "infantized" in order to physically survive and emotionally flourish. We have regressed, it would seem, into a state of permanent childhood.

Where, you might ask, does this leave us? No one needs to be told that the business of beauty is inherently superficial and pitiless, but it's another matter entirely when it starts to depart from all prevailing norms. So here's the burning question: Are Android Beauties ahead of the pack, leaving the rest of us who have not morphed to lag behind, fated to be nonbreeding singletons with our lurking expression lines, relatively small eyes, prominent (or at least visible) noses, and collagen-free mouths? Or do they point to an alarming future in which little girls will be eroticized without the constrictions—the civilizing restraints—of guilt or of culturally mandated taboos? A future in which the Humbert Humberts of the world will be just one of the gang, just another regular pervert, free to cruise the playground without pretext or disguise?

In a remarkable essay, "Afternoon of the Sex Children," which appeared last spring in the journal *n + 1*, Mark Greif makes a persuasive argument that the possibility of such a pedophilic scenario coming to pass is neither futuristic nor even all that unlikely. In fact, as Greif envisions it, the scenario has already taken place without our even noticing. The trend of the last fifty years, he observes, has been toward focusing our lascivious gaze with ever greater intensity on the prenubile rather than averting our eyes from them. "The representatives of the sex child in our entertainment culture," he writes, "are often 18 to 21—legal adults. The root of their significance is that their sexual value points backward, to the status of the child, and not forward to the adult." One doesn't have to look far afield for confirmation. A study by the anthropologist Douglas Jones, in which he fed the images of various models into a computer that correlated the sizes and proportions of people's faces to their ages, estimated the models' ages to be six or seven.

In which case, Stanley Kubrick was more prescient than even he suspected when he ended his sci-fi fantasy *2001: A Space Odyssey* with a puzzling (and somewhat pretentious) image of a fetus. It might well be—it is certainly worth considering—that what

our information-stuffed, overstimulating, and multitasking time
has produced is not a yearning for new legal-age experience but
rather a counter-yearning to evolve backward toward some beckoning galaxy where life has literally just begun and adult conse-
quence is yet to appear on the horizon. Perhaps the emergence of
Android Beauty finally suggests that rather than facing our respective futures with anticipation, we are, many of us, carrying a
secret longing to tarry another day or two (make that a trimester)
in the womb.

III

OUT OF PRINT

FREUD WITHOUT TEARS

(ADAM PHILLIPS)

Adam Phillips doesn't do e-mail. It's not clear to me whether this is a Luddite impulse, a shrewd maneuver designed to enhance his glamorously elusive aura, or simply a pragmatic decision not to squander hours at the beck and call of everyone with a keyboard and a screen name. "I don't want to be in touch," he explains when I question him directly. "I want less communication."

That may sound like a decidedly antisocial remark for a man who trades in human connectedness. But then Phillips, an idiosyncratic literary talent and the celebrated maverick of contemporary British psychoanalysis, is nothing if not defiantly self-contradictory. He has made his name by questioning the orthodoxies of hard-line Freudianism, yet his most recent role is as general editor of the first major new Freud translation to appear in thirty years. This month, four volumes of a scheduled eight are being issued here as part of the Penguin Classics series. These hip-pocket paperbacks are each translated by a literary scholar, and the visually witty covers take their images from Magritte and other surrealist masters. They are as removed in tone from the weighty and astronomically expensive twenty-four-volume version edited by James Strachey as Freud's office in London's solidly bourgeois Hampstead neighborhood (now the Freud Museum) is from Phillips's office in trendy Notting Hill.

Phillips gives the bulk of his time, four days a week, eight hours a day, to his analytic work. "Therapy provides an opportunity to talk to people the way you don't do anywhere else," he says. Wednesdays are reserved for writing, and over the last decade and a half of Wednesdays, Phillips has produced ten books of nonfiction. Most are collections of essays and reviews, with the exception of several more sustained meditations, including *Darwin's Worms* and *Houdini's Box*, which focus on a single theme or set of questions. The books' provocative titles—*The Beast in the Nursery* and *On Kissing, Tickling, and Being Bored*—hint at the uncategorizable contents within, which are characterized by Phillips's droll humor, his penchant for the epigrammatic, and his wide-ranging, interdisciplinary affinities. The curious thing about reading Phillips is that he makes you feel smart and above the daily grind at the same time as he reassures you that you are not alone in your primal anxieties about whether you are lovable or nuts or, perhaps, merely boring.

It is hard to think of another writer who, in the guise of intellectual inquiry and dazzling erudition, manages to always come back in some way or other to the conundrum of why our longings so often end in acts of self-sabotage. "People have traditionally come for psychoanalytic conversation," he observes in the introduction to *On Kissing*, "because the story they are telling themselves about their lives has stopped, or become too painful, or both."

What do therapists talk about when they talk about love? If you're Adam Phillips, you are likely to talk about the infinite human capacity for mangling desire—for hating what we love most. It is a Thursday evening at the end of May, and I am waiting for Phillips at the Walmer Castle, a packed bar around the corner from his office. The bar is on hippest Ledbury Road, amid shops that carry high-end bath gels and clothes in a range of sizes from small to smaller. Everyone looks to be twenty-five, and no one seems to have caught on to the dangers of smoking. Phillips has sent me off to read a book called *Love of Beginnings*, by his favorite fancy French theorist, J.-B. Pontalis, while he finishes up with his last patient of the day.

I am sipping an outsize mug of draft beer when he comes in, a slight, graceful man with a ragged mop of hair, several days'

worth of stubble, and more than a passing resemblance to Bob
Dylan in his prime. He is wearing a leather jacket and pointy
suede shoes and has the rushed air of someone navigating the
world incognito. Lighting up a cigarette, Phillips launches into
his thoughts on the vexed subject of human relationships.

"Sexual desire leads us awry," he says, speaking softly yet
authoritatively in his impeccable Oxbridge accent, the ideas spilling out in fluid sentences. "The erotic life is ashamed, conflicted,
awkward, embarrassed, uncertain. The way to survive psychically
is to find people to love. But in order to feel safe enough with
other people, most of us feel we have to control them. If you fear
losing somebody who you think you need, you try to enslave or
addict them." It is as though Phillips has taken Freud—whose
emphasis on the vicissitudes of libidinal life was second to none,
thereby casting him as suspect from the start—and given him a
contemporary gloss, a kind of play-it-as-it-lays panache. So where,
I wonder aloud, does all this amorous conflict leave us after the
hostile passion subsides? Phillips shrugs, like a man who's seen
too much to be overly impressed by people's ability to handle hard-
core reality. "Then," he says, pausing for a moment, "you fall into
ordinary life."

Phillips combines the energy of the great Victorian polymaths
like Thomas Carlyle and John Ruskin with the radical belief in
the indeterminacy of all truth that defines the postmodernist
sensibility of Walter Benjamin or Jorge Luis Borges. ("There are
no deep truths about human nature," Phillips maintains. "There
are more or less interesting or inspiring descriptions.") His writings have brought him a cultlike following among serious readers
(although not among serious psychiatrists, few of whom seem to
have read him). Part of his appeal is that he is a graceful stylist,
who writes airy yet charged prose. In the essay "On Translating
a Person," he glides from arcane references (Marx's *Eighteenth
Brumaire of Louis Bonaparte* and Raymond Williams's *Problems
in Materialism and Culture*) to poignant vignettes culled from
years of clinical experience. In "Clutter," he writes about a
fourteen-year-old boy who annoys his otherwise-tolerant bohemian parents by dropping clothes all over his room because he

believes "our clothes should come and find us." In one of his teasing, aphoristic asides, which is characteristic of his amused disengagement from domestic dramas, Phillips points out that "the art of family life is to not take it personally."

Freud, who virtually invented the art of taking everything personally, loved a good joke as much as anyone and would no doubt have appreciated the deadpan wit of this remark—and might even have chuckled at Phillips's claim that the founding father of psychoanalysis was himself "resistant to therapy." But Freud was also a man singularly of his own time, steeped in Old World culture and moral gravitas, and informed by the classical, premodernist perspective of his literary heroes, Goethe and Schiller. As such, his pessimistic interpretations of his patients' conflicts were inseparable from a dark, if not tragic, view of civilization. Phillips, on the other hand, blithely asserts that the invention of therapy, in its emphasis on "suspending internal censorship," neutralized the very judgmentalism of "what used to be called the moral life."

Phillips is an odd choice to edit the Freud translation on many counts, not least because he doesn't know German, the language in which Freud wrote. When I mention this fact to the eminent literary critic Frank Kermode, who is a Phillips enthusiast, he is somewhat taken aback. "That's a tremendous bit of cheek, isn't it?" he says, half admiringly.

This lack of a seemingly essential credential, however, seems not to have deterred Paul Keegan, the former editor at Penguin Modern Classics in the U.K. who conceived of the project. (In the U.K., fifteen volumes are planned, and six have already been published.) Keegan knows Phillips from their student days at Oxford, where they both studied English literature. He was interested, as he explains it, in publishing a Freud "free of the fetters of the Freud industry." Phillips, with his constant venting about "the institutional hypocrisy of psychoanalysis" (and, no less important, his unparalleled ability, as Keegan sees it, "to work the angles"), was just the person for the job. "He's his own one-man band," Keegan remarks. "It's all been done on a harmonica."

The Penguin translations aim to present a more accessible and vernacular Freud, freed from the cult of genius and from the straitjacket of Strachey's dowdy and somewhat creaking rendition. It is a prospect that Phillips gave thought to over the years, well before the new edition became a gleam in his publisher's eye. "By pooling the language of psychoanalysis rather than hoarding it . . . psychoanalysis can be relieved of the knowingness that makes it look silly," he writes in *On Kissing*, "the knowingness that comes from its 'splendid isolation,' the fantasies of inner superiority in the profession."

To this end, Phillips has boldly dispatched with internal consistency and a uniform technical lexicon and has imposed a thematic rather than chronological organization. You might wonder how a craft as facilitating (and, ideally, invisible) as translation can change the basic thrust of a book. "All translation is to some extent misrepresentation," observes Louise Adey Huish, in her preface to *The "Wolfman" and Other Cases*. With Freud, however, it appears that the effect was to make him less—rather than more—lucid. "Freud was *not* the father of psychobabble," Huish acerbically notes. "Very few of the terms he coined require a dictionary to make them comprehensible to the ordinarily educated reader."

Phillips has written the introduction to only one of the books (*Wild Analysis*) but was in charge of selecting the translators and the writers of the introductory essays; the essayists include specialists in literature, philosophy, and the history of science, as opposed to writers on "hot" topics dear to psychoanalytic journals like psychic trauma and boundary violations. There isn't a shrink in the bunch, and none of the translators was given instructions beyond the one to follow their own noses. Some of them hadn't read Freud before. One, Michael Hofmann, who had signed up to do *Wild Analysis*, decided not to go ahead after reading it in the original.

The idea to update and condense the magisterial standard edition—sometimes referred to, tongue-in-cheek, as the King James Version—was spurred by the expiration of the Strachey copyright. Strachey's Herculean labors, under the watchful eye of Anna Freud, Freud's youngest child and the only one to follow in his footsteps, took place over a period of twenty-one years (1953–1974). His work has long been regarded as an exhaustive triumph of fastidious scholarship. "We must fall back on square brackets and footnotes," he vowed, "for we are bound by the fundamental rule: Freud, the whole of Freud, and nothing but Freud."

Still, there have always been questions about the aptness of some of the vocabulary—for example, Strachey's use of "instinct" instead of "drive" for the term *Trieb*—as well as the possibility that he denatured Freud's vivid style into the polished and stately prose of a Victorian gentleman: "a cross," as the Cambridge historian of science John Forrester summarizes it, "between Thomas Hardy and Julian Huxley." Some criticized Strachey's translation as a well-meaning but essentially falsifying effort to present Freud as an empirical and systematic (indeed Darwinian) thinker rather than a subtle and allusive poet of the unconscious life. In the hope of making him more acceptable to a skeptical medical community, Strachey set about "scientizing" Freud, adding concrete qualifiers like "degree" and "level" to Freud's metaphorical imagery, and introducing clanking Greek words like "cathexis" and "parapraxis" into the text in place of Freud's more colloquial and plainspoken German.

It was Bruno Bettelheim who first brought these concerns to wide attention twenty years ago in an essay in *The New Yorker* in which he suggested that Strachey had literally taken the soul out of Freud. Bettelheim focused particularly on Strachey's translation of *das Ich* (the I), *das Es* (the it), and *das Überich* (the above-I) into "ego," "id," and "superego," which, he proposed, set up a depersonalized paradigm of mental processes that was colder and sharper edged than Freud's more organic conception.

Of course, these issues, intriguing though they are to scholars and critics, pale beside the larger issue of Freud's relevance—or lack of it—as a figure who speaks to the twenty-first century. The true believers, like the psychoanalyst and overseer of the Freud Archives Harold Bloom, maintain that Freud is the central consciousness of our time; he is, as Auden had it, "a whole climate of opinion." For them, the small mistakes here and there—as in

Freud's consistent reduction of women to biologically inferior creatures forever in mourning over their lack of a penis—add up to no more than a few shadows on the lustrous face of genius. On the other side, there is the hallowed vituperative tradition of Freud bashing, which proceeded in piecemeal fashion with Karl Popper and Hans Eysenck in the 1950s and '60s and went on to claim ever more cultural ground. It is perhaps best exemplified by the gleefully sustained attacks of the literary critic Frederick Crews, a reformed believer whose 1980 article "Analysis Terminable" could be considered the first real shot in the Freud wars. For this group, the whole enterprise of psychoanalysis is no more than a colossal con job perpetrated by a wily and ambitious half-baked theoretician on his cowed peers and on a gullible lay public.

Enter Phillips, the man who, as he himself might say, loves Freud but refuses to be enslaved by him and has thereby succeeded in moving beyond the raging ambivalence (or sadomasochistic "enactment," to borrow from the florid jargon of shrinks) he maintains is inherent in all our relationships. Having long been convinced that "psychoanalysis . . . is useful only as . . . one among the many language games in a culture," Phillips is apparently unhampered by unconscious conflict—which invariably results in the need to deify or diminish a chosen object—and is thus left free to rescue an embattled Freud from his champions and detractors alike.

"Freud is not a sacred text," he told me. "I never thought psychoanalysis had anything to do with science. It has been servile in its wish to meet scientific criteria to legitimize him. I want people to read Freud as you would any great novelist. His books are not accurate accounts of people. Every psychoanalytic text, as Auden said, should begin with 'Have you heard the one about . . . ?'"

Phillips's office is at the top of three flights of stairs in a scruffy whitewashed brick building down the street from Dakota, the chic restaurant on the corner where he and I repair for a late lunch. His determination not to take himself too seriously (or, at any rate, not to seem to be taking himself too seriously) is disarming. He cheerfully admits that he's "not good at punctuation," and when I ask him why he is resistant to drawing even the most provisional of conclusions in his own writing, he offers a simple explanation. "I don't know how to elaborate thoughts," he says. "I write sentence to sentence." Dedicated to what he calls "the transformative effect of listening," Phillips is alert to the loopholes in conversation, the dropped questions and trailing clauses, the partly said or the left unsaid. This receptive attitude helps to explain the rapport with children and adolescents that shines so clearly through his writing, in which he comes across as the least patronizing and most charming of allies, one who is willing to acknowledge the hopeless error of grown-up ways.

Phillips, who will be forty-nine this September, was the principal child psychotherapist at Charing Cross Hospital in London for a decade before going into private practice seven or eight years ago. He pulled back from working with children after he became a father—to Mia, who recently turned nine. (Phillips and the critic Jacqueline Rose, his ex-partner, share parenting responsibilities.) "Part of my internal myth," he says, "is that I could listen to anything. But when I had my own child, I could bear much less about the way children had been treated. I've seen many brutalized children, and it was like losing some kind of protective covering."

These days he mainly treats adults, who come to him by way of referrals, by word of mouth, or from reading his books. He sees most of them for forty-five-minute sessions, but since he is reliably unorthodox ("Anxious practitioners," he points out, "need rigorous technique"), he also sees patients for an hour or occasionally for double sessions. He has been known to sit on the floor and says he works well "on demand," seeing patients when they want to come rather than at regular times. Although Phillips cuts a sufficiently glamorous figure to earn him the sobriquet "the Martin Amis of British psychoanalysis," he firmly states his preference for the common over the uncommon patient. "I don't want to see famous or rich people," he says. His only criterion for treatment is that he be "moved" by the person he is working with and that "there's a conversation that's important."

I am inclined to believe him. He appears genuinely appalled at the blatant materialism of contemporary life and has few acquisitional habits beyond college-dorm staples like books, CDs, and plants; he does like to eat out, he admits, as though it were a fantastic indulgence. He is particularly incensed by the greed of his colleagues: "Any analyst who charges a lot of money is in my view betraying the profession." His own fees are modest, at least by American standards, ranging from no charge to forty-five pounds (roughly seventy-five dollars). "If you want to make money," he snaps, "go be a film star."

Phillips seems to have led a remarkably charmed life. He grew up in Cardiff, Wales, in an assimilated Jewish family (his grandfather's surname was Pinchas-Levy until a customs official at Swansea decided to replace it with a Welsh one) and remembers feeling "very well loved" as a child, with parents who indulged his passion for tropical birds. ("*National Geographic* was my childhood pornography.") He describes his parents—both of their families came from Eastern Europe—as having suffered from "pogrom anxiety." Although Phillips, who has one sister, lived in a Jewish house in the boarding school he went to and spent a summer picking apples on a kibbutz when he was sixteen, he insists that his background protected him from feeling the presence of English anti-Semitism. "I'm an accidental Jew," he says heatedly. "It's a contingent fact that one is born one thing and not another. I don't believe Jews are the chosen people. I don't believe our having suffered on a colossal, cataclysmic level should be recruited as a kind of special pleading."

After doing a year of graduate research on the poet Randall Jarrell, he went into training as a child psychotherapist. The catalyst for his change of professional direction was D. W. Winnicott, the innovative pediatrician turned analyst who rendered psychoanalytic dialogue accessible to the skeptical lay reader. (He is responsible for such iconic phrases as "the good enough mother" and "transitional object.") Phillips had come upon Winnicott's *Playing and Reality* when he was at Oxford. "I remember reading it and thinking, 'This is it,'" he says. Years later, after his own "eclectic" psychoanalytic studies and training (which included being analyzed by the mercurial Masud Kahn, who was an analysand of Winnicott's and whose sexual peccadilloes and rabid anti-Semitism eventually led to his being ejected from the British Psychoanalytical Society), he would put that excitement into words. Phillips wrote to Frank Kermode to ask if he could contribute a volume on Winnicott's work for a series called Fontana Modern Masters that Kermode was then editing. He included a short piece he had written on tickling, which Kermode passed on to Richard Poirier at *Raritan*, thereby launching Phillips's writing career. *Winnicott*, the first of his books, was published in 1988.

Not everyone, of course, is convinced that Phillips is either a true original or a knockout stylist. *Monogamy*, a collection of 121 aphorisms that is short on text and long on blank spaces, was largely savaged. Indeed, it shows Phillips at his worst, being clever and obvious at the same time, as if he were writing a self-help guide to erotically challenged readers of *The New York Review of Books*: "A couple is a conspiracy in search of a crime. Sex is often the closest they can get." Phillips's propensity for post-Lacanian abstractions and flashy linguistic inversions irritates critics like Elaine Showalter, who noted in a review of Phillips's last book, *Equals*, that his observations were "pithy rather than persuasive."

In the end, what remains up for grabs is how many of Phillips's ideal readers—"those who are curious about Freud as opposed to those who are convinced of his truth or falsehood"—are out there, waiting to hear a story about something called the unconscious. "The idea of a standard edition," Phillips points out, is "implicitly sacralizing." Instead, this intellectual impresario is offering a new and slimmer model—a "slightly wicked" Freud, as John Forrester calls him, one who has been snatched from the lionizing acolytes who laid claim to him and dragged into a less rarefied orbit, where he can be seen acting recognizably human. Phillips's Freud is "always torn between being a lover of conversation and a lover of being right." You might say that Phillips wants to restore the radical nature of the psychoanalytic enterprise—"Freud backed off and got afraid"—and transform the *Doktor* into a man for the transgressive moment rather than the calcified ages. "You can no more own Freud," he declares, "than you can own Henry James."

Certainly, this Freud is a less daunting one, more conducive to the insouciant pleasure of discovery than Strachey's weighty entombment allowed for. And perhaps reinventing Freud as a literary figure on the order of Joyce, Proust, and Kafka rather than presenting him as a rigorous cartographer of the mind is a canny way to keep him alive in the public imagination. It's a gamble that Phillips, for one, is prepared to make, and he has the charismatic presence to persuade a lot of formidable scholars and writers to come along with him for the ride. Even some of these people, though, have their doubts as to where it will end. "If Freud is simply another writer-philosopher," observes Malcolm Bowie, who was a professor of French literature at Oxford and is now at Cambridge, "there is no need to shackle him with quack-like claims to scientism or, indeed, to the pragmatic alleviation of suffering. But it is also to diminish him."

The truth is that Phillips has made it clear that he doesn't give a fig whether the institution of psychoanalysis endures, just as he, like Freud, is not all that smitten with the "romance of cure," preferring to see his sessions with patients as "a pretext for togetherness, a way out of loneliness." Still, I suspect he loves his Freud, the one who encourages a view of complicated selfhood in the same way that Dostoyevsky or Shakespeare does, with the kind of disinterested love he admits, in a touching moment, to feeling for his patients. "They matter to me a great deal," he says, with quiet conviction.

There is no doubt that they make strange allies—the pared-back, fast-moving enfant terrible and the serious old professor with his cigar and his beloved collection of antiquities—and it is hard to imagine what would happen if these two men ever ended up sitting next to each other at one of those hypothetical dinner parties. One possible scene is that Phillips would tell Freud to stop worrying what the Joneses and Jungs think, while Freud would tell him to grow up and get an e-mail address. Or perhaps they'd drink a toast to their shared interest in plumbing the depths of ordinary unhappiness—what remains after the neurotic misery that brings people into therapy has abated.

"We have to learn to enjoy the things we don't like," says Phillips, in the way he has of making deeply unconsoling things sound seductive. "Our desires are in excess of any object's capacity to satisfy them. But I'm not for this vale-of-tears approach. The point is to find out what it is that makes one's life livable."

BLOOMSBURY BECOMES ME

(LYTTON STRACHEY)

2002

I still think of it as the summer Lytton Strachey saved me. I was nineteen or twenty, and life should have been tipped in gold, glinting with possibility, but it wasn't. I see myself lying in the garden, muffled under antidepressants, sunk in a silent mourning that was impinged on only by the constant trilling of the cicadas in the bushes behind me, and by Michael Holroyd's two-volume biography of Strachey. The books came as a boxed set, like *The Compact Edition of the Oxford English Dictionary*, which added to their aura. They have been with me through several apartments, and by now they might almost be taken for antiques, with their embossed endpapers, faintly penciled underlinings, and yellowing pages. Volume 2, *The Years of Achievement, 1910–1932*, lost its dust jacket somewhere along the way, but otherwise they sit intact on a bookshelf within view, as they have always done. (Holroyd went on, with astonishing industry, to publish a wholly new one-volume biography in 1994, drawing on previously inaccessible material—much of it to do with Strachey's homosexuality—and although this book duly stands next to the earlier version, it does not have the talismanic value of the cased edition that got me through that unhappy summer.)

Strachey, of course, is best known for having challenged the staid, fact-gathering, and incorrigibly sentimental tradition of historical biography with his irreverent and psychologically informed approach to hallowed public figures. *Eminent Victorians*, published in 1918, was something of a literary bombshell, as much a critique of the hypocritical and sanctimonious mores of the Victorian age as it was an exploration of four individual lives. Strachey's ironic tone and ambivalent stance toward his subjects, who included Cardinal Manning and Florence Nightingale, was a radical departure from the idealizing and airbrushing principles that held sway until he came along. The critic Cyril Connolly described *Eminent Victorians* as "a revolutionary textbook on bourgeois society." And one contemporary reader, who appreciated Strachey's refusal to be awed by the high-minded in high places, observed, "You can feel reading the book that he is pleased that Miss Nightingale grew fat and that her brain softened." Strachey went on to refine his skills with his biography of Queen Victoria, which came out three years later and gave a complex and moving portrait of a woman who had been cloaked under the vestments of monarchy and the funereal garb of her widowhood.

Queen Victoria is dedicated to Virginia Woolf, one of Strachey's great chums and the only woman he ever proposed marriage to; the offer was rescinded, to the relief of both of them, within twenty-four hours. ("I was in terror," Lytton wrote to Leonard Woolf, "lest she would kiss me.") A large part of why I found solace in reading about his life was Strachey's membership in that fabled, ceaselessly self-evaluating, and tirelessly documented circle of chatterboxes known as Bloomsbury.

Bloomsbury has been described as having the self-important air of an exclusive club; the group's many critics, then as now, found it easy to write them off, as Leon Edel notes, as "a parcel of snobs, eccentric, insolent, arrogant, egotistical, preoccupied with neurotic personal relations." Still, indubitably clannish as they were, the price of admission to what Edel calls the "House of Lions" had nothing to do with Edwardian standards of lineage or class (although many of the members leaned on independent incomes) and everything to do with a democratic principle of competitively sharpened wits. The attitude of sexual tolerance (according to legend, Strachey was the first mortal to utter aloud the word "semen" in mixed company) only added to the fun;

there were several "open marriages," and bisexuality seems to have been a Bloomsbury specialty. "What was so new and exhilarating to me," Leonard Woolf observed after spending one evening in their company, "was the sense of intimacy and complete freedom of thought and speech . . . above all including women."

All of us long to be at home in the world, to find our singular passions reflected in a larger pond than the selves we swim in. Hell may be other people, as Sartre bluntly asserted in *No Exit*, but mired in my solitary darkness, I took great comfort in the ideal of a literary community—a fellowship of like-minded neurasthenic souls—that Bloomsbury represented. Having found myself not up to the bustle of life, I clung to the refuge of reading about people—writers, critics, painters, economists, philosophers, and historians—who took the athletics of reading and thinking as seriously as living.

My original affection for Bloomsbury and its intricate family gossip has never faded. I believe that I have read every second- and third-generation account that has been published about them—including Angelica Garnett's indicting memoir, *Deceived with Kindness*. (Garnett, the daughter of Vanessa Bell and the painter Duncan Grant, was led to believe that her father was Clive Bell and eventually married David Garnett, a cousin of Strachey's who had once been Grant's lover.) My first publisher, William Jovanovich, warned me years ago that if I wrote the biography of Dora Carrington—who improbably fell in love with Lytton Strachey and set up house with him—I was so set on writing, I would be accused, in his picturesque phrase, of "scraping the bottom of the Bloomsbury barrel." Although a biography of Carrington eventually did appear, I have little doubt that he was right. (In tongue-in-cheek tribute to the avalanche of books that has come out of the group, Malcolm Bradbury called one of his essay collections *No, Not Bloomsbury*.)

Did the Bloomsbury in my mind ever really exist? The Algonquin Round Table? The expatriate Paris of the 1920s? Was the post–World War II Greenwich Village of Anatole Broyard's memoir *Kafka Was the Rage* really as companionable as he would have us think? Or are all these literary Camelots of one kind or another nothing but wishful havens in a heartless world? Such cozy visions of companionship exist in part because we are in dire need of them. Beyond that, I'm not sure it matters how much of these legendary communities is real and how much is myth, so long as they help moor us to our vastly imperfect lives by allowing us a grown-up fantasy of the perfect familial embrace.

THE LOOSE, DRIFTING
MATERIAL OF LIFE

(VIRGINIA WOOLF)

1997

How in the world, you may find yourself thinking, can the delicate but overarticulated psyche of Virginia Woolf withstand yet another exhumation? Can there possibly be any gold left to extract from the overmined precincts of Bloomsbury, where Virginia and Vanessa and Leonard and Clive and Duncan and Morgan and Maynard and Lytton moved about with an avid sense of post-Victorian newness, talking and writing to beat the band? It is an oft-told story, gripping in its details: the beautiful but remote mother who died when Virginia was thirteen; the father grunting away at his literary labors, inconsolable in his grief; the sexual advances of her half brothers, George and Gerald Duckworth; the early breakdowns; the rivalry with her sister, Vanessa; the marriage to the "penniless Jew" Leonard; the intense friendships with other women, including lesbian affairs with Vita Sackville-West and Ethel Smyth; and then her suicide in 1941, at the age of fifty-nine.

As Hermione Lee, a professor of English literature at the University of Liverpool and the author of a biography of Willa Cather, notes, Virginia Woolf's "status has grown beyond anything that even she, with her strong sense of her own achievements, might have imagined." The greater a writer's status, of course, the more likely he or she will be appropriated by others: Given the sheer volume of material that's been produced about Woolf—all those books, articles, and scholarly papers, not to mention memoirs,

letters, diaries, and psychoanalytic readings—is there anything
vital left to say? This question is raised by Lee herself ("periodic
attacks of archive-faintness overcame me") and must inevitably
occur to even the most ardent of Bloomsbury/Woolf fans when
faced with this rather hefty volume. One hesitates to commit
oneself, wondering whether the time put in will have been worth
it at the end—a bit ashamed of this cost-accounting approach but
wary nonetheless.

Virginia Woolf had very mixed feelings about biography, or
"life-writing," as she called it. On the one hand she was an
enthusiast. "As everybody knows," she wrote in her essay on
Christina Rossetti, "the fascination of reading biographies is
irresistible." But, as Lee points out in the opening chapter of her
remarkable new book, Woolf also declared biography to be "a
bastard, an impure art" and claimed that the very idea was "pop-
pycock." Objecting to "the draperies and decencies" of the Victorian approach, she still had qualms about "the new biography"
as practiced by her good friend Lytton Strachey. She argued
within her own work "about the rival merits of archival and
imaginative research" and eventually wrote fictional biographies
(*Orlando*, *Flush*) as well as a real one (*Roger Fry*). Throughout
her life Woolf pondered the silence of her own sex when it came
to autobiography; always fascinated by "the gap between the
outer self ('the fictitious V.W. whom I carry like a mask about
the world') and the secret self," she intended to write her own life
from her diaries. Still, with "her perpetual fear of egotistical self-
exposure" (an inhibition that began in the merciless teasing of her
childhood and ripened in the preening atmosphere of Bloomsbury's Memoir Club), it is unlikely she would have risked being
truly forthcoming when being "fearfully brilliant" would do.

Lee documents the evolving perception of her subject from
"the delicate lady authoress of a few experimental novels and
sketches, some essays, and a 'writer's' diary, to one of the most
professional, perfectionist, energetic, courageous, and committed writers in the language." She does this without recourse to
the politicized agendas of the academy or special pleading (all of
Woolf's flaws are on display here). This account sets itself above

the fray, the better to home in on the glittery and elusive creature at its center—the prize catch in what one critic has described as the Bloomsbury pond.

From its very first page Lee's book is informed by current thinking on how to approach the writing of someone's life: "There is no such thing as an objective biography, particularly not in this case. Positions have been taken, myths have been made." But it is also infused with a very personal passion for her subject, which enables the author to cut crisply through the labyrinth of theories that have sprung up: there is "no way of knowing," she asserts, whether the teenage Virginia Stephen was really violated, "forced to have oral sex"—or, indeed, any kind of sex. What we get instead of reductionist speculation—Virginia Woolf as incest survivor or proto-feminist or trailblazing postmodernist—is a vivid picture of an age in flux and the pressures, internal as well as external, that it brought to bear upon one particularly sensitive female.

Virginia Woolf was born in 1882 into an Edwardian world of water closets and silver salvers filled with visiting cards, a world without electric lighting. During her childhood there were still some households that kept carriages "with a coachman and footman who wore powdered wigs, and yellow plush knee breeches and silk stockings"; when she and her half sister, Stella, took a walk in Kensington Gardens, they sometimes bumped into Henry James. As late as 1904, when a twenty-two-year-old Virginia was living with her three siblings in what her parents' generation regarded as a bohemian, if not déclassé, setup at 46 Gordon Square in Bloomsbury ("Henry James was particularly aghast"), bathroom references were still cause for embarrassment. In 1917, observing the freedom in matters of attire and sexual preference enjoyed by her new women friends, like Katherine Mansfield and Dora Carrington, she could note, "It seems to me quite impossible to wear trousers." In 1927 a cheroot-smoking Virginia Woolf would shingle her hair, and in the summer of 1934 she switched from an old-fashioned nib to a fountain pen. In 1939, light-years away from her cloistered beginnings, she met Freud, who presented her with a narcissus.

Lee renders this world, in which change was both slow in coming and shocking in its effect, with technically inventive moments, such as the one early in the book in which she recounts a visit the four young orphaned Stephens paid to their beloved childhood summer house, and moves brilliantly from a freeze-framed scene to conjuring up a re-created moment in the past, using *To the Lighthouse* as a referent: "Like Lily Briscoe conjuring up Mrs. Ramsay, we can superimpose, on to the image of the four young Stephens standing outside the hedge in the dusk, the image of summers of twenty years before. We can take the ghosts, turning them back into children, through the escallonia hedge . . . and back into the 1880s. The sun comes out, the house and garden are full of children and adults in Victorian clothes—family, visitors—walking and playing cricket and picking flowers and talking and reading. Julia Stephen is sitting there, casting her shadow on the step." Lee skillfully links the gradual rescripting of the "old laws" with the developments in Virginia Woolf's sense of herself and her writing, enabling us to see how the modernist refashioning of culture influenced her creative vision and helped her begin to untangle the problem of "how to present 'intellectual argument in the form of art.' "

This biographer also makes judicious use of psychological conjecture; by keeping a careful distance from jargon-ridden speculations ("But do we need . . . to put Virginia Woolf on the couch and make more sense of her than she can make of herself?") and by maintaining a certain modesty before the irreducible nature of her subject, Lee comes across as immensely insightful without appearing to have all the answers at hand. Of Woolf's parents, for instance, she remarks, "They both died before she had begun to prove herself as a writer, but it is probable that her writer's life was driven by the desire to say 'look at me!' to those two exceptional and critical parents."

Lee is good, as well, on the crucial role of Leonard—this man who seemed "so foreign" to his wife-to-be even as she is only months away from marrying him and who eventually became her truest companion. In the legend that has grown up around Virginia Woolf, Leonard features as a grim head nurse of a husband, ceaselessly gauging his wife's symptoms and doling out the amount of time she may spend chatting with visitors. Lee does not deny this side of him, conceding that Leonard's vigilant supervision of his wife's social life "certainly turned him, over the years, into more of a guardian than a lover," but he takes on fuller form here than he has elsewhere, exhibiting ambitions and judgments of his own—not only in the arena of politics, where Virginia favored pacifism in the face of the mounting threat from Hitler and Leonard favored going to war, but also when it came to people and literature. (Leonard was bored by much of Bloomsbury's partying; found Ethel Smyth, the eccentric seventy-two-year-old composer with whom his forty-eight-year-old wife fell briefly in love, "appalling"; and thought *Three Guineas* his wife's worst book.) And although it has become de rigueur to treat the Woolfs' marriage as a sexless union of highbrows, the one sober and the other mad, this is the first biography I have read that succeeds, through a subtle shift in emphasis, in conveying the profoundly intimate quality of their relationship—the way Virginia felt about Leonard's presence of an evening when they both read quietly, "L in his stall, I in mine."

Lee subverts the established view still further by suggesting that at least in the beginning, as evidenced by the playful use of pet names (Virginia was often "Mandril" and Leonard "Mongoose") and general indulgence in what Virginia called "private fun," the Woolfs' marriage had a cuddly, even frisky aspect—"an erotic secret life." (Another recent biography, *Art and Affection: A Life of Virginia Woolf* by Panthea Reid, while not nearly as strong as Lee's, makes fascinating use of documents that are either unfamiliar or heretofore unpublished. So we fall upon a startlingly sexy note written by Virginia to Leonard a year and a half after their marriage, in which the Mandril "wishes me to inform you delicately that her flanks and rump are now in finest plumage, and invites you to an exhibition." Virginia when she sizzles sounds very hot indeed!)

Of the many original ideas that Lee takes up, the place of reading in Virginia Woolf's life and the meaning of her madness are especially well developed. Although Woolf's was too mocking a

sensibility to give itself over to the Pateresque view of art as a
form of religion, she clearly found solace—a way out from her
overwhelming sense of futility, "the old treadmill feeling of going on and on and on, for no reason"—in the ordering proper-
ties of reading and writing. Reading became for her, as Lee
describes it, a means "of transcending the self." (She wrote to
Ethel Smyth, "Sometimes I think heaven must be one continuous unexhausted reading.") As for Woolf's psychological frailty—
"my own queer, difficult nervous system"—Hermione Lee makes
a persuasive case for her underlying sanity and for the literary use
to which she put the epiphanies revealed to her in her breakdowns. Notwithstanding her "blue devils," which was her term
for depression, and the agitations of her manic phases, she nur-
tured a hard-won affirmative instinct. She admitted to a "terror
of real life" and a general thin-skinnedness—"Cut me anywhere,
& I bleed too profusely"—and by her own recognition she de-
scended from an overbred, attenuated line: "such cold fingers, so
fastidious, so critical, such taste." To which assessment she added:
"My madness has saved me."

    And perhaps, indeed, it did. As she aged, she seems never to
have succumbed to middle-aged prejudices; she remained porous
in a way creative people are often imagined to be but rarely are.
Although it may seem odd to call someone who killed herself (she
put a large stone in a pocket and walked into the Ouse River) heroic, it is all the same the word that one most associates with Virginia Woolf after reading this biography. She ceaselessly challenged
herself in her art, always giving "this loose, drifting material of
life" her best imaginative capacities. Her courage in questioning
the manifold smug assumptions of the patriarchal culture in which
she lived—ranging from its educational system (she felt a particular disdain for masculine vanity as personified by Oxbridge dons
and turned down several honorary degrees) to the way it waged
war—is easy to overlook because of the subtlety and whimsy of
her methods. But it is all the more striking when one considers
that she might have comfortably inhabited the privileged niche
she had within that culture (T. S. Eliot called it "a kind of heredi-
tary position in English letters") without rocking the boat.

Hermione Lee has written a discerning and utterly absorbing account of the cost of female genius and the interplay of the forces that shape an individual life (as well as the perception of that life). Although her biography has not uncovered any startling new facts, Lee's tone and level of interpretation are such that she has performed the impossible: she has rescued Virginia Woolf from her iconic standing and restored her to human dimensions. We come to see her as she really was, unabashedly snobbish (she found Joyce's *Ulysses* "underbred, the work of a self-taught working man") and unremittingly envious—she was always snapping at the heels of other people's self-regard—yet also luminous and tender and generous, the person you would most like to see coming down the path.

I wish that the extensive notes were less confusingly organized, and I would like to have heard a bit more, given the capaciousness of this work, about the fluctuations in Virginia Woolf's reputation. Although she is today firmly ensconced in the canon, she would have been a dubious literary bet at any number of historical moments in the last half century. There were always those, like the critic Raymond Mortimer, who thought she had the "Midas touch" as a writer—"every word she uses is alive and pulling like a trout on a line"—but the Leavisite assault on Bloomsbury and its ethos began a period of diminishment as early as the 1930s. Queenie Leavis liked to refer to Virginia Woolf as "the clever daughter of Sir Leslie Stephen," as if she were describing an unusually articulate debutante. And there is something about Woolf's writing—its lack of rigid ego boundaries and blurring of subject-object distinctions as manifested by the fluid plotlines and evasion of authorial omniscience—that has consistently threatened a certain kind of male reader, from Erich Auerbach (who noted in *Mimesis* that she "does not seem to bear in mind that she is the author and hence ought to know how matters stand with her characters") to John Bayley (whose censorious essay some years ago rapped Woolf on her knuckles for her competitiveness and lack of a "sense of moral order," only to allow that "she might have grown up in her last years and moved us in the more considered ways that older writers do").

Who's afraid of Virginia Woolf? Everyone and no one, it seems. Meanwhile, we have a book worthy of its subject— graceful, astonishingly well researched, yet imbued with a sense of flow that is rarely achieved at this level of scholarship. Brimming with intelligence and excitement, it sets before us the idea of an electric mind, of indisputable greatness. Virginia Woolf thought the biographer had to go "ahead of the rest of us, like the miner's canary, testing the atmosphere, detecting falsity, unreality, and the presence of obsolete conventions." Here, then, is that miner's canary—just listen.

MOPING ON THE MOORS

(THE BRONTË SISTERS)

2004

Has there ever been a background more marked by personal tragedy and literary ill omen than the one that produced the Brontë sisters? Charlotte, Emily, and Anne: there was less than four years between them (their brother, Branwell, who dissipated his talents in drink and drugs, came between Charlotte and Emily), and it is tempting to think of the three, radically different as their personalities were, as linked to one another like a chain of paper-doll cutouts. None of them lived to forty: Emily and Anne died of consumption within five months of each other, the one at thirty and the other at twenty-nine (Branwell died three months before Emily, at the age of thirty-one), and Charlotte, the only one of the sisters to marry, was in the early months of pregnancy at the time of her death just short of thirty-nine. Yet their legacy is incomparable in the history of writer-siblings both for the degree of individual talent and for the triumph of imaginative vision over inhospitable circumstance that they personify.

The trio had much going against them: Branwell, the designated family genius, was educated in the classics by his father, and the money was found to send him to London to pursue his grand dreams of becoming an artist; his sisters, meanwhile, in keeping with their genteelly impoverished lot, were forced to find humble employment as governesses and teachers. All three were unconventional in both their ambition and their independence of mind, and although Emily and Anne were not without feminine allure,

they were none of them real beauties. (Thackeray, who gave a
dinner in Charlotte's honor after she "came out" from behind
the male pseudonym Currer Bell, believed that what troubled her
more than anything else was that she was not pretty enough to
win a man.) And yet, despite the corseting assumptions of their
time and place—Victorian England at its most high-handedly
patriarchal—these three slightly built (Charlotte was under five
feet) and psychologically delicate young women contrived to
produce a clutch of novels that to this day retain the daring
originality and riveting characterization that scandalized their
contemporaries. (Anne's novels, *Agnes Grey* and *The Tenant of
Wildfell Hall*, which are as bold as her reputation is mild, have
been routinely slighted in favor of her sisters', but when they came
out, they were thought to be even more shocking.) Two of the
sisters' novels, Charlotte's *Jane Eyre* and Emily's *Wuthering Heights*,
have entered the canon and can lay claim to equal status with the
fiction of Dickens and George Eliot. (Although *Jane Eyre* was
originally billed as "an autobiography," it is *Villette*, Charlotte's
most accomplished novel, that is also her most painfully self-
revealing one.)

Lucasta Miller's *Brontë Myth* is a wonderfully entertaining
and often spellbinding account of the ways in which the Brontës'
"lonely moorland lives" lent themselves to the process of mythifi-
cation even before the last sister had expired. It helped that misfortune lurked in every nook and cranny of the family history:
Charlotte was five when their mother died, and within four years
two elder sisters had died as well, at the ages of eleven and ten, as
a result of the miserable conditions at a boarding school that
would later be immortalized as the horrifying Lowood school in
Jane Eyre. (Both Charlotte and Emily attended it briefly as well.)

Patrick Brontë, the children's father, was the curate of Haworth;
the village parsonage fronted on a graveyard and looked out in
back on the Yorkshire moors. Looked after by a spinster aunt and
a housekeeper, Tabby, and cut off from the local goings-on by
virtue of their not entirely secure social class (Patrick Brontë,
who attended Cambridge on a scholarship, had risen from humble Irish stock, changing his name along the way from the ple-

beian Brunty to the more commanding Brontë, which is Greek
for "thunder"), the four remaining siblings looked to one another for companionship. Patrick might not have been quite the
deranged character he was made out to be until fairly recently,
when his image was refurbished in Juliet Barker's heroically—
and sometimes myopically—researched 1997 biography, *The
Brontës: A Life in Letters*, but he was undeniably on the peculiar
side, preferring, among other habits, to take his meals alone.

The children entertained themselves by creating, in minus-
cule script on tiny scraps of paper, elaborate and gory fantasy
worlds, the most enduring of which were Angria and Gondal.
The origins of the sisters' literary gifts are clearly to be found in
their juvenilia, but the remarkable fact is that they persevered
in their scribblings despite so many obstacles. These included the
sovereign fact that writing in the Brontë house was "very much a
male domain"; their being saddled with managing their father's
household after the deaths of their aunt and their housekeeper;
anxieties as to the worth of their writing (Charlotte was particularly afflicted with doubts, which makes her entrepreneurship
on behalf of herself and her sisters all the more moving); and
discouragement from outsiders.

Miller is particularly good on this last point, although she is
blessedly free of the sort of dogmatic gender-study approach that
takes a perverse pride in counting off the indignities inflicted by
an obtuse male establishment. Among those who either responded
negatively to Charlotte's work or advised her against pursuing it
were Hartley Coleridge, son of the poet (who had earlier complimented Branwell on his poetry), and Robert Southey, the poet
laureate, to whom she sent some of her poems while she was teaching at a boarding school. While conceding that she had "the
faculty of Verse," Southey solemnly admonished her: "Literature
cannot be the business of a woman's life: & it ought not to be."
Resisting the impulse to wax irate on Charlotte's behalf, Miller
prefers to understate the case, wondering mildly whether Southey
"might have considered a lust for fame more excusable in a young
man than in a girl" and noting that Charlotte hastened to reassure
the poet of the self-extinguishing program she had put into effect:

"I carefully avoid any appearance of pre-occupation, and eccentricity, which might lead those I live amongst to suspect the nature of my pursuits . . . I try to deny myself."

Although Miller's style is vivid and graceful, a good deal of research and thinking has gone into this undertaking, which she accurately describes in her preface as "not so much a biography of the Brontës as a book about biography, a metabiography." To this end she charts the emergence of a literary growth industry, one that is "littered with examples of apocryphal stories and fantastical claims" and was characterized by Henry James as a "beguiled infatuation" that "embodies, really, the most complete intellectual muddle, if the term be not extravagant, ever achieved, on a literary question, by our wonderful public."

The muddle began with Charlotte herself and the careful construction of her social persona as "the modest spinster daughter of a country parson," which served, as Miller points out, as a kind of "protective 'veil' to distract attention from the unacceptable elements of her fiction and deflect attacks on her personal morality." But the phenomenon that would eventually blossom into full-blown Brontëmania—with a cadre of relic-worshipping fans (including a former Hells Angel who interrupted a 1994 meeting of the Brontë Society to protest a newspaper article that described Charlotte as ugly) as well as the marketing of Emily Brontë soap (smelling of "the elusive fragrance of the wild moors") and Brontë Natural Spring Water—was really set in motion with Elizabeth Gaskell's landmark *The Life of Charlotte Brontë*. Published in 1857, two years after Charlotte's death, and written in a colorful, you-are-there style that eschews literary analysis for poetic descriptions and psychological portraits, it is, Miller writes, "arguably the most famous English biography of the nineteenth century" and one that "set the agenda which would turn the Brontës into icons." It became an immediate sensation, and although not quite an authorized version, the biographer's hagiographic view of events was colored throughout by her subject's participation and guidance; Gaskell was intent on playing up Charlotte's "womanliness" and her noble penchant for "self-denial," as opposed to the fiery romantic and intellectual passions that had ruled her life.

The canonizing and sanitizing instincts that informed Gaskell's rehabilitative project inaugurated the "purple heather school" of Brontë biography and would lead to a century and a half of imitations, rebuttals, correctives, and parodies, with the emphasis shifting in accordance with ideological fashions. There are now scads of biographies, critical studies, novels, plays, children's books, films, and psychoanalytic inquiries (the last very much taken up with Charlotte's Electra complex, lack of self-esteem, and overriding masochism, as well as with Emily's anorexia). All of them attempt to trace the source of the sisters' genius—in spite of the critic J. Hillis Miller's wise observation about the most inscrutable of the Brontës' novels, written by the most impenetrable of the sisters: "The secret truth about *Wuthering Heights* . . . is that there is no secret truth." Some of these Brontë interpretations were done in a spirit of fun (a satirical two-woman theater piece called *Withering Looks* and a novel called *The Brontës Went to Woolworth's*); others with a heavy touch (a book called *Charlotte Brontë's World of Death* and a novel called *Divide the Desolation*) or a sensationalistic eye (*The Crimes of Charlotte Brontë* wildly claimed that Emily was murdered after she was impregnated by Arthur Nicholls, the assistant curate who finally got to marry Charlotte after loyally hanging around for years).

Miller gives a hilarious account of the 1946 Warner Brothers movie *Devotion*, in which the reserved and very English Nicholls is played with "a disconcerting Austrian accent by Paul Henreid" and is given lines better suited to Rhett Butler, such as his declaration, after kissing Charlotte in the conservatory: "There are two ways of dealing with young women of your perverse temperament. It is fortunate for you that I am not a woman-beater." But the funniest instances of the "lurid legend-mongering" that passed for scholarship have to do with inflamed guesswork about the romantic life of Emily, who has been called "the sphinx of English literature." With great relish Miller hauls up a 1936 biography of Emily by Virginia Moore called *The Life and Eager Death of Emily Brontë*, which purported to be a rigorous examination in which "especial and respectful" attention had been paid to primary sources. In her zeal to bring new light to bear on the elusive Brontë's lost lover, Moore misread the title of one of her manuscript poems as "Louis Parensell" instead of "Love's Farewell." Miller notes that the "mythic Louis went on to spend a colorful speculative existence on the letters page of the *Poetry Review*," with one correspondent writing in with a suggestion as to where the two lovers might have met, based on a sleuth-like reading of a throwaway phrase in one of the diaries. Not content with her discovery, Moore excitedly went on to unearth another dark secret, proposing that Emily had been "a member of that beset band of women who can find their pleasure only in women."

There is little to find fault with in *The Brontë Myth*, except perhaps for its failure to bring the ghostly Anne out of the mists so as to give her the benefit of its respectful but vastly amused scrutiny. It suffers, too, from a somewhat tentative organizing principle, which slightly undercuts its ambitious agenda. But these are quibbles. The Brontës are an endlessly intriguing subject—as a 1931 novel about them put it, "What a family! Even if they'd never written a line, what a story!"—and Miller's book is a superbly unmuddled contribution to the continuing literary conversation.

THE LADY VANQUISHED

(JEAN RHYS)

2009

Jean Rhys lived a hard-luck life and wrote, almost exclusively, about hard-luck women. Her pellucid prose, in which shards of pained observation cut a jagged edge in an otherwise fluid style, is so accessible that it is easy to overlook the art—the tight control—behind the seeming artlessness. Like those of Marguerite Duras and Katherine Mansfield, Rhys's natural psychological habitat was despondency of a particularly female kind—what Mansfield in her notebooks describes as "an air of steady desperation," hinging on desiring and desirability. With the exception of Rhys's last novel, *Wide Sargasso Sea*, which reimagines *Jane Eyre*'s Mrs. Rochester, her characters are bewildered women of the demimonde who reside in what she describes as "lowdown" sorts of places: cheap hotels and seedy boardinghouses. Armed with kohl-blackened eyelids and feigned indifference, they dine out on erotic allure that loses its luster even as they banter with the men on whose good humor and money they depend, only to end up sooner or later drunk and alone. These cornered creatures are based on the author herself, and all suffer from the lassitude—the lack of élan vital—that plagued Rhys for most of her life, causing her to note in her unfinished, posthumously published autobiography, *Smile Please* (1979), "Oh, God, I'm only twenty and I'll have to go on living and living and living."

Lilian Pizzichini's *Blue Hour* is the second full-length biography of Rhys to appear since her death in 1979 at the age of eighty-eight; the first was Carole Angier's excellent and tirelessly researched *Jean Rhys: Life and Work* of 1990. Pizzichini's title is borrowed from the Guerlain perfume L'Heure Bleue, a scent that was meant to evoke dusk in Paris and happened to be Rhys's favorite. As Pizzichini writes, "The blue hour was also the hour when the lap-dog she saw herself as being during the day turned into a wolf . . . Underneath our surface sophistication lurks a predator. Jean Rhys was always concerned with what lay beneath the top notes."

This sense of being at the mercy of latently hostile forces against which she had to arm herself informed the way Rhys approached the world from childhood on. She began life on August 24, 1890, the fourth of five children born to a family that belonged to the tiny patrician class of Dominica, a volcanic island in the West Indies—a class that enjoyed a simulated Victorian life among the natives. Rhys, née Ella Gwendolen Rees Williams (the novelist and critic Ford Madox Ford, who became her lover and literary champion in the 1920s, suggested the change to give her name a more modernist ring), lost her mother's attention to a new sister when she was five and was thereafter looked after by a mercurial native named Meta, who, she would insist in *Smile Please*, "couldn't bear the sight of me." Meta was a believer in voodoo and obeah, the Caribbean form of black magic, and instilled fears in the vulnerable young girl of vampires, zombies, and werewolves: "Jean spent much of her childhood screaming, crying or collapsing with terror," Pizzichini observes, "and taking weeks to recover in bed." Until she left for an English boarding school at seventeen, Rhys spent an isolated youth reading and communing with nature; her increasingly removed mother, meanwhile, was mystified by her shy misfit of a daughter.

Rhys arrived in a grimy, sunless, and crowded Edwardian city that didn't live up to her fantasies: "London was disappointing. She could not see her future in its smog-smudged streets." (One might argue that among Rhys's problems was a failure to envision her future anywhere she was; she was doomed to be overwhelmed by first impressions.) Rhys attended Perse School in

Cambridge, and although she did well in her studies and made some friends, she held on to her West Indian accent with its "lilting rhythms and French patois" and was mocked for talking "like a nigger." Never one to feel easily at home—Pizzichini describes her as existing "in a permanent state of dissociation"—Rhys was at a loss when it came to basic skills, such as riding a bike, and got chilblains from the freezing dormitory. She stuck it out for three terms, winning the school's Ancient History Prize, and then, with the support of her "indulgent" father, switched to the Academy of Dramatic Art. After two terms of classes in "fencing, ballet, elocution, and *gesture del sarto*," her father refused to pay any further, having received a letter from the school that held out little hope for Rhys's "success in Drama."

Defying expectations that she would return to Dominica, there to wait on a suitable marriage proposal, Rhys threw herself into the raffish life of a chorus girl. The next few years saw her gradual transformation into one of her own heroines, short on money and long on anguish. She entered into a two-year affair with an older, wealthy businessman she called Lancey; he set her up in spacious quarters, paid for her singing lessons, and listened to her tales of exotic Dominica. Despite Rhys's dreams of being saved by her lover, Lancey abruptly ended the affair by letter, agreeing to pay her an allowance in return for being left alone. This turn of events led to Rhys's emotional collapse, setting the pattern for relationships to come: "Lancey's rejection . . . left her feeling nullified. As such she began her pursuit of disappointing adventures and loves that replicated this scenario of loss and mortification; or else retreated, disconsolate and speechless, alone with the chaos her feelings brought."

For all her self-destructiveness and nihilism, there was something resilient about Rhys; she held on to life almost out of spite, to prove she could get the better of her own "rum existence," as she describes the plight of Julia Martin, one of her autobiographical antiheroines. She moved to Paris in 1919 with the first of her three husbands, Jean Lenglet, who "was known to the police of three countries" and with whom she had two children, a son who died in infancy and a daughter who lived mostly with her father after the couple parted in the mid-1920s. (They divorced in 1933.) Most important, she wrote a clutch of books during those decades—four novels and a collection of stories—that gave voice to her dark, outsider's sense of human relations, where vulnerable women were pursued and then abandoned by predatory men while society turned an indifferent eye. They were published to admiring but cautionary reviews. No less a critic than Rebecca West singled her out as "one of the finest writers of fiction under middle age" in her review of *After Leaving Mr. Mackenzie* (1930) but pointed out that Rhys was "enamored of gloom" and that her novel was an inducement to suicide. After 1939, in which she published *Good Morning, Midnight*, Rhys did not publish a novel for almost thirty years, during which time she lived a peripatetic, chaotic existence, which included a stay in Holloway prison for assaulting a neighbor—and, indeed, was rumored to be dead.

Rhys's career as a writer received a fresh infusion when a dramatization of *Good Morning, Midnight* was featured on BBC radio in 1957. ("She missed the eventual broadcast," Pizzichini bemusedly notes, "because she still had not worked out how to tune a radio.") Francis Wyndham and Diana Athill, editors at the British publishing firm André Deutsch and long-standing admirers of her work, signed Rhys to a contract that same year for the novel that would emerge, years later, in 1966, as *Wide Sargasso Sea*. Its author was by now an elderly woman living in a condemned farmworker's dwelling in the Devon countryside fitted out with wartime linoleum and a bare bulb; her main visitor was the local vicar, and a bottle a day of whiskey was, as she wrote, a "must."

After years of obscurity, Rhys entered the 1970s as a literary celebrity. Visitors trekked to her village to pay homage; V. S. Naipaul wrote about her, and the Queen gave her a commander of the Order of the British Empire. She was writing again—going back and forth between a final collection of stories, *Sleep It Off, Lady* (1976), and *Smile Please*—but paranoia and depression remained constants. She worried how she looked in photographs, was irritated by the causes of the day such as women's lib and black activism, and was none the happier for her newfound re-nown: "Fame and financial security had come too late to make any difference to an old woman. She told her new friends this over and over again. She was too old for this, and they were far too late." Rhys died on May 14, 1979, in a nursing home, watched over by a young friend, Jo Batterham, who persuaded the attending nurse not to feed Rhys or to replace the oxygen mask she had pushed off her face. A connoisseur of bleakness, the writer had remarked to David Plante (who recounted his vexed relationship with Rhys in *Difficult Women* [1983]) that "the end would be joy," and she appeared to welcome it.

The Blue Hour is an admirable effort to document the inner workings of a complex, opaque woman who distrusted words as well as people yet believed in the redemptive possibilities of writing more than she let on. That the fascination with Rhys's fragmented, messy existence and wounded psyche continues to grow—textual and psychoanalytic studies show no sign of abating—attests to the uniqueness of her unflinching vision. She articulated the plight and sensibility of a certain kind of female—the kind who speaks to the inner bag lady in all of us—better than anyone before or since. Still, one wonders what Rhys, who considered her life an "abject failure" except for her writing and who, like Oblomov, preferred sleeping to most anything else ("Sleep is so *lovely* better than food or thinking or writing or anything," she wrote in her memoir), would have made of all the fuss.

LAST TANGO

(ANNE CARSON)

2001

The writing of poetry is regularly deemed a dead art, so it is little wonder that its living practitioners are a somewhat petty and xenophobic bunch—or that the enterprise itself has come to seem, except in the hands of a few populist types like Sharon Olds, Philip Levine, and Billy Collins, almost willfully insular. "Contemporary poets," noted the Polish poet Wisława Szymborska in her 1996 Nobel acceptance speech, "are skeptical and suspicious even, or perhaps especially, about themselves." One can hardly blame them, of course, seeing as how most people return the compliment by avoiding the stuff altogether.

In the small world of people who keep up with contemporary poetry, Anne Carson, a Canadian professor of classics, has been cutting a large swath, inciting both envy and admiration. Her publishing trajectory has been something other versifiers can only marvel at, having propelled her from a position on the periphery to her perch as a MacArthur fellow and a commercially viable author at a prestigious mainstream house. It was clear from the start that Carson's writing was unclassifiable, even by today's motley, genre-bending standards. Was she writing poetry? Prose? Prose poems? Fiction? Nonfiction? Did even her publishers know for sure? (Her current paperback house, Vintage, calls her first book, *Eros the Bittersweet* [1986], "An Essay" in its listing of her titles, while the 1998 Dalkey Archive paperback edition of the book gives it no such designation.)

Beginning with *Eros the Bittersweet*, Carson seemed determined to pull out all the stops by bringing everything she knew—specifically her knowledge of Hellenic literature but also her vast reading in other fields, including philosophy, fiction, and poetry—to bear on her writing. In the abbreviated, free-associative mode that she instantly established as her trademark, any thought might set off any other thought, or even a demi-thought: a discussion of Sappho's understanding of erotic desire in the opening of *Eros the Bittersweet*, for instance, segues quickly into the most fleeting of allusions to Anna Karenina. The enclosing context of Greek myth is everywhere in evidence, but so are the writerly presences of Simone Weil, Virginia Woolf, and Eudora Welty, to name but a few. Freudian and Lacanian theory also puts in an appearance, as does a passing observation on Sartre's understanding of the experience of viscosity. And all this by page 40!

Carson has since gone on to write five more books, each distinctive in the elusiveness of its style; these have included *Glass, Irony, and God, Plainwater* (subtitled *Essays and Poetry*), and the much-acclaimed *Autobiography of Red*, published in 1998. This last, billed as "a novel in verse," was based on an obscure Greek myth about a winged red monster named Geryon, which Carson reworked, improbably but spellbindingly, into a gay coming-of-age story. The book added Alice Munro and Harold Bloom to her growing cadre of fans; the latter recommended her, a bit obliquely, as "a disciplined version of Gertrude Stein."

Autobiography of Red also succeeded in bringing the truly innovative aspect of Carson's work into sharper focus. This, as it turned out, had less to do with her dazzling but sometimes tiresome erudition than with her carefully controlled use of a post-confessional voice—one that darts into the text by way of casual snatches of dialogue or raw asides:

> *Don't pick at that Geryon you'll get it infected.*
> *Just leave it alone and let it heal,*
> *said his mother*

> *rhinestoning past on her way to the door.*
> *She had all her breasts on this evening.*
> *Geryon stared in amazement.*

In her second-to-last book, *Men in the Off Hours*, Carson continued to demonstrate her easy familiarity with the history of ideas, both high and low, through her use of ironic appropriations and cross-pollinated allusions. The book's characteristically hybrid offerings included a cinematic rumination on Catherine Deneuve and a poem-essay on "the phenomenology of female pollution in antiquity." But Carson also continued to exhibit an emotional daring that is rare in this level of discourse—and even rarer in a writer who wears her brain on her sleeve. So a short poem with the fussy title "Essay on Error (2nd Draft)" skips across an invented mental landscape, archly strewing references (including one to her own poem of a few pages earlier, another to a letter from Freud to Ferenczi, and yet a third to a phrase of Descartes's) before collapsing into a pure, unmediated image of nostalgia:

> *After all*
> *what are you and I compared to him?*
> *Smell of burnt pastilles.*
> *I still remember the phrase every time I pass that spot.*

It is this very sudden and unexpected surrender to the rush of experience that makes Carson unusual—her willingness to drop her eggheady defenses, the references to Artaud and Derrida, and risk sounding like Lucinda Williams:

> *Not enough spin on it, said my true love*
> *when he left in our fifth year.*
>
> *The squirrel bounced down a branch*
> *and caught a peg of tears.*
> *The way to hold on is*

> *afterwords*
> *so*
> *clear.*

Goodbye, Mr. Derrida; hello, Mr. Heartache. (Okay, so she felt the need for that closing pun with "afterwords." Let her have it.)

Now, less than a year later, comes *The Beauty of the Husband*, boldly and a bit vaingloriously subtitled *A Fictional Essay in 29 Tangos*. Its subject is the waywardness of lust and the disaffection of the heart as seen through the lens of a marital breakup. "There is something pure-edged and burning," Carson writes, "about the first infidelity in a marriage." Never mind that the union in question probably shouldn't have occurred in the first place, given that the husband is an inveterate philanderer who is "loyal to nothing" and "lied about everything." The poet would bid us understand that logic has nothing to do with it:

> *Not ashamed to say I loved him for his beauty.*
> *As I would again*
> *if he came near. Beauty convinces. You know beauty makes sex*
>   *possible.*
> *Beauty makes sex sex.*

The book, in fact, takes as its overt theme what has been the ever more insistent subtext of Carson's prior writing—the "dilemma of desire" and the ways in which intellectual discernment (a familiarity, say, with "the passive periphrastic" tenses in Latin) and erotic taste often pull in opposite directions. The inexplicable nature of romantic longing, the insuperable divide between thought and feeling, is a predicament as old as the hills and one that, I'd guess, women are more disturbed by than men— especially the sorts of women who have "grasped certain fundamental notions first advanced by Plato" and still find themselves doubled over with "the agony of sexual reasoning."

There are other, walk-on characters, including the watchful

mother who instinctively distrusts her daughter's choice in suitors: "To abolish seduction is a mother's goal." A pair of sisters, improbably named Dolor and Merced, figure briefly as objects of the husband's attention, but they remain paper-thin and seem to have been chosen primarily for the foreign sound of their names, like characters who have wandered in from an Almodóvar film. More memorably there is Ray, a gay friend of the husband's who befriends the ex-wife and keeps her posted on the randy goings-on. A painter by day and a short-order cook by night, he is introduced in one of Carson's cinematic bursts:

*Ray flips two half-fried eggs with one hand
and catches an explosion of toast (too light, shoves it back down)
then spins left
to pick a clean plate off the dishwasher stack.*

With his casual insights about the wife's predicament ("You married people get too tight with things, get all strained in and sprained up") and "his beautiful wicked grin like a skirt flying up," Ray helps to ground the book in whatever semblance of narrative it has. But then again, a story line in any conventional sense is not what fuels Carson's writing—or what she cares about, except as it may enable her to ask the questions that interest her: To what avail are Parmenides and "the true lies of poetry" when set against the "welter of disorder and pain" that "is our life"? "How do people / get power over one another?" (This conundrum fascinates Carson sufficiently for her to pose it twice within the first thirty-five pages of the book.) And perhaps most poignantly: "What does not wanting to desire mean?"

Carson's willingness to implicate herself in the discussion at hand—her refusal to edit out the personal, even at its most pathetically lovelorn—has become more obvious with each successive book, and *The Beauty of the Husband* takes her further out on the precarious limb she has claimed as her own. It is always difficult, of course, to gauge how much is autobiographical in a writer's material, and Carson is trickier than most in this regard, but *Husband* strikes me as being the least cloaked about its ori-

gins in lived life. There is far less of the brainy braggadocio that
has marked her previous work, especially if one looks beyond the
tap dancing around the Keatsian equation of Truth and Beauty
that is invoked in epigraphs preceding each section. From the
very first "tango," she is cutting pretty close to the bone:

> *A wound gives off its own light*
> *surgeons say.*
> *If all the lamps in the house were turned out*
> *you could dress this wound*
> *by what shines from it.*

Similarly, the voice of sensual lament that Carson has resorted
to with poignant effectiveness in the past is here presented without the fig leaf of fancy cerebration:

> *Naked in the stone place it was true, sticky stains, skin,*
> *I lay on the hay*
>
> *and he licked.*
> *Licked it off.*
> *Ran out and got more dregs in his hands and smeared*
> *it on my knees neck belly licking. Plucking. Diving.*
> *Tongue is the smell of October to me.*

Carson is one of the great pasticheurs, and her influences are
diverse. Emily Dickinson is said to be a favorite, although I don't
see much of her in the work, but there are traces of Gerard Manley Hopkins in her use of bricolage-like constructions and of
Anne Sexton in the sudden dips into the fondly maternal ("Little
soul, poor vague animal") and in her flashes of emotional clarity:
"We are mortal, balanced on a day, now and then / it makes sense
to say Save what you can." Overall, one would wish for less arch-
ness, which too often gives the writing a brittle patina of self-regard,
and I wonder when Carson will realize that not every performance has to be a bravura one. Sometimes, too, the images strain
credulity—"He could fill structures of / threat with a light like

the earliest olive oil"—and at other times the writer seems lost in an enterprise of her own devising.

Still, I don't think there has been a book since Robert Lowell's *Life Studies* that has advanced the art of poetry quite as radically as Anne Carson is in the process of doing. Although I can understand why Carson's peers might bristle at the grandness of her ambition and squabble about her imperious disregard for even the laxest of forms, it seems to me that there is only one relevant question to be posed about her writing. What her fellow poets would do well to ask themselves is not whether what Carson is writing can or cannot be called poetry, but how has she succeeded in making it—whatever label you give it—so thrillingly new.

DUST-TO-DUSTNESS

(W. G. SEBALD)

It's tempting to try to make sense of the randomness of fate by reading an eerie quality of foreboding into the tragic end of a writer who has presented an elegiac view of life in his books. As was the case with Albert Camus (whose life was cut short at the age of forty-six) so with the German writer W. G. Sebald, who died in a car crash in December 2001 at the age of fifty-seven. A keen, almost triumphant presentiment of extinction pervades the four novels that were published during Sebald's lifetime and in remarkably short order established his reputation as an austere literary voice of the utmost moral seriousness.

Sebald's work reads like a lamentation or a dirge, as though existence itself were no more than a way station on the journey from dust-to-dustness ("We lie prostrate on the boards, dying, our whole lives long") and he had long ago said his goodbyes. His books are all depictions, in one way or another, of the ashen premonition of loss; and they might be said to take place in a state of permanent déjà vu, in which a geographic site that is reconstructed from "mountains of rubble" or an emotion that is dredged up from the ocean floor of psychic debris seems no more than a revisiting of something that was glimpsed once before, in a far-off time or place.

Considering that Sebald was a late starter—he began to publish fiction only in his mid-forties—the rapid ascension of his melancholic literary star (although he has never received the reverential attention in his native Germany that has been paid him in England or America) is all the more striking. The details of his life are sparse, and those that are available are opaque, adding to his mystique. He was born in 1944 in a tiny village in the Bavarian Alps; his father served in the Wehrmacht but maintained a silence on the subject of his wartime experiences after returning from a POW camp. Sebald immigrated to England in his early twenties and settled in Suffolk, where he taught at the University of East Anglia for thirty years, eventually becoming the founding director of the university's British Centre for Literary Translation.

It is an attribute of all truly inspired writing to seem original, whatever its provenance or influences, and Sebald's work reflects this wherever you turn. It feels almost unprecedented in tone, although his weltanschauung derives from Schopenhauer and his literary affinities can be traced to a select group of writers, including Adalbert Stifter, Heinrich von Kleist, Robert Musil, and, most discernibly, Thomas Bernhard. His meandering and curiously formal prose (one German critic has described it as prose that is always dressed in a tuxedo) bypasses the ordinary exigencies of narrative, drawn instead to the graveyard silence that looms over the hectic impulse of storytelling.

Sebald's landscapes, whether those he traverses in his solitary walks and travels or the ones that appear in his eschatological dreamscapes, are dotted with treeless heaths and the remains of walls. (There is a good deal of the naturalist in Sebald, which provides for the scattered passages of lyricism about clouds or the phosphorescent glow of herrings that leaven his harsh outlook.) The cities he stops in are peopled with the ghostly presences of exiles (often Jews who have managed to escape the Nazi net) and transplanted, reclusive eccentrics who flit in and out of the deserted railway stations, run-down buildings, and emptied-out towns that are left behind after the drumbeat of progress or the whims of conquerors have moved on. "From the earliest times," he observes in one of the casually desolate asides that are strewn like black confetti through his writing, "human civilization has been no more than a strange luminescence growing more intense by the hour, of which no one can say when it will begin to wane and when it will fade away."

Sebald's books are usually referred to as novels or "prose fictions," in spite of his transparently autobiographical narrators and the fact that Sebald himself never clearly defined his work as belonging to any one genre; they fall into that gaping crevasse between fact and fiction known as hybrid, which is another way of saying that they are committed to but not hindered by the obligation to tell the truth. They are interspersed with blurry, uncaptioned black-and-white photographs—as well as reproductions of newspaper items, handwritten notes, receipts, timetables, and tickets—which may or may not refer to the text. Sebald calmly disposes with such rudiments of reader-friendliness as paragraphs and quotation marks; the sentences within his long monologues sometimes run amok, and his narrative voice often switches without warning from the first person to the paraphrased thoughts of a third-person character. In lieu of the momentum of a plot, he relies on layers of bricolage that derive their force—or lack of it—from a cumulative rush of coincidences or correspondences, the frisson of an unsuspected synchronicity of detail that crosses centuries and continents. (*Austerlitz*, the last and most accessible of the books to appear before his death, is something of an exception in this regard, with a more conventional creation of character and pacing of incident.) It is an approach that might seem artless but is as deliberate as the story line in a fast-paced mystery. In *Vertigo*, the third book to appear here, he gives a glimpse of his creative strategy: "August the 2nd was a peaceful day. I sat at a table near the open terrace door, my papers and notes spread out around me, drawing connections between events that lay far apart but which seemed to me to be of the same order."

Sebald's typical protagonist (if that is not too concrete a term for his disembodied, wafting narrators) is somewhat paranoid (an anonymous waitress in a bar strikes him as suspicious, "as if she were the bearer of secret messages between the several guests and the corpulent landlord") and seems always to be recovering from or about to enter a period of debilitating malaise. Even the images he exhumes from his childhood are tinged with an irredeemable sadness, like the "sorrow-worn camels and elephants" he once spotted at a performance he saw with his mother. In the present, meanwhile, he contemplates the portents of certain doom, sifting through sadness. Needless to say, the colorless, nomadic universe he inhabits, where the pizzerias are dreary and the hotels unwelcoming, offers few flashes of humor except of the most heavy-handed, ironic variety (the eponymous Jacques Austerlitz recalls ordering an ice cream that turned out to be "a plaster-like substance tasting of potato starch and notable chiefly for the fact that even after more than an hour it did not melt"). The mere mention of an "ice-cold can of Cherry Coke" or "an immense Rolex watch" jumps off the page like a garish piece of flotsam from a different planet.

The shadow of estrangement follows Sebald everywhere: there is scant mention of women or sex (in *The Rings of Saturn*, he passingly alludes to the "ardent bewilderment of my senses that I used to feel in an embrace") and there are few companionable encounters except for those with people in straits similar to his own, who are, more often than not, on their way to suicide. (Three out of the four characters in *The Emigrants*, his first book to appear here, take their own lives.) The experience of being in an airport, hardly a restful one for most of us, takes on an almost somnambulistic aspect when Sebald undergoes it. The crowds strike him "as if they were under sedation or moving through time stretched and expanded" (which gives one cause to worry whether any of them will make their flights); the airport is "filled with a murmuring whisper," and the atmosphere itself has a "strangely muted" quality. Even when he does something as prosaic as stopping at a McDonald's, the transaction assumes a terrifyingly anomic quality: "I felt like a criminal wanted worldwide as I stood at the brightly lit counter."

On the Natural History of Destruction is the second of two posthumous works of Sebald's to be published. (*After Nature*, a triptych of biographical prose poems and the first of his nonacademic books to be published in Germany, came out here in the fall of 2002.) It comprises four disparate essays, the latter two having been appended to the book as it appeared in the original German in 1999. One is on the Austrian writer Jean Améry, who survived torture by the Gestapo and Hitler's concentration camps (he was together with Primo Levi at Auschwitz for a brief time), only to commit suicide in the 1970s; the other is on the German artist and writer Peter Weiss, whose work, in a description Sebald quotes from one of Weiss's published journals, is a constant struggle with "the art of forgetting"—an attempt "to preserve our equilibrium among the living with all our dead within us."

On the Natural History of Destruction also includes a fore-word Sebald wrote to accompany the first two essays, "Air War and Literature," which takes up the silence of German writers in the wake of World War II, and "Between the Devil and the Deep Blue Sea," an examination of the compromised principles and quasi-brilliant career of the writer Alfred Andersch. (This is an odd and disconcerting piece, the splenetic tone of which is unlike Sebald's other work and hints at a more private grievance, as if it had been written to even a score.)

Although one might reasonably claim that all of Sebald's work has an air of contingency, this slim volume is patently something of a publishing afterthought. As such, it cannot in fairness be said to represent the writer at his best, but it is precisely this pieced-together quality that enables the reader to consider some of the chinks in Sebald's literary armor that might have been overlooked before—including his tendentious approach to a fraught national legacy, his practice of a kind of keyhole history, and his uneasy relation to both his personal and his national origins.

The central essay of the collection, "Air War and Literature," which was excerpted in *The New Yorker* and is based on a series of controversial lectures that Sebald gave in Zurich in 1997, comes at the reader from a different tangent than one might have ex-pected, given the denunciations of German culture and character that are peppered throughout Sebald's work, from *The Emigrants* on. In that book he assails his countrymen for their willed amnesia about the depredations of the Third Reich and the gruesome efficiency "with which they had cleaned everything up." Similarly, in *Vertigo*, he evokes his first visit home in thirty years with undisguised revulsion. The women of his village are described as "almost without exception small, dark, thin-haired and mean"; his philistine father is indicted as a man "who would probably never have taken it into his head to go to the theatre, and less still to read a play"; and his parents' Teutonic habits are scrutinized with narrow-eyed disdain, from the "cold and loveless" chimes of the living room clock to an étagère in which the plants "led their strictly regulated plant lives."

It is all the more surprising, then, that "Air War and Literature" poses the problematics of memory in another light entirely, shifting the onus of inquiry from one kind of moral quiescence (the Germans' self-preserving complicity with Hitler's program of genocide and tacit acceptance of the Master Race theory) to a different kind altogether (the "extraordinary faculty for self-anesthesia" that led to the postwar evasion of the fact of Germany's own suffering at the hands of the Allied bombing campaigns). Sebald accuses his country's writers of having failed to come to imaginative terms with the devastation wrought upon their cities by air raids in which 600,000 civilians died, 3.5 million homes were destroyed, and 7.5 million people were left homeless: "It seems to have left scarcely a trace of pain behind in the collective consciousness, it has been largely obliterated from the retrospective understanding of those affected, and it never played any appreciable part in the discussion of the internal constitution of our country." Indeed, he blames this peculiarly German ability to cordon off unpleasant memories—to impose order on the unruly workings of the mind—for his own lack of knowledge about both the Nazi past and the retribution "on a scale without historical precedent" meted out by the British and the Americans.

The terms of the argument have subtly but significantly changed. In keeping with a revisionist and somewhat disreputable line of thinking that has surfaced in German writings on the Holocaust in recent years, Sebald no longer calls for a confrontation with the intergenerational pathology—based on an "almost perfectly functioning mechanism of repression"—that allowed people like his parents to close their eyes to (or to outright embrace) the bloodthirsty philosophy that led to the creation of the crematoriums. Instead, the historical burden of citizens of "the Fatherland" (an odd nomenclature for Sebald to avail himself of, given his previous, strenuously asserted disassociation from his German roots) is now deemed to be the necessity of conjuring with their fate as survivors of another kind of crematorium—the "inferno" caused by the "obvious madness" of the Hamburg and Dresden firestorms.

Although he dutifully acknowledges the immutable reality that led to the Allied attacks ("a nation which had murdered and worked to death millions of people in its camps"), Sebald seems to be suggesting that the precipitating horror of Hitler's reign has been sufficiently atoned for and that the time has come to acknowledge a "shameful family secret" that leaves aside the tribal particulars of guilt and focuses instead on the ecumenical nature of human suffering. In a sleight of hand so deft that it is easy to miss its implications, Sebald repositions the Germans as unmourned victims of "defenseless cities" rather than as culpable victimizers of a defenseless people.

His catastrophist's perspective, in which we briefly inhabit the world in the face of horrors past, passing, and to come, leaves no room for an etiology of disaster—and therefore no room for the sort of psychological triage that would allow us to pool our limited resources of compassion and pity in accordance with some stark hierarchy of justness. Considering that it was Hitler who pioneered the art of sophisticated aerial bombardment and who was the first to target civilians (in Rotterdam), one might find it understandable that German casualties have had less claim on our sympathies up to now than they otherwise might have had. But in the world according to Sebald the end is always more or less in sight, and we are all more or less Jews bound for slaughter.

On the Natural History of Destruction is a complex apologia of a book, one that attempts to absolve a son of the sins of the father by establishing a larger and more generic ground for incrimination. It is a testament, among other things, to the lingering impact of early familial identifications and to the powerful grip of unresolved conflicts between intellectual and emotional allegiances. Which is to say that even a writer as scrupulous about his own motives—"one could not say whether one goes on writing purely out of habit, or a craving for admiration, or because one knows not how to do anything other"—and as removed from private agendas as Sebald seemed to be, may be possessed of an impulse to clear the bad name of the parents he has ostensibly repudiated. (He pitilessly observes the profound fulfillment his mother and father found in "the acquisition of living room furniture befitting their station, which . . . had to conform in every detail with the tastes of the average couple representative of the emerging classless society.") He may also be trying to account for his own unfathomable lapses of attention and failures of memory.

Still, Sebald's conviction about the discontinuous character of any one time period and the fallibility of conscious recall (as opposed to the Proustian belief in the magically rehabilitative effects of involuntary recall) puts him in a curious bind. Skeptical though he may be of "the much-vaunted historical overview," based as it is on "a falsification of perspective," the slippery stratagems of memory are the only material a writer of an archaeological bent such as his has to work with. Sometimes, as appears to have been the case with *Austerlitz*, Sebald was capable of his own convenient repressions. In one of several flurries of controversy that surrounded him in his lifetime, Susi Bechhöfer, herself a survivor of the *Kindertransport*, claimed that he had made use of the experiences recounted in her published memoir without acknowledging it. Sebald eventually responded to a letter she wrote to him and admitted that he had in fact read her account and based some of Jacques Austerlitz's recollections on it.

I suppose it is possible to read all of Sebald's work as the through-a-lens-darkly vision of a man suffering from a medicable mood disorder that he mistakes for a universal entropy, "as if the world were under a bell jar." It might even help to explain the suspect aura of highbrow cultism that attaches to his books, the prick of misgiving as to whether they are profound or just implacably misanthropic. Who else but a gloomy, deskbound intellectual would warm to a narrator who chooses as his "favorite haunt" the Sailors' Reading Room in Southwold, which is "almost always deserted but for one or two of the surviving fishermen and seafarers sitting in silence in the armchairs, whiling the hours away"? But to reduce Sebald to a clinical depressive is to ignore the admittedly bleak gift that is the larger part of his greatness, which is his mining of a primal existential despair that goes beyond the merely personal to suggest something endemic about the condition of being human. I think of him as someone who was on good terms with darkness—a solitary watchman who stayed awake while the rest of us dreamed, the better to acquaint himself with the mad dogs that bark in the night.

PORTRAIT OF THE ARTIST
AS A FIASCO

(HENRY ROTH)

2005

Henry Roth, whose ruthless assertions of creative will were off-set by equally savage powers of self-sabotage, remains one of the more confounding figures in modern American letters. Roth's jangled and disrupted life, filled with the most noble artistic intentions—including a sustaining belief in the redemptive possibilities of art—along with the most sordid personal impulses, belies the illusion of internal cohesiveness we prefer to set our sights of human behavior by. Even during his long and agonized lifetime—Roth died in 1995, at the age of eighty-nine—his bizarre trajectory as a one-book wonder who had wandered off to an unheated cabin in the Maine woods took on the aura of a cautionary tale. What unseen mutation of character led Roth to trade in his former existence as a literary comer for the persona of a Yankee hick—the laconic, subsistence-level operator of a feather-plucking business called Roth's Waterfowl? Or, as his sister, Rose, put it in an interview quoted by Steven G. Kellman in *Redemption*, his absorbing biography of Roth, "How could he give up a God-given talent and fool around with chickens and ducks?"

Roth had shown early indication of dazzling promise with *Call It Sleep*, published in 1934 when he was all of twenty-eight. The novel is told from the harrowing perspective of David Schearl, a young boy growing up in the fractious melting pot of New York City. David is the half-adored, half-abused only child of Yiddish-speaking greenhorn parents who emigrated from

Eastern Europe to the ironically labeled "Golden Land" of their bare-bones tenement flats in Brownsville and the Lower East Side. The hypersensitive eight-year-old cowers in the face of his brutish, feckless father and looks to his unhappy, radically disoriented mother for love and protection. Without her attentive, reassuring presence he feels lost: "He would not see his mother again until morning, and morning, with his mother gone, had become remote and tentative."

From the opening sentence of the first chapter, the reader crouches down behind David's eyes, peering out along with him at a universe looming with imminent menace, indifferent to his needs and wishes: "Standing before the kitchen sink and regarding the bright brass faucets that gleamed so far away, each with a bead of water at its nose, slowly swelling, falling, David again became aware that this world had been created without thought of him."

A true multicultural novel *avant la lettre*, *Call It Sleep* had an epic ambition that was immediately recognized. Roth was praised by one reviewer as "a brilliant disciple of James Joyce"; his book was hailed by another as "the most accurate and profound study of an American slum childhood that has yet appeared." Still, the novel was published during the depths of the Depression and sold fewer than two thousand copies before disappearing. More cuttingly to the point for Roth, a zealous recruit to the Communist Party, the book was condemned by the Marxist publication the *New Masses* for being insufficiently political in its use of its working-class background. That particular reviewer felt it was beset by the fatal flaw of bourgeois aestheticism and dismissed it as "introspective and febrile." (He also found *Call It Sleep* overly focused on sex, an opinion seconded by the presumably capitalist *New York Times* critic, who characterized it as "a fine book deliberately and as it were doggedly smeared with verbal filthiness.")

As Kellman points out in his introduction, *Call It Sleep* "offers a case study in the fickle mechanism of literary reputations, in the eclipse of cultural leftism, and in the invention of ethnicity." The last two factors were particularly important. The novel's seminal accomplishment would become clear only in 1964 after it was released in a handsomely designed paperback edition and was hailed as a classic articulation of the American immigrant experience. (*The New York Times Book Review* ran a front-page rave by Irving Howe.) *Call It Sleep* became a bestseller as well as a fixture in the canon. Meanwhile, as it turned out, neither Roth's retreat into "silence, exile, and waterfowling" nor the rediscovery of his long-ignored novel (which Roth, in his characteristic snatching-defeat-from-the-jaws-of-victory fashion, went to great pains in his later years to disassociate himself from) was destined to be the end of the story. Instead, it came with an eleventh-hour plot twist in which the slumbering literary giant surprised everyone by emitting a final scandalous roar that echoed through thousands of pages and brought decades of near-oblivion to an end.

These pages added up to six volumes, four of them published under the overall title *Mercy of a Rude Stream*, beginning in 1994 with *A Star Shines over Mt. Morris Park*. Without taking into account this astonishing late-life opus, it is impossible to gain any vantage on the scope of Roth's endowments as a writer—and the pathos of his decision to turn his back on them. *Mercy of a Rude Stream* is shot through with unwieldy genius, a clunky insistence on getting at the elusive and often ugly heart of the matter that is without parallel in contemporary literature. All four books, of which the second and the third—*A Diving Rock on the Hudson* and *From Bondage*—are the strongest, display an almost manic urge for documentation, as if a naturally garrulous man whose jaws have been wired shut has finally been released into the liberation of speech.

Although *Mercy of a Rude Stream* contains patches of wooden writing, it also demonstrates Roth's undiminished lyric brilliance and skill with dialogue; his keen social antennae for the slights of class and race; his psychological acuity, as well as his descriptive energy, and what can only be called the enforced intimacy of his prose. Most strikingly, though, this transparently autobiographical cycle does battle with tawdry aspects of Roth's own character, as revealed through his young alter ego, Ira Stigman, whose angst-filled journey from terrified child to fledgling artist is tracked in this multivolume bildungsroman. (*A Star Shines over Mt. Morris*

Park begins a year after *Call It Sleep* leaves off, and Ira is clearly an extension of David Schearl.) It was Roth's misfortune—or perhaps his ornery gift—that he was incapable of prettifying his experience. His compulsion to come clean about ancient, grimy secrets can be viewed in many different lights, as heroic or masochistic or exhibitionistic, but what can't be denied is that his unflinching unself-protective candor leaves most of what we think of as confessional literature, with its sidelong glance at the good opinion of the reader, in the dust.

Redemption clears away some of the lingering myths around Roth (that he was a "spurned prodigy" who stopped writing because he felt ignored) and confirms other perceptions (the Oedipal undertone in *Call It Sleep* turned out to be just the merest fictional hint of a real-life familial enmeshment). From a purely sensational angle, the most fascinating—and repellent—incident in Roth's vivid and volatile life, one that outdoes everything else in shock value, was his decade-long incestuous relationship with his sister, Rose. The siblings' involvement started with "groping" when Rose was ten and Henry was twelve, and developed over the next four years into full-scale sexual relations. The "murky slough of his self-indulgence," as Roth described these acts by way of his stand-in, Ira, left him with an enduring sense of horror and mortification that was the cause, he believed, of both his warped personality and his writer's block.

Of course, there's a case to be made that this perverted family romance both silenced Roth and hurt him into his finest art. He had scratched his sister out of the picture in *Call It Sleep*, recasting himself as an only child, although it was Rose who typed up the manuscript of the novel and, years later, was responsible for revealing her brother's whereabouts to an admiring editor after his work had fallen out of print. But something moved Roth to expose this "canker in the soul" in the most graphic (and, as he pointed out, exaggerated) terms when he began writing again in his early seventies. Although Ira is siblingless in the first installment, a sister suddenly appears, rising up from the rubble of the past like a blast from the unconscious, in the second volume, *A Diving Rock on the Hudson*. Despite Rose's pleas that he not betray their involvement, Roth went ahead and spilled the steaming beans. He had never taken the devoted Rose into account, not even after she graciously shared half of their father's meager estate with him after Roth had been cut off with just a dollar, and he wasn't about to start doing so. "For me she scarcely existed," he told an interviewer in 1977. "She was never important." (Under threat of legal action, he did eventually pay her ten thousand dollars and agreed to take out all further references to the incestuous aspect of their relationship in the remaining volumes.)

Oddly enough (and to comprehend all, needless to say, is not to forgive all), within the context of the violently dysfunctional marriage of their parents and the generally xenophobic climate of the Roth household, the incestuous detour makes a kind of anthropological sense, as though an ingrained Jewish pattern of tribal endogamy had been taken to its logical conclusion. "It was," Roth would write in *A Diving Rock on the Hudson*, "like a sneaky mini-family."

Kellman, who avoids the urge to reduce Roth's life to neon headlines, fills in the contours of his subject's higgledy-piggledy route ably enough. We begin with his troubled childhood under the venomous scrutiny of a father who is possibly even worse than the father in *Call It Sleep* and a mother every bit as doting as her fictional portrait suggests, then witness Roth's escape into art with the help of his lover and mentor, Eda Lou Walton. Throughout his life, Roth would be dependent on the kindness of women who supported him both emotionally and financially. Walton, a prolific writer and a generous teacher, was twelve years older than Roth when she took the twenty-two-year-old aspiring writer under her wing. He lived with Walton while he wrote *Call It Sleep* (the novel is dedicated to her), and she introduced him to Greenwich Village literary salons, where he hobnobbed with Margaret Mead and Louise Bogan. But Roth never had any trouble severing connections with people who had outworn their usefulness, and when he found himself floundering, having burned the manuscript of his second novel in disgust, he turned to another self-sacrificing mother figure. In 1938, at Yaddo (where

Walton had arranged for his stay), he met Muriel Parker, a gifted composer and musician whose patrician lineage led back to the *Mayflower*, and he credited her with saving him. "I feel that Muriel just retrieved me in time," he told an interviewer. "I don't think I would have lived very long; I just didn't feel like it."

Their marriage of fifty-one years appears to have been a blissfully symbiotic union, although it didn't leave much room for Roth's two sons, who both became alienated from their father as adults. In 1968, after twenty-two years of dour New England weather, Roth and his wife moved to Albuquerque, New Mexico, captivated by its warmth and light, where they lived in a mobile home. (Roth, as one and all attest, inherited his reviled father's inability to part with money.) After Muriel's death in 1990, a grief-stricken Roth found it difficult to continue writing and was hospitalized for six months for suicidal depression. He eventually rebounded, with his usual sly force, and spent the last few years of his life in a ramshackle stucco house that had originally been designed as a funeral parlor, a fitting residence for the morbid and ailing writer, who displayed an inscription of the Cumaean Sibyl's pronouncement "Apothanein Thelo"—"I wish to die"—in his study.

Kellman has done a scrupulous job of research, but there is, all the same, something recalcitrant about the material, some way in which the shards of Roth's fragmented narrative—its "grave and disabling discontinuity," as he called it in *From Bondage*—resist being glued together even after the chronology is in place, the dramatis personae established, and the events sketched in. The mystery of who the man was—of why he was the way he was—persists. Undoubtedly, this has something to do with the fact that, more than most people, Roth retained a certain plasticity of temperament throughout his life, a receptivity to the imprinting of new experience that spoke either to the lingering infantilism he felt cursed by or to a genuine porousness. A striking instance of this was his love-hate attitude toward his Jewishness, which led him from a complete renunciation of his religious past (a declared atheist at the age of fourteen, in 1963 he was still of the opinion that the best thing Jews could do would be to circulate themselves out of existence) to an embrace of Zionism as an antidote to "exilic insecurity" and a belief in the value of Jewish community in the aftermath of the 1967 Six-Day War.

Roth's vastly mercurial nature, whatever the reasons behind it, created many shifts in both physical locale and psychological orientation. As a result, the narrative feels somewhat disorganized, as though Kellman were overwhelmed by the necessity of keeping track of everything, of logging one rambunctious detail after another. The list of jobs Roth worked could fill a paragraph all on its own: "Roth's occupations would have to include not only novelist and waterfowl farmer but also newspaper peddler, messenger, bus conductor, soda pop vendor, plumber's assistant, ditchdigger, English teacher, precision tool grinder, firefighter, maple syrup vendor, blueberry picker, woodcutter, psychiatric hospital attendant, and tutor in math and Latin."

"Really you know," Roth once wrote to Eda Lou Walton, "the artist is just a maniac who somehow evades the bug-house." There is indeed something heartrending about the example of Roth's life, as well as something monstrous. What I'm not sure there is, though, is the edifying message this book's title might lead us to expect. Granted, there are bright moments as well as blighted ones, and not everyone disappoints or acts badly—although to the end Roth senior never ceased denigrating his son, not even when he came to stay with Henry and his family during the summers after his wife died, calling him "a schmo who had married a shiksa and didn't amount to anything."

Notwithstanding its prelude and coda of literary triumph, Roth's life remains in many ways a rags-to-rags story, marked from its penurious beginning to its frugal, penny-pinching end by a lasting sense of psychological impoverishment that manifested itself in a grimly contrarian attitude. These are dark and murky waters Kellman has ventured into, and it's small wonder that other writers before him—including Leonard Michaels, who considered writing Roth's biography, and Philip Roth, who toyed with the idea of fictionalizing the older Roth's life—backed off. Michaels, according to Kellman, was "depressed by his subject." And no wonder.

Kellman's book presents us with a profoundly disturbing sense of the damage that can take place in families and the toll this damage exacts on its recipients, especially if they happen to be gifted. In Roth's case, this took the form of an underlying emotional instability, like a fault line running through him. "A sorrow had dislodged something in him," he observed in *A Diving Rock on the Hudson*. "He had worried too far: like prying apart something that wouldn't come together again, wouldn't come together right, had left a weakness, a chronic vulnerability to unhappiness."

The notion of the wounded artist—the writer or painter who plies his or her "golden handiwork," as Yeats called it, to placate demons or fill in absences—is so common as to verge on the truistic, and yet the example of Roth's embattled life and career reminds us that great injury doesn't always yield to the wish, or even the ability, to transpose it into something of aesthetic value. Sometimes pain merely yields to more pain. To say that Roth suffered for his writing is to say little; to say that he suffered too much to find an enduring refuge in his art is perhaps closer to the truth. Which may be why the experience of reading *Redemption* isn't so much redemptive as unsettling, in spite of its poignant image of the enfeebled but indomitable old geezer, plagued with crippling arthritis, persevering with his craft even as urine runs down his leg.

It was Roth's declared wish to die with his "books on," which is what he essentially did. All the same, one is tempted to ask in his case, even more so than is usual when reading about the often disastrous private lives of creative people, if the work was worth the anguish. All that pain for all that prose: Did it exact too high a human cost? "Portrait of the Artist as an Old Fiasco" was one of Roth's provisional titles for the autobiographical musings that became *Mercy of a Rude Stream*. As a summing up, it suggests the piercing self-awareness of the man, his undeluded familiarity with the pitfalls and dips in the "landscape of the self," as he called it. "I'm a wretch," Roth announced toward the end of his life. Ah, but how well he wrote.

A TIP OF THE HAT

(JOHN UPDIKE)

2009

Of few writers can it truly be said that they embody Henry James's description of the artist as "a person on whom nothing is lost." Most writers have curiosity about some things but not about others; their interests are usually obsessive and thus preclusive. They may wish to know how memory evolves, as Proust did in *Swann's Way*; or how football works, as Frederick Exley did in *A Fan's Notes*; or how real estate is sold, as Jane Smiley did in *Good Faith*.

Once in a while, however, a writer comes along who has an omnivorous appetite for description and the bric-a-brac of knowledge—who is at ease in the imaginative as well as the critical realm, in the visual as well as the literary arts, who is as intrigued by dashboards as he is by women's pinkish interiors. Such a writer was John Updike, from his earliest fiction and reviews up to his final essay, "The Writer in Winter," which appeared in the November/December issue of *AARP* magazine. No literary snob, he, for all that he was criticized for being one. It's impossible to imagine other writers of his stature (Philip Roth, for instance) stooping to reflect for that publication's Life Lessons column. In this piece Updike observed, with his scrupulous eye, that when he looked back at his prose from twenty or thirty years ago, "the quality I admire and fear to have lost is its carefree bounce, its snap, its exuberant air of slight excess. The author, in his boyish innocence, is calling, like the sorcerer's apprentice, upon unseen powers—the prodigious potential of this flexible language's vast vocabulary."

Indeed, with the exception of Nabokov, no writer inheres in the details quite as much as Updike. His almost OCD compulsion to translate everything he saw, heard, appreciated, and disapproved of (including much of contemporary life) into honed, even finicky words on the page may render him too promiscuous a talent for true gravitas, as James Wood once suggested. Or it may simply underline the way in which he takes in the chaos and clatter of the world with an attentive and unfailingly courteous vision. What is certain is that his metaphors usually succeed in what they set out to do: widening the lens rather than simply calling attention to themselves, as leaps of associative derring-do in the way of many younger writers. What is also certain is that, much like Cheever, Updike is a sucker for poignancy, for the sense of "irrecoverable loss." In 1976's "Here Come the Maples," a quintessentially Updikean story in its theme (the failure of marital intimacy) and tone (elegiac), Richard Maple appreciates his wife, Joan, most fully as he is driving her to divorce court: "All those years, he had blamed her for everything—for the traffic jam in Central Square, for the blasts of noise on the mail boat, for the difference in the levels of their beds. No longer: he had set her adrift from omnipotence. He had set her free, free from fault. She was to him as Gretel to Hänsel, a kindred creature moving beside him down a path while birds behind them ate the bread crumbs."

In keeping with his sense of decorum, his apparent disinterest in ordinary fame ("Celebrity is a mask that eats into the face," he wrote in *Self-Consciousness*), and his wish to keep chosen aspects of his life private, the news of Updike's death at seventy-six from lung cancer on Tuesday came as a shock. Like many fans, I last caught sight of him on November 12 on *Charlie Rose* (his sixteenth appearance!), where he was promoting his latest novel, *The Widows of Eastwick*. He conversed with Rose in his rueful and polished style about growing old and continuing to write amid diminished expectations, about the continuing need to write because that was what one did. He had seemed the very epitome of witful aging, his intellectual energy blazing out from slanted brown eyes and his impish grin firmly in place.

All of which led me to wonder after the fact who outside his family had known that he was harboring a fatal disease, that he was about to go off into the gloaming (one of his favorite words), leaving behind him a staggering—nay, Victorian—legacy of sixty-one books, including the much-lauded Rabbit tetralogy (two of which received the Pulitzer Prize), the Bech trilogy, nine volumes of poetry, numerous collections of book reviews and short stories, two books on art, and a collection of golf writing. Watching him that evening, I was struck not by the aura of obliviousness and entitlement that presumably led David Foster Wallace to dub him a "Great Male Narcissist" or by the aura of senescence that led Tom Wolfe to christen him one of his "Three Stooges" (along with Norman Mailer and John Irving) in a *Harper's* essay. "He's an old man, he's my age, and he doesn't have the energy left to be doing something about the year 2020 in a town north of Boston," Wolfe noted, referring to Updike's 1997 novel, *Toward the End of Time.* I was struck, rather, by the opposite qualities: by Updike's lively engagement, his lack of swagger (unless an intensity of will qualifies as such), and an almost imperceptible air of bewilderment as to how and when he and the American reading public had parted ways.

Tributes have appeared and will no doubt continue to appear, attesting to Updike's dazzling gifts, sexual candor (which, in its anthropological focus, inspired many an embarrassed titter in its day), and preeminent standing among modern American writers. But the reality is that the world outside the literati (and sometimes including them) no longer much cared after a certain point—say, 1990—what Updike had to say. He would always be reviewed with reflexive respect, and his name would come up as a perennial Nobel contender (notwithstanding Cynthia Ozick's conviction that his American brand of small-town Protestantism kept him out of the game). But somewhere along the way—somewhere between the marginalization of suburban angst and the dawn of multiculturalism—the fizz had gone out of Updike's name. The news he was bringing was no longer cutting-edge but seemed

steeped in nostalgia for lost cultural signposts. His vaunted cos-
mopolitanism began to feel dated, stuck in a moment when the
de haut en bas tone of *The New Yorker* editorials still prevailed.
He began to seem like a man who always wore a hat to work.

What is odd is that underneath his upright churchgoing
persona and paterfamilial embrace of domestic convention—
underneath what Foster Wallace insisted was an immovable
solipsism—Updike evinced more interest in the Other, as he/she
has come to be called, than most of his contemporaries. He was
always forsaking his natural territory—disgruntled marriages,
derailed desire, and crumbling Wasp traditions—for darker and
less parochial matters. The lure of foreignness steadily intrigued
him, be it Jewishness (*Bech*), militant blackness (*Rabbit Redux*),
or Third World upheavals and misadventure (*The Coup, Brazil*).
In *Terrorist*, his second-to-last novel, he bravely and not always
successfully attempted to inhabit the perspective of a radicalized
Muslim adolescent named Ahmad. Although the novel more than
anything gave Updike a chance to rail at the materialist, sex-
obsessed culture of a decaying New Jersey factory town under
cover of Ahmad—"*Devils*, Ahmad thinks. *These devils seek to take
away my God*. All day long, at Central High School, girls sway
and sneer and expose their soft bodies and alluring hair"—it
was also an effort at understanding the intractably alien, those
who "belonged to the margins of the Christian world, the comic
others in their funny clothes."

In the end, John Updike probably shone most brightly as a
miniaturist—as a writer of stories and essays, where his supremely
conscious, sibylline prose had the chance to chew more than it
bit off and thus feature him at his mimetic best. I still remember
the excitement with which I devoured stories like "The Fairy
Godfathers" and "The Man Who Loved Extinct Mammals." To
be sure, he remains one of our most unabashedly heterosexual
writers, reveling in the taste of femaleness. I wish I had had the
chance to meet him when I was writing for *The New Yorker*, the
magazine that was his home for over fifty years. Above all, I believe
he never really got his due, in part because he was so prolific for
so long that the emergence of a new book seemed unremark-

able; in part because he never wrote the one great, defining novel; and in part again because his kind of lapidary prose and American boosterism went out of style. Then, too, behind his witty discernment one could sense a churlishness gradually creeping in, especially over the last two decades.

Still, the final verdict has not yet been handed down. In June, a new collection of Updike stories, *My Father's Tears, and Other Stories*, is being published, and for all one knows, there may be more to come. There are ideal readers yet to discover him and long-standing admirers yet to make the case for him as a rare and generous and altogether seductive voice.

IV

HIGHER
VALUES

WHEN A BAG
IS NOT JUST A BAG

2006

It is the Thursday evening before New Year's Eve, a time when most equally minded people are busy laying in the champagne and taking stock of their lives. Or reading on a chaise somewhere pretty and tropical, nibbling on papaya, or perhaps skiing down a white slope in Aspen, Colorado, with the wind behind them. On this day you would have found me scurrying along Madison Avenue on my way to Barneys, the metropolitan mecca of all that is fabulously new and covetable, to return two bags. The items in question were a characteristically whimsical Marni evening pouch that had cost this side of $800—and that I had originally planned on carrying to a nephew's bar mitzvah to offset a stark, synagogue-appropriate St. John Knits ensemble but in the end decided against, in favor of a borrowed and less contrapuntal Lambertson Truex lizard clutch—and an uncharacteristically unconstructed Jil Sander number ($670) that had briefly spoken to me in my continuing search for an Edenic black bag. It goes without saying that neither one was a strictly necessary purchase (what bag after the first one is?) and that they were about far, far more than themselves.

The mania for bags—an irrational passion if ever there was one—defines our acquisition-mad cultural moment as surely as the tulip fever that raged through seventeenth-century Holland defined the burghers of Amsterdam. Put it another way: we may have lost our moral bearings in these centerless and often incoherent times, but we know what bag we want to carry our bearings in should we ever find them again. Where shoes once reigned supreme as the dominant wardrobe accessory, bags now lead the way as the top fashion signifier. A woman's bag also serves as the portable manifestation of her sense of self, a detailed and remarkably revealing map of her interior, an omnium-gatherum of myriad aspects of her life—the crucial Filofaxed information as well as the frivolous, lipsticky stuff.

Last fall, as if to underscore the point, the Rebecca Hossack Art Gallery in London staged *I Want to Be a Bag*, by Alessandra Vesi, featuring sewn, crocheted, and glued constructions that were like visual puns made delightfully concrete. As Anna Johnson suggests in her witty introduction to *Handbags: The Power of the Purse*, "a good bag becomes an intimate extension of the body," which is why an astute female reader will realize that Anna Karenina is about to end it all when she tosses aside her red handbag. "A woman who is sick of her handbag," Johnson observes, "surely, is absolutely sick of living." (This explains, as well, why Diana Vreeland's unappeasable dislike of this accessory and her dictum to "ban the bag" were wisely ignored by designers and why, when Tom Ford suggested in a recent interview that the hippest thing a girl can do is carry no bag at all, he instantly revealed the limits of his understanding of what makes women tick.) "The only way I know I exist is if I have my stuff with me," explains a writer friend, the possessor of a portfolio of bags ranging from a LeSportsac to a "slab of brown buttery leather" measured to the size of a September *Vogue* and handmade for her by Jutta Neumann.

Let the record note, then, that I spent the greater part of this past autumn, when not pursuing gainful employment as a writer or nagging my daughter about her homework, buying and returning bags. Among the many returned bags were ones from Pollini and Theory that didn't hold up to at-home scrutiny. The bags I kept included a beaded and sequined jeu d'esprit of an evening clutch from Anya Hindmarch; an inexpensive espresso leather satchel that is unadorned except for two subtle pieces of Aztec-looking hardware that I picked up at Fred Segal when I was in Los Angeles

in September and have yet to bring out of my closet; a Jane August chenille satchel that looks like a magic carpet ride purchased
from Linda Dresner; and the pièce de résistance, a dramatically
oversize rosy-purple Bottega Veneta. To be scrupulously truthful,
I bought and returned the Bottega and then rebought it when I
happened to notice it in a glass display at Barneys, discreetly but
substantially reduced—making it, at a fraction under four figures,
still the priciest bag I have ever bought. (Thankfully, there is no
little metal label on the bag telling you its provenance. Only if you
peer very closely can you dimly make out its attribution, stamped
in a small, bookish typeface into the leather interior, thereby satisfying another of my tendencies, reverse snobbism.)

Buying a bag is nothing less than a compulsion, a fixation, a
tragicomic spectacle, an indication of status anxiety, a sign of existential hope, a fetish, a clue, a puzzlement, a pity, a pleasure. One
might even go so far as to conjecture that the British analyst
D. W. Winnicott's notion of "potential space"—an imaginative
domain between inner and outer worlds that corresponds to the
infant's sense of play—finds its most perfect habitation in a handbag. It is, above all, the great unstated answer to the Freudian
question: What do women want? Well, I am here to clear away
this lingering mystery about the nature of female desire forever:
women want bags.

Some of them, like my friend Molly Jong-Fast, crave the latest
"It" bag and bugger the cost, be it the Fendi Spy, the Chloé
Paddington, the Balenciaga Twiggy, or some multipocketed Marc
Jacobs number. Others, like the writer Elizabeth Hayt, are drawn
to all bags Chanel because they are, she says, age appropriate
for a woman in her forties, impeccably made, and available in
slightly off colors, like terra-cotta or distressed gray. She likes them
"logo discreet" and big enough to carry her Evian in, but not
overtly practical. "I would die carrying a tote," she says. Still others, like the beautiful fawn-like creature I met at a party who told
me she was afraid to make a choice of one bag over another for
fear of what it might say about her, are so aware of the possible
implications that they respond counter-phobically by using any
old bag.

And yet again others, like myself, are ascertainably bag crazed but shy away from the obviously commodifiable only to spend hours searching out the unlikely and indefinable—a bag that will not only meet them in all of their complexity but will also telegraph that message of complexity out to the world. Behold the woman who carries such a bag: so supple and yet unyielding, so ephemeral and yet sturdy, so large of presence and yet graceful of mien, so French and yet Italian, so elegant and yet artisan-like, so Hermès and yet Beguelin. So everything, in short, and yet insouciant. You've got to love a woman who recognizes the value of a bag like that.

Although nowadays we associate the carrying of bags almost exclusively with women, from ancient times through the Middle Ages both men and women wore drawing purses around the waist or hips. The handbag as the strictly feminine accessory we know it to be came into being in the Paris of the 1790s, with the introduction of the sheer Empire-line dress. Of course, one might think, given the symbolic importance of bags in modern women's lives from their adolescent years on, that inquiries into the larger meaning of these receptacles—as maternal substitutes, say, or as holding environments (to borrow from another idea of Winnicott's) for the fractured or improvised self—would be all over the psychoanalytic literature, right up there with dream interpretation.

Oddly enough, though the erotically forward-looking seventeenth-century poet John Donne alluded to a woman's two "purses" (signifying the vagina and the anus) in an elegy titled "Love's Progress"—"Rich Nature hath in women wisely made / Two purses, and their mouths aversely laid"—amazingly little has been made of the subject by those who are regularly in the habit of reading psychodramas into the average cigar. Since the female body provides our first sheltering container, it would make perfect intrapsychic sense that containers would be viewed as generically feminine, but a quick review of the Psychoanalytic Electronic Publishing archive yields curiously few references to purses or handbags, and when they do appear, it is in papers that focus on other topics.

In perhaps the most famous instance of a psychoanalytic interpretation of this crucial female accoutrement, Freud's case history of the paradigmatic hysteric Dora alludes in passing to her playing with her "reticule" as representative of masturbating; it also spells out that her dream about a jewel case (and the small ivory box carried by another female patient) were stand-ins "for the shell of Venus, for the female genitals." Interestingly enough, classical analysts of yesteryear tended to view the fantasized scenario or dream of a stolen purse as a metaphor for a missing penis. Talk about the inflexible rule of patriarchy! It seems that even when we lose this crucial, dangling part of ourselves, it is really the opposite sex's crucial, dangling part that we have, unbeknownst to ourselves, gone in search of.

Ah, well. The notion of penis envy is not in good repute these days in any event, and I, for one, am inclined to believe that women may have resolved this hypothetical problem with their appropriation and fetishization of the once-androgynous handbag. (Freud believed that women were on the whole less inclined to fetishize, which served his purposes—and left us poor creatures in a permanent state of craving for what we could not have.) "A bag," observes my friend with the portfolio of bags, "is about controlling the world outside your home. It's not any more about materialism than Neruda's 'Ode to Things' is. When he says, 'Oh irrevocable / river / of things,' he's talking about his attachments, and some of us cannot bear to be separated from our things for too long."

Considered in this light, bags are almost worth the time and money we give them. In being so sublimely iconographic, they tell us nothing less than where we live, who we are, and where you might metaphorically find us, carrying our portable identities in the pouch that best meets our dreams of self.

A FASHIONABLE MIND

2011

All of us have key moments in our fashion evolution—moments when we realize that fashion isn't simply a frivolous imposition on the self but can be a cunning expression thereof, moments when we are struck by the lexicon a particular designer employs and discover that we have cultural references in common, be they Popeye and Felix the Cat or the decline of the Roman Empire. Just as an entire life story can be told in the fall of a sparrow, so can an entire fashion story be told in the length of a hem or the cut of a sleeve.

My interest in the possibilities of fashion, in its ability to transcend its own particulars and become a narrative worth paying attention to, collided with my loftier literary side. I was a very bookish young woman, an admirer of Henry James and F. Scott Fitzgerald, a worshipper at the altar of Virginia Woolf. But I also had a secret self, one enraptured by certain designers and how they looked at the world. I fell in love with the witty and elegant clothes of Geoffrey Beene somewhere in my twenties. It happened just as I was beginning to develop an eye for the way in which fashion can mirror our own anxieties and pleasures back at us in the choice of fabric (in Beene's case, his use of gray wool jersey for evening wear) or a particular trim (Beene's innovative deployment of zippers, bow ties, and rhinestones). Here was a man who clearly thought beyond the surface, someone for whom whimsy was a means to a meaningful end, a man after my own heart.

I remember my first sighting of the pristine Geoffrey Beene label in a dress of my mother's. More a dabbler in couture than an acolyte, my mother owned a Beene or two along with a smattering of other American designers. A German-Jewish immigrant who'd lived in what was then Palestine for a decade before arriving on these shores, she cared about clothes more than she was willing to let on. My mother perused fashion magazines along with weekly installments of *The New Yorker*, and I know she read the reviews of new collections that appeared in *The New York Times*. I don't recall her ever discussing fashion as such, however, other than to refer to a woman who attended our synagogue as "Mrs. Valentino," in tongue-in-cheek homage to the woman's fealty to that designer's clothes. (My mother also loved to use the word "chic"—which she mispronounced slightly, failing to elongate the *i* into an *e* so that the word came out as "shik"—as the ultimate compliment for an outfit.) One of her firm convictions was that clothes should be secondary to the person wearing them, which I'd come to realize was a rather sophisticated view, one held by Beene himself, who didn't believe in dressing "for success" ("Dressing for success," he opined, "is something unsuccessful women do") and was known to take runway bows in a sweatshirt embroidered with the words "MR. BEENE" or in an off-the-rack number with "Polynesia" printed on it.

Lately I've been thinking of Beene a lot—especially of the pared-down, a-gesture-is-all-it-takes Beene—because of the excitement generated by the latest spring collections. For what seems like the first time in a while, American fashion is back on track, sure of itself and its origins, rather than craning its neck to check out what Europe is doing. (The truth is that Europe and America are doing similar things, but this appears more a matter of synchronicity than one side of the Atlantic influencing the other.) "Never look to Europe for inspiration," advised Beene, who died in 2004. "We're a modern nation. We move faster. Look here. It's all on the street."

You can see it in the very wearability of spring's clothes, the simplicity of the cuts, and the bold use of high-voltage color as well as color blocking. There's a graphic eye appeal, whether from

Derek Lam or Matthew Ames, and a signal lack of fussiness, whether from Francisco Costa at Calvin Klein or Alexander Wang.

After seasons of outfits that look like costumes and an editorially driven endorsement of near nudity, embellishment for its own sake has yielded to function, and in-your-face sexuality to a subtler, hide-and-seek approach to eroticism. Somewhere, the ghost of Geoffrey Beene is dancing a jig, persuaded that at last his message of intelligent fashion—for the woman who wants to put on something vital and becoming but has more important things to do than stroke her clothes into submission—has broken beyond the clutch of fashion insiders who always knew he was a designer's designer, ahead of the pack in thinking and execution.

Like many of the most interesting people, Geoffrey Beene was almost entirely self-made, down to his name. He was born Samuel Albert Bozeman, Jr., in Haynesville, Louisiana, and, at his mother's urging, attended medical school at Tulane University in New Orleans. His passion, though, lay elsewhere. By his own account, he'd always been enamored of design and at the age of eight directed his aunt Lucille, a talented seamstress, to whip up a Simplicity pattern for some beach pajamas in a blue-and-orange floral fabric he'd selected. Beene eventually abandoned medicine, to the consternation of his family, who sent him to Los Angeles for a so-called rest cure. While there, he got a job creating window displays at I. Magnin, but by twenty he'd moved to New York to enroll at the Traphagen School of Fashion. From there, he was off to Paris to learn the art of tailoring and expose himself to the world of haute couture. After returning to New York in 1951, he worked on Seventh Avenue for more than a decade, mostly for the women's ready-to-wear house Teal Traina, where he earned a reputation for going his own way.

In 1963, Beene was in the vanguard of designers who opened their own companies, and a year later the first of his pieces was featured on the cover of *Vogue*, worn by Jean Shrimpton. A bred-in-the-bone maverick, Beene had ornery relations with the fashion press, who were busy fawning over Christian Dior and Yves

Saint Laurent; his adversaries included Diana Vreeland and John Fairchild, with whom he had a legendary thirty-seven-year feud after Beene refused to let Fairchild's *Women's Wear Daily* get an early look at the wedding dress he designed for first daughter Lynda Bird Johnson.

Beene remained open to new ideas throughout his career, reinventing the connection between clothes and lifestyle many times over. He included softly draped shirtdresses from his earliest collections onward—debuting in 1967, for instance, his famous evening dresses that resembled sequined football jerseys while continuing with the gowns made from gray flannel. But in the early 1970s, after *The New Yorker*'s fashion critic Kennedy Fraser likened the somewhat stuffy "architectural" dresses Beene had become known for to concrete, he moved decisively toward more fluid silhouettes. A modernist who had much of the visionary about him and little truck with nostalgia (he embraced synthetic fabrics before others, only to discard them when they failed to hold up, and eventually did away with runways and models, preferring to send his clothes out on professional dancers in unconventional spaces), Beene had an essentialist view of fashion that lifted it from the realm of the frivolous. "The more you learn about clothes," he observed, "the more you realize what has to be left off. Cut and line become increasingly important."

This season, it's impossible not to think of Beene's legacy—his innovative pairing of haute and humble materials, his obsession with the contemporary applicability of a given design—and the way it has been funneled down to a freshly minted generation of designers, whether or not they're aware of it. We trust Alber Elbaz, Narciso Rodriguez, and Francisco Costa to have a centered point of view about who women are and how they want to dress, but a newcomer like Prabal Gurung might as well be channeling Beene when he talks about his muse: "I'm designing for a thinking man's sex symbol. What makes a woman interesting is her brain." Beene's work was "thought-out without being too tortured," Gurung goes on, with "the right amount of sex appeal."

Michael Kors, who proves once again this season that he's a master of classic American style, describes his customer as "opinionated, a woman who's going to put her own spin on what I do." His effortlessly elegant separates are done up in dreamy fabrics such as cashmere, crepe, matte jersey, and glove leather, and the emphasis on black and white with touches of crimson and cobalt is eminently Beene-esque. Kors believes that we've come to expect more from fashion than ever, in part because the financial crash made everyone "reassess things." These days, he says, "thought has to go into fashion, not just time. There's a concern with mobility—can I get it into a suitcase?" Kors points out that "intrinsically, separates are based on function. Without function, a design can be beautiful but not intelligent." He sings the praises of sportswear designers, citing "the Proenza boys," Phoebe Philo, and Stella McCartney. Evening wear is the last bastion of form over function, he notes, a genre in which the woman is still seen in an old-fashioned decorative light, but even here the rules are changing.

The closest I got to Beene the designer was when I wore Beene Bag, the impeccable bridge line he started in 1971 and gave as much care to as he did his higher-priced collection. The line retailed for somewhere between fifty and two hundred dollars when he introduced it, and I recall the blouse and skirt I bought—in a navy-and-white silk, printed with a graph-paper-like pattern—as one of my more expensive purchases. The only flourish was a discreet ruffle punctuating the sleeves, which were becomingly cut not too short, and I remember feeling like the height of style—of "shik"—when I wore the ensemble, which was often.

The closest I got to Beene the man was when I chanced to be seated next to him at a lunch given by *Paper* magazine during the late 1990s to honor Eleanor Lambert, the elderly doyenne of fashion PR. When the day arrived, I woke up feeling gray and internal, hardly the right mood for a fashion event. I shrugged on one of my black, baggy outfits meant to suggest the artiste that lurked beneath and taxied over to the downtown bistro with Eleanor.

The place was bobbing with intricately outfitted women from the fashion press as well as besuited ladies who lunch, but somehow I got seated next to The Man himself. I must admit he took absolutely no notice of me when I introduced myself, offering me the most frigid of smiles before turning to the person on his other side, with whom he appeared to be warmly engaged.

What can I say? I felt a bit hurt that Beene, who understood that fashion was about more than being fashionable, had dismissed me with barely a nod. I told myself that I should have dressed more carefully, had my hair blown out, put on more than my usual haphazard coating of makeup. But, as fate would have it, I looked like me rather than the fashion writer, muse, and mega Beene collector Amy Fine Collins—and when you come down to it, no one is capable of peering beyond the trappings into your soul, not even a genius who can make clothes tell a story. I realized that among his many complicated qualities, Beene was something of a snob, no matter how unconventional his approach to the fashion system, and on that day, at that lunch, I didn't meet his standards. I forgave him, though, and continued to watch his development with a fascination bordering on awe.

If I had to state it in a nutshell, I'd say that Geoffrey Beene made it okay for me to take fashion seriously. His layered and self-reflective aesthetic made it clear that fashion wasn't just an obsession of dimwits and airheads. You could practically see the twinkle in his eye as he scattered brightly colored pom-poms across the lace netting of a cocktail dress or subverted the flowery pattern of a chemise by adding a graphic polka-dot fabric at the neck and hem. These days I no longer have quite the pure, contemplative passion for fashion I once had—there have been too many tricks masquerading as innovation, too many borrowings pretending to be informed referencing—but this season's offerings are way too tempting to ignore, reminding me of why I looked up from my reading in the first place to embrace the unexpectedly cerebral pleasure of clothes.

OUR MONEY, OURSELVES

1999

I have never understood money. More than that, I was trained in
the hazardous, complex art of not understanding money at an
early age. This isn't to suggest that everything about my relatively
privileged childhood was a pleasant pecuniary blur—that my desires as a girl weren't regularly deemed too expensive, or simply
excessive, or that the rudiments of saving against a rainy day were
not imparted to me. My favorite piggy bank was a chubby, cloudy-
white glass milk bottle (labeled with my name, in big block letters,
to distinguish it from my sisters' piggy banks, which were otherwise identical) with a slot in the middle of its round tin lid. I remember the satisfying noise, like the clink of good china, that
the bottle made when it was weighty with change; I would pick it
up and shake it, feeling well accounted for. But since my mother,
a refugee from Hitler's Germany, didn't believe in giving her
children allowance (she considered this to be one of many misguided Americanisms), I never accumulated enough money to buy
anything ambitious, and there came a time when I realized that
the piggy bank's value was more symbolic than actual. Indeed, one
of those piggy banks still resides on a closet shelf in the room I
shared with my sisters in our parents' apartment. The pennies and
nickels and quarters in it are more than three decades old by now,
and I find it odd that such elderly coins aren't worth more—
having been around for so long and witnessed so much.

My parents were affluent, although the word "affluent" had

not yet, in the 1960s, replaced the simpler and more viscerally descriptive term "rich." We lived on Park Avenue, in a duplex with a curving staircase, and spent the summers in a house that was an hour outside the city, several blocks from the ocean. The staff included a stern woman of Dutch origins who looked after the six of us, a cook who presided over the kitchen, and a chauffeur. There was also Willie Mae, the laundress, who loudly cracked chewing gum as she ironed my father's underwear and custom-made Sulka shirts. For tailoring needs, there was Mrs. Kaabe, a short square woman who was able to hold entire conversations with straight pins in her mouth.

And yet such was my family's inordinate, even pathological, discretion on the subject of its own wealth that I continued to believe my father sold chairs, rather than shares, well after I had outgrown other Gidget-like malapropisms. The larger meaning of money—its social potency—was kept deliberately veiled, as though it were a secret weapon, a force that could send things spiraling fatally out of control. There was so much hemming and hawing around the basic economic facts that I was surprised the first time—I was ten years old and at sleepaway camp—I heard my family knowingly referred to as "rich."

Rich? I didn't feel remotely rich. For one thing, I shared a room with my two sisters; it was only from my friends who lived in smaller apartments, without staircases, that I learned it was desirable—virtually an upper-middle-class standard—to have a bedroom of your own. These same friends had more Danskin outfits than I did, in an enviable array of colors, and seemed far more casual about spending money. My mother may have ordered one or two expensive dresses apiece for us to wear to synagogue, when we were on display, but she was indifferent about what we wore to school, where no one she cared about saw us. She briefly campaigned for uniforms at the Jewish day school I went to and ceaselessly inveighed against the clothes obsessions of adolescent girls. I can remember desperate arguments over the purchase of an extra pair of shoes: we were allowed one "good" pair, for Shabbos, and one everyday pair, and any more than that was deemed frivolous. At dinnertime, my five siblings and I often argued over seconds, and our refrigerator never burst with fruit; there were no inviting mounds of cherries, peaches, and plums like the ones stocked in the Short Hills basement of Brenda Patimkin's parents, in *Goodbye, Columbus*. (Even if it had been full, we weren't allowed to range freely in the kitchen and open fridge doors at our whimsy.)

It was as though my mother were acting the part of being the wife of a rich man without really believing in the role. Or she believed in it schizophrenically, with one ledger kept for my father—for whom nothing was too good or too much—and another ledger kept for us children. This tendency was undoubtedly exacerbated by the differences in my parents' backgrounds, which were subtle but important: they were both German immigrants, united by their Orthodox Judaism, but my mother's father was a lawyer and a philosopher, a member of the Kant Society in Germany, while my paternal grandfather was a canny businessman, a fur merchant who would have preferred his grandsons to go into the *sechoira* (merchandise) business rather than what he called "the paper business" (Wall Street).

Although I don't believe my mother ever balanced a checkbook, and I know that she was never confined to a weekly budget, I can still hear her saying "Cherries are expensive!" on a summer weekend when one of us protested the meager amount she had bought—as though someone somewhere were keeping close watch on her expenditures. My mother scorned the randomly acquisitive habits of upper-middle-class Americans; she never threw leftovers away, and she loved to intone penny-wise, pound-foolish phrases like "Enough is as good as a feast." (My father's peccadilloes, which included a tendency to warehouse electric shavers and eyeglasses, were lovingly exempted from these strictures.) She was so careful to convey the message that she was not entirely at ease with the lifestyle she'd come into when she married my father—or, more to the point, that she in any way endorsed "marrying up"—that I came to believe, unlike the Bennet daughters in *Pride and Prejudice*, that there was something intrinsically admirable about men who *didn't* make money.

There was another factor that added to the confusion, and

that was my father's prominence as a philanthropist. A generous dispenser of funds to charities large and small, he sat on the board of countless Jewish institutions—from rickety, fanatically religious yeshivas in the backwaters of Brooklyn to big-city hospitals with gleaming secular reputations—and endowed any number of scholarships and chairs in the family name, both in New York and in Israel. Throughout my childhood, my parents attended an astonishing number of dinners on behalf of these institutions, where they frequently took a table that cost tens of thousands of dollars and often had the honor of being seated on the dais. (Actually, in the segregated men's-club atmosphere of these functions, my father would sit on the dais with other honorees in starched shirtfronts, while my mother had to make do at a more plebeian table below.) My father was also capable of throwing the odd donation to a political candidate and of suddenly being pressed into service on behalf of some non-Jewish cultural organization. By the time I reached my teens, it had become clear to me that my siblings and I were viewed by the world as having been born with silver spoons in our mouths, no matter that we had developed an intricate system of hiding food—especially sweets—from one another at home, in case there wouldn't be enough to go around. This faux reputation as an heiress has dogged me ever since; it took a firm hold when I was in my twenties and my father, as part of his ongoing commitment to a Jewish school of the arts, endowed a concert hall on the Upper West Side.

At the time, I was renting a dark subterranean apartment all the way over on the East Side that would eventually be robbed, twice, by the super, and by then I had all but given up on making the two parts of the picture fit together in my own mind, much less in other people's: the shame and contempt that attached to the subject of money within the family versus the public recognition and deference accorded my parents. Who, one might wonder, was I in all this? Someone looking in on a scene of plenty, her nose pressed wistfully to the window, or someone who was born into the scene, nestled in the silken folds of privilege?

My mother went to great lengths to convince me and my siblings that money was not only intrinsically poisonous but not ours to claim by virtue of blood ties. What were we to my father's money, and what was it to us? We were connected, she implied, only by sheer happenstance. None of us was ever offered a strand of pearls or a jazzy little sports car or some other gift on reaching a signpost of maturity, like college graduation. (Once my father took me to buy a fur coat, but the only one who emerged from the showroom wearing fur was him.) It wasn't as though we weren't thrown the occasional perk, of a kind my parents deemed worthy—a trip to Israel, say. But in my experience, it's pretty much a rule of thumb that no one compares downward. In the world of Jewish princes and princesses that I inhabited, I didn't look to friends who had less than I did; I looked to those who had more, who seemed to glide on a surface made shiny and smooth by parental largesse. At some point I took to muttering darkly to my mother that charity began at home, but she would always fix me with a contemptuous look and ask, "And what exactly is it that you lack?" She managed to make me feel ungrateful and grabby at once, as though my bad character doomed me to be a scheming Goneril rather than a selfless Cordelia.

This ambivalence about money—its rightness and wrongness, when it was meant to be a visible facilitator and when it was supposed to hang back shyly—led inevitably to an atmosphere of self-consciousness and false restraint both at home and in the world. Well before I had heard the term "conspicuous consumption," it seemed to me that being genuinely rich entailed a certain compulsive delight in spending and accreting. As a girl, I was a devout reader of *Archie* comics, which featured Betty and her rival, the "gorgeously rich" Veronica Lodge, as well as the brilliantined, ever-scheming Reggie, who was also "lumpy with loot." Its pages were filled with wisecracks about the allure of wealth and the importance of finding a rich boyfriend. ("Let's do something romantic!" one character says. "Like counting money or watching armored cars unload.") Beneath the jokes, however, lay a serious mid-century appreciation of the mercantile ethos. "If it draws people and shows a profit," explains the perennially put-upon Mr.

Lodge to his daughter, "that's good business." I also watched *The Beverly Hillbillies* on television—this was a decade and a half before money lust came out into the open with *Dynasty* and *Falcon Crest*—and noticed an insouciance about living high on the hog that was nowhere in evidence in my own family, despite our maids and our fancy address. (The glamour of a good address has been brought home to me many times since, of course. Once, when I was in my late twenties and having lunch with Philip Roth, he asked me where I grew up. When I answered, hedging as I always did, "On Sixty-Fifth and Park," he leaned across the table, his dark eyes blazing with curiosity, and asked, "On Sixty-Fifth? Or on Park?")

Although my family's now-you-see-it, now-you-don't approach to money may have been particularly heated, I slowly came to realize that this private obfuscation was embedded within a larger cultural evasiveness. I noticed that other people were caught in a similarly ambivalent grip, however different their circumstances. No one was honest about the subject of money; worse yet, not many people seemed to recognize that they were being dishonest. People either deified money or demonized it—conducted themselves like Ayn Rand characters, as if the profit motive were the only thing that mattered, or pretended that they didn't give a fig for worldly wealth and that those who did were beneath consideration.

The latter type tended to strut around the groves of academe, where a spirit of apology for being white and the beneficiary of the American system of free enterprise was standard among the Columbia University humanities faculty in my student days, and the one English professor who wore bespoke suits was rumored to be on the payroll of the PLO. Then again, anyone who has been exposed to a basic humanistic education in the last fifty years has absorbed money's bad reputation. Rich people rarely came in for a kind word in the novels we read for our courses, although the preoccupation with the simple fact of money was so much in the forefront that, as Lionel Trilling observed, "the novel is born with the appearance of money as a social element." Most of us came of age with the sense that money was inherently impersonal, if not morally suspect; we were raised to believe that financial success can't compensate for loneliness and may even be conducive to it.

Of course, this attitude underwent a shift in the late 1970s and early '80s, when all vestiges of Depression-era thrift and upper-class noblesse oblige were replaced by ostentatious one-upmanship, and the adage "Never buy what you can't afford" gave way to "You can't afford not to buy it." This was the period when real estate, as one writer put it, became "the great conversation starter in the social life of the middle class." Everywhere you looked, someone was buying an apartment the size of a yacht or hiring out Blenheim Palace for parties, and even artists were expected to have ten-thousand-dollar-a-month lofts in SoHo. In what was one of many disquieting cultural shifts, the young children of the wealthy were no longer instilled with a becoming sense of modesty but were to be found at trendy Upper East Side tables, ordering costly plates of spaghetti that they barely nibbled at. How far this seemed from the unease, the feeling of unworthiness that led my siblings and me, cowering in the back of the car, to ask Jimmy, the chauffeur, to drop us off a block away from school—for fear that someone might connect us to the Cadillac or the Lincoln and the capped driver behind the wheel. Or from Poorhouse, the make-believe game my sister and I played, in which we tied kerchiefs around our heads and imagined that we were the directors of a Dickensian-style orphanage, where the primary activities consisted of disciplining our dolls and eating deconstructed sandwich cookies. Still, I sometimes wonder whether our game didn't have within it the glimmerings of a social conscience—a sense of the precariousness of financial fate and of how little it depended on one's innate human worth. This sort of counter-identification is hard to imagine today, when my daughter and her pals talk excitedly about the "stretch limo" a school friend of theirs has boasted of riding in.

Yet for all the loosening up that the 1980s brought—the uncensored embrace of "champagne wishes and caviar dreams," in the greasy phrase of the *Lifestyles of the Rich and Famous* host Robin

Leach—money remains quite firmly in the closet even now. It, far more than sex, lingers as our deepest collective secret, our last taboo. Even now, you are more likely to get a woman to confess that she has committed incest with her father than to disclose what her father earns, or whether she's being subsidized by any of his money. A shrink I know tells the following joke: "A guy comes to a psychiatrist and tells him about his sexual perversions and fantasies down to the last sordid detail. Then, at the end of the session, the shrink asks him how much he makes a year. To which the fellow answers, 'Hey, I'm sorry, that's too personal.'" We may think we talk openly about money—and in daily discourse we do indeed chatter about mutual funds and book advances and the resale value of beach houses. But we don't really tell each other very much.

So it is that to this day, I can't figure out how it is that many of the people I know are able to live in New York on their salaries, much less send their children to private schools. As far as I can see, most of my peers handle money with the same mixture of entitlement and panic that I do. There is, for instance, the friend—a therapist married to an editor—who mutters about making ends meet and briefly considered sending her only child to public school rather than to the private school that was inevitably her daughter's destination, but indulges in regular jaunts to Paris and biweekly forays to Paradise Market, where the fruits and vegetables glisten like jewels and are priced accordingly. Yet another friend, a writer, opts for cut-rate haircuts and takes her free reviewers' copies of books to Barnes & Noble in order to exchange them for birthday gifts even as her parents furnish the apartment they bought for her with auction finds from Sotheby's and Christie's. More dramatically, there's the friend who has conspired to live—or at least to dress—way beyond her means. Both she and her husband are in "creative pursuits," and her weakness, she happily admits, is "what I put on my back." She explains, "I spend it in dribs and drabs, and it all goes on credit cards with huge balances. I keep myself blind to exactly what I spend on clothes, the Armani jackets and the occasional $1,300 black cashmere sweater. Every pair of Clergerie shoes I buy for $350 or $400 really costs $500, if you figure out the interest. My big terror is that I'll get killed in an accident and my father will find out that I was mired in credit card debt."

The simple truth is that I haven't the vaguest idea what kind of money even my closest friends live on. Once in a while, something seeps out, when I happen to hear about a grandmother's stock that was "borrowed" to underwrite a new computer system, or an inherited piece of artwork that was traded in to help purchase a larger apartment. (The clotheshorse concedes that her and her husband's earnings—even with their cramped "college dorm" apartment and credit card stratagem—don't completely support their lifestyle. Her father-in-law kicks in some of the children's tuition, and her divorced parents each give them money, ranging from birthday checks to more significant annual gifts.)

My friends, I might add, can't have a much better idea of how I make ends meet, working as a book critic and living in pleasant, if not grand, circumstances—a two-bedroom condo on a block listing toward the decrepit off upper Lexington. They must surmise about me as I do about them. Do they surmise that I don't live on what I earn? If so, they'd be right. I feel some discomfort about this, but it also allows me to circumvent the sense that money might have the ability to define me, might throw me into a context of second-rate aesthetic choices and chronic anxiety.

The strangest thing about my situation is that I myself don't have full knowledge of it: I receive a certain amount of financial help from my family, without having any idea what my father, who recently died, at the age of ninety-one, was actually worth. (Less than I infer? Much less? Or more? Much more?) There has never been a discussion about this in the family, nor, since my father's death, has anyone mentioned his will or his estate. To try to get a purchase on the mystery, as I did some years ago, by making a visit to my father's white-shoe lawyers, is to come up against an impregnable code of silence. Money is not supposed to matter, much less be discussed, lest—lest what? Lest I think that it's mine to do what I like with? Lest I order a gold-plated dinner service for twenty-four? I received a tight-lipped welcome at the lawyers' office, where they had me confused with my two sisters, and the only thing I actually found out was that my family's money was held in what even the firm's patrician senior partner admitted was the most illiquid state possible. I could conjecture that my inability to learn more had something to do with my being female—with the invested power of the patriarchy, with men trading crisp information in rooms high above the city—and that wouldn't be entirely inaccurate. Two of my three brothers work on Wall Street, and they've clearly been told more about the situation. (One of them manages the family accounts.) Still, there is a part of me that believes—or merely hopes—that the less I inquire, the more there will be, in a sort of see-no-evil, hear-no-evil fog that will lift one day to reveal a green vista of cash.

Maybe this is why I keep most of the money I have personally earned in an insanely liquid state—in a checking account, to be exact. In the face of my family's clamped-down way of handling its resources, this is my version of keeping a wad of bills under the mattress: it's as if I never know when the knock on the door will come and I will have to flee, with just the shirt on my back, my family having ceased looking, in however ambiguous a fashion, after my interests.

We all harbor fantasies of how we were meant to live; it's an image that we carry around in our heads, beckoning like a kitchen in *Architectural Digest* done up with the latest in appliances and finishes. I may not admire people who make money, but I envy whatever making money brings them—to put it plainly, I want what they've got. Take the summer in New York, for example. Where is the beach house I dreamed of decorating unambitiously, with pleasant knockoffs from Crate & Barrel or Pier 1? I realize that this isn't a question to lose sleep over, but it throws me back on that old familial feeling of not understanding how much money there was in my immediate vicinity and how it was to be used. "Surely," a man who knows my family says to me at a dinner party, "you have a place in the Hamptons." Ah, but surely I don't. Is there money buried somewhere in some account or trust that I could avail myself of in order to buy—or rent—such a place? I don't know the answer; I know only that I've been trained not to pose the question. Neither I nor any of my five siblings, with twenty children of our own between us, have ever rented a summer house, and it was only a few months ago that my oldest brother, a successful hedge-fund manager who owns a sprawling multimillion-dollar residence in the city, finally bought one. Even he spent more than a decade of summer weekends bringing his wife and four kids out to my parents' place—a functional brick house with a pool in a beach community frequented by Orthodox Jews who require a synagogue within walking distance. Now not only has he found something in the same town as my parents' house, but he appears to have inherited the Merkin gene for excessive discretion: all of us, including my mother, first heard about his purchase from someone outside the family.

What really puzzles me is that my brother and I—and, it seems, everyone else I meet in Manhattan—inevitably refer to ourselves as upper-middle-class. Can this category really be so elastic as to include people who shop endlessly in "the bubble," as my internist refers to the rarefied reaches of Madison Avenue in the Sixties and Seventies; people who sit in huge apartments on Central Park West when they're not in their upstate weekend homes; and the harried professional urban couples who live in Battery Park City, rent a cottage on the Cape for two weeks in the summer, and aren't the beneficiaries of invisible infusions of parental wealth? If everyone is upper-middle-class, where does rich begin? A European banker in his mid-forties explained the distinction to me over lunch in his bank's private dining room, offering up the assessment that "wealth" signifies $10 million in liquid assets, while "real money" means a net worth of $100 million. "To be genuinely entrepreneurial," he added, "you need 200 or 300 million to play with."

One summer when I was in my early thirties, I was invited to spend a few days at the Canadian vacation home of my publisher, William Jovanovich, a brilliant maverick who had gone from being a textbook salesman to owning the publishing company he worked for outright. I flew up on the company's private jet; it was lushly appointed and smelled of fine leather. There was a staff of

two, a pilot and a cabin steward who fussed over me, and I remember sitting there, sipping soda, and thinking that I could get
used to this very quickly. (I suppose there are people who are un-
moved by luxury, but I've never met any, and I'm not sure I'd trust
them if I did.)

I was standing and talking to Bill, as I called him, in his heated
swimming pool, behind the tennis courts and statuary and gardens, which yielded fresh raspberries. A man who was worth many
self-made millions, he struck me as having a fairly unimpeded approach to matters of finance, so I was surprised when he asked
me, apropos of nothing, what I thought was "behind" my father's
philanthropy. I didn't want to explain—nor did I fully know—
what moved my father so forcibly in this direction. In truth, I resented the question; it sounded unaccountably suspicious, even
defensive (why, one might ask, didn't Bill think to give more of
his own money away?), and it unnerved me that something I had
been brought up to think of as admirable might be considered
suspect. I was, of course, cynical enough to have formulated my
own theories about the status climbing that accompanied charitable enterprise. I also knew it was as good a way as any of leaving
an imprint—of laying claim to a bit of immortality. But it had
never occurred to me to impugn the impulse itself. The whole
thing was awkward, and it made me wonder—not just about my
publisher but about the worldview I had been raised in.

I believe his inquiry was made possible, at least in part, by the
simple fact of my father's being Jewish. Jewish money is often
fairly recently minted, and although my publisher's wealth was as
new as could be, it's fair to speculate that he, a Gentile, mim-
icked the habits of the Wasp aristocracy when he made it: short
of being Rockefellers or du Ponts, wealthy Wasps, I've been
told, are less inclined to be charitable than wealthy Jews. They
seem, rather, to be busy with horses and boats and what one
Anglo-Saxon friend calls "the great Wasp affliction"—watching
as their offspring fail to replenish the diminishing family fortune.
I sensed a bit of reflexive anti-Semitism in my publisher's question—a suggestion of the vulgar parvenuism that Jews have ines-
capably been associated with. ("Their fortitude, such as it is,"

wrote the happily biased H. L. Mencken, "is wasted upon puerile objects, and their charity is mainly a form of display.")

But that was only part of it, the part that made me feel righteous and misunderstood on behalf of my tribe. The other part was more disturbing: the brute realism of my publisher's approach to his money (some of which he used to underwrite the lavish lifestyles of his children) suggested a clearer and more liberating approach than the one my parents favored. My father's generosity undoubtedly did a lot of good, but it derived to some degree from the disdain he felt for the very enterprise of making money—from a need to be cleared of the taint of filthy lucre. His sense of self-worth came more from his philanthropy than from his financial success in itself. My publisher seemed free of this, and I couldn't help thinking that had I been his daughter, he would surely have bought me that place in the Hamptons instead of supporting every Jewish organization that came calling. The encounter in the pool made me aware for the first time of the strangely hidebound approach to money that had been instilled in me. For his part, my publisher wasn't afraid to admit that his money was his and would benefit his own. He didn't need to put distance between himself and his wealth—to reconfigure its baseness into something glittering and prideful, a diadem of sorts.

Not many people are as unabashed as this baronial man was able to be. "Among the cultural elite, it's not yet proper to acknowledge that he who has the most money wins," a theater producer told me recently. "It's a luxury of people who've inherited money—like my parents—to say that money doesn't matter." He believes that inherited wealth made his father "soft." "Inherited money is shameful," he declares matter-of-factly, adding that, as a result, "it's very important to me that I live off my paycheck."

Clearly, inherited money presents more of a problem than earned money. A woman in her late thirties who is informed and competent in her professional life admits, "I don't know how much money my husband has, and we've been married five years. It's not like I haven't asked. He hems and haws and says it's al-

ways changing." She adds, "He has a small inheritance, and I
guess it represents something he's uncomfortable about, something he's not sure he's earned." But how many of us look at
people with money, inherited or otherwise, and really think it
has been earned? Don't many of us think, why them and not us?
"Money," another friend suggests, "is sort of like morality. Everyone has their own private benchmarks. Not letting people know
what you have protects you from judgment."

Naturally, our own irrational demands strike us as having the
force of needs, while other people's needs strike us as capricious
indulgences. Few of us are able to look calmly and cogently at the
issue, caught up as we are in envy and comparison. "People see
money as making them special—like genitalia," an analyst who
has treated a lot of wealthy patients observes. "What possible difference could two inches make? But, also like genitalia, money is
private—it's one of those things you're not supposed to show."

This can result in what a friend of mine describes as "the West
Side ethos," where the whole point of dressing is to "muffle the
impact of privilege." She explains, "The Upper West Side is the
last bastion of moneyed liberalism. We have money, but we're
slightly embarrassed about it." And another woman, an interior
decorator who spends freely on herself, insists, "Anytime I've
complimented a woman on what she's wearing, she says she
bought it on sale. There's this anguish about spending—about
openly spending on nice things." It's almost a relief to come
across someone as down-to-earth as one woman I talked with, a
widow in her seventies. "When I came to America, at age nineteen, I appraised myself," she said. " 'I'm pretty, I'm young, and
I want to marry a man with money.' Not that I wanted that much,
but I didn't want to struggle. I wanted a guy who could take me
out beautifully, offer me an apartment and a nice life." The majority of us consider ourselves to be more enlightened; we like to
think we're subscribers to Matthew Arnold's gently didactic view
that life is "not a having and a resting, but a growing and a becoming." And yet we continue in our entrancement. Woody Allen, at
least the latter-day Woody Allen, has become our contemporary
F. Scott Fitzgerald, filling the screen with the haunts and customs

of the rich. He admits openly to what he calls "an enormous aesthetic fascination with wealth—with wealthy, rich kids, high prices." He adds, "To me, it's like staring into a fireplace—endlessly riveting."

"Diamonds are cold," my mother used to say, although I noticed that it didn't stop her from wearing the ones she owned or from marrying a man who could afford to impress her with a chunk of an engagement ring. Money may not keep you warm, but it can take on the aspect of an embrace; indeed, it can be a stand-in for love, especially if the real thing is in short supply. "It's only money," sure—but do any of us really believe that? Freud conferred odious status on money. He thought it symbolized feces in the unconscious, but at the same time he was obsessed with generating more of it. "My mood also depends very strongly on my earnings," he wrote to his confidant Wilhelm Fliess. "Money is laughing gas for me." And we know what he means; we all recognize the absolute power money has to inflate our spirits and dispel anxiety.

Nowhere is this charged dynamic more explosive than in the romantic sphere, from the first date, when a man offers to pay for dinner (or doesn't). All my relationships with men have teetered uneasily around the issue of who pays for what. In the first place, I am never sure whether I am to view myself as the hunted or the huntress: someone whom men are after "for" her money, as my mother frequently intimates (when, that is, she's not intimating that there's no money to go after me for), or someone who seeks to be saved from the pinched aura of her childhood, from its behold-the-kingdom-but-none-of-it-is-yours atmosphere, and find a truly giving, unambivalent provider.

This lack of clarity helped to undermine my marriage, beginning with the scene that took place in my father's study shortly after the birth of my daughter. As my husband and I perched on a sofa, ignorant as to why we'd been summoned, my father launched into one of his benevolent patriarch speeches about futurity and procreation and responsibility. It sounded innocuous enough, until he pronounced that of course he was willing to help us buy a bigger apartment than the one-bedroom we were living in, as he had helped my siblings before me (I was the last to marry). Pausing only slightly, he went on to add that his unsolicited offer came with a condition, which was that we would not only agree to keep kosher in our new place but would sign a document stating as much. I was stunned: even by the control-besotted standards of my family, this was blackmail. I hadn't been religiously observant for years—the only one of my parents' flock to go astray. I mumbled something about my nonexistent religious beliefs, to which my father roared, "I don't give a shit what you do or don't believe in!"

After a tense moment or two, my husband and I picked ourselves up and left. I remember a brief, sweet discussion about living on our joint funds, which were fairly negligible. For a moment, I saw us as a version of the newlyweds in *Barefoot in the Park*, growing ever more amorous in our tenement digs while the water from the apartment above leaked through our ceiling and the radiators hissed to a standstill. It was a dream in which the absence of money was a boon, a way of purging the past—a release from the whole edifice of family and money and New York strivings.

In the end, we didn't sign and we got the apartment anyway, but the marriage unraveled a few years later. Since then, my doubts have grown: Am I loved for my yellow hair alone or for my real estate potential? One unforgettable conversation on the subject occurred several years ago at a birthday dinner for the man I was then seeing. We had been invited out by his parents, and we somehow landed on the subject of apartments. My boyfriend, who had essentially moved in with me, had been telling me for months that the early-morning noise of the garbage trucks outside my building was depressing, and that I was too "big"— too large a presence, I assumed he meant—for the apartment I lived in. I owed it to my child, he said, to provide a better environment; my building also faced a school that bused in underprivileged children with emotional problems, a circumstance that he found troubling.

Under his scrutiny, my apartment began to look shabbier to me than it actually was, and I found myself scouring the real estate section on a weekly basis. I don't know how much of this my boyfriend's mother knew, but the two of them were close, and she was probably kept abreast of all the rumblings. At any rate, she leaned forward over dessert and said, "I myself have always needed light." I understood what she meant, in the code of such exchanges: she required an apartment on Fifth or on Central Park West (which, in fact, she had), and who could require anything less? I was offering her son a room without a view; couldn't my parents do better for me? I answered that I liked light myself and blushed—like a prospective bride offering an insufficient dowry—on behalf of my apartment.

And then there was the older man who came trailing rumors of inherited wealth of his own. For a while, it looked as though I had met someone who understood the unique form of emotional deprivation that is felt by children of rich but withholding families. We had long talks about the limitations of money and the ways in which it could be used to subvert rather than create happiness. He pointed out to me that I had never escaped from my childish money confusions; I was looking for a kind of protection, a primary reassurance, that couldn't be bought—even I could see that.

Still, I couldn't help noticing that he hadn't escaped from the shadow of his past, either. He vacillated between making expansive gestures and making stingy counter-gestures—inviting me, when we began dating, on a weekend to Florence and then asking me if I would pay for my own plane ticket, all the while making it clear that he had considerable resources to call upon should he care to. I was puzzled as to the reality of his situation: he seemed to be supporting his two grown daughters, but he made a big deal of contributing a twenty-dollar coffeemaker to my apartment, where he frequently ate both breakfast and dinner. Things were no doubt made worse by the fact that a close friend of his described him to me as "loaded," and yet another acquaintance told me that he had heard that my friend was the scion of a soft-drink fortune. As I know from my own fictitious fortune, nothing multiplies faster than the myth of personal wealth, which breeds ever more baroque fantasies in the eye of the beholder, even if there isn't much in the way of reality to back them up. I knew I shouldn't care either way about the state of this man's finances, but I didn't want to be tantalized only to be shut out of the kingdom once more.

In the end, we were both too irrationally invested in what money meant. I yearned for a "what's mine is yours" embrace, for a plenitude of cherries; he had been divorced twice and feared being exploited—giving with no guarantee of return. One night, just when it seemed that we had settled into the rituals of domestic togetherness, he reminded me, as I was getting into bed, that I owed him money for a dry-cleaning bill. There it was again: It's only money. It's only everything.

We broke up the next day.

LET THE FUR FLY

2005

Where have all the Lassies gone? Who can forget that noble collie who had her own show on Sunday night TV and was a kid's best friend, there for the hugging when you needed her to be? She was an honorary member of the show's perfect nuclear family—the whey-faced Timmy, played by Jon Provost; his earnest mother, played by June Lockhart; and his levelheaded father, played by Hugh Reilly. But it was also abundantly clear that no one was thinking of inviting Lassie in for a snack of milk and Lick 'n Crunch! treats (Oreo-style cookies from Three Dog Bakery, made with carob instead of chocolate, which is bad for dogs) or of decking her out in a Swarovski-crystal heart-shaped dog tag, or of painting her nails with OPI Pawlish. You can be just as sure that Timmy wasn't saving up his allowance to buy Lassie a fourteen-dollar squeaky toy Chewy Vuitton or Jimmy Chew and that his mother wasn't stretching the household budget to cover Le Chien et Le Chat cedar-scented laundry detergent.

No, Lassie belonged to an honorable but almost-extinct breed of household pet, one that knew its place in the family of man. She would never have been caught dead sleeping in a customized four-hundred-dollar white-crackle-painted dog bed with toile linens—would never have been caught dead sleeping anywhere but outside the farmhouse screen door, keeping an ear cocked for strange sounds.

At the risk of drawing ire, I would like to suggest that there is something profoundly awry about the way our culture treats pets. To wit: we spend more money annually on pet-related supplies and services (an estimated thirty-five billion dollars last year) than we do on toys for children. To wit: *The New York Dog* magazine, which features un-tongue-in-cheek articles on whether or not to buy health insurance for Fido (5 percent of pet owners have insurance) and how to hold on to your canine in a custody battle ("Start a diary showing that you are the primary caretaker," advises Raoul Felder, divorce lawyer to the stars. "Note how many times you walk the dog"), is but the latest entry in a crowded field that includes *Dog Fancy*, *Modern Dog*, and *The Bark*. To wit: if you're looking for a place to board your dog while you're on vacation, you could do worse than Canine Cove in Sausalito, California, a cageless facility offering a quiet area to watch TV as well as an outside lounge area.

How has it come to pass that outfitting a dog with a $1,380 Hermès crocodile-and-calfskin leash-and-collar set doesn't seem too absurd—too shameful? How is it that our sense of humanity has been transferred to members of the animal kingdom—the domesticated and overbred as well as the wild and exotic—so that we lavish affection, money, and moral outrage on them while we gripe about the homeless instead of empathizing with their plight and ignore our elderly altogether?

Credit for this weird and somewhat depraved cultural phenomenon must go equally to the Animal Liberation movement, which has managed to seize the moral high ground in spite of sentiments that are neither entirely heartwarming nor logically consistent (Clive D. L. Wynne's *Do Animals Think?* offers a witty rejoinder to many of the movement's more pious arguments), and to a prevailing Marie Antoinette spirit of consumerism. Together these two forces have produced a climate that has allowed the anthropomorphic fallacy—in which we confuse our very human desires with an animal's best interests, sometimes to the detriment of the animal—to run riot. A recent instance of this involved the more than seven years of international effort and twenty million dollars spent on trying to return Keiko, the sociable killer whale and star of the movie *Free Willy*, to the Icelandic wilds. Keiko, who never seemed to feel the call to freedom quite as keenly on his own behalf as his human protectors did, ended up dying two years ago, "seeking human consolation," as one writer put it.

Meanwhile, PETA activists seem to be more focused on saving lab rats than on preserving advances in medicine that might save their parents or grandparents, while people are prepared to endanger their neighbors' (and sometimes their own) lives by adopting tigers or chimpanzees as backyard curiosities. And although pet fetishism has a well-documented history, nowadays dogs and cats are embraced with more brazenness than ever—as status possessions, or substitute children, or displaced love objects ripe for narcissistic projection (and sometimes all three at once).

Lest you're still in any doubt as to where I'm coming from, let me identify myself as an unreconstructed speciesist. I am, that is, one of those unenlightened types roundly criticized by the animal rights philosopher Peter Singer for conceiving of humans somewhat differently from, say, boa constrictors. This is not to say that I don't take it on faith that animals can suffer—"The question," according to Singer's guru, the nineteenth-century English philosopher Jeremy Bentham, "is not, Can they *reason*? nor, Can they *talk*? but, Can they *suffer*?"—only that I can't bring myself to regard the psychic or physical travails of my niece's beloved dog, Lily, with the same empathic investment I regard those of my niece.

You might say that I come by these attitudes naturally, descending as I do from a long line of pet-avoidant people. In my Orthodox Jewish family, animals of all sorts were associated with a Tennysonian principle of aggression—"Nature, red in tooth and claw"—rather than with cuddliness or companionliness. Both my parents were escapees from Nazi Germany, where the *Führer* was known to adore his German shepherd, Blondi. (The opening of *Downfall*, the harrowing movie about Hitler's last days in his bunker, refers to his twin obsessions with vegetarian food and his hound.) While Jewish law takes a fairly benign view of household pets and prohibits unnecessary cruelty to animals, European-born Jews have historically enjoyed somewhat leery relations with dogs and cats.

In my own family, gerbils were the main concession to my and my five siblings' wishes for a pet, along with some negligible goldfish and a loveless chameleon or two. The gerbils died fairly regularly by way of negligence rather than of intentional malice, and one particularly ghoulish instance—in which a batch of gerbil newborns were devoured by their mother—has remained etched on my mind. My youngest brother was the most insistent in his wish for an animal playmate and eventually cajoled my mother into letting him have a snake. The snake required a diet of live mice, which only added to my brother's happiness, but the whole project was short-lived since it turned out that my mother's cherished housekeeper wouldn't step foot in our apartment as long as a snake was on the premises.

All the same, it's easy to see the allure of furry, tail-wagging little creatures, and I'm not averse to the proposition of joining the swelling ranks of urban dog owners someday. (As for cats, I might as well admit I'm a confirmed ailurophobe.) My fifteen-year-old daughter and I, in our elaborate conversations about our dream dog, lean toward saucy breeds, like cocker spaniels and West Highland terriers. (Then, too, it has hardly been lost on me that dog-walking is the divorced woman's answer to single bars.) Nor am I minimizing the importance of the animal-human bond, although I've never been persuaded that there's much correlation between being kind to animals and being kind to people. I'm more inclined to believe in the negative side of the equation— the link between kids who enjoy tearing the wings off butterflies and adults who become serial killers.

Indeed, one of the supreme dog lovers of all time, the gifted British writer and editor J. R. Ackerley, was undoubtedly also one of the most intensely misanthropic people ever to have lived. Ackerley's memoir *My Dog Tulip* is a compelling and somewhat queasy-making testament to the power of displacement, as evidenced by the author's absorption in the excretory and mating habits of his beloved Alsatian, which he conveys in prose that is nothing short of rhapsodic. Ackerley's passion for animals was

exceeded only by his contempt for people, which makes you wonder whether it is possible to be equally ardent about both mice
and men, or whether it is truly a matter of declaring one's exclusive allegiance, as Ackerley seems to have thought: "Everyone
in the long run must decide which side he is on." He went so far
as to observe, "I myself am out to save the animals . . . if necessary at the expense of mankind."

Which brings me back to the heart of the matter: How did
creatures once relegated to the basement and the back porch,
who were expected to earn their keep as retrievers and ratters,
ascend to their current prima-donna status? Why is moneyed
America throwing its discretionary income in the dog bowl,
gussying up its dogs and cats and stuffing their yaps with delica-
cies as they perch on upholstered pillows as if they were tempera-
mental Egyptian deities? Perhaps these pampered beings offer us
spiritual cleansing, a way of absolving ourselves from the guilt of
living high while others starve by sharing our good fortune with
mammals less powerful than ourselves. Then again, who—no
matter how rich or celebrated—isn't in the market for unconditional love, even if it comes by way of a pooch or a kitty that can't
tell a joke or remind you to take your keys?

Still, even if our "relentlessly anthropomorphic psyches," as
Stephen Budiansky describes it in his charming book, *The Truth
About Dogs*, are to blame for the warm place that dogs (whom
Budiansky characterizes, only half jokingly, as "con artists,"
"parasites," and "biological freeloaders") hold in our collective
hearts, I know I can't be the only one to find myself increasingly
nostalgic for the days when a pet was a pet and not a handbag-
size celebrity pooch named Tinkerbell or Bit Bit. These, of course,
are the precious little bowwows that appear at fashion shows
and shopping sprees on the arms of their respective owners, Paris
Hilton and Britney Spears, in a parody of mothering that is rem-
iniscent of girls pushing doll strollers. (Courtesy of my daughter's copy of *In Touch Weekly*, I have learned that Tinkerbell now
faces stiff competition in the form of another teacup Chihuahua,
named Bambi, which led one animal behaviorist to gravely observe, "The older dog has probably been lavished with affection,

which may lead to heightened anxiety if Paris is now paying attention to another pet." God only knows what trauma has been induced in Bit Bit by the news of Britney's pregnancy.)

Not long ago, my neighbors across the hall asked if I'd house and feed their lone Japanese betta fish, Candy, for a week while they went away for a spot of sun with their three young children. I readily agreed: I like my neighbors and was reassured by their calm assertion that if the fish happened to die on my watch, I could always replace it for $3.79 at a nearby Petco. This was an attitude to pets that I could recognize, even identify with, one that predated our present culture of relentless commodification, in which everything—from your child's school to your dog's exclusive kennel—is meant to testify to the enviable pedigree of your lifestyle rather than to the messy reality of a life.

The fish, I'm happy to report, survived his foster domicile. I kept the rather majestic tank in my kitchen, and sometimes of an afternoon I would wander in and watch Candy swim in and out of the plastic igloo-looking dwelling that was its only diversion other than some flakes of fish food. What, I wondered, did Candy think about all day? Did he recognize that he was away from home? And then, coming rather quickly on the heels of that thought, I realized that my own interest in piscine consciousness was limited in the extreme, unregenerate speciesist that I am. Besides, I tend to agree with Wittgenstein, who was of the opinion that if lions could talk, we wouldn't understand their conversation. The final word on the subject of the larger meaning of pets, however, should really go to Groucho Marx, who was never beyond taking things to their preposterous conclusion: "Outside of a dog, a book is man's best friend. Inside of a dog, it's too dark to read." Go on, give the man a bone—I mean, a bow.

MARKETING MYSTICISM

2008

What brought me to the small, neat office in the Kabbalah Centre in Los Angeles—at the tacky southern edge of Beverly Hills where the upscale ambience of Doheny Drive turns into a decrepit stretch that includes two gas stations and multiple Korean nail salons—was Madonna, who, I had learned while interviewing her, doesn't believe in death. And then there was my mother, who had recently died. Somehow, in an effort to reconcile divergent realities, I must have been looking for a resolution of the irresolvable, a way of navigating a path between the absoluteness of mortality and the lingering hope of something beyond it, between the immutable reality of personal loss and the promise of spiritual consolation.

In a world where everyone is angling for a piece of the kabbalah mystique, an esoteric occult offshoot of Judaism dating at least to the thirteenth century, the Los Angeles center has been attracting Hollywood glitterati since it first opened its doors in 1993. And who can blame the neighboring institutions for trying to cut in on a share of the booty—the bevy of run-down ultra-Orthodox yeshivas and religious girls' high schools with names like Torat Hayim and Ohr Haemet Institute, many of which have their own makeshift signs attesting to introductory kabbalah classes? It all looks so easy, not to mention remunerative, thanks to the pricey little doodads offered in the center's store (ranging from red kabbalah bracelets at twenty-six dollars a pop to bottles of kabbalah water at nearly four dollars apiece) and to the hefty donations solicited from members old and new.

Housed in a two-story cream stucco building with a red-tile roof that fits in with the 1920s- and '30s-style Spanish Moorish architecture characterizing the neighborhood, the Kabbalah Centre is set in the midst of a surrounding shabbiness hard to reconcile with any kind of drawing power. All the same, in its Los Angeles incarnation, the center is spiritual home to Demi Moore and Ashton Kutcher, Roseanne Barr, Donna Karan, and any number of other celebrities who dip in and out as the spirit moves them. Most important, as anyone who has heard anything about the center knows (and often it is the *only* thing they know), its public face is none other than that of the stridently non-Jewish and notoriously profane human meteor named Madonna.

Despite having based an unparalleled career on her in-your-face assault on her native Catholicism and its iconic imagery, this über-celebrity appears to seek life guidance from the center's precepts: she avails herself of its teachers (her spiritual guide is Eitan Yardeni, who proffers kabbalistic wisdom to handpicked and mostly famous disciples); shows up for High Holy Days services in either Israel or Los Angeles; and attends the occasional Friday night Shabbos dinner. Madonna brings the Kabbalah Centre's message of egoless dedication to *tikkun olam* (repairing the world) home to her fans both in her music and in her personal appearances. Not incidentally, she has been lavish in her financing of the center's larger ambitions and philanthropic enterprises, ranging from buying it property in London to providing millions for its outreach programs worldwide, including her pet project, Spirituality for Kids. Of course it is useful to the center's relationship with its most generous benefactor—who is given pride of place as a member, with care being taken not to expose her to the curiosity of the center's more plebeian devotees—that a primary kabbalistic tenet places great emphasis on the role of giving, the better to receive. "Embedded in their ideology," explained Boaz Huss, a professor of Jewish thought at Ben-Gurion University of the Negev, whom I talked to in an effort to understand the center better, "is that giving—and giving to the center—is important. They believe that they have the keys to redeeming themselves and humanity. They're bringing in the light."

Although the center has been mocked and derided since the day Philip and Karen Berg founded it in 1993 (an embryonic version existed during the 1980s in Israel and New York), no small part of that mockery is envy—and resounding disbelief. How could so many people, especially jaded celebrities who have seen it all and then some, fall for an ordinary middle-class Orthodox couple from Queens who hawk their intangible wares—a kind of "Spirituality for Dummies" or "McMysticism," as it has been described—with so little guile and so much fanfare? And what is it precisely that the center is offering its adherents? On some level, you might argue that it doesn't matter what the center is ultimately providing—whether it is religious self-help, theological kitsch, non-Jewishness for non-Jews and disaffected Jews, a sense of community akin to that offered at AA meetings, or a way of ensuring your immortality by paying God in the form of contributions to the center—so much as the fact that it has brought a rarefied branch of Judaism out of the shadows and onto the red carpet.

What sets the center apart from other postmodern belief systems like Scientology, which have subverted the traditional relationship between spirituality and authenticity by insisting that authenticity itself is fungible or even beside the point, is that it has wrapped its ardent ecumenical message around the kernel of a centuries-old, highly ritualized religious tradition. Much as the center denies its association with Judaism or any other existing religion (indeed, one of its leading members referred to the "stigma" of Judaism in conversation with me), its tiny insider circle of members (numbering a bit more than two hundred in all), referred to as the *chevra*, or circle of friends, abide by the laws and customs that are the underpinning of observant Judaism. These include observing the Sabbath and a multitude of holy days; keeping kosher; maintaining a separation of sexes in synagogue; the wearing by men of crocheted yarmulkes of the modern Orthodox style that prevails both here and in Israel; and the wearing of skirts and *sheitels* by married women. (*Sheitels* are the wigs, usually made of real hair, that cover women's natural hair to signify that they are no longer objects of allure and are off the marriage market, although the kabbalistic rationale is more exotic and quasi-scientific, having to do with negative filaments and positive circuitry.) The *chevra* are the chosen among the chosen, provided with housing, clothes, schooling for their kids, even plane tickets.

Still, given the proselytizing ambitions and will to visibility (there are a total of ten centers in the United States and sixteen internationally), it is difficult to get anyone close to the center to admit to this underlying belief system for fear of appearing too insular and exclusive. Even thirty-four-year-old Michael Berg, the younger of the Bergs' two sons, a graduate of rigorous Orthodox yeshivas in America and Israel just like his thirty-five-year-old brother, Yehuda, and one of several spiritual directors of all the centers, insists that the center is without conventional religious affiliation. "We honestly do not believe we are spreading Judaism in the world," he told me during a lengthy phone conversation. "The Creator gave the Jews these tools that were meant to be used and to show the way we should connect to the world." When I asked him why the center insists on using "tools" instead of the word *mitzvot*, he answered without missing a beat, "If we used Jewish terms, we would alienate people."

The history of kabbalah is long and thorny, filled with shifts in attitude toward the dissemination of its wisdom. It has been looked on with suspicion and even hostility by most Jewish authorities since it first emerged, its lore codified in an ur-text known as the Zohar, the authorship of which some attribute to Moses de León in the thirteenth century and others to the sage Simeon ben Yohai in the second century. Some principal ideas include a very specific and radical notion of cosmology, one that involves an initial cataclysmic "rupture," or literal "shattering of the vessels" (*shevirat hakelim*), which occurred during the creation, leaving in its wake a fragmented and disordered state of affairs that can be made whole only through selfless devotion to *tikkun olam.*

A second major theme focuses on a conception of God's powers as being dynamic—God is evoked as a receptive female presence called the Shechinah—and on the idea that human beings can unite with the divine spirit through meditation and by following the panoply of religious commandments, thereby restoring the universe to its original integrity. Although kabbalah was studied from early on by elite circles of Spanish Jews and from the fifteenth century through the eighteenth century by scattered communities in the European and Islamic worlds, the prevailing attitude within the normative Jewish community was restrictive. Fear of its antinomic implications being ever present, kabbalah was generally considered to verge on the dangerously heretic in its speculative and personalized approach to a text-based and communal religious tradition. It was tenuously approved for study only for devout married men over the age of forty who were well versed in the Talmud and Jewish law or for exceptionally gifted and sturdy-hearted yeshiva students.

Fast-forward to the last decade and a half. Enter Philip Berg and his second wife, Karen (he and his first wife had eight children before they divorced), who set up shop out of their Queens house with an original following that numbered no more than their two sons and a clutch of Israeli disciples. (Philip Berg, born Shraga Feivel Gruberger, who changed his name in the 1960s, was a former insurance salesman; Karen was his onetime secretary.) When it comes to spreading the gospel of the theosophical system of kabbalah, lineage is all; if you can establish a proven generational link to a master kabbalist, you are immediately vaulted into a privileged position to transmit its enigmatic philosophy. Intent on validating his title to the dynasty of kabbalism, Berg linked his own genealogy through his teacher Rabbi Yehuda Brandwein (an uncle of Berg's first wife), who in turn was the disciple of Rav Yehuda Ashlag.

It is Ashlag who is the linchpin of the outwardly egalitarian but intensely hierarchical operation that is the Kabbalah Centre—or, as many would argue, the justification behind an illegitimate group of squatters who lay claim to its ancient, sacral territory. A crucial and highly controversial figure who was born in Poland

and immigrated to Palestine in the early 1920s, Ashlag began to revolutionize traditional attitudes toward the promulgation of kabbalah, prying open its historically hallowed, coded concepts. Among other innovations, he attempted to integrate kabbalistic ideas with communism and to modernize a system steeped in untouchable exclusivity by emphasizing the non-elitist nature of kabbalah and its ostensible link to scientifically ordained truths. His writings, which might be said to be the beginning of the "de-authenticization" process that many have accused the center of setting in motion, are the foundation of the Bergs' movement, just as Ashlag himself is its sanctified figurehead. Thus the importance of Berg's constantly reiterated link to his predecessors Brandwein and Ashlag, whose photographs share an honored place surrounded by flickering candles on the *bimah*, the raised platform in the center's synagogue from which the Torah portion is recited every Shabbos.

For the vast majority of their followers, however, the minutiae of lineage means very little. The Bergs have succeeded in selling kabbalistic wisdom as a source of inspiration to an audience that has nothing to do with academics and their careful distinctions between where one line of kabbalistic wisdom (the theosophical Lurianic strain) ends and another (the ecstatic Abulafian strain) begins. They have effectively boiled down an attenuated, arcane, and often tedious system sprinkled with numerological symbolism and elaborate, loop-the-loop interlinkings of God, the world, and the evil eye, into an accessible lifestyle philosophy offering succor to the unaffiliated and the disheartened of whatever racial or ethnic origin. Theirs is a canny reading of the infectious malaise of secular life and the widespread yearning for a transcendent context as well as an up-to-the-microsecond sense of branding.

In spite of my wide-ranging Jewish circle, I knew no one who had ever attended a class or service at the Kabbalah Centre at either its New York or its Los Angeles locations. Still, the fact that the movement seemed to speak to a hodgepodge of impulses and to represent a less than pristine—indeed, a somewhat tabloid—version of the religion I had been brought up in piqued my curiosity. My interest crystallized after a meeting with Madonna in the winter of 2006, months before my own first visit to the center. I met with her for nearly two hours in a hotel room on Central Park West in the process of writing a profile of her for a women's magazine. She was dressed in her usual idiosyncratic mix of naughty and nice, wearing a formfitting top tucked into a corduroy skirt that stopped modestly at the knees—all of it set off by a gold lamé belt, opaque brown kneesocks, and a pair of gold pumps. She was in New York to publicize the release of her album *Confessions on a Dance Floor*. In tribute to the nebulous spiritual guidance the center has offered her, which includes renaming her Esther, the CD features a track called "Isaac," with a mantra-like phrase in Hebrew, suggesting that Madonna is planning on ascending heavenward to join the sisterhood of biblical foremothers—Sarah, Rivka, Leah, and Rachel—at the right transmigratory, soul-evolving moment. (A core kabbalistic concept, *gilgul neshamot*, refers to the recycling of departed souls.)

It became clear to me during our conversation that Madonna had been schooled in basic center tenets: she let drop the exalted name of Brandwein, Philip Berg's mentor; referred to the "light," a term that would be much bandied about the center in my hearing, signifying a supremely opaque notion having to do with positive and negative cathodes (don't ask) as well as the transmission of spiritual energy; and discussed reading the introduction to the Zohar, which she said was full of "potent information." She went on to explain, in her prim, faintly British-accented voice, that kabbalah offered her "a reconciliation of science and spirituality"—of "the Garden of Eden and superstring theory." After informing me that her children and husband were taking Hebrew lessons, she evinced curiosity about my observant Jewish background, wanting to know whether my mother covered her hair. (She didn't, in a break from her own family tradition.)

Finally, in what seemed to me a startling detour, she asked whether or not I believed in death. I answered somewhat bleakly that I did. When I turned the question back on her, she announced that she believed in the concept of reincarnation as taught by the

Kabbalah Centre. "The thought of eternal life appeals to me," she told me, as though she were trying on a new outfit in front of a mirror. "I don't think people's energy just disappears." I wasn't sure what she meant by this—whether Madonna believed in a concrete form of reincarnation whereby she would return to earth as herself, all blond ambition and strenuously toned body, or in the more abstract concept of *gilgul neshamot*. But it made eminent sense that her link to the center would be based on something more than an altruistic vision of egoless self-betterment and earthly bliss, which is the message she conveys in her statements and songs. When I asked her why she hadn't stuck with Catholicism, which incorporates belief in an afterlife, she snapped in reply: "There's nothing consoling about being Catholic. They're all just laws and prohibitions. They don't help me negotiate the world."

Seven months later, in the immediate wake of my mother's death from lung cancer, I took a trip to Los Angeles to begin my own year-and-a-half-long journey of exploration into the Kabbalah Centre. I thought of it as an investigative-cum-personal search, the goal of which was to find out what its appeal was to Madonna and others and whether it might have anything to offer me, despite its mumbo-jumbo aspect and suspect "vulgarization" of a preexisting religion (as Moshe Idel, the foremost scholar of kabbalah, described it to me). Although my curiosity was initially intellectual, the unfortunate—or, as some might have it, propitious—timing and my own sense of grief undoubtedly made me less skeptical of the form of solace the center had to offer.

I visited the Los Angeles center on two occasions, separated by a period of some months. So it was that one winter afternoon, on my second visit, I found myself in Michael Berg's airy wood-paneled second-floor office, filled with photographs of bearded kabbalists and shelves of *seforim*, solemn-looking books of Jewish learning of the kind that filled my father's study when I was growing up. Under Michael's guidance, we delved into several passages of the Zohar. (According to the bio on one of his book jackets, he "achieved a momentous feat when he was only 28" by doing the first translation of the complete Zohar from ancient Aramaic to English.) I became immediately absorbed by the abstract, centrifugal line of reasoning that ran through the text. It reminded me of the Talmudic commentators I had studied in high school—forever engaged in exegetical flourishes—in the way it somehow managed to remain clear of sticky human emotions while at the same time dilating on the mechanics of human behavior at its most paradigmatic. Michael and I got on to the topic of my mother's recent death, and I listened spellbound as he gently conjured the logistics of reincarnation—which has no place in the doctrine of normative Judaism but which is embraced in all its hazy and exploitable reality by the Kabbalah Centre. True disbeliever that I am, I nonetheless figured it might well be possible that I would meet up with my difficult yet vivid mother in some coffee shop in the world to come, where we would no doubt commence to have a heated argument but would at least be in the presence once again of each other.

I was ripe, in other words, for seduction. Or was I? Because I come from an Orthodox background—I am the product of a yeshiva day-school education, and although I am no longer observant, my siblings all are—my own interest in taking a closer look at the Kabbalah Centre had been percolating for a long time. I had heard it referred to both in conversation and in the media in only the most dismissive terms, ranging from derision at its unsubstantial and misleading synthesis of Jewish, New Age, and Sufi elements to rantings about its being "dangerous." Still, disenchanted as I was with the patriarchal foundation and constricting prohibitions of observant Judaism, I wondered whether there might be something worthy in a more ecumenical approach.

The center seemed to answer an intractable longing among its followers for an old-style sense of order in the midst of the chaotic jumble of contemporary choices and for something that elevated the disappointing limitations of human existence. Could it be that the very obsession with "authenticity," which is where the center clearly came up short, was itself an outdated obsession? Perhaps the Kabbalah Centre was a celebration of an ad hoc mix-and-match approach, a renunciation of "the bottled product" of ritually driven Judaism—as Gershom Scholem, the founder of kabbalah as an academic discipline, once described it—in favor of something more nondenominational and contemporary? Or, as Boaz Huss put it, "Why does kabbalah have to be clean? The center annoys people so much because they subvert the basic perceptions of modern society, which puts religion here and pop culture there, in opposition to each other." Alluding to the many A-list types who come and go, Huss insisted that the now-you-see-it, now-you-don't quality of their involvement with the center is precisely the point: "Being in there for two minutes is a significant part of what the center is about. In a spiritual marketplace, most of the consumers don't stay long."

Huss also seemed unperturbed by the huckster spirit that attaches itself to everything the center touches, from flash cards to candles to baby bumpers. "They give spiritual guidance," he asserted, "and they take money for it. Embedded in their philosophy is that giving as much as you can is important. They believe that they have the keys to redeeming themselves and humanity. People go freely, and most of the consumers are happy with what they get." (It doesn't hurt the center's gimme-gimme approach that kabbalah places great credence on the role of "giving," although it's dubious that the sort of "giving" the center encourages bears any resemblance to what the kabbalists originally had in mind.)

My own, more religiously informed background might have militated against my falling in with a bunch of lost, lemming-like souls who mumbled about chakras, cosmic karmas, and energy flows. All around me were people whose eyes lit up when they talked about the "rav" and Karen as though they had just glimpsed the Messiah and his missus hurrying through the corridors, carrying bottles of kabbalah water and wearing the red bracelet said to be directly connected to Rachel's tomb. But my self-imposed exile from the orbit of Friday night dinners and Shabbos services I had once known and abiding nostalgia for the encircling warmth of the Jewish community made me more open-minded than I otherwise might have been. The fact that the *chevra*'s immersion in the classic minutiae of Orthodox Judaism was kept under wraps lest it scare off followers was precisely the

aspect—the strategic missing piece in the puzzle—that forged
the bridge from the center to the lost milieu of my childhood. It
was what led me, in the initial throes of my exposure to this hith-
erto unsuspected enclave of closeted Jewishness, to call up an
ex-Orthodox friend and tell her that she should take the first
plane out of New York to attend the celebrity-studded celebration that was being planned for the rav's birthday, with Donna
Karan in attendance, the better to acquaint herself.

I was given fairly generous but carefully monitored access to
the center and its doings. I attended Friday night services at the
New York branch, where the prayer books include "directions for
scanning" and a transliterated English text for non-Hebrew-
speaking members. I noticed a sprinkling of Filipinos and other
Asians as well as several diamond-bedecked Upper East Side
women, all of whom looked as if they were just warming up to
the strange brew on tap, clapping their hands and tentatively
singing along with the Shabbos prayers. The women, cordoned
off in a makeshift women's section, seemed merry and carefree,
while their children ran amok, playing with Rubik's Cubes and
prancing around the *bimah*. Although there was no evidence of a
formal dress code, as there usually is in an Orthodox synagogue,
where pants and tank tops are frowned upon, there was a casually
imposed but strict gender divide, which put me in mind of all the
Orthodox synagogues I had ever attended and reminded me
uneasily of the compensatory ethos of liberation in confinement
that is the Orthodox woman's lot.

In Los Angeles, I attended a Friday night dinner where the
emphasis on kabbalah not being a "religion" (always referred to
in quotation marks, as though it were another of those tossed-
out, old-hat ideas, like fidelity) was heightened—undoubtedly
to offset the lure of other local pastimes, like shopping at Fred
Segal—and a microphone and slides accompanied the singing of
prayers. The men circled Philip Berg, hands clasped around one
another's shoulders, singing and dancing in the ecstatic, overheated manner of a Lubavitcher gathering. I also went to Saturday *mincha* and *maariv* services, leading up to the Havdalah
ceremony, in which a braided candle is lit, a symbolic sip of wine

is drunk, and a box of scented cloves is inhaled, marking the demarcation of Shabbos from the workweek. Again, the women were observers from the sidelines while the main action went on among the men, who wore white track suits and baseball caps in tried-and-true Guy Ritchie fashion. (The men wear white, one of the *chevra* told me, because "they are the ones reaching the light through prayer, while women are only vessels.") The proceedings grew weirder as they went along, with a lot of football-huddle sort of male bonding interspersed with hora dances, guttural noises, and a talk by one of the *chevra* that ramblingly connected the weekly Torah portion with some aspect of goodness or spirituality I couldn't quite put my finger on.

Both Friday night dinners I attended followed the same pattern: tickets had been purchased ahead of time, and the prearranged seating at round tables appeared to correspond to some intricate hierarchy of important and less important guests. (Madonna and Guy Ritchie are said to eat behind a screen.) The meals were served Chinese-style and consisted of a mixture of Middle Eastern food—hummus and baba ghanouj—and the more ordinary Friday night roast chicken or overcooked brisket. For all the press hubbub that surrounds the center's doings and the 150,000 hits it gets every month on its website, these occasions draw a relatively small number of people—several hundred in Los Angeles and less than half that in New York. (Although the center's website alludes to a worldwide following in the millions, it is impossible to get an accurate number as to its actual devotees; one disenchanted observer puts it as low as three thousand to four thousand people.)

During the course of my visits, I also sat in on a session of a class called Kabbalah 101 at the Los Angeles branch, taught by a patronizing and seemingly bored former therapist named Jamie Greene. After quickly summing up the "universal wisdom" he had dispensed in the first two classes, Greene went on to talk in generic terms about taking responsibility for your behavior, pausing to draw simplistic chalk diagrams with a white marker on a big blackboard. Listening to him coolly dispatch such enlightening concepts as "a credit card is a dangerous little thing" and "fear of intimacy guarantees that we'll never experience intimacy," I wondered if all of human behavior could be twisted into an ema-nation of kabbalistic principle, from gambling to dating.

The class was a multiethnic assortment of mainly blue-color workers of different ages. Most of the students were wearing the red string bracelet (notwithstanding the fact that the color red, according to Moshe Idel, has *negative* connotations in kabbalah), and all of them had copies of *The Power of Kabbalah*, written by Yehuda Berg, the more populist of the two brothers, with a cover blurb courtesy of Madonna: "No hocus-pocus here. Nothing to do with religious dogma, the ideas in this book are earth-shattering and yet so simple." Subtitled *Technology for the Soul*, Berg's book includes brief chapters with titles such as "The DNA of God," "The Light Bulb Metaphor Applied to the Endless World," and "Nanotechnologists Confirm the Kabbalists." There was much vague talk about flows of consciousness, forces of darkness, and blocking the light. "The light is always there," Greene assured the class before they struggled out. "The light is endless."

I met separately with some of the center's star teachers, in-cluding Eitan Yardeni (Madonna's teacher), an intense forty-two-year-old Israeli who has been instrumental in opening Kabbalah Centres elsewhere in America and is currently the spiritual direc-tor of the London center. Yardeni grew up in a nonobservant family and started studying kabbalah as a teenager while in the Israeli Air Force, where he gave instruction in Hawk missiles. He explained the center's grandiose mission to me: "We're much bigger than Jewish; we're here to touch souls all over the world, to give people universal tools to access the practical." He added, "We're talking about affecting change on a global level." I had my horoscope read by Yael Yardeni, the center's resident astrolo-ger who also happens to be the sister-in-law of Eitan, keeping it all in the family, and discovered that in one of my three past lives I had been a *rebbetzin* with oodles of children. (Yael has a waiting list of three months and charges two hundred dollars a session.) Astrology is a big part of the center's construction of meaning, though it plays a marginal role in kabbalistic thought. When I met Karen Berg, she immediately pointed out that Donna Karan was a Libra, as though this were a profound insight into her character. And at a Friday night dinner in New York, Miriam, one of the hipper and more elegantly dressed among the *chevra*, confidently assessed me as a Scorpio. (For the record, I am a Gemini.)

Back in New York, during an earnest phone conversation with Michael Berg, I found myself growing teary-eyed when we became involved in a discussion of why, despite my late mother's fervent wish, I had never put up those small, totemic objects known as mezuzot (which enclose a *klaf*, a handwritten rolled scroll of parchment inscribed with a section of Deuteronomy) on my doorways. I was truly touched when Michael promised to send someone that very Sunday to put them up, only to discover that that was the last I would hear of it.

A year and a half after I began my explorations, the cynic in me wrote the Kabbalah Centre off as hokum, a brilliantly shrewd commercial enterprise, playing on the existentially orphaned state that is the general condition of many people today, in or out of Los Angeles, offering spiritual cachet for cash. Still, the ever-hopeful, lapsed Orthodox Jew in me wonders whether I might have found my own personal, mystically tinged form of antireligious religion had I been willing to overlook the crass reductionism and imbibe the New Age atmosphere of nonjudgmental compassion. Gershom Scholem, in *Major Trends in Jewish Mysticism*, observes on the last page, "The story is not ended, it has not yet become history, and the secret life it holds can break out tomorrow in you or in me. Under what aspects this invisible stream of Jewish mysticism will again come to the surface we cannot tell."

Are the Bergs onto something genuine, some "secret life" of Jewish mysticism that they alone have managed to fathom? Or are they gifted con artists milking the invisible stream of human gullibility for all they can get? That there are glaring holes in the center's façade—philosophical discrepancies and yawning gaps in scrutability—cannot be denied. Not to mention the impenetrable finances. Why, for instance, as many observers have wondered, is the center so reluctant to discuss how the many millions it raises every year as a nonprofit organization are actually spent? In answer, Michael Berg insists that the center is a flawed "work in progress" that has made mistakes it must rectify.

Here's what I do know: My mother has shown no signs thus far of resurfacing, and I would guess that Madonna continues to hold fast to a belief in her own immortality as guaranteed by the center. Meanwhile, the couple from Queens and their *chevra* have pulled a rabbit out of a hat, made believers out of ex–car mechanics and former real estate brokers. That's them in the spotlight, flashing their red bracelets, embracing their nouveau, pseudo, po-mo religion.

V

WOMEN IN
THE SINGULAR

AN INDEPENDENT WOMAN

(LIV ULLMANN)

I first see Liv Ullmann standing in the door of her New York apartment, and for a moment I am struck by a quality of almost tangible luminescence, an aura that transcends her iconic status as the muse of a great and melancholy director—"the village genius from Sweden," as Ingmar Bergman once described himself. Days later, I find myself trying to figure out her singular physical effect, the way it caught me off guard, as though flesh-and-blood reality had, just this once, outdone the mythologized screen image. Perhaps it had something to do with simple atmospherics, the stage setting of a gray December afternoon against which Ullmann stood out with a particular vividness. Or perhaps it was that she was taller and slimmer than I had expected, more regal— still recognizably the figure of mesmerizing allure who graced *The Passion of Anna* and *Cries and Whispers*.

At sixty-two, she has a soft, doleful beauty that is in some essential way undiminished by time, despite faint signs of age around her eyes and mouth and a slight slackness around her neck. Unlike many women renowned for their looks, she hasn't had plastic surgery—because, she tells me, she always liked her grandmother's face: "I thought if I could grow into that kind of face . . . I wanted to see what God wanted from mine, more out of curiosity." She is honest enough to admit to having thought about it, especially when she has to be photographed, or when a woman stops her in the airport and says, "Didn't you used to be Liv Ullmann?" All the same, the face that stirred Bergman's romantic and artistic imagination still captivates: the rounded forehead, the flushed complexion with a faint smattering of freckles, the lush mouth, and the open cornflower-blue gaze that is capable of conveying immense delight but more often hints at some unfathomable sadness.

Bergman first caught a glimpse of the twenty-five-year-old Ullmann—then a promising stage actress from Norway who had achieved notice as a member of Oslo's National Theater—in a casual snapshot in which she stood against a red wall next to her friend, the actress Bibi Andersson, who had already appeared in several Bergman films. This photograph gave him the idea for the psychological usurpation of identity that is the theme of *Persona*, starring Andersson and Ullmann, which he shot in less than three months over the summer of 1965. "Film work is a powerfully erotic business," Bergman remarks in his memoir *The Magic Lantern*.

Although Ullmann insists that the filmmaker did not set out to seduce her, she became involved with him during the making of *Persona* when he sat on a rock and told her about a dream in which he said to her, "You and I will be painfully connected." According to Ullmann, it was this somewhat gnomic remark that won her heart. "That's what I went for," she says. "I fell for it. How was I to know better? I believed everything he said, and if he said it, it must be true." Shortly thereafter, Ullmann left her doctor husband for Bergman, then forty-seven and already a veteran of four marriages (which produced six children) as well as any number of amorous relationships with various actresses, including Andersson.

After *Persona*, Bergman chose to work almost exclusively with Ullmann—who displaced Andersson as his lead actress, just as Andersson had displaced Ingrid Thulin. (Despite this divisive situation, the two women have remained close, which Ullmann attributes largely to Andersson's generous spirit. "Bibi never said, 'If it hadn't been for you, I would have had your career.'") Bergman and his latest protégée lived on the remote Swedish island of Fårö from 1966 to 1970; he built a house for her there, and they had a child together. After they ceased being lovers—"He probably left me," she says, as though the matter has never been fully resolved—they remained friends and frequent collaborators. "The best thing about him was how wonderful he was when it was over," Ullmann recalls. "I needed to talk to him every day, and he allowed me to do that. He never hung up on me. Most of them hang up. The terrible thing is when someone leaves you and you hear the door bang." Bergman continued to cast Ullmann in his bleak, tormented dramas—going so far as to use her, rather than Max von Sydow, as his cinematic alter ego—until he announced his retirement from film directing in 1982. (His last feature, *Fanny and Alexander*, was written for her, but Ullmann stunned Bergman by passing up the opportunity in favor of another project.)

Ullmann is in New York for a few days to meet with members of the Women's Refugee Commission, an organization she helped found that works on behalf of women, child, and adolescent refugees. She is also here to do some advance publicity for *Faithless*; the movie, which opens this week, was directed by Ullmann from a screenplay by Bergman. This is the fourth feature film she has directed—her debut was *Sofie*, in 1992—and the second written by Bergman. (The first was *Private Confessions*, in 1996.)

Faithless runs two and a half brooding hours; it is vintage Bergman in its preoccupation with the interior life of its characters and the harrowing consequences of their often inscrutable actions. The film opens a bit creakily, taking time to establish itself as a narrative within a narrative. It is as much an old man's musing on mortality—"a diversion before death"—as it is an examination of the high price of reckless passion. The movie's carefully orchestrated story line unfolds in extended flashbacks, prompted by the recollections of "Bergman," an aging and isolated film director (played by Erland Josephson) driven to confront the disastrous aftermath of a long-ago affair. We learn of the events that lead inexorably to tragedy from the beautiful and vulnerable Marianne, who upends her contented existence as a wife and mother when she commits adultery with David, a close friend of Markus, her celebrated conductor husband. David is a clear stand-in for Bergman's younger self, and it is a lacerating depiction of the artist as a shameless egotist who leaves wreckage in his wake. "I mess things up for myself and others," he warns Marianne right before they fling themselves at each other.

Faithless presents itself as a reconstruction of an incriminating autobiographical episode (the kernel of its plot can be found in a chapter of *The Magic Lantern*), an artistic farewell that is also an effort at self-absolution by a man whose films have always grappled with the condition of spiritual guilt. It strikes me as a deliberately mystifying artifact, intellectually detached and emotionally accessible at once. Looked at one way, the film is an act of homage from a woman who learned much of what she knows about the craft of filmmaking at Bergman's knee. In another way, it is an ingeniously conceived piece of role reversal, in which the famed director has the tables turned on him by a former lover who was once a worshipful disciple but now sees him clearly for the *monstre sacré* he is. Of course, Bergman has wittingly colluded in this enterprise—and endorsed Ullmann as the premier interpreter of his work—by writing the screenplay in the first place and then giving it to her to direct.

What is perhaps most interesting about the film—which includes the relentless close-ups, angst-ridden bursts of dialogue, and long pauses Bergman is known for—is its focus on the unforeseen harm done to children by the behavior of irresponsible adults. Josephson's opening voice-over is a rumination on the destructive forces unleashed by divorce. Thereafter, the viewer is rarely allowed to lose sight of Isabelle, the ethereal young daughter of Marianne and Markus, who watches the breakup of her parents' marriage with enormous, reproachful eyes. The camera keeps coming back to linger tenderly on the girl, whose unspoken despair runs like a black thread throughout the movie. Bergman's screenplay did not include the little girl as an on-screen presence. "The child was never in the script," Ullmann points out. "Without changing any of his words, because he's very protective of his words, I put her there, listening, vulnerable, desolate."

In a similar shift, she put the older Bergman character in as a real person; the film was supposed to be shot over his shoulder, in such a way that he wouldn't actually appear on-screen but would exist as an unseen, magisterial creator. These revisions seem to be a matter of some pride to her, perhaps as evidence that she has succeeded in sidestepping Bergman's towering shadow—his personal mentorship of her career as well as his weighty artistic imprimatur.

But it is also Ullmann's way of bringing her intimate history with him, and her specifically female imprint, to bear on the material. "He's a controlling person," she observes, "but he gave me the script, and for him the thrill was letting it be mine." As I listen to the note of quiet triumph in her voice, it occurs to me that the decision to emphasize Isabelle's suffering may have had as much to do with Ullmann's desire to convey a private message to the real-life Bergman—who was largely an absentee parent, leaving her to bring up their daughter, Linn, on her own—as with her wish to exert directorial independence.

Linn Ullmann, who is now thirty-four and one of Norway's leading journalists and literary critics, has an understandably complicated relationship with both of her parents. When she came to New York in 1999 (she lives in Oslo with her young son) for three weeks to promote her novel, *Before You Sleep*, she refused to be identified as their daughter in interviews. Her novel draws a less-than-flattering portrait of Anni, the character who appears to be modeled on Ullmann. Anni is described as an "irresistible woman" with "reddish-blond hair" and "glittery blue eyes." So far, so good. But she is also painted as a self-absorbed and self-dramatizing "empress" who devours men ("when she smiles men die") and cries fake tears. "Anni is the most sincere hypocrite I know," the narrator dryly notes. Worst of all is Anni's wobbly maternal sense, exemplified by her tendency to outshine her daughter at every opportunity: "Anni is standing in the light, I'm standing in the shade. Isn't that just typical, I say, and move closer to her."

Linn spent her early years moving around the world as her mother's career dictated, attending thirteen different schools. She and her mother settled in Manhattan when Linn was fifteen, and she went on to study English literature at New York University, living with her mother—with whom she always spoke Norwegian—until she was nineteen. She spent summers with Bergman but rarely saw him otherwise. Although Ullmann says that she and her daughter used to be "tremendously close, perhaps too close," she seems confounded by the coolness that has developed between them over the years.

The two don't see eye to eye on many things, including Ullmann's intense involvement with her work throughout Linn's childhood and adolescence. "I feel mostly guilty that I wasn't available a lot of the time," Ullmann says. "I was so full of my own life—my career, being in and out of love." She also refers to Linn's anger at the saccharine evocation of herself as "the sweet little person" in *Changing*, Ullmann's bestselling 1976 memoir. "That's how I experienced her," Ullmann says, somewhat defensively. "She herself claims she was tough, with a cool eye."

What is perhaps most surprising about the current situation is Linn's closeness to her father, which Ullmann professes to be pleased about. When she delves into the dynamics of it further, however, it becomes apparent that she is bewildered by the way things have turned out. "He has been so tremendously absent," she says, speaking of Bergman. "Her wedding was the only event he's been to—not her university graduation, not high school, not even her christening." Bergman seems to have contributed next to nothing monetarily, and Ullmann says that when she told him Linn was accepted to college, his answer was, "Oh, that's nice, but I'm retired now, I can't help you." She pauses, as if trying to make up her mind how much to divulge. "He's a multimillionaire, you know," she says in a conspiratorial tone. And then, as though suddenly defeated by the unfairness of it all, she sounds terribly sad. "He was never there," she repeats, almost as if she were trying to address an invisible judge. "Fathers get a lot of credit for nothing."

Ullmann's small apartment, in a sterile, glitzy building on Manhattan's Upper West Side, is more of a pied-à-terre than a permanent residence. She divides most of her time these days between Boston and Florida, where she lives with Donald Saunders, a real estate developer. The couple were married for ten years and parted in 1995—only to reconcile in cinematic fashion the morning after the divorce papers were signed. Ullmann was on a plane bound for Switzerland when her new ex-husband suddenly appeared in the first-class section and declared, "We are partners for life." They took up where they left off but have not remarried.

Despite Ullmann's peripatetic existence, her living room has a homey, cultured feel. A facsimile of George Orwell's manuscript of *1984* lies open on a stand, and the yellow walls, Miró drawings, piles of books, and assortment of bibelots suggest a catch-as-catch-can personal aesthetic rather than a decorator's sleek touch. The actress is dressed in an understated navy knit pantsuit, her thick straight hair (a Russian director who once wooed her described it as "red straw") is simply styled, and other than mascara she wears little makeup. Her nails are short and unmanicured, and when she puts her glasses on to read, she does so without the self-conscious comments that older women often make.

Although Ullmann describes herself as a natural listener—"I'm not a talker," she says—she is in fact easily engaged in conversation. Sitting on her chintz couch, we dash from topic to topic as though we once knew each other and now have much to catch up on. She mentions Erland Josephson's rediscovery of his religious roots during the filming of *Sofie*, which follows the life of a bourgeois Jewish family in nineteenth-century Denmark. "Erland was brought up by Orthodox grandparents," Ullmann explains, "and he suddenly remembered his Hebrew." She goes on to express mixed feelings of pride and chagrin about Linn's novel. She comprehends her daughter's need to come to terms with the past, but she is also quite evidently wounded by the fictionalized version of herself in *Before You Sleep*. "I can't allow myself to be crushed," Ullmann says resolutely, "that she didn't write the romantic fantasy of me that I hoped she'd write."

Several days later, I attend an evening at the 92nd Street Y at which Ullmann is interviewed as part of a film series moderated by the critic Annette Insdorf. Their discussion is preceded by clips from a recent documentary, *Liv Ullmann: Scenes from a Life*, narrated by Woody Allen, followed by a screening of *Autumn*

Sonata. In contrast to the mousy, earnest daughter she plays in
the film, Ullmann, sitting onstage, looks glowing and womanly
in a black velvet pantsuit, the very incarnation of Goethe's ideal
of *Das Ewig-Weibliche*—the eternally feminine. Replying to questions about her years with Bergman and her current career as
a director, Ullmann displays her customary charm but also a sly
humor, as though she no longer feels compelled to meet anyone's
expectations other than her own. She refers to her past with affection but not much regret, and without a trace of reverence.
Recounting an incident that occurred on the set of *Autumn Sonata*, in which she looked on wide-eyed as Ingrid Bergman challenged "the genius Bergman" (as Ullmann calls him) on his view
of her character, Ullmann sounds as though she still relishes that
long-ago moment of unprecedented impertinence. "I'm not going to say that," she recalls her assertive co-star insisting. "I
would slap her in the face and leave the room." Ullmann crosses
her legs and pushes back her hair. "I used to sit in a corner and
admire her," she tells the audience, "because this is the kind of
woman I wanted to be. I learned a lot from her."

Ullmann is emphatic about not wanting to act again; she describes acting as "a school" from which she has graduated with
honors. Now she wants to do what she wants, which is to
direct—to make her own footprints rather than follow someone
else's and inhabit her own complex self. (A large part of the reason her relationship with Bergman failed, she told me, was that
he needed to see her as a woman "of one piece, with no neuro-
ses.") Perhaps the most poignant and admirable aspect of Ullmann's life is the hard-won battle she has fought to cease playing
the role of the woman behind the man and trading it in for the
role of playing herself. I remember her telling me about her unease when she first began to direct and found herself falling back
on her reflexive habits of self-effacement and wifely clucking over
other people's comforts—"I'm sorry I'm existing. Can I get you
coffee? All those things." In the intervening years, she seems to
have grown more sure of herself—projecting that strength she so
admires in her daughter. She has pulled back from her exquisite
receptivity to the needs and demands of talented men, but she

retains the passion—the impetuous, romantic approach to the world—that has always marked her life.

"I never thought of myself as a muse," she tells the Y's rapt audience, endearingly pronouncing the word as "moose." "I'm not sure what it is. If it's complementary, then I want to be it. If it means being a pupil, I don't want to be it." It's a declaration of independence of sorts, stated in her unshrill and unantagonistic style, but the message behind it is unmistakable.

SLEEPING ALONE

(DIANE KEATON)

2005

Diane Keaton, who the critic Pauline Kael once suggested "may be a star without vanity," is fretting about her makeup. Keaton sits on an elevated director's chair in front of a large mirror in a bare dressing room, worrying that an indiscernible powdery dab on her nose will show up on camera—she's about to shoot a public service announcement on behalf of the dogs and cats left homeless in the wake of Hurricane Katrina—if she doesn't locate some putty-colored foundation to cover it. The actress, who will turn sixty in January, returns to the screen in December in *The Family Stone*, an ensemble drama in which she plays the dying but buoyant matriarch of a large and strenuously colorful brood. Keaton is deeply attractive in a way that you don't see much in Hollywood anymore (or on the Upper East Side or in any upscale area, for that matter): she looks, that is, the way a woman her age might look if preemptive cosmetic surgery for actresses over the age of thirty hadn't somehow become the law of the land. Keaton's slightly Nordic-looking features and good bones are still very much in evidence, but if you peer closely, you can see a faint tracing of lines etched around her unplumped-up mouth and at the corners of her slanted, blazingly alert hazel eyes.

"Does anyone have any concealer?" she asks as she continues to cluck and make faces at herself in the mirror, her naturally droll inflection infusing the question with a note of comic desperation. ("She doesn't 'do' funny," her friend and *Father of the Bride* co-star Steve Martin observes. "She's just Diane.") Notwithstanding the fact that Keaton has defied the fetishization of youth endemic to celebrity culture, she will readily admit that her appearance—the visual impact she makes—has always been acutely important to her. This fixation goes all the way back to her girlhood, when she would hunt with her mother for the right plaid fabric from Goodwill to be whipped up into clothes based on Keaton's own designs. "When I was younger," she told me, "I was very concerned with how I looked, with a fantasy of what I wanted to look like." She mentions a pink suit that she and her mother bought from Ohrbach's that, she says, in her self-amused, mordant way, "I undoubtedly thought was the answer to everything." She adds that she worked in J. J. Newberry's bra department during high school: "I was very excited by bras."

Still, this brief glimpse of backstage vanity makes her seem poignantly ordinary rather than hopelessly shallow or self-absorbed. For one thing, it is immediately clear that Keaton's concern about a potential blotch on her face is less an indication of the narcissistic anxieties of a movie star—one whose formidable lineup of ex-lovers includes Woody Allen, Warren Beatty, and Al Pacino and whose on-screen interests have included Albert Finney, Mel Gibson, and Liam Neeson—than of the "Oh my God, what now?" insecurity of a woman who has never been quite sure of her physical allure. (Make of it what you will, but Keaton claims that the persistent disinclination of her mother, now eighty-three, to acknowledge her oldest daughter's fetching looks while she was growing up is the source of her drive. "I could never get her to say I was pretty," Keaton says ruefully. "That fueled my ambition.")

Keaton has by general consensus grown, if anything, more beautiful over the years, her broad-planed face having gained in elegant angles what it has lost in round-cheeked *Annie Hall* dewiness. And, as finally became clear during her split-second nude scene in *Something's Gotta Give*, she can lay claim to an amazing body, one that is kept in willowy shape by lots of walking and swimming. All the same, she insists that she has never liked her own reflection. "It's not fun to see myself in the movies," she says. "It's not fun to see myself in the mirror."

The sun is high in a cloudless sky on this late September morning in Los Angeles, but inside the cavernous, windowless studio
on Sunset Boulevard it might as well be midnight in a bomb
shelter. Keaton is dressed in one of her usual obscurantist getups,
in shades of blackness—with the exception of a pair of gold hoop
earrings—from the ribbon band on her gray flannel bowler hat
to the pointy toes of her high-heeled Gucci boots. Although it is
a warm day, she wears a black turtleneck under a fitted black velvet
jacket over matching pants that emphasize her slim, long legs.
Given that she also sports tinted glasses, there is not that much
left of her to see when she actually sits down in front of the cameras. But then she flashes what a critic once described as her
"ravishing, clown's smile" and begins to speak her piece in her
distinctive ripe voice, and you suddenly realize that her most
steadfastly glamorous asset is her megawatt personality, bursting
out of her like an uncontainable force of nature, a geyser of quirk-
ily endearing traits that fall on the air and lend everything around
her a momentary sparkle.

Keaton, as I learned when I first met her some years ago on
the set of *Hanging Up*, the movie based on Delia Ephron's novel
that Keaton starred in and directed, is a consummate professional.
This aspect of her has been noted by everyone who has ever dealt
with her, from Beatty—who once characterized her to me, in
terms that made her sound like a Girl Scout leader, as "industri-
ous" and "punctual," the sort of person who "makes plans and
sticks to them"—to her former agent John Burnham, who says
that underneath her charmingly self-effacing persona Keaton is
"organized and tough and smart." Today, true to her reputation,
she sits uncomplainingly under the hot lights, holding Spike, the
winsome hound (a mix of basset and beagle) that has been flown
in from an animal sanctuary in New Orleans, in her lap, and does
take after take—at least fifteen in all—without a murmur of protest. After what seems like the nth impeccable delivery, the actress obligingly adjusts her tone yet again, injecting it with more
seriousness or greater enthusiasm at the director's request, all the

while keeping up a funny, slightly lewd patter about the develop-ing intimacy between Spike and her. (She jokes about her hand brushing up against the dog's genitals, his "package," she says coyly.) In between laughing heartily at her own shtick—"She has the most ingratiating laugh," Woody Allen observes, "it's fatal"—she hugs and kisses Spike. Although I have grown fidgety with impatience, as have many of the twenty-odd crew members stand-ing around me, Keaton remains unruffled until the end. Gracious as a Southern hostess, she bids everyone a warm goodbye before swinging her oversize woven-leather black bag over her shoulder and striding out into the day.

After the shoot, Keaton and I repair to lunch nearby at Lucy's El Adobe Cafe, a Mexican eatery decorated with a brick wall, Formica tabletops, and out-of-season Christmas lights that Jerry Brown used to frequent in its heyday. The restaurant is hip in a counter-chic way and, perhaps more important from Keaton's perspective, cheap. Despite her well-oiled lifestyle, which em-ploys enough people to run a small luxury hotel, a certain hard-nosed attitude toward money is one of her many old-fashioned virtues. On the walk over to Lucy's, for instance, she happily in-forms me that the Tom Ford pantsuit she is wearing was a freebie acquired on a celebrity trip she took to Las Vegas when she was up for a Best Actress Oscar in 2004 for *Something's Gotta Give*. "I was only one of two nominees to go," she notes almost proudly. Then, of course, there is her skill at trading up real estate—or, rather, her obsession with renovating houses—at which Keaton has demonstrated nothing less than a Midas touch. She recently sold her deconstructed hacienda-style house in Bel Air, which she bought for six million dollars, for sixteen million. She lived in it for less than two years after working on it for almost double that time, and it sold practically minutes after it appeared on the April cover of *Architectural Digest*.

When I first met her in Los Angeles six years ago, I spent hours in rapt contemplation of the fine-tuned Southwestern sen-sibility on display in the Beverly Hills house she lived in at the time. From the outside, the residence was an unprepossessing Spanish Colonial, but a dazzling yet austere sanctuary awaited inside. She had filled the rooms with Monterey furniture (not to be confused with Mission) and Navajo rugs, against which vivid touches—a collection of silver-and-turquoise jewelry, six graduated urns burnished with a turquoise-green glaze—stood out. When that house landed on the cover of *Architectural Digest*, it was snapped up by Madonna. Like a master shoemaker who hobbles around in worn-out slippers, Keaton has suffered the fate these last years of living for long periods in a rented house, as she does now.

The thing about Diane Keaton is that she has more energy than anyone under the sun—"She uses the time in her day like no one I've ever seen," John Burnham says—as well as the boundless curiosity to go with it. Jack Nicholson, who starred with Keaton in *Reds* in 1981 and in *Something's Gotta Give* in 2003, describes her as "crackling" and appears to be in genuine awe of her Energizer Bunny stamina. "Energy is the most amazing thing about Diane," he drawls over the phone. And then, audibly chuckling at the memory, he recalls that during a three-day break while in Paris filming the end of *Something's Gotta Give*, Keaton managed to trot over to Spain while he barely left his hotel room. "Her basic unit of energy is so enormous," he says. "It's hard to decipher."

Nicholson seems to have forged a uniquely strong bond with Keaton, one that enables him to get her in the way few others do. "We talk a pretty fast shorthand on deep subjects" is how he puts it. Nicholson was the solitary male among a bevy of female friends, including Meg Ryan and Lisa Kudrow, to be invited to her fifty-ninth-birthday party. Keaton claims that she asked him to the celebration, which was held at her friend Nancy Meyers's house (she describes Meyers, who wrote and directed *Something's Gotta Give*, as "the only comedy writer in the world who wants to tell stories about middle-aged women's love lives"), because "I knew he would make it an eventful evening. I knew he would stir things up. Not that an evening full of females is his kind of fun." Nicholson, in his turn, admitted that he did feel "severely male, yes," but says that he found the invitation "both enticing and odd."

I am struck by the way the two of them talk about each other in the same curious tone of erotically charged admiration, which

leads me to wonder whether their relationship might have blossomed into something else—if only (he weren't an inveterate
skirt chaser) and if only (she weren't so confoundedly full of high
standards). And indeed, when I ask Nicholson if he's surprised
that Keaton is romantically unattached, he ducks the question—
as well as the ambiguous nature of their connection—by referring obliquely to "the particular nature of her refinement."
Pressed to explain what he means by that quaintly Jamesian
phrase, he succeeds only in deepening the mystery: "She's complicated enough that at this point she's not going to be involved
with someone as a halfway measure. She at least knows what she
doesn't want."

Then again, there are many things the actress is sure she does
want in her life, although these days they have little to do with
either romance or the trappings of fame. Like a perennial extra-
curricular student, Keaton has always been captivated by many
subjects, especially by those that call upon the meticulously
honed aesthetic that permeates everything from the scrapbooks
and other oddities she likes to collect to her famously idiosyncratic way of dressing. Keaton has enormous, if peculiar, style,
which is as unmistakably hers as it is difficult to describe. It usually includes some combination of the following: a hard-edged
touch by way of a belt or footwear, a Chaplinesque bow tie or
hat, some appropriation from street fashion in the form of gloves
or hosiery, and a nod or two to the layered look she popularized
in *Annie Hall.* "She wakes up every morning," a longtime friend
of hers, the art dealer Daniel Wolf, told me, "and she sees her
clothes like paint coming out of a paint tube: What am I going to
mix today?"

Many of Keaton's interests are too intensely pursued to be
categorized as mere hobbies. They range from photography (she
has edited four collections of photographs on offbeat topics like
hotel lobbies, salesmen, and grisly tabloid shots from the *Los
Angeles Herald Express*) and architecture (she's on the board of
the Los Angeles Conservancy and is currently editing a book on
Spanish Colonial architecture for Rizzoli) to music (to the consternation of some filmmakers she has worked with, she is in the

habit of listening to Bob Dylan or Linda Ronstadt on her head-
phones until the moment the director says "Action!") and politics, about which she is surprisingly well-informed. (She is a
CNN addict and told me that one of the high points of her career was meeting Bill Clinton at a screening of *Hanging Up*.)

Sarah Jessica Parker, who plays the detested girlfriend whom
the oldest son has brought home for Thanksgiving in *The Family
Stone*, assumed that she would never get the chance to know
Keaton, whom she has always admired as an iconic figure in the
way that many younger actresses, like Kudrow and Ryan, seem
to. "I was worried she'd think of me as a terrible, vacuous, superficial blonde," Parker confides. Instead, to Parker's delight, the
two of them found themselves alone in a makeup trailer every
day of the shoot for a solid two hours before they were called to
the set and ended up talking about everything from clothes to
real estate to children to that day's news. Parker is particularly
admiring of Keaton's self-discipline, noting that the older actress
came to work promptly at five in the morning dressed in "a
cinched-waist skirt, heels, and hat" while "the rest of us were in
sweatpants." Then she adds, sounding more like Miss Manners
than Carrie Bradshaw, "You can't be a woman and gotten where
she's gotten without showing up on time."

For the last decade, ever since Keaton chose to take on motherhood at the age of fifty and proceeded to make it, however belat-
edly, first and foremost among her priorities, her schedule has
been even more packed than it once was. These days, her large,
well-staffed household revolves around her ten-year-old daughter, Dexter, and her four-year-old son, Duke, and their attendant
playdates, outings to the L.A. County Fair, parent-teacher con-
ferences, and pediatrician appointments. It helps that Keaton has
always been an early-to-bed, early-to-rise kind of creature. (Bill
Robinson, her friend and partner at Keaton's Blue Relief production company, once characterized her as "a Pilgrim nightmare,
up at dawn and in bed at ten.") Keaton is indeed up at five to
answer e-mail and troll the Web in search of items that stir her

eclectic visual imagination ("I love the computer," she declares.
"I wish I were partners on eBay"), after which she prepares lunch
for the kids and gets them ready for school. Dexter and Duke attend the University Elementary School (UES), a progressive,
socioeconomically diverse lab school affiliated with the Graduate
School of Education at the University of California at Los Angeles. Having considered herself "a neglected student," Keaton is
particularly impressed with the teachers at UES, "who," she says,
"are constantly trying to find new ways to be creative about stimulating children to learn."

It was during her forties that the actress discovered a growing
baby hunger in herself—"the need to participate in being part of
a family." Having tried and failed to become pregnant and having never made it down the aisle despite her many romantic liai-
sons, Keaton decided to adopt. Both Dexter, a towheaded girl
who stares out with a slightly wary gaze from the tiny black-and-
white snapshot Keaton pulls from her bulging date book, and
Duke, a fair-haired charmer of a boy, were adopted when they
were infants. Keaton's eyes still gleam with pleasure when she
talks about her first week snowbound in a hotel room in New
York with a six-day-old Dexter newly arrived from a Texas agency.

She is by all accounts a deeply engaged mother who eats dinner with her kids every night, gives great birthday parties, and is
intimately acquainted with her children's friends and the other
parents at UES. Ann Carlson, an environmental law professor at
UCLA School of Law whose daughter has been close pals with
Dexter since they were in prekindergarten together, describes
Keaton as remarkably "in there" with her children and as a "direct
and in some ways no-nonsense" but also "love-struck" mother
for whom the experience of parenting has been "life altering—
it's changed her in ways that she probably never anticipated."

Keaton would undoubtedly agree with this assessment. "To
have a child," she says, "you've got to stop messing around." She
has, of course, often played mothers, including the wonderfully
textured performance she gave as a betrayed wife and devoted
mother of four in 1982's *Shoot the Moon* on through her latest
role as the crusty but heroic mother in *The Family Stone*. In real

life, Keaton's relationship with her own mother, whom she describes as "irresistible," is a pivotal one. Over another lunch, this time at the Blvd, a swanky restaurant in the Beverly Wilshire, she talks about her mother with an almost fierce passion. In answer to my question as to whether any of the men she was involved with was the One, she states unequivocally, "There was no love of my life except my mother."

Keaton grew up in conservative Orange County, California, the oldest of four siblings (she has two sisters and a brother) in a tight-knit family. Despite the suggestion of tony Wasp breeding about Keaton's disciplined approach to life and the air of reserve that underlies her friendly accessibility—she has been described as being as guarded as Garbo, which may be an exaggeration, but it is undeniable that she has managed to preserve a rare zone of privacy in the fishbowl atmosphere of Hollywood—her own background is not markedly patrician. Her paternal grandfather was a barber who was murdered in a labor dispute; her maternal grandmother worked as a janitor. Keaton credits her father, Jack, a civil engineer who designed the Olympic-size pool at Santa Ana College, with instilling in her quick reflexes, a "deep, instinctive ability to run." Her mother, Dorothy, was a housewife who once won a "Mrs. Los Angeles" contest and was "the dominant person" in her children's lives.

Although Keaton sees bits of her father in her own "sappiness," she identifies overwhelmingly as her mother's daughter. It is Dorothy to whom she owes her limelight ambitions—"She was the best audience anybody could have," Keaton observes. "I developed all my skills through her"—and her abiding interest in the artistic preservation of memories, the storage of history in various forms, from old buildings to scrapbooks. Her mother has kept forty years' worth of journals about the family—"collage after collage, page after page"—and Keaton proudly points out that the photograph of her as a young woman that is the final image in *The Family Stone* (it has been doctored to make her appear pregnant) is, in fact, her mother's handiwork. "The photograph," she declares, "is the best damn acting I've ever done." Since her face in the photograph is the face of a woman to whom life has not yet happened, I'm not sure what she means by this assertion, but I sense that it is her way of linking her own accomplishments with her mother's unsung talents.

We continue our conversation that afternoon as she drives me back to my hotel in her recently acquired hybrid Lexus after we have stopped to visit a cluster of art galleries in Santa Monica. I ask her if she ever gets flak for being an older mother. "No one will say anything to me because I've taken a stance," she replies. Still, on some larger level, it clearly bothers Keaton—who referred to herself in an e-mail message as "twitchy, demanding, not fully grown-up"—that she feels herself to be something of a late arrival at the gates of motherhood in particular and adulthood in general. She is touchingly candid about her regrets, enumerating them with the stoic self-awareness of someone who has put in many hours on the shrink's couch. "I wish I could have been braver. I wish my limitation with intimacy hadn't been so crippling. I wish I had taken more risks. I wish I had started earlier addressing these things." Keaton is a firm believer in analysis; she considers it "a huge privilege" she intends to take advantage of as long as she can. "I've been talking my life away about deep conflicts that don't go away," she says of therapy. "I'm never leaving. It's like going to church. Whether I'm helped or not is not the issue. It's about trying to understand more about why something is the way it is, about my own participation in a problem."

The biggest problem in Keaton's life, as far as either of us can determine, has been with men. "Being in love," she announces, "brought out the worst in me. The thing for me with men has probably always been, *How much do they love me?* As opposed to, *How much do I love them?*" Nicholson characterizes this "I never got to choose anybody, they always chose me" plaint as "Diane's chapter heading on what the past was like." Keaton discusses her amorous history with a kind of pained but succinct retrospective wit—as if it were a phase of her life that she has sadly but firmly put behind her. Which, in fact, as evidenced by her persistent state of uncoupledness, she may well have done. By her own admission, she hasn't been seriously involved with anyone since her breakup with Pacino fifteen years ago. (When I asked her about rumors of a relationship with Keanu Reeves, she responded with a disbelieving yelp.)

Some of her troubles seem to stem from the way her parents' "difficult but passionate" marriage colored her own perspective on relationships. "They were a little in love and a little enraged," she says. "I viewed them in a romantic light. I wasn't prepared for complexities." Then, as befits an actress who has been remarkably skilled—notwithstanding her overriding screen persona as Woody Allen's darling flustered muse—at portraying shy, self-conscious women overcome by the power of their own awakened eroticism in films like *Looking for Mr. Goodbar*, *Reds*, *Mrs. Soffel*, and *The Good Mother*, she expounds on the mysteries of the flesh and the incongruousness of desire: "So much of romantic love is selfish and underdeveloped and doesn't grow. I couldn't love someone and like him at the same time. Sexual drive is such a big thing; it's attached to such specific requirements for me," Keaton elaborates. "Do you think I wanted a nice guy to come home to? I'm really happy I didn't have a child with any of the men I was with."

Men may have taken up a lot of Keaton's energy, sometimes to the slighting of her career—like the period during the 1980s when she seems to have dropped temporarily out of sight after the making of *Reds*—but she has actually spent very little time in domestic setups with any of them. "Maybe Woody," she says, "for a short period. He was the only one who would live with me while walking on eggshells, as he claimed I forced him to do." Keaton sounds as if she finds the very idea of an opposite sex both inherently fascinating and inherently objectionable, as if men were alien creatures to whom she has been drawn against her own better judgment. "I have ordinary affection for women," she explains, "but I don't have ordinary affection for men. I have extraordinary feelings. I was either so excited, so enamored, and swept away by them, or I wasn't interested in them at all. Instead of seeing them as people, I saw them as more extraordinary. They don't want anything to do with that," she adds, chuckling. "It's a nightmare for them."

Of course, there is always the possibility that rather than there being anything irredeemably wrong with either Keaton or the entire male species, there is something wrong with the specific sort of man she picks. Her producing partner, Bill Robinson, says, "Even if she had been a cashier at Woolworth's, Diane would have been drawn to the wrong men." By "wrong men" I suppose he means wrong for the long haul—what one friend calls (with the exception of Woody Allen) "pretty men," and another describes as "titular boyfriends, the football star or the class president."

In any case, Keaton appears to have made her peace with falling in love the way she can most readily tolerate it—on-screen, where she has always been able to "get in there deep," as Nicholson describes it, but she has also been able to get out, stay on top of the situation, be in control. ("She is a raw nerve," Sarah Jessica Parker says, "but she is practiced. Her emotions are available to her, but make no mistake about her: she has technique.") Perhaps it goes back to a certain spacious quality of self-invention that her mother encouraged, the fantasy of "finding an audience for your life" that helped inspire her daughter. "She let us explore our strongest wishes," Keaton points out. She says she believes that the "fake situation" of being in a movie romance is "under-appreciated by actresses" and that this particular kind of magic, this make-believe rapture, is, in fact, the biggest perk of the job. "You're in bed only in the best possible way," she told me. "You're not paying the price for being in love." She pauses for a minute, as if sifting through her mind for an irrefutable piece of evidence to back up her position, and then says, as if it were the obvious icing on the cake, "I got to kiss Jack Nicholson a lot."

Keaton, of course, is referring to her role as the deferred but triumphant love object in *Something's Gotta Give*, the money-milking hit of a fairy tale (for which, in the unmisty-eyed, bottom-line world of Hollywood, Nicholson was reportedly paid several times what Keaton was paid) that was supposed to give the definitive boost to her career after more than forty films and put her on the map once and for all as the box-office catnip that Woody Allen has always perceived her to be. "If she had wanted to," he told me, "Keaton could have been the most popular female star in America, another Lucille Ball." After a first act as Allen's ditzy foil, a second act as a gifted and erotically nuanced character actress, a third act as an appealing maternal figure in the two *Father of the Bride* movies (or, take your pick, a woman's woman with a sexy edge in *The First Wives Club*), Keaton was ready for her moment.

And here's the odd part, the part that sets people to shaking their heads, from Jack Nicholson to Sarah Jessica Parker, tsk-tsking about the limitations of the business, the glaring paucity of roles for older women, the neglect of more mature audiences. After the excitement of *Something's Gotta Give*, nothing gave. Literally, nothing happened. Her moment was gone before she could say hello to it. "There's no call for me," she says. "I got a lot of attention and money, and then I went right back to where I was before, a TV movie once a year."

Everyone I talk to agrees that Keaton's talent has been strikingly underused and that the situation is more a reflection of the film industry than of her place in it. Meanwhile, Keaton remains a Great Actress in Waiting, a kind of hipper Katharine Hepburn—an old-time leading lady from an age when, as she says, "elitists didn't do TV," before the red-carpet stratagems of celebrity and the synergistic manipulations of personal publicists (she has never had one, except for the two weeks many years ago that she hired Bobby Zarem) took over the landscape. Would she have gotten further if she had compromised more, been less picky, stooped to more commercial vehicles and smaller roles? "She likes popular success," Allen says, "but she won't move an inch for it. She works on her own terms."

Keaton's terms are remarkably complicated ones, having to do with what Warren Beatty once astutely referred to as her "subtextual inner conflict"—the multiplicity of impulses that rattle around in her and play themselves out in a general ambivalence about being taken seriously and the nature of her own ambition. One minute she's perversely insisting on her ordinariness; the next she's gleefully leading with her idiosyncrasies, as if she figured out long ago that the deliberate cultivation of oddness is the key to endearing yourself to a potentially hostile world. What you discover about Keaton the longer you're around her is that she's always disappearing inside her complicated self-presentation, leaving you empty-handed. Craig T. Nelson, who plays her husband in *The Family Stone*, sums her up as well as anyone. "There are so many multifaceted people inside of her," he says. "All of them are very well-rounded. I think you can meet her and think you know her and only get to know one of those people within the multitude she carries in her."

I suspect this is just the way Keaton wants it to be, the whimsically opinionated and ultimately baffling impression she prefers to leave in her wake. It would explain why, at the end of the day, after she has tucked her children in for the night, she beds down together with her multitude of selves in front of the TV. "We're isolated creatures," she explains, "living our lives vicariously. The sense of community is so reduced." She claims that her "most profound moments have been spent watching the news with Miles O'Brien during the hurricane." Keaton breaks out one of her captivating smiles as she says this, the effect of which is to make whoever is on the receiving end want to linger in her company for just a little longer. "He's not knowable," she says of the CNN newscaster, adding, after the briefest of pauses, "like me." For a moment, the woman who describes herself as "basically negatively inclined" sounds positively jubilant.

WHAT THE CAMERA
SEES IN HER

(CATE BLANCHETT)

2003

Cate Blanchett is not, at first glance, conventionally beautiful; indeed, her strong face can, from certain angles, seem almost plain. Her cheekbones look less enviably sculptured than they do on-screen, and her gorgeously ripe mouth shows up less than it does when it is slashed with crimson, as it is in *The Talented Mr. Ripley* and *Charlotte Gray*. Her ears (as she points out, lest I fail to notice) are big, and she wears her hair scraped back in a non-do. She is not, in fact, immediately recognizable until you get up close and see those extraordinary wraparound eyes, long, narrow, and a searching pale blue. Showstopping eyes that register emotions with a clarity that conveys some Platonic essence of whatever the emotion in question may be. So, I think, this is what it means to be photogenic—to have the kind of face that veils its magic until it meets the camera.

It's a Saturday afternoon in October, and the thirty-four-year-old actress and I are having lunch at the Four Seasons Hotel, smack in the middle of New York's shopping heaven. One of the first things I realize about Blanchett is that she is a very unsuperficial person. She is, in fact, incapable of sounding superficial even about topics like the hazards of fame, but since she moves in a world of mirrored surfaces, she wants to make sure I haven't mistaken her for some tinfoil, mindless movie star. "You're not going to talk about clothes, are you?" She sounds genuinely panic-stricken, as if I had unearthed an incriminating detail from her deep past that no one has confronted her with until now.

Blanchett speaks in a beguiling tumble of words with an elegant, lightly accented voice that is not quite placeable, and this is the first time in our two hours of hopscotching conversation that she has sounded anything other than unfazedly low-key. Except when she is being wildly enthusiastic (two of her favorite adjectives are "extraordinary" and "fantastic"), she tends to be wryly deflating of herself and other people's perceptions of her. "I don't live in the media," she declares. " 'Well, you will one day, won't you?' people always say. As though all actors aspire to the same thing." Detouring briefly to the subject of her childhood, she explains that as a middle child she was left mostly to her own devices. I don't ask whether it was her father's death when she was ten that triggered her interest in acting, on the assumption that she is tired of having this neat scenario presented to her as a profound insight, but she sees fit to confide that Gregory Peck and Alan Alda stood in as "substitute fathers" during her adolescence.

She talks about her growing family: she has been married to the screenwriter Andrew Upton for six years; she is the mother of Dash (short for Dashiell), who will be two in December, and is three months pregnant. We discuss her beginnings in theater, where she caused a stir almost from the moment she started performing. Geoffrey Rush, whom Blanchett worked with in David Mamet's *Oleanna* when she was in her early twenties, was a mentor. She recounts that when Rush, whom she had idolized but didn't know, called to say he was looking forward to working with her, she sat in her apartment, perspiring ("I didn't know there were sweat glands in my elbows, but I discovered them"), listening to his "mellifluous voice" on the other end. "I thought, 'I'm talking to Geoffrey Rush. I'm about to start working with Geoffrey Rush. It can only go downhill from here.' "

The subject of clothes has come up because Jessica Paster, Blanchett's stylist cum friend (or friend cum stylist, depending on how much credence you give to the friend part), has shown up at the table to take the actress out "for some fresh air" (which I take to be a euphemism for a shopping spree). While Blanchett goes

off to take a call from her husband, which has come through on
Paster's cell phone, the stylist informs me that she has worked
with Penélope Cruz and Uma Thurman, and I inquire into the
provenance of the silk kimono-like top that Blanchett is wearing
over jeans and pointy, kittenish heels (Chloé). The two of us are
discussing the ubiquity of nail salons in L.A. when the actress
returns and expresses dismay at the fluffy turn the conversation
has taken. She is clearly less at ease chatting about what she calls
"the lipstick side of things" than when she is analyzing her subliminal connection with her characters or when she is explaining,
with a lot of animated arm gestures, her favorite moment during
her theater period. "What I love," she explains, "is when you're
transported into the collective unconscious—that magical place
between audience and stage when you both jump up."

Still, her initial response to the mention of clothes strikes me as
suspiciously exaggerated. Blanchett is, after all, regularly featured
on magazine covers as a contemporary style icon and is a muse to
cerebrally inclined designers like Karl Lagerfeld (who flew her to
Paris in order to dress and photograph her as Coco Chanel) and
John Galliano (who designed the hummingbird-bedecked frock
she wore to the Academy Awards in 1999). Earlier this year,
Donna Karan succeeded in wooing Blanchett to represent the
latest incarnation of the "real woman" the designer claims to have
in mind when she whips up her costly and largely impractical
couture collections.

So it seems puzzling at first: Why would a young woman who
has succeeded in becoming "one of the most revered young actors of her generation"—as James Lipton solemnly describes her
later that evening at an *Inside the Actors Studio* interview—be at
such pains to distance herself from the starry aura and frivolous
curiosity that attends upon having a certain kind of face and
body attached to a certain kind of fame? In the space of less than
a decade, Blanchett has become a coveted screen presence who
adds instant cachet to any movie she is associated with. She is the
sort of über-actress capable of moving the director Anthony Min-
ghella to create a part where previously none existed (*The Talented
Mr. Ripley*). Sebastian Faulks sent his bestselling novel *Charlotte*

Gray to Blanchett in hopes of interesting her in playing the title character in the film version (which she went on to do). Brian Grazer, co-producer of *The Missing*, a gripping neo-Western about an errant father's attempt to make peace with his daughter, which comes out later this month, tells me that he and the director Ron Howard always had her in mind for the leading role of a resourceful frontierswoman. He explains that he needed an actress who would be "believable and formidable" going up against Tommy Lee Jones in a difficult role set in a barbaric time and place (New Mexico in the 1890s). "You've got to feel the dirt in her hands," Grazer says. "At the same time, she has to have enough sex appeal to hold the screen."

Blanchett is a closet workaholic, dashing from set to set without scheduling much time to luxuriate or enjoy domestic life. (Although her son and husband have already flown back home to London when we meet, she makes a point of noting that her son is almost always with her. "The longest we've been away from each other is three days.") She has touched down in New York just long enough to tape the *Inside the Actors Studio* segment before she returns to Los Angeles to put in a final day on Martin Scorsese's film *The Aviator*. (Blanchett plays Katharine Hepburn, and Leonardo DiCaprio plays Howard Hughes.) Less than a week later, she will fly off to shoot the spring 2004 ad campaign for Donna Karan and then begins work on a new movie, *The Life Aquatic with Steve Zissou*, directed by Wes Anderson and co-starring Bill Murray. She has also been talking with Liv Ullmann, whom she greatly admires as a director (she is a fan of Ullmann's *Sofie* and *Faithless*), about playing Nora in a film version of *A Doll's House*.

For such a breathlessly busy person, Blanchett is almost devout about living in the moment, which may be the truest legacy of her father's death. "I've always felt the shortness of time," she says. She's also too intelligent to let her ambition show; to listen to her, you would think her meteoric film career has been more fortuitous than planned. She insists that she would be happy doing something else, that she needs to be convinced that the enterprise in question is worth her effort. "Each time I work," she says, "I want to be seduced back." She seems adamantly unimpressed to find herself in the business of "being projected thirty feet high." "Film," she declares, "was never a mecca to me." It's hard to believe that she would be as ready to walk away from making movies as she claims, but it makes her seem charmingly insouciant, as if she were discussing a more mundane line of work, like bookkeeping.

She is currently starring in Joel Schumacher's new movie, *Veronica Guerin*, about an intrepid Irish journalist who exposed Dublin's largely unreported drug problem and was killed in 1996 at the age of thirty-seven. Although Blanchett picks her projects carefully, she is wasted in a movie that would be almost entirely unmemorable except for her performance. She spends most of the film gamely acting the role of Lois Lane, girl reporter, banging on doors and asking bold questions of criminal types. The actress, who is, as Grazer notes, "relentless in her effort to be authentic," talked to many people who knew Guerin and familiarized herself with the dingy Dublin neighborhoods where drugs were sold and used. But her character is essentially written as a stock type, free from introspection and the vicissitudes of a personal life thanks to a forbearing husband who takes care of their young son while she is off making a name for herself. I wonder aloud whether the part of Guerin might have been too much of a star vehicle, too much of a Julia Roberts kind of role. Blanchett listens and then diplomatically responds. "Who knows," she asks, putting her finger on the existential mystery that underlies the construction of any screen persona, "who Julia Roberts really is?"

In the course of plying her craft, Blanchett has frequently been compared with Meryl Streep, whose mantle of thespian prestige she has inherited and with whom she shares a singular ability to impersonate all sorts of accents, from the broadest of Southern inflections to elf-speak. She is invariably described as chameleon-like because of her uncanny ability to get under the skins of characters as diverse as a sixteenth-century queen who renounces her private life to rule her parlous empire (*Elizabeth*) to a single mother of three with psychic powers who lives in rural Georgia (*The Gift*). "Maybe by 'chameleon' they mean forgettable," she says.

It is an appealingly self-deprecating remark but not entirely off the mark. Blanchett's ability to sink into the environment of the film and fully inhabit her characters' lives includes within it the risk of blurring her own physical presence in favor of the role she's playing, sometimes to such an extent that you forget whom you're watching. (A day or two before I meet her, I admit to a movie-aficionado friend that I can't recall what role she played in *The Talented Mr. Ripley*, and he sheepishly concedes that he can't remember, either.) It was said of the great English character actress Peggy Ashcroft that she didn't have a face, and in the sense of not seeming to be fixed in her own physiognomy, Blanchett doesn't have one, either.

What is less frequently mentioned, though, is the way in which Blanchett has, despite her own resistance, subtly mutated over the course of time into a bona fide movie star. She wears Chanel and Prada, doesn't carry her own room key, and moves with an entourage of handlers. But unlike some of the other talented actresses of her generation, like Nicole Kidman, whose considerable abilities often disappear under the scrutiny of the tabloids, Blanchett has risen to the top of a brutally competitive profession without appearing to have sacrificed her creative aspirations or her grounded, just-folks quality. However she managed it, she has skillfully avoided being pawed by the fawning pop press, with its fickle affections and malicious innuendos. One way I have of gauging what I take to be the actress's relatively low celebrity quotient (or Q Score, as it's called) is the utterly blasé response of my fourteen-year-old daughter—who would have been beside herself with excitement at the thought of my meeting Gwyneth Paltrow or Kirsten Dunst—to the fact of my breaking bread with Blanchett. She didn't even request that I bring back an autograph.

The actress's disarming presentation of herself as a person who has just happened to wander into the limelight and doesn't find Being Cate Blanchett all that fascinating is either a tribute to her authentic sensibility—or a brilliantly disingenuous piece of self-presentation. Perhaps because she is more securely moored than is usually the case with people who look to be applauded for portraying someone other than themselves, Blanchett is able to draw on the same abundant curiosity and receptivity that she uses as an actress to endear herself to the many strangers who claim her time and attention. I've no doubt that all of us go away thinking that we alone have been privy to her funny, self-aware ruminations, just as I have no doubt that she offers a more reflective self to me than she does to the hip young journalists from *Jane* magazine and *BlackBook*. But in the end, the only thing that really matters is how incandescently real she comes across on the screen. "She seems just such a normal woman at heart," observes the film critic Richard Schickel, "no matter what emotional issues festoon her roles. She's played queens and she's played ethereal fantasies, but she never goes ditzy in the role. Even when she's trying to build a glass house in the outback, there's something down-to-earth in her manner."

I'm not sure how Blanchett has managed to bring off this balancing act—between the claims and seductions of celebrity and the considered and serious impulses that have guided her personal and professional choices so far—and it will be interesting to see if she will continue to do so as the pressure to live up to her Hollywood billing increases. My hunch is that meanwhile she intends to keep her ten-thousand-dollar red-carpet ensembles as beside the point as possible, at least when giving interviews.

A THORNY IRISH ROSE

(NUALA O'FAOLAIN)

2001

Nuala O'Faolain is making up for lost time. It has been a mete-oric five years since the sixty-year-old journalist banged out her tentatively titled memoir, *Are You Somebody?*, in an inspired two months spent sitting at a wooden table in her one-bedroom cottage in County Clare. The book, which had an initial print run of fifteen hundred copies, remained on the Irish bestseller list for six months before it was bought for a pittance by an American publisher, presumably without great expectations, and became a bestseller on this side of the Atlantic as well.

O'Faolain's first novel, *My Dream of You*, comes out this week in America, and hopes are that it will be one of those rare cross-over books that has both literary ambitions and wide commercial appeal. Based on the success of *Are You Somebody?*, O'Faolain received an advance for *My Dream of You* that is rumored to be in the seven figures, and she is being sent by her publisher, River-head Books, on a seventeen-city promotional tour. The novel is narrated by Kathleen, a middle-aged writer who is fiercely inde-pendent but lovelorn—a character who sounds very much like the author—and whose "misunderstanding of passion" has led her on a lifelong search for a man who will provide both loving companionship and sexual bliss. The slightly meandering plot follows Kathleen to the remote village of Ballygall, where she has gone to research an obscure historical scandal known as the Talbot Judgment—involving a liaison between an Irish groom and a married, upper-class Anglo-Irish woman—which took place during the Great Famine of the 1840s. As the story navigates between Kathleen's own sense of romantic dislocation and the tightly constructed historical subplot, it speaks in naked and direct ways to women who are no longer young and firm-fleshed but who still keep "a vigil outside the shrine of Eros." After an unexpected one-night stand with a man she meets on a ferry, Kathleen broods, "What if I never have another lover? What if I have to go the whole way to the grave without ever making love again?"

Had the author not given a remarkably unzipped account of her own life and loves when she appeared on Ireland's top-rated chat show to promote her memoir, *Are You Somebody?* might never have become a literary sensation. The interview began on a startling note, with the host, Gay Byrne, nosily asking, "You've slept with a lot of men, haven't you?" To which O'Faolain shot back, "Only three that ever mattered, which is modest for a woman of my age." The conversation steamed along from there, delving into the sort of damaging family history that most of Ireland's "fretful, conscious citizenry," as O'Faolain once described it, didn't talk about but longed to hear discussed. She recalls that she appeared on the show in "a rictus of terror," having prepared for it by giving up drinking and taking up exercising four weeks earlier, as well as praying to "a God I didn't believe in." Once on camera, she quickly charmed her way into the studio audience's hearts—"I could feel them on my side," she says—and within no time *Are You Somebody?* was being sold straight from boxes before it even reached the shelves.

The use of the word "accidental" in the memoir's American subtitle, *The Accidental Memoir of a Dublin Woman*, was not just a clever marketing ploy to catch the reader's attention. The book was, in fact, originally conceived of as no more than a grace note, an introduction to a collection of O'Faolain's widely read pieces from the daily paper *The Irish Times*. "I was ashamed," she says, "of reprinting columns with ancient arguments in them. It's the most pitiful form of bookmaking," Once she decided to write an introduction, she explains, "I had to answer the question nobody had asked: Where do my opinions come from? The answer was simple: Ideology had nothing to do with it. My opinions come from my life." Despite her fears about writing in a private voice— "you don't get to be an Irish woman of my age and say 'I, I, I' with any confidence, because 'I' has been frightened out of you"—the introduction swelled to two hundred intensely personal pages. "I sneaked out my autobiography when no one was looking," she says, sounding like a child caught reading by flashlight under the sheets. "My unconscious recognized a chance."

Prior to this, O'Faolain had made her name for more than a decade as a maverick pundit at the prestigious and traditional *Irish Times*, where she expressed her often discomforting views about "this damp little shambles of a democracy on the edge of the Western world." The editor of the paper, Conor Brady, who offered O'Faolain her own column on a hunch after hearing her interviewed on the radio about her work as a producer of a magazine-style television series called *Women Talking*, was struck by her ability to "infuse ordinary people's everyday activities with value and interest." (O'Faolain prefers to shape her story— somewhat disingenuously—with a dramatic Cinderella twist, in which Brady plays the Prince Charming character; to hear her tell it, she was a middle-aged washout when he offered her the job out of the clear blue.)

Brady's instinct proved right within weeks of hiring her. "She just took off," he recalls. "She'd get these amazing mailbags from people because she touched something very elemental in their lives." Her public voice was politicized without being doctrinaire; she could be as ardently outspoken as Germaine Greer, but her perspective was softened by bursts of humor and the Irish gift for lyrical lament that is so evident in the fiction of Edna O'Brien. In a column called "Birth," O'Faolain described the quiet, vigilant atmosphere of an intensive-care maternity ward in which "you hear the silence of the babies. You long for them to cry, but they can't cry, because they are sedated. Tiny little starfish things, literal scraps of life."

With clear-eyed affection, O'Faolain registered the hidebound habits of mind—"the florid national inefficiency"—she saw around her. "She has a great capacity," Brady observes, "to force us to confront some of the illusions we like to have about ourselves in Ireland—that this is, for instance, a very good society in which to bring up children." O'Faolain commented on the political issues of the day as well as on the country's ongoing problems, like domestic violence, homophobia, the iron grip of Catholicism, and the high birthrate. She was utterly unpredictable in the positions she took. "People find it difficult even in Ireland to categorize her," Brady says. In the witty essay in which she came out against the antifur lobby, O'Faolain recalled being pushed against a doorway and wordlessly handed a pamphlet about cruelty to animals. She went on to reflect, "This confrontation raised in an acute form my rights as opposed to a Korean rabbit's rights."

Today, O'Faolain refers dismissively to the "fake objective" and "authoritative" tone she had to adopt in order to write those commentaries. "When I entered the world of op-ed journalism," she declares, vividly overstating the case, as is her custom, "that male world of 'on the one hand' and 'on the other,' I became an honorary man." What is certain is that *Are You Somebody?* shocked everyone in the matey, closemouthed newspaper circles in which she was a member in good standing. Among other revelations, the book described O'Faolain's consuming dedication to a proposition she had been taught to accept as self-evident: "I'd spent my whole adult life on the errand that smoothed the way to being a woman in the home—a search for a man, for love, for the one man to love and be loved by and have babies with—without *wanting* to be a woman in the home."

Her quest yielded various lovers, including such famous intellectuals as the art critic Clement Greenberg (who once signed off a letter to her, "in hopes of another orgasm"), the literary critic Leslie Fiedler (who took her on a visit to the film director John Huston, which the two of them cut short on account of the "glacial meals" served in a dining room with ornate antique Chinese wallpaper), and the well-known Irish novelist John McGahern (who, she wrote, "was recovering from pain connected with the beautiful sister of a policeman"). She also discussed, albeit somewhat evasively, her almost fifteen-year involvement with a woman who is one of Ireland's most prominent feminist activists. When I

ask O'Faolain, who was shipped off to a convent boarding school
at the age of fourteen because of her brazenly flirtatious ways—
"She was always climbing out the window to meet boys," her
sister Deirdre says—whether she considers herself a lesbian, she
cuts the subject short.

O'Faolain's cottage sits above Liscannor Bay, on a meandering
little lane that ends at the shoreline. Three miles away, in the village of Lahinch, there are, as she puts it, "a couple million pubs."
If you drive as she does, with a hair-raising lack of caution along
winding two-way roads, it is an hour's trip from Shannon Airport to this underpopulated part of western Ireland. We pass a
Wordsworthian landscape of stone walls, hawthorn hedges, and
fields where mud-covered cattle graze. "Feisty little bullocks," she
mutters affectionately. "They can take what God throws at them."
When she is not pointing out the sights, O'Faolain, who has a
streaked mop of hair and striking gray eyes that have a slightly Ori-
ental tilt to them, analyzes the tragically flawed national temperament—"disfigured by drink," as she puts it, "and a feeling of inner
despair." As we pass a majestic pink mansion that was once a children's hospital, she remarks in a tone of quiet bitterness, as though
the 1845 potato blight that decimated Ireland's population had occurred only yesterday, "Sixty children died of cholera in that house."

The famously depressive Irish weather is nowhere in evidence
when we pull up at her house; the sun glows perceptibly in a pale
blue sky. O'Faolain unlocks the bright red front door of her
cottage, and we have barely stepped over the threshold when
Molly, her beloved collie, dashes out, barking and wagging her
tail in a frenzy of welcome. Inside, the house is decorated in an
arts-and-craftsy style; there are whimsically patterned curtains
on the windows, yellow walls, and a colorfully tiled fireplace. Beyond the tiny kitchen, outfitted only with an ancient four-burner
range and some unfinished shelves that hold a tin or two of sar-
dines and several jars of jam and relish, an open laptop takes
pride of place on the living room table. But O'Faolain is eager to
show me her pièce de résistance—a new bathroom with a shower

that she had installed in the past year. She leads me to it, practically crowing with pleasure, and the two of us stare at it with a reverence usually reserved for great works of art.

O'Faolain was the second oldest of nine children who grew up in rural County Dublin in a family that looked richly cultured— "My mother read all the time," she recalls in her memoir, "and my father taught us the words of German songs, and we played extracts from *Swan Lake* on the gramophone"—but was, in fact, haphazard and impoverished. Her father was a celebrity, a debonair society columnist with a car and driver. He was also an inveterate philanderer who was rarely home, treated his desperately smitten wife like a dependent child, pummeled his sons, and kept his family in a humiliatingly penurious state. Her mother— whom O'Faolain refers to as Mammy—was both undomestic and unmaternal and retreated into the solace of novels and alcohol. Gestures of affection were rare ("I can't remember my mother ever picking one of us up of her own accord," she says), and over the years the household became ever more dilapidated, with the younger siblings increasingly left to fend for themselves. One of her little sisters once went to school without underpants on; another languished at home with untreated TB for over a year, until a family friend noticed and took her to the sanitarium.

O'Faolain talks with a kind of detached sorrow about her siblings, some of whom she doesn't speak to anymore. She is closest with her sister Deirdre, a mother of seven who lives with her husband in a cramped row house without central heating in working-class Dublin. She describes the chronic emotional struggles of two other sisters but seems most saddened by the plight of her brother Don, who wasted his "brilliant potential" in a futile search for their father's approval and systematically drank himself to death by his early forties.

On the surface, O'Faolain was the one who got away, triumphing over the circumstances of her background on the strength of her charm and wits. Her close friend Marian Finucane, who is the host of Ireland's most popular morning radio show and has known O'Faolain for twenty years, credits her great "survival skills." Finucane and I talk over an elegant lunch in a restaurant across from St. Stephen's Green, in a building that was part of University College Dublin (UCD) back when James Joyce was a student there; it was on the building's top floor that the poet Gerard Manley Hopkins expired. "When we were all stamped out of the same cloth," Finucane explains, "Nuala O'Faolain was different. She took the bravest route all the time." From the start, O'Faolain shone academically, winning scholarships to University College and then to Oxford. In her thirties, after teaching briefly in the English department at UCD, she became a television producer for the BBC, filming innovative shows on volatile subjects—religious sects, pornography, transsexuals.

But although O'Faolain had succeeded in moving forward by never looking homeward, her achievements failed to assuage the bleakness she carried with her. With her trademark bluntness, she describes her thirties as "a wasteland of misery and loss and mourning and drinking." She spent much of this period, which culminated in a psychiatric hospitalization in the wake of her father's death, as an emotional "derelict," boozing away her demons in a Dublin basement flat. In spite of the early recognition she received for her intellectual abilities, O'Faolain considers herself "a very late starter" when it comes to life skills. She learned to drive when she was forty (she failed the test three times, and her instructor was on Valium, "presumably," she says, "because of women like me"), took her first swimming lesson at fifty, and promised herself that she'd learn to use a computer and get a dog by the time she was fifty-five. While other women bemoan their lost youth, she considers her fifties to have been her prime. "I went into the phone booth and came out Lois Lane. It was the first time I lifted my head above the storm and dust that obscured everything. Until then, I had just gone from one day to the next."

These days, O'Faolain is a national celebrity and a powerful presence on the Irish literary scene. She divides her time between the country, her apartment in Dublin, and, increasingly, months-long intervals in Manhattan. As I stroll with her along Dublin's busy Grafton Street one afternoon, we bump into several people who greet her, including a dashingly dressed man whom she introduces as the city's "best hairdresser and a great gossip."

Within the past year, O'Faolain has moved on to writing a more personal column—"Regarding Ireland"—on whatever catches her fancy, for the Saturday magazine supplement to *The Irish Times*. A recent column was inspired by a new set of capped teeth she acquired in New York, which feat of dentistry led her to meditate upon differences in national character as seen through the prism of attitudes toward self-improvement. Noting that Americans wholeheartedly embrace "looking like a winner," she pokes wry fun at the Irish for their "fidelity to natural decay" and goes on to upbraid them for their persistent, religiously instilled allegiance to the Last Day instead of the present one. "You're supposed to assert your gritty authenticity," she observes, "by a display of yellowing, crooked, brownish bits and pieces of teeth that have the amazing merit of being untouched by the 20th century."

On my last morning in Dublin, O'Faolain uses some of her newly acquired clout to get a dusty employee of the National Library of Ireland to give us an advance peek at the Joyce manuscript recently purchased for $1.5 million at Christie's. She stares with shining eyes at the precious pages of carefully annotated prose from the "Circe" section of *Ulysses*; they are preserved between sheets of plastic and covered with Joyce's small, slanty script. "This is the greatest moment of my life," O'Faolain says.

Shortly thereafter, we say goodbye in front of my hotel, where she has locked her bicycle to the railing. As I stand there, watching as she rides off to a TV interview, her back ramrod straight, her red interview jacket neatly folded in the basket, I'm suddenly reminded of my first sight of her several days earlier. She had come rushing toward me in the early-morning gloom of Shannon Airport, an hour late to fetch me, calling my name wildly and apologizing in the same breath. Dressed with youthful stylishness in leggings and a pink cashmere scarf flung over a black plush jacket, she stood out among the weary-looking locals like a vivid apparition.

O'Faolain has traveled far on her cleverness, her ambition, her insistence on being heard. It's odd, then, that given all this hurtling life force, this hard-won happiness, my strongest impression of the writer is that she is running backward—toward the defeated mother of her childhood and toward the Ireland of the past, a desolate country of broken men and broken women. In one of her *Times* columns she described pubs, with the trembling sense of awe most people feel for holy wells and churches, as "numinous spaces." Although O'Faolain assures me that she gets drunk these days only "from exuberance," when I ask her how she envisions her future, she says she sees herself as a shapeless old woman in a tweed coat held together with string, ten empty beer bottles at her side. "I can't wait to be an old lady," she says. "I'm dying to wither up so I can stop hurting." And then she adds, almost dreamily, "I'm going to live in a pub as soon as I get the old-age pension. Old ladies are always treated with great respect in pubs."

POSTSCRIPT

Nuala O'Faolain died at the age of sixty-eight, in May 2008, of cancer. She and I had remained in touch after my New York Times Magazine *essay about her came out and met intermittently when she was in New York, where she spent part of the year, living in Brooklyn and teaching. I always felt a deep connection with her based on our shared experience of difficult backgrounds (although they were difficult in very different ways), a common streak of depression, and our mutual love of reading and writing. One of the last times I saw her was when she came to hear me read from a memoir I was working on, to which she had a characteristically empathic response. She went on to publish several more books, one of which—a memoir titled* Almost There—*I read in manuscript form and had some apprehensions about, not least because of her frankly critical view of the over-doting relationship between the man she was living with and his young daughter. In the event, the book got mixed reviews.*

Nuala gave an emotionally charged and deeply moving radio interview with Marian Finucane a month before she died, in which she spoke openly about her anger at her life being cut short: "I don't want more time. As soon as I heard I was going to die, the goodness went from life." I discovered after her death, much to my surprise, that Nuala had left me (among a select group of others) a small gift of money, which I took as a token of her expansive nurturing impulses. I miss her incalculably.

ILLUMINATING
THE ORDINARY

ALICE MUNRO

2004

It is a brilliantly clear Saturday afternoon in early September, one of those days when the blueness of the sky seems to be set off to luminous effect by drifting puffs of cloud. Time slows down everywhere at this hour on a cusp-of-fall weekend, but here in Clinton, Ontario—a somnolent slip of a town (population thirty-five hundred) that is easy to miss after a three-hour drive from Toronto during which you pass nothing but mile after flat mile of fields punctuated by grazing cows and horses—the stillness is so vast that it seems almost cautionary.

This area, southwest of Toronto and east of Lake Huron, is Alice Munro country, a place that the acclaimed Canadian writer has described as crucial to her: "It means something to me that no other country can—no matter how important historically that other country may be, how 'beautiful,' how lively and interesting. I am intoxicated by this particular landscape. I am at home with the brick houses, the falling-down barns, the trailer parks, burdensome old churches, Walmart and Canadian Tire. I speak the language." Thanks to Munro's unparalleled ability to evoke the condition of felt life at both its most essential and its most particular—the "sudden holes and impromptu tricks and radiant vanishing consolations," as characterized in her story "Carried Away"—her terrain has become totemic, as real and familiar as our own backyards and avenues, to a rapt and ever-growing audience of readers.

She is, of course, among Canada's best-known and most feted
writers, at the forefront of a list that invariably includes her friend
Margaret Atwood and goes on from there to take in figures like
Carol Shields and Timothy Findley before splintering apart, depending on how you rate Marian Engel, say, or whether you
judge Robertson Davies to be more smoke than fire. (Munro
herself dismisses him, in a word, as "dead.") Munro, whose tenth
collection of short stories, *Runaway*, will be published at the end
of the month, has succeeded in putting this intractably rural,
unhurried, and laconic region firmly on the literary map, render-
ing its human commotion—gothic passions, buried sorrows, and
forlorn mysteries—in dazzlingly plainspoken tales that connect
directly with her readers' interior narratives and histories of the
heart. By paying precise yet generous (although never sentimental) attention to those aspects of women's lives that usually go
under the undignified rubric "love troubles," and to the sexual
and domestic crises that come in their wake, Munro has made her
presence felt well beyond Canada. Her books have been translated into nearly twenty languages, including Finnish and Slovak,
and she shows no ebbing of her imaginative powers or her ability
to seduce new readers. Each of the writer's books has outsold the
one before, and although none of them has become a bestseller in
the United States, Munro has won a National Book Critics Circle
Award (not to mention every literary prize Canada has to offer).

Munro's stories have appeared in America over the past three
decades, first in *The New Yorker* and then in book-length collections that have emerged every few years since 1979, when *The
Beggar Maid* (which was actually her fourth book) was published
by Alfred A. Knopf. Her work garnered critical huzzahs right out
of the gate for its clear, unfinicky delineation of complex adult
emotions. Along the way, this spinner of humdrum kitchen-sink
entanglements, whose signature is the illuminating ordinary detail that clarifies everything that leads up to it or the unremark-
able yet pivotal moment that changes everything that comes after
it, has earned a reputation as one of our greatest contemporary
writers of fiction. "Our Chekhov," Cynthia Ozick called her, in
a vaulting comparison that has since become something of an

obligatory tip of the critical hat, bringing ever more stratospheric analogies to Tolstoy and Flaubert in its wake.

Notwithstanding the fact that Munro's writing is the sort to prompt a keen interest in the person behind the writer, she herself has remained tantalizingly out of reach of her readers. In this age of de rigueur promotional campaigns and personal publicity, she is famously private, someone who needs to be coaxed into giving interviews and finds book touring an ordeal. The other point that is constantly being made about Munro—always in a preemptive fashion suggesting that any further inquiry into the subject of her personality is an indication of your own insatiably vulgar TV-addled perspective—is how modest and unassuming she is. Both of these adjectives crop up repeatedly about her, as though the mystery of how this ostensibly contained and genteel creature came to be the excavator of our most randy desires and our most brazen impulses—our "open secrets," as the title of one of her collections has it—is a negligible one. Never mind the ambition and drive, the all-consuming focus it must take to create those stunningly observed and crafted stories, year after year, decade after decade, on the part of a writer who, at age seventy-three, shows no signs of letting up on her production—or on her clear-eyed perceptions.

"I still haven't claimed being a writer," Alice Munro observes at our first meeting, less than ten minutes into what will turn out to be a very long and companionable lunch. "My husband claims it for me. I still write in a corner of the dining room, and I often answer the phone." The tragicomic aspects of this are not lost on her, despite her reputation for good behavior. "I get very upset with the thought of the way a man's work is accepted and honored. People don't expect to phone up and talk to the man. He's writing. He's got a room where he writes."

We had arranged to meet at 12:30 at Bailey's, located on the tiny patch of main square in Goderich, the next backwater town over from Clinton, where Munro has lived for the past thirty years with her second husband, Gerald Fremlin. (It is also the setting for many of Munro's stories.) It's easy to miss the restaurant—to miss the whole town—but when I finally find it, Carolyn, the restaurant's proprietor, is waiting in the doorway to greet me, as though she were running a boardinghouse in a Carson McCullers story, scaling the world down to a cozy and welcoming presence. She takes me over to Munro, who is seated near the bar at her regular table, where she meets all of her friends and which also seems to be the designated point of contact for strangers who insist on tracking her down way out here in the sticks.

Munro is a trim, beautiful woman with relatively unlined skin and coiffed silvery-gray hair; long gone are the slightly unkempt curls of her early photographs. She is elegantly but unfussily put together, wearing a light enhancement of makeup, dressed in an ivory silk blouse, off-white pants, and arty yet sophisticated earrings. Munro gets up to give me a warm hello, and I am immediately struck by a lack of pretense that all the same seems too considered to be entirely guileless. Perhaps it is no more than the undercurrent of quiet amusement emanating from her gray-green eyes, which suggests a watchful inner self behind the easygoing, even intimate manner—a witty, sometimes brutally observant self, held in check by the need to pass herself off as conventionally and graciously female. When I compliment her on having remained thin, she corrects me, stressing the difference between "thin" and "thinnish" as though she were a weight counselor. "I've always been thinnish," Munro insists, only half jokingly. "I was never a thin girl." And then, warming to her theme, as our first glass of white wine is poured, she continues: "I was bulimic for a while before the word existed. I thought I was the only person who discovered it. Most women I knew got a heavy maternal figure. I was determined not to, as part of maintaining my identity."

We order Caesar salad, followed by arctic char, on Carolyn's recommendation; she hovers throughout the meal, treating Munro like a prized local specimen who requires special care—not because she is so exacting but precisely because she isn't aware of her own aura. Munro is an esteemed figure here, half town matriarch and half local Famous Person. "I have permission," she gaily announces, "to close this place up." (Indeed, when the last staff member departs several hours later and as the two of us are still going strong in the now-empty restaurant, Munro gets up to lock the front door for the afternoon.)

The issue of her privacy, what she does and doesn't want to disclose about herself, is very much on the table, so to speak, throughout our lunch. Munro's fictional approach is rooted in a process of incremental disclosure, of a gradual peeling away of layers in order to get closer to an approximate emotional truth. In person, she strikes me as torn between the habit of self-effacing reticence, instilled in her by her Scottish-Irish Presbyterian background, and a conflicting, equally strong impulse to strip away the curtains, the better to expose the lives within, lives she has described, in a memorable and oft-quoted phrase from her only novel, *Lives of Girls and Women*, as "dull, simple, amazing and unfathomable—deep caves paved with kitchen linoleum."

By way of apologetic explanation for having, at the last minute, scuttled the original plan for me to pick her up at home, she mentions a "long-ago rule that my husband and I have that no one come to the house." I don't press her on why this no-access clause, if it indeed exists, had initially slipped her mind. Beneath Munro's charming surface, I suspect, lurks the steely resolve of the eleven-year-old girl who knew she wanted to be a writer even though she came, by her own account, from "a little town where nobody was interested in writing or the world of literature." "My charm has a time limit," she sweetly warns, in case I tread too far in with my questioning. I take the opportunity when a pause occurs in our conversation to inquire about her husband. Gerald Fremlin is a retired civil servant, a geographer who edited *The National Atlas of Canada*, and grew up in the same house the couple live in now. In our conversations, Munro invokes him frequently and affectionately as "my husband" rather than by his name, like a proud Midwestern banker's wife whose one great claim to glory is that she has married well.

"He sounds," I say, "like the love of your life." Somewhat to my surprise, Munro gamely rises to the challenge, revealing that

the two of them met for the first time when she was still eighteen-
year-old Alice Laidlaw, a scholarship student at the University of
Western Ontario—and freshly engaged to James Munro, with
whom she would go on to have a twenty-year marriage and three
daughters. Fremlin was a World War II vet seven years older than
she, and Munro immediately "fell for him," as she tells it with
visible relish, her still-youthful eyes ablaze with the memory of
romantic mischief.

Fremlin was her earliest official appreciator, the first to see a
whiff of Chekhov in the novice writer. He wrote her a fan letter
about a story of hers that appeared in the college literary magazine—
she recalls the youthfully portentous title, "The Dimensions of
a Shadow," with a forgiving laugh ("Okay, okay," she says, "we
were all young once")—but what she really hoped he would do,
apparently, was ask her out. "I wanted him to say something like,
'When I laid eyes on you . . . ,'" she explains, her voice trailing
off, sounding like one of her own multilayered characters, about
to revise the course of her destiny on a dime, without so much as
a goodbye to her former life. When I ask whether she would have
gone off with Fremlin then and there, she says, simply and un-
hesitatingly, "Yes," and for a moment I see the character of Pauline
in her, the adulterous wife and mother in her 1997 story "The
Children Stay," who decides to bag an existence of "married
complicity" to run off with her lover.

In the event, Alice Laidlaw became Alice Munro at the age of
twenty, a decision that doesn't appear to have been propelled by
the starry-eyed dictates of romance so much as by the brute exigencies of carnal need. "You got married," she points out, "to
have sex. Methods of birth control were too chancy." She was
pregnant a year later—which lapse of time, although abbreviated
by today's standards, she calls "an accomplishment in and of
itself." Although Munro is close today to her three daughters—
who, she says, with a wry smile, get together "mostly to discuss
me"—and is an enraptured grandmother ("I'm crazy about little
kids," she says. "I used to be cooler about them"), she candidly
admits to an ever-present ambivalence about the maternal role,
which she saw as foisted upon her by the expectations of her

time, rather than actively chosen. "I never had the longing to have children," she muses. Munro's oldest daughter, Sheila, herself a writer, has published a bittersweet memoir, *Lives of Mothers and Daughters*, in which her mother appears somewhat distant and not beyond applying a wooden spoon for disciplinary purposes. I ask Munro about her feelings regarding the book. Astonishing me once again with her readiness to implicate herself—I have no doubt that in a court of law, Munro, who happily owns up to having "no moral scruples," would be her own worst witness for the defense—she concedes that Sheila might not have received her best efforts. "She wasn't the utter joy of my life she might have been. I was emotionally more open to the second."

Munro left her marriage when she was in her early forties and moved to London, Ontario, with her two younger daughters, Jenny and Andrea. In 1974, she took a yearlong academic appointment at the University of Western Ontario, where she encountered Gerald Fremlin for the first time since they had been students there together. She says that she considers herself "enormously lucky" in both of her spouses and is "eternally grateful" to her first husband, who has also remarried, for believing in her writing enough to let her attend to it in the hours she had "left over from my duties." ("Such a stroke of luck," she exclaims, although whether she is being entirely ingenuous or not, I can't tell for sure. "In that time!")

Jim Munro, who came from a higher and more aspiring class than the writer's family and owns Munro's Books, one of Canada's best bookstores, was also responsible for getting her away from her suffocating hometown. "None of the boys liked me," she notes, without a trace of self-pity. "I was nice looking, but they left me alone. I would have been so unhappy if I had married one of the boys I went to high school with." She then adds, quoting Fremlin with the slightly wicked half smile that accompanies all her best anecdotes: "My husband always says that if I hadn't gotten out in time, I would have developed into a sad character out of a New England novel. I would have become the old maid who walked into town because she never learned to drive and had no sexual life and lived with her parents until they died."

Alice Munro's childhood, which she has drawn on heavily in her fiction, was a demanding, hardscrabble one. If not quite Dickensian in its lack of privilege, neither were her Scottish and Canadian bloodlines conducive to encouraging the overt "look at me" egotism that gifted writers-in-the-making are sometimes indulged in; indeed, her origins go far toward explaining her unease with directly claiming the spotlight. When I tell her that her much-praised modesty strikes me as a canny form of protective coloration to keep other people's envy at bay, she nods her head in agreement. "I'm frightened of being overvalued," she explains. "Someone will shoot you down. Being a writer is a shameful thing. It's always pushing out your version. I try to correct for this."

Munro, the oldest of three siblings, grew up in the heavily Scottish-Irish farming community of Wingham, Ontario, a town twenty-odd miles from where she currently lives. She did well at school "as a way of distinguishing myself," but as in the fictional town of Jubilee in her stories, limited expectations and a pervasive self-effacing reticence were the order of the day. "We were encouraged to be practical above everything," Munro explains. "In the social background I came from, people never asked, 'Am I happy?' Self-fulfillment wasn't a concept."

Her family were outsiders on all counts: temperamentally, socially, and geographically. Her father was an unsuccessful silver-fox breeder, and the family lived on the outskirts of town in what Munro has described as a "kind of little ghetto where all the bootleggers and prostitutes and hangers-on lived. It was a community of outcasts. I had that feeling about myself." (Although she wasn't aware of his deep literary interest growing up, her father would turn out to harbor writerly ambitions of his own, which expressed themselves in the form of a novel he wrote that was published shortly after he died. "His book was the last thing we talked about," she says, sounding quietly victorious.)

Munro credits her mother, who haunts her fiction like the most persistent and poignant of ghosts, with having had "great pride in me when I was young." The risk-taking gene that enabled Munro to spring for the precarious rewards of the writing life must also have originated with her. Having married at thirty after carving out an independent existence for herself as a schoolteacher, her mother seems always to have yearned for more psychologically and financially luxuriant vistas. Much like the mother of the narrator Del, in *Lives of Girls and Women*, Munro's most autobiographical work, Munro's mother entertained advanced ideas about the role of women outside the home that strayed beyond the closed-in, orderly universe of Wingham, where, as in Jubilee, "the clean, reproachful smell of wax and lemons" ruled over more free-floating ambitions. (These advanced ideas did not include ones on the subject of sex, which Munro's mother apparently viewed with unmitigated distaste.)

When Munro was still an adolescent, in what appears to have been the defining emotional circumstance of her young life, her mother began to suffer from a welter of enfeebling and mortifying symptoms that would eventually be diagnosed as Parkinson's. It fell to Munro, as the oldest, to keep the household running from the age of twelve or thirteen on, an experience that both toughened her and damaged her relationship with her mother, bringing in its wake the deep sense of regret that appears and reappears in her stories. "My mother's illness frightened me so much," she admits, "that I couldn't identify with her. I learned to be capable simply because I had to be." Munro admits to feeling guilt about having "emotionally abandoned" her mother during her long decline; she didn't go home to see her for the last two years before she died. Whereas these daunting circumstances might have trampled the fighting spirit of a weaker girl, in Munro's case they served to fuel a writerly sense of marginalization and a conviction that she was cut out for different things, even if not always by her own choice: "I was a person who didn't fit anywhere. I always felt I'd kind of get out."

And "kind of get out" Munro did, with a vengeance. But unlike her compatriot, the writer Mavis Gallant, who left her unhappy

young self permanently behind in Montreal when she immigrated to Paris in 1950, Munro escaped the confinements of her
origins via a less external distancing but, it could be argued, an
even more radical route. It took, I would suggest, the form of
an internal rebellion—one that went against the inhibiting strictures of both her upbringing and her chosen vocation. In her
own slyly and unnoisily subversive fashion, Munro has broken
new ground in terms of her subject matter, which is often close
to raunchy in its sexual frankness, and in her allegiance to the
short-story form as a vehicle for sustained narrative expression.
Three interlinked stories in *Runaway*—"Chance," "Soon," and
"Silence"—are proof that she continues to do just that. The stories follow a character named Juliet from the time she is a gawky
twenty-one-year-old girl in 1965 with a graduate degree in classics, which she fears may compromise her chances on the marriage market, through three decades to where they leave her off,
short of money, still studying "the old Greeks," permanently estranged from Penelope, the "bright but not bookish" daughter
she had out of wedlock.

The thirty-odd years that are covered in this trilogy is kid's
stuff compared with the chronological leapfrogging Munro has
done in the past—in, say, "A Wilderness Station," where she strad-
dled more than a century in the space of thirty pages. "I write
the story I want to read," she says, as straightforward a literary
credo as has ever been expressed. "I do not feel responsible to my
readers or my material. I know how hard it is to get anything
to work right. Every story is a triumph, and then I think, 'Now I
can relax. I've done it; I've got it out.'" As for Munro's playing
fast and loose with the genre, it is an issue critics have raised
from the start. "Whether Alice Munro's 'The Beggar Maid' is a
collection of stories or a new kind of novel, I'm not quite sure,"
the critic John Gardner wrote, "but whatever it is, it's wonderful."

"I've tried to write novels," Munro says, sounding slightly an-
noyed with her own intractable methods. "They turn into strange,
hybrid stories." And then an almost imperceptible note of defiance enters the conversation, as though she were having an argument with the powers that be, whoever they be—with all those

who would tell her how to behave or how to write: "I haven't read a novel that I didn't think couldn't have been a better story," she says. "I still go into bookstores and look at how few pages you can get away with in a novel. I actually stand there, deducting the white pages in between and adding up the number on my fingers. Do you think you can get away with 110?"

It is five on the same Saturday afternoon in Clinton. In search of more clues to the psychological whereabouts of this most autobiographical but personally elusive of writers, I stroll around to the back of the narrow white Carpenter Gothic house, with a blue roof and brown wood shutters, where Munro lives. I am snooping around at her express invitation. She and her husband, who arrived to pick her up at the end of our lunch, wanting to know immediately how much we had had to drink, are out shopping for groceries. Her offer of an unguided tour of her unoccupied premises struck me as a consolation prize of sorts for having come all this way and never getting past the front door, but I decide to take her up on it in my best investigative-reporter role. I cast a sweeping eye over the side porch, furnished with a round table and humble plastic chairs, and take in the jumble of small ceramic and wood animals on a windowsill. Then I concentrate on channeling my inner Miss Marple, trying to glean potentially vital information by studying the couple's expansive five acres of garden, taking vague but assiduous notes. "Peaceful birdsong," I note. All I lack is a microscope—and a working knowledge of flora and fauna. Munro has described a big row of walnut trees, but I wonder whether all the trees—there are quite a few—are walnut. Maybe some of them are birch or spruce? "Old trees," I scribble.

Otherwise, everything in the garden is just as she has described it to me: the large pond, the railroad track beyond the hedges, and the "visually witty" touches Fremlin has provided in the way of scattered homemade objets d'art. An old-fashioned claw-footed bathtub lies tilted on its side against a tree trunk; it has been painted to resemble a Holstein cow, then provided with a pair of rusting propeller-like ears. Elsewhere a weather vane has been erected on an old striped barber pole. Munro claims responsibility only for the flowers, characterizing them as the kind favored by casual gardeners like herself. "They plant things," she explains, "and say, 'You're on your own.'"

I wander around in the growing shadows, musing on why Munro seems to feel so strongly about her garden and why it seemed so important for me to see it, when suddenly it strikes me: These trees and rocks and flowers and pieces of sculpture compose a whimsical sanctuary, speaking the private language of insider jokes and family history. It is, if you will, a place that is both imaginary and concrete, bringing together the writer's need to soar beyond reality with her down-to-earth upbringing. Here, tucked away on the corner of a quiet street of modest porch-lined houses in a universe far away from the red-hot literary center, lies an enchanted garden that is Alice Munro's clandestine room of her own.

THAT BRITISH DAME

(MARGARET DRABBLE)

2009

Let us begin as Margaret Drabble might begin one of her novels, by setting the scene. (And, because this is in part a tale of literary influences, let us begin as well with apologies to Virginia Woolf, who mocked the Edwardian novelists for just such hopelessly materialist renderings. "They have given us a house," she declared, "in the hope that we may be able to deduce the human beings who live there.") Picture, then, an overcast Saturday afternoon in England in mid-July, the sort of weather about which the British are constantly on the defensive. The writer, who has recently turned seventy, leads the visiting journalist into the living room of the country house that she shares with her husband, the eminent biographer Michael Holroyd, tucked away on its very own hillside in tiny Porlock Weir at the tail end of Somerset.

The view looks northward across the Bristol Channel to Wales, and the air rings with the sound of cawing seagulls. The three of us have just come from an excellent lunch down the road at a little hotel that Drabble and Holroyd treat like a closely guarded secret. While her husband repairs to watch cricket in their cozy TV room with its striped curtains and tightly patterned wallpaper, Drabble shows me the room that Holroyd uses for writing; it is impressively large and light filled, with sloping glass ceilings, and stands in stark contrast to her own basement office, which is damp and dark but has the one advantage of looking out on the garden. It is in the garden that she seems most in her element—as anyone who has read a Drabble novel knows, she is a connoisseur of flowers and plants—and after a brief tour we settle ourselves down on comfortable couches in the living room. We proceed to talk for the next two hours about matters large and small, from Drabble's views on housework ("It's good exercise—you can run up and down stairs with the Hoover, it doesn't do you any harm") to feminism ("I don't think women have a fair share yet, but I don't see writing novels along that agenda") to her famously vexed relationship with her older sister, the novelist A. S. Byatt ("The only book of mine that she said she liked was *The Waterfall*—it could've been because it was more experimental").

Drabble, who has been writing continuously for almost five decades, was made a dame of the British Empire in 2008 for her contributions to contemporary English literature—the year after her husband was knighted for similar service—and the couple's house is everything you might imagine a residence of two formidable literary creatures to be. It is a kind of Bloomsburyian vision of whimsy and cultivation, with rooms painted different colors— mint green, rose, lilac, and Tuscan yellow—and faded rugs, books, and paintings everywhere you look. A Chinese-checkers board and copies of *The Coleridge Bulletin* and *The Bookseller* occupy a round coffee table; across the way is a pink recliner adorned with a handwritten sign reading, "Do Not Sit" ("so the grandchildren won't destroy it").

As I assess the room, my eye is drawn to an elaborate, partly done jigsaw puzzle of van Gogh's *Irises* that is laid out on a mahogany folding table. It was on this table that Drabble would do jigsaws with her "auntie Phyl," a "stroppy" woman who, for the last fifteen years of her life, made annual summer visits to her niece at Porlock Weir. She is the heroine-of-sorts of Drabble's memoir-of-sorts, due out September 16, called, with a nod to Henry James, *The Pattern in the Carpet: A Personal History with Jigsaws.* Doing jigsaw puzzles with her aunt—she continues to do them to this day as "one of my strategies to defeat melancholy and avoid laments"—was also a part of Drabble's childhood, which she here excavates selectively, in an effort to rescue its brighter aspects. "Many of the happier times of my childhood I owe to her," Drabble writes, "and although I often tried to tell her this, she was not much of a one for compliments or emotional declarations. She did not know how to deal with them."

Out of memories of her aunt and of childhood visits to Bryn, her grandmother's redbrick Georgian farmhouse where Auntie Phyl lived as an unmarried daughter and taught her niece "to peg rugs, and to sew, and to do French knitting, and to make lavender bags, and to thread bead necklaces, and to bake rock cakes and coconut fingers, and to play patience," Drabble has constructed an oblique but absorbing account of her early life—albeit one that by American standards is grievously lacking in self-disclosure. "I didn't want to write a memoir," she explains, "because it would annoy too many people. I thought I'd infiltrate bits of memoir into the jigsaw book." Then again, as Drabble notes, "the English have a reputation for being very reticent. I was very conscious of what I left out. I don't think any English person would be as confessional as Philip Roth." Penelope Lively, the English novelist, who is a longtime admirer of Drabble's and doesn't approve of what she calls "the vogue for 'misery memoirs,'" agrees with this assessment. "We're less confessional," she notes. "We create lacework."

What is certain is that in *The Pattern in the Carpet*, Drabble bypasses both chronology and raw autobiographical revelation for a more meandering approach that touches briefly on family pathology and private pain as it crisscrosses the centuries and unfolds the microhistory of jigsaw puzzles, an English invention, circa 1767. This is not the first of Drabble's books to allude to the writer's difficult past—her 2001 novel, *The Peppered Moth*, was a fictionalized portrait of her unhappy mother, and there are autobiographical elements in many of her novels—but it is the first time she has written at length about herself "without," as she puts it, "the veil of fiction." On the other hand, although Drabble is a prolific fiction writer, having produced seventeen novels to date, she has never confined herself to one genre. She has written biographies of Arnold Bennett and Angus Wilson, as well as literary and social histories of modern Britain, and took on the massive task of editing the fifth and sixth editions of *The Oxford Companion to English Literature*.

I'd been fascinated by Drabble ever since coming upon her deft early novels in my twenties and discovering that she not only had already published five novels in *her* twenties but had somehow also managed to be a wife, a mother, and, from the sound of it, a good cook as well. ("I'm a very agitated cook," Drabble insists. "But I can provide a good meal, yes.") By her mid-thirties she was divorced and raising three children on her own (she separated from her first husband, Clive Swift, in the early 1970s and married Holroyd a decade later), yet she continued to write novels, this time of a different and more ambitious order than her first efforts. In doing so, she stood for the writer not as a special case—a neurotic creature always on the verge of a nervous breakdown—but as a hyper-competent Everywoman adroitly running her life. There was something admirably plucky about her heroines; they had an efficient way about them even when they were at their most defeated, and the same, I gathered, could be said of Drabble herself. She struck me as someone who had hewed to the line of her own ambition without sacrificing crucial pieces of her feminine identity along the way.

"We remind ourselves," Carolyn Heilbrun, the critic and novelist, once observed, "that of the great women writers, most have been unmarried, and those who have written in the state of wedlock have done so in peaceful kingdoms guarded by devoted husbands. Few have had children." So how did Drabble pull it off? How did she handle it all—marriage, divorce, children, a vocation dear to her heart, success, the envy of others, the specter of aging? She had always offered direction through her work, from the reader-friendly early books that made her reputation to the massively intelligent and almost bristlingly informed novels she produced from the 1970s on. Although she must have suffered from the anxiety and despair that she passed on to some of her characters, she seemed uniquely capable of rising to the next occasion on behalf of her fiction—whether it be shifting social priorities, as in *The Ice Age*, or the changing expectations of a woman no longer in the prime of her life, as in *The Sea Lady*—and becoming more expansive, more embracing of the larger world in the process.

Like Doris Lessing (whom she counts among her good friends) and—to pick someone on this side of the Atlantic—Anne Tyler, Drabble has been writing steadily for years, and like them she is beyond trends, seemingly immune to the whole business of literary marketing. Perhaps this above-the-fray aspect could help to explain what, to me, is her puzzling lack of presence in America, at least these days, when she is no longer delivering the kind of renegade news about the domestic life that she did when her first novel, *A Summer Bird-Cage*, was picked out of a publishing-house slush pile in its brown paper parcel by a discerning reader ("I sent it to George Weidenfeld," Drabble explains, "because he published Saul Bellow") and appeared in 1963 to general acclaim.

Drabble remained a well-known literary name throughout the next two decades, even as her novels became more complex and wide-ranging in their concerns. In 1980, after the publication of her ninth novel, *The Middle Ground*, *People* magazine profiled her glowingly, noting that she had been compared to Jane Austen and Virginia Woolf—and could just as well have noted that she had also been compared to Charles Dickens, George Eliot, and Evelyn Waugh. But somewhere along the way—between her dense and somewhat insular trilogy of a postimperial, post-industrial 1980s England, her seven-year interlude working on the *Oxford Companion*, and the 1990 publication of A. S. Byatt's humdinger of a novel, *Possession*—Drabble appears to have been gently sidelined. No one's denying that her books merit critical attention or that she isn't in some way a figure to conjure with, but somehow the excitement that brews around certain writers, even when there are disappointments in their work (as there have been in Drabble's), isn't quite there. And yet, in her own quiet, get-it-done fashion, Drabble has been excitingly taking risks all her creative life, right up to her latest book, in which she audaciously both does and doesn't deliver up a personal narrative, admitting in her foreword that she is "not sure what [this book] is."

What she is, I think, is nothing less than a British prodigy, dedicated to the delineation of the provisional, the tentative, the nontriumphant—what life is rather than what it might be. But she is hard to pin down precisely because of her many-faceted angles as a writer, her refusal to lend herself to packaging as either a feminist or a throwback to a more "old-fashioned," exterior sort of storyteller. Although Drabble's consistent attention to the passing sociopolitical scene has been essential to the landscape of her novels since *The Needle's Eye*—her characters discuss multiculturalism, the economy, and global warming the way characters in less heady novels might discuss playdates or love affairs gone wrong—she is equally interested in exploring her protagonists' interior lives. Her literary influences are hybrid; she is a confirmed admirer of F. R. Leavis, the conservative Cambridge professor who established the pristine "Great Tradition" of the English novel in the 1950s, with its focus on the novel as a moral mirror, while at the same time sharing Arnold Bennett's "great respect for ordinary life and ordinary people." (Leavis thought Bennett to be "beneath contempt.") When you add to that her openness to brazen postmodernist techniques like bossily intruding into the story and resisting the "closure" of neat endings, it's small wonder that she evades being categorized except as herself.

My first encounter with Drabble (who is known as Maggie to her friends and family) and Holroyd occurred several days before my visit to Somerset, at the annual Ways with Words literary festival at Dartington Hall in Devon, about a two-hour drive from their country house. (The couple also share a home in Notting Hill in London, after many years of maintaining separate residences.) Each of them was on the roster of speakers—she to talk about her memoir, which was published in England to mostly admiring reviews, and he to speak about his latest book, an account of the nineteenth-century theatrical careers of Ellen Terry and Henry Irving. We arranged to meet in the reception area, and I immediately picked out Drabble from the back, although we had never crossed paths before. She was wearing a tan hooded anorak and a pair of trousers; her hair was cut in the guileless Dutch-boy style that was familiar to me from two decades of author photographs, and there was something compelling—a kind of not-quite-regal bearing—that singled her out. Holroyd, a tall, cerebral-looking man who dresses with a witty flair suggestive of a Ronald Firbank character, recently came through a two-year battle with cancer and appeared to depend on Drabble for navigation. "Do you want me to answer or should you?" he asked about a form they were supposed to fill out.

Drabble and I arranged to have a quick drink before she was to help Holroyd "get ready for his 'show.'" (Holroyd prepares his talks ahead of time, while Drabble prefers to speak off the cuff.) When we met later at a wood-paneled pub, she had changed into a bright yellow cardigan and gray flannels and was wearing a dab of rosy lipstick. With her slim build, clear blue eyes, and soft brown hair barely tinged with gray, it is still possible to glimpse in her the poised, chic young woman who captured the imagination of so many of her generation when she published her first clutch of novels, starting at the age of twenty-three. ("She was a terrific figure in those days, the '60s," Hilary Spurling, the biographer, recalls. "She became enormously famous very young. People read huge amounts of her stuff. She was both glamorous and 'in.' I remember her wearing those triangular dresses from Mary Quant.")

Unlike many celebrated types, Drabble seems genuinely modest—very much a person who "backs into the limelight," as Holroyd describes it to me. "She's shy of publicity," he explains. "She's afraid that it will stimulate envy or competition: 'Who is the overrated writer getting all this attention?'" Drabble also evinces a curiosity about whomever she happens to find herself with, and for the first few minutes of our conversation I find I am the one being graciously interviewed rather than vice versa. It is a way of avoiding the spotlight, to be sure, of maintaining her reserve while not seeming to be impolite, but it is also a way of establishing parity and thus putting the other person at ease. When I turned the conversation back to her and noted how patient she was with a woman she didn't know who had just approached her to expound her theory of jigsaw puzzles (or possibly life), Drabble explained that she likes jigsaw puzzles because "they're a neutral subject, like the weather." It is easy to mistake a comment like this for a lack of passion, but it struck me as an extension of inbred English discretion around the presumption of intimacy.

We touched on her relationship with her sister—Drabble has never read Byatt's *Babel Tower* but confided that when *Possession* was up for the Booker, she bet some money on it and won—and then we moved on to the topic of money itself, which is never far from the surface in Drabble's novels as an irritant or, more rarely, a facilitator. "So few people think they have enough," she said. "I think as long as I don't have to worry about the taxi meter, I'm fine." Drabble is an echt, old-line Social Democrat, but she went on to sound like the champagne socialist she sometimes can be taken for, adding, "I'm interested in what it's like *not* to have money." It is a theme she explored in what is, to my mind, her most powerful novel, *The Needle's Eye*, where money or the lack of it fuels the plot and a main character ventures to give away her inheritance.

Drabble's family was first-generation bourgeois, one foothold removed from working class. She grew up in Sheffield, Yorkshire, the second of four gifted and driven siblings, in an atmosphere shaped by Quaker values, with their emphasis on probity and the common good. Her mother and father were the first in their families to attend university—both at Cambridge, both on scholarship. Her father, John Drabble, who went on to become a barrister and a county-court judge, was, according to his daughter, a remote but loving figure. Her mother, Marie Bloor, was a different matter altogether—a source of conflict and strife as well as the prime mover behind her children's wish to excel. Bloor attended Newnham College, from which all three of her daughters would eventually graduate. (Aside from Byatt, Drabble has a younger sister, Helen, who is an art historian, and a much younger brother, Richard, who is a barrister.) "She really wanted to be an English teacher," Drabble explained. "She enjoyed grammar and could explain a poem, but in those days that was not what people did. She would have been happier with a career, but it didn't happen that way."

Bloor's sense of thwarted ambition and acute class anxiety led her to move further and further inside herself, clinging to the house and projecting her feelings of frustration and disappointment outward. In the process she stoked the keen competitive spirit that would ripen over the years into a sense of rivalry between her two older daughters. (In *Margaret Drabble: A Reader's Guide*, Marie Bloor is quoted as saying that "Susan"—the name by which A. S. Byatt was known—"resented the birth of a second child, and Margaret was quite old before she realized that Susan didn't like her.") At the same time, Drabble seems to have been acutely aware that her mother envied her children's success. "She got jealous when we went out and did things," Drabble said. "Something in her didn't like us to have a fuller life than she did." Drabble, who was her mother's acknowledged favorite, also crossed swords with her. "Mum could fight back better," observes Becky Swift, Drabble's forty-five-year-old daughter, who runs a literary consulting firm in London. "She was always feisty."

Curiously enough, for such a committed scribbler, Drabble didn't always want to be a writer. Her original ambition, formed at Cambridge, where she shone academically and took part in dramatic productions, was to be an actress. This idea was scuttled not long after she married Clive Swift, an aspiring actor, in June 1960 at the age of twenty-one. Swift was Jewish and grew up in mercantile Liverpool (his father sold furniture)—a far cry from Drabble's dour Yorkshire roots. ("There was a certain kind of coldness about the Drabbles," Swift observed.) He was bar mitzvahed, and the family went to an Orthodox synagogue on Yom Kippur, but, as he hastened to assure me in a phone call, "We were very liberal—we weren't Zionists or anything." Drabble seems to have fallen in love as much with Swift's generous and warmhearted family—whom she refers to as "adorable" to this day—as with the man himself. The couple divorced for what Drabble calls "the usual reasons—career divergence, stupid rows, both of us having affairs." Drabble grows starry-eyed when recounting her exposure to the hothouse tribalism of the Swifts, different as it was from the undemonstrative style she had been used to at home: "I did think this was the great escape. I loved the gefilte fish, the chicken soup, the way they hugged you."

The couple spent the first years of their marriage in Stratford-on-Avon as members of the Royal Shakespeare Company, where Drabble understudied actresses like Vanessa Redgrave and Judi Dench. When she became pregnant with their first child, however, she gave up on her acting career and turned to writing. As Drabble tells it, the shift to writing sounds suspiciously easy. She didn't know anyone in Stratford, and she was alone most evenings while her husband was out socializing, so, presto, she "sat down and wrote a book." It is, I suspect, a tribute to the dauntingly strong will that thrums beneath the overtly uncompetitive image she projects. "I don't like to be beaten by things," Drabble admitted, almost uneasily. "It's another go, another day." (Drabble's conflict about her own ambition is such that in recent years she has refused to be put up for a Booker Prize. Her sister, meanwhile, has been nominated for her second Booker for *The Children's Book*, due out in the United States in October.)

In becoming a writer, Drabble was, consciously or not, trespassing on the literary turf that had appeared to be her sister's domain. "The original setup," says Becky Swift, alluding to the decades-long tension between her mother and her aunt, "was that the pretty sister was going to act—and then she turns to the things Antonia always wanted to do and becomes a bestseller." Tellingly enough, Drabble's first novel, *A Summer Bird-Cage*, revolved around the differing destinies of two sisters, the elder one of whom is beautiful and mercenary and the younger of whom is more vulnerable but ultimately more fulfilled. Byatt would have her own back with her second novel, *The Game*, published in 1967, in which one sister drives the other one to suicide. Drabble openly admits to not liking it, "especially since the murderer was me," and still sounds stung, all these years later, despite the fact that her sister called her up after it came out and apologized. (Byatt declined to be interviewed for this article.)

Narrated in a casually perceptive, nervy first-person voice, *A Summer Bird-Cage* laid out what would become recognizable

Drabble territory in its taking for granted a certain level of intelligence and education in its female characters; it also demonstrated an unexpected candor about sex, abortion, career-versus-motherhood conflicts, and the glaring insufficiencies of married life. Drabble recalls that she was very much influenced early on by *The Group*, by Mary McCarthy. "It meant a lot to me," she said. "It was about growing up as a woman. I began making it up for myself in the beginning, then I looked around and saw Fay Weldon, Nell Dunn, Edna O'Brien, and Sylvia Plath. We were all living the same kind of lives, on our own, with children."

Her aura of self-sufficiency in the literary realm, as in others, is inescapable. (She told me that she "quite enjoyed" being by herself after her divorce, adding, "I didn't think I'd remarry.") All the same, it is almost impossible from our current vantage point to understand just how freeing Drabble's tone in those first novels actually was. Drabble's early works were nothing less than "startling," says Carmen Callil, who founded Virago Press and ran the publishing company Chatto & Windus from 1982 to 1994. "They were about clever women having children and love affairs but straining at the leash. Those first women were spiky women, good mothers who loved being in love and loved men but were sort of fed up much of the time."

Drabble's talent for evoking the mixed reality of women's lives, for capturing the practical drudgery of child care while also tuning in to the unfettered aspirations that a higher education and a more developed sense of autonomy had created, brought her a loyal readership as well as a high profile. "It's a gift she has," Hilary Spurling says. "She embodies, expresses, and pins down something everybody feels, but she is often the first person to say it. Those early novels were about how to live a life that was not purely domestic—feminism before the letter." Victoria Glendinning, a novelist and biographer who remembers seeing Drabble at "fantastic, lavish parties" in the 1970s before becoming friends with her, concurs: "She was writing for people like me—people in modern society who also had brains. I don't think anybody wrote like that before, not with that sort of intelligence and empathy. Her books accompanied our lives."

When I asked Drabble whether she kept up with the women writers who tackle such topics today in novels and memoirs, she seemed slightly weary of the question and its implicit suggestion that she's old hat, when the reality is that she got there first. "'My mother loved your books' is a line I get a lot," she said, flashing a wry smile. "There's a younger generation that I don't read so much. I feel I know about that character—I've got colicky children, I'm divorced, juggling mothering and a career. There's a movement about women hating their children. They don't know anyone wrote about it before . . . Doris Lessing would say that's how it should be: you put an idea out there, and other people pick it up."

One theme that has absorbed Drabble since the beginning is the extent to which choice can affect your destiny. Can we, that is, unmake our beginnings, or are we always acting willy-nilly on the promptings of the past? Are our individual stories foretold, or do we create them as we go along? You sense that, willed into shape as her own life is—she went from being a timid, unhappy girl with a stutter to someone who can disarm a crowd of four hundred—she is always cognizant of those, like her mother, who don't make it out, who are felled by circumstance. "I married at twenty-one," she said, "which was very wise. I left home. I knew I had to get away."

In *The Pattern in the Carpet*, Drabble writes about her fear of inheriting a legacy of misery: "My mother was seriously depressed for much of her later life, and her depression oppressed and infected me, or so I have come to believe." Although Drabble uses a SAD lamp in the winter to mimic natural sunlight, which cheers her up, and was briefly in therapy, she nonetheless is convinced that depression can have a positive as well as a negative effect. "My mother used it as a weapon to manipulate others," she said, as the afternoon wore on and the sky grew darker outside the living room windows in Porlock Weir. "It took the form of anger." Her own bouts seem to feed her art—"happy and buoyant don't force you into action on the page; you go shopping when you're up"—and also force her to reassess things. "It's useful," she pointed out, "for stripping off ways of getting through life that prevent you from having to think."

These days Drabble writes best in the mornings, on her own in Porlock Weir. She suggested in an interview last spring that she was done with novels, but she insisted to me that she didn't really mean it. "I only said that to see what it sounded like," she said. "I felt quite strongly that I wasn't in a frame of mind to write fiction—it was connected with Michael's illness, which absorbed all my energy. I couldn't get away from it in a way that he could. He could concentrate, but I couldn't. A man is much more able to make work a priority. Women have a tendency to allow other considerations weight. Doing jigsaws was a refuge and writing the jigsaw book an escape." So maybe Drabble isn't quite the expert juggler in her own mind that I have envisioned her as being after all.

"As I get older," Drabble confided, moments before Holroyd came in to collect me for the drive to Taunton, where I would catch the train to London, "I do fear my physical world is getting thinner. When I was younger, I led multiple lives. When I'm here in Porlock, everything flows in again. It doesn't matter if I'm thinning out . . . The trees are full, the sea is full, and I am getting more ghostly. The physical world is taking over and absorbing me, and eventually my ashes will be scattered in the churchyard." And then, taking her aptitude for seeing beyond the glare of self-interest—beyond the moment's buzz—to its natural extension, she muses unblinkingly on the inevitable void that awaits even those who fill the world with words: "My being the center has ceased to be of importance."

SISTER ACT

(BETTY FRIEDAN)

1999

In our ever-mutating cultural landscape, it's almost impossible to keep track of the way movements (women's lib) yield to counter-movements ("power" feminism without special pleading), which yield to savvy coeds with book contracts for reactionary theses (the new modesty), which yield to fashion trends (geisha chic). Betty Friedan? Her name comes at us like a far-off echo—as though she were a suffragette fighting for the right to wear bloomers instead of the woman who, not all that long ago, presided over the birth of modern feminism. Before there was Wendy Shalit or Katie Roiphe or Naomi Wolf or Susan Faludi, before Germaine Greer propounded her theater-of-ideas version of female virility or Gloria Steinem flashed her come-fly-with-me smile on magazine covers, Friedan cast her eye over a nation of suburban housewives and determined that inside their well-kept but under-occupied lives they were going bonkers.

It was in 1963, the tail end of the quiescent 1950s, that Friedan burst forth with *The Feminine Mystique*—the same year that Steinem, then an un-politicized girl around town, published *The Beach Book*, which sought to impart frilly wisdom about suntans and rich men. ("A landing party from Aristotle Onassis's yacht has just come ashore to ask you to join them. You say no.") Friedan's book had begun as a questionnaire circulated at her fifteenth Smith College reunion (she was class of 1942), and after five years of work it metamorphosed into an expansive, sometimes overwrought argument with what she viewed as the Donna Reed culture of her time. Half sociological tract and half impassioned manifesto, *The Feminine Mystique* took on "the problem that has no name"—an amorphous malaise that afflicted college-educated American women, who smothered their children with attention, had unrealistic expectations of their husbands, and then sought to assuage their sense of quiet desperation by downing pills or having joyless extramarital affairs. That, she charged, was what came of being indoctrinated into society's rigid and largely unconscious notions of femininity.

After pages and pages of deconstructing the fluffy content of women's magazines (where the malaise "is solved either by dyeing one's hair blonde or by having another baby"), citing gloomy statistics and psychological surveys, Friedan moved to define the problem in the largest possible terms, as "simply the fact that American women are kept from growing to their full human capacities." The book, which had a first printing of three thousand copies, went on to become the No. 1 bestselling nonfiction paperback of 1964. Its author, in turn, became a celebrity, appearing on the then–newly born television talk shows, and an effective crusader, giving speeches around the country. In the summer of 1966, Friedan co-founded the National Organization for Women—known by its acronym, NOW—and provided her supporters with a serious platform from which to shake up the status quo.

These days, it is hard to remember that Friedan was the one who got a revolution going—that it was she who fought for equal pay, equal rights, day care, and legal abortion, so that other women could go on to examine their cervixes in consciousness-raising groups and muse wishfully on prehistoric matriarchies in the pages of *Ms.* For women under forty—the "I'm not a feminist, but . . ." generation—who are aware that Friedan was important but are vague about her exact contribution, she is a shadowy presence, an icon-without-portfolio. Given her age (she is seventy-eight) and our short collective memory, this isn't so remarkable.

What is surprising, though, is how quickly she was pushed to the sidelines of the very movement she had founded. In 1972, when the fledgling National Women's Political Caucus gathered at the Democratic National Convention in Miami Beach, Friedan lost her bid to be the official spokeswoman for the cause. Somewhere along the way, between the first stirrings of liberal activism and the increasingly radical, anti-male, and pro-lesbian tone that came to mark the women's movement as it gained momentum in the early 1970s, Friedan was edged out of the spotlight in favor of other leaders—notably, Steinem and, briefly, Bella Abzug. "The cameras are clicking at Gloria," Nora Ephron observed in a gimlet-eyed account of the Miami Beach gathering that she wrote for *Esquire*, "and Bella has swept in, trailed by a vortex of television crews, and there is Betty, off to the side, just slightly out of frame."

How and why did this happen? And what does it suggest about the internecine conflict that seemed to fracture the women's movement at the very moment of its ascent? The enigma of Friedan's rapid eclipse is at the heart of Judith Hennessee's new biography, *Betty Friedan: Her Life*. It is a tale that hangs on a visibly unfixed nose, a tendency to yell, a commitment to broad-based social change rather than identity politics, and a refusal to demonize family and the male sex. (For the record, right after finishing *The Feminine Mystique*, Friedan considered getting a nose job, but she was concerned that the operation would change her signature gravelly voice.)

She was born Bettye Naomi Goldstein in 1921, a year after women were given the vote, and grew up in Peoria, Illinois, where her family lived in a three-story redbrick house in the best part of town. Though the Goldsteins were assimilated, they could not join the restricted Peoria Country Club, and socialized mainly with other Jews. Betty's mother, Miriam, liked to entertain and to fuss with her appearance; her father, Harry, who owned a jewelry store, enjoyed challenging his children intellectually. "He would pose math problems, which Betty solved in an instant, and discuss the political issues of the day," Hennessee writes. Betty had inherited her father's temper, and she fought with her critical, perfectionist mother over issues of grooming ("Miriam thought Betty deliberately made herself look like a frump") and personal style ("where Miriam was diplomatic, Betty was blunt; where Miriam was gracious, Betty could barely accept a compliment"). In high school, Betty was passed over for a sorority, and she attributed that to the subtle workings of anti-Semitism rather than to her overbearing personality or her unconventional way of leading with her intellect. Hennessee writes, "The idea of hiding her brains, or at least not featuring them so prominently—of deferring to boys—did not occur to her."

Hennessee somewhat leadenly tries to link Friedan's future difficulties with her early experiences. The trouble Friedan had maintaining her leadership of the movement and, especially, her disdainful treatment of other women are viewed as reenactments of her conflicts with her mother, her rivalries with her younger and prettier sister, Amy, and her sense of herself as an unappreciated outsider. Still, Friedan went off to Smith with no more than the standard allotment of insecurities for a brainy but somewhat homely young girl. Her anxieties manifested themselves mainly in asthma attacks that began to appear in her freshman year, but for the most part she had an abundance of energy and ambition. She majored in psychology and took a lot of writing courses, eventually running the college paper and starting a literary magazine. It was also at Smith that she developed an unsubversive, mink-coat brand of left-leaning politics, which would later be sniffed at by her more radical sisters; she immersed herself in Marxist texts and ran sympathetic stories on behalf of Peoria factory workers and the Smith maids, who went on strike in her senior year.

In 1942, Friedan graduated Phi Beta Kappa and summa cum laude, with a yearlong fellowship to study under the renowned psychologist Erik Erikson at Berkeley. The following spring, she received another fellowship—"the most coveted prize in her field"—which would have enabled her to pursue a PhD. She turned it down, in the ancient (and, I daresay, still flourishing) female belief that the single-minded pursuit of achievement would cut her off from what she described in *The Feminine Mystique* as "the warm center of life"—from marriage and children. In later interviews, she blamed a boyfriend: "He said, 'You can take that fellowship, but you know I'll never get one like it. You know what it will do to us.'" The account may well have been a convenient reconstruction of a more general sense of conflict, but the message she had received was clear: as a woman, you couldn't have both personal and professional fulfillment. Nothing she saw around her—not the friends from college who "just wanted a rich marriage," or the lives of the spinster librarians from her hometown, or the largely unmarried professors at Smith—suggested that it could be otherwise.

Shortly thereafter, Friedan moved to New York and began writing for the Federated Press, a left-wing news agency. She was both eager to "prove herself with men" and sexually forthcoming in her quest for romance. In the spring of 1946, she went on a blind date with Carl Friedan, who was recently out of the army; two months later, Carl moved in with her, and in June 1947 they married. The first of their three children was born in the fall of the following year, and by 1951 Betty Friedan had transformed herself into one of those suburban housewives whose chains she would rattle a decade later with the revelations of *The Feminine Mystique*.

Lured by a co-op nursery and more space, she and Carl, who worked in advertising, moved from a roach-infested Manhattan apartment to Parkway Village in Queens, a garden-apartment development that had been built to house United Nations employees. The Friedans lived a version of the American dream: "They grilled hamburgers on charcoal barbecue grills and dipped their potato chips into the universal dip of the 1950s, sour cream mixed with dried Lipton's Onion Soup. Betty made salad dressing and supervised a maid who cooked." At the same time, both Betty and Carl drank to excess, and their marriage—which persisted for twenty-two years—was tempestuous to the point of physical violence. (Friedan was late to one of the first sit-ins that she organized—in 1969, in the Oak Room of the Plaza hotel, where women were excluded from noon to three—because her bruised face had to be heavily made up before she could appear in public.) She was what would nowadays be called a battered wife, except that she never called herself one and she gave as good as she got.

The trajectory that propelled Friedan from a homebound freelance-writing career—she wrote for *Charm, Parents,* and *Redbook,* among other publications—to the front ranks of "women's lib" is, as often proves to be the case, a story of self-emancipation. The reader senses somewhere between the lines of *The Feminine Mystique* that Friedan is hacking a trail back to the stellar student she once was—the ambitious young woman about to make a bright future in a profession she loved, only to renounce it in favor of a lower-profile, more "female" presence. The glorification of domesticity—shiny floors, insistent married "togetherness," and an overconscientious style of mothering—and the fear of "masculinization" through intellectual development: these were pressures she had struggled against and sometimes yielded to. Her book makes for provocative reading even now, thirty-six years after it was first published. In spite of the far-reaching changes that have taken place, the psychological barriers to women's self-fulfillment that she described continue to exist.

The Feminine Mystique has obvious weaknesses: it is something of a hodgepodge, it owes more to Simone de Beauvoir's *Second Sex* than it concedes, and its style is frequently overheated. (For example, women who adapt to the "housewife state" are likened to concentration camp victims.) It's also, unquestionably, an artifact of its time and place. Some of Friedan's terminology ("the servant problem") and attitudes (she refers to "the homosexuality that is spreading like a murky smog over the American scene") suggest that part of her had remained back in Peoria, at one of her mother's afternoon bridge parties. And although she vehemently attacked the way the media encouraged women to dust, iron, bake, and vacuum away their best years—"Occupation: Housewife" was her derisive term—it was unclear whom she had in mind to take care of the "details of life" when evolved women stopped attending to them, unless it was less evolved women. (Friedan's cavalier disregard for the "minutiae of housework" seems to have informed her own life: Carl Friedan claimed that his wife had "never washed one hundred dishes during twenty years of marriage.") I might add that no one has ever come up with an answer to this problem, and one might wonder whether the busy-hands-at-home empire of Martha Stewart isn't a more insidious and time-consuming version of what *The Feminine Mystique* was railing against.

Whatever the book's limitations, I find it silly to fault its author, as some people do, for not speaking to women of all classes, sexual predilections, and races: ironically, this sort of "inclusive" rhetoric is in part to blame for pushing the women's movement off the main road and into the byways. (In Marcia Cohen's 1988 account *The Sisterhood*, the journalist Susan Brownmiller recalls the days when "the only person who could get up and say something and not be shouted down was a black lesbian single mother on welfare.") Friedan was assuredly writing from and for a particular perspective: the middle-class, white, and heterosexual reader of *McCall's*, who sensed that something was missing but couldn't quite put her finger on it. She knew her audience—"the modern American housewife that I myself was helping to create, writing for the women's magazines"—and she tempered her politics and her ideology to fit its needs. Although many of her convictions arose from her leftism and her early journalistic involvement with labor organizations, it strikes me as an exaggeration to see her, as Daniel Horowitz does in his recent book, *Betty Friedan and the Making of "The Feminine Mystique,"* as a closet Marxist who played down her sympathies to avoid the searchlight of McCarthyism and to gain a place in the mainstream.

Friedan's abiding sense of realpolitik was both her weakness and her strength: rather than overturning the patriarchal order—on Capitol Hill or in the Oak Room—she sought to reposition women within it. "Betty thought attention to such issues as Vietnam and welfare would interfere with the main goal, which was electing women," Hennessee writes. "Her basic issues remained . . . equal pay and equal rights and the situation of ordinary working women." She was never a theoretician, like Kate

Millett (whose *Sexual Politics* gave the movement serious intellectual credentials), or a loony purist, like Ti-Grace Atkinson (whom Friedan pushed out of the presidency of New York NOW after she spoke to the press in support of Valerie Solanas, who had just shot Andy Warhol), or an inflammatory anarchist, like Robin Morgan (who had founded WITCH—Women's International Terrorist Conspiracy from Hell—before going on to become an editor at *Ms.*). As the climate of protest heated up in the 1970s, she kept her sights firmly on the center, even while it failed to hold.

In fact one could argue that Friedan's unwavering commitment to a populist constituency in the face of growing pressure from more radical groups—especially militant lesbians, whom she referred to as "the lavender menace"—is what did her in. "Betty had no patience with the lesbians," Jacqui Ceballos, an early supporter, recalls. "She covered her face with her hands and said, 'I don't want to hear what people do in bed.'" Was this simply provincialism? Or did Friedan foresee that as the movement tried to corral the disenfranchised women at the margins—not just lesbians, but black women—it would alienate the middle-of-the-road Jane Doe she hoped to reach, and feminism would lose its crowd appeal?

There were also personal factors that loosened her grip on power. Friedan yelled when she didn't get her way, and her hunger for publicity was insatiable. "Among those who were disillusioned with her," Hennessee writes, "the standard view of Betty was that of a microphone hog." She displayed "a breathtaking incivility for which she was fiercely resented" and had little patience for the navel-gazing turn that the movement took, scornfully dismissing consciousness-raising as "mental masturbation." She lacked as well Steinem's knack for snappy sound bites that dissed men or marriage. ("We are becoming the men we wanted to marry," and so on.) Nor, being short and chubby and frazzled, did she cut a telegenic figure. The leggy, serenely beautiful interloper who stole Friedan's show—Friedan called her simply "The Hair"—was everything that she wasn't: placating, impersonal to the point of remoteness, a soft touch for underdog causes.

Steinem had, as a fellow activist recalled, "this bubble of untouch-
ability around her," and rather than overtly aspiring to leadership,
she arranged to have it thrust upon her. Steinem won the position of spokeswoman for the National Women's Political Caucus,
the job Friedan had coveted, even though she "said she did not
want it and had deliberately stayed away from the meeting."

Of course, even if Friedan had been Miss Congeniality, she
would have lost out to Steinem, who was the trophy feminist best
able to shill for the movement. For one thing, Steinem had an
ability to communicate the movement's concerns with a casual
note, as though they were no more threatening than T-shirt slogans; for another, men responded to her, no matter what those
slogans were. Friedan attacked Steinem in public and in private,
accusing her as early as 1972 of "ripping off the movement for
personal profit" and continuing to discuss Steinem's "perceived
hypocrisy," as Hennessee puts it, more than twenty years later.
"Here is someone who always dressed beautifully, chic-ly, and all
that," Friedan complained, "and told other women they didn't
have to bother to wear makeup or shave their legs."

Hennessee's account, in its determination to be fair, in true
sisterly fashion, to all sides, sacrifices a chance to offer a trenchant
analysis of the movement's gradual implosion. Friedan's rapid rise
and fall suggests a larger, seemingly inevitable pattern, whereby
the visionary founder, scripting the future, must in time be cast
off as an old fogy, captive to the past. So the integrationists of
the civil rights era—the James Farmers and John Lewises—
would be elbowed aside by their Black Power successors, the
Stokely Carmichaels and Huey Newtons. And Friedan, once the
rampaging polemicist of the picket-fence set, would soon find
herself scorned by the burn-the-house-down types—the Red-
stockings, New York Radical Women, and all the rest. She was
easily caricatured by a newer and angrier generation as a kind of
Joan Crawford of feminism, the aging star pouting in her trailer.
Revolutions, rightly or wrongly, devour their old.

Hennessee steps gingerly around these troublesome points;
she's the proverbial peacemaker, smiling now at the girl with the
golden tresses, who is popular with the boys, and now at the

plainer, smarter girl, whose obvious need to dominate her peers ensures her rejection. One comes away from her book with a sense of too many prima donnas (and their attendant groupies) battling each other for center stage. Meanwhile, the maw of the media grinds busily behind this story, hungry for marketable products, chewing up and spitting out both icons and issues. Friedan was an improbable media product from the start, and Steinem was finally the one who endured, her image resistant to overexposure or criticism. The stature of the movement itself turned out to be more precarious: Steinem's attempts to correct Friedan's bourgeois biases and court the clamorously disenfranchised would prove too radical for the mainstream, too mainstream for the radicals. Hennessee's book nonetheless makes for fairly absorbing reading—not least because it reveals the rancorous underside of sisterhood. The amount of envy and hostility that percolated just beneath the utopian hopes and high-minded principles will not come as a shock to any woman who's ever made it through high school, but all the infighting does give one pause concerning the fairer sex's vaunted reputation for making nice.

It would be convenient, at least when it comes to the writing of cultural history, if the private lives of public figures matched their onstage selves: saintly idealists would invariably be kind to their children; female firebrands would assert themselves at the dinner table; and revolutionaries would be above petty snobberies. Of course, a great part of the allure of reading biographies lies in this very discrepancy between image and reality. "The persona she had developed had taken over the person," Hennessee observes of Friedan. "It protected her from competition, but it also demanded constant care and feeding, separating her from what she truly craved—love and intimacy."

Which brings us to men, who Friedan always insisted were not the enemy but simply part of the equation. Male companionship—a "gentleman friend," in her somewhat quaint phrase—continued to be important to Friedan after her divorce. In *The Second Stage*, published in 1981, she placed men near "the cutting edge" of the next phase of feminism and indicted the first stage of the movement for being too selfish—all of which led some critics to suggest that she was retreating from much of what she'd said in *The Feminine Mystique*. In fact, the notion that men needed to be reeducated, freed from their own mystique, was one she had long advocated.

Still, despite Robert Bly, Sam Keen, and others, the world in its vastness is resistant to change, and now that men have given women greater parity, they seem as leery of female power as ever. The political assuredly isn't personal: at best, the struggle for equality brings about higher wages; at worst, it leaves women stranded without alimony. It sometimes seems that we have merely exchanged one costume for another, aprons for suits, and the results have not always approximated the dream of liberation. Indeed, they often look like the old curses of loneliness and overwork in new guise. To be sure, women are freer to choose who they are and how they wish to connect to others. But a political or social movement that can accommodate the vagaries of personal fulfillment, which are always idiosyncratic and unheeding of the party line, has yet to exist. "People didn't trust her to speak for the group," Steinem complained of Friedan. "She always spoke for herself." It was meant as a reproach, but it could also be read as a tribute to Friedan's irrepressible individuality—and to the elusive nature of female desire. What do women want? Try asking them one at a time.

VI
THE
MATING GAME

LIFE ON A DARE

(SCOTT AND ZELDA FITZGERALD)

1980

In the archives of literary history the files on Scott and Zelda Fitzgerald must be crammed to bursting. His drinking and her madness have become the stuff of legend, of Art colliding with Life, yet we watch wide-eyed as the reel unwinds once again: see the golden-haired couple frolic and then scorch themselves playing too close to the sun. Scott and Zelda intrigue because the scale of their lives was more grand, their triumphs more dazzling, their failures more replete than most of ours will ever be. They created the kind of splash that only the reckless of the race create: Bonnie and Clyde, life on a dare, ending in the Fitzgeralds' case not in bloodshed but in subtle, lingering damage. It is, in a way, incidental that Scott—and Zelda—were writers. He might have painted or fought bulls, except that his occupation gave Scott a chance to document, over and over again, both the "romantic readiness" that Jay Gatsby personified and its gradual erosion. What the author noted most consistently in his characters— "there was something gorgeous about him," he observed of Gatsby, "some heightened sensitivity to the promises of life"— was what he had observed most truly in himself.

Scott Fitzgerald wrote novels that hinge on the conceptually softest of visions—less than visions really, more like glimpses. He was preeminently the poet of withdrawn promise—the green light that winks ever less brightly at the end of Daisy's dock. If there is ultimately something unsatisfying about his work, that may well be because Fitzgerald never ceased to think of life's wreckage in the most boyishly wondrous of terms. He described Zelda to Scottie, their daughter, as "one of the eternal children of this world," yet the phrase applies just as easily to him. When Scott could no longer be a child, when debts piled up and Zelda's mind went off course, he became a drunk. The evidence isn't all in on their marriage, and it looks as if certain questions—such as how talented a writer Zelda was to begin with—will never be solved other than in a partisan spirit, but Scott and Zelda appear to have been more similar than not. They both believed, rather fatally, in what Scott called "the business of creating illusion": "Why don't you come to Tryon?" Zelda wrote in April 1939, on her way back to a mental hospital in North Carolina. "It's the best place in the world . . . and we could keep a little house on the lake . . . We might have a very happy summer in such circumstance— you like it there, and I am very clever at serving birdsong and summer clouds for breakfast."

The just-issued *Correspondence of F. Scott Fitzgerald*, edited by the indefatigable Matthew J. Bruccoli and by Margaret M. Duggan, with the assistance of Susan Walker, is as complete a compilation of previously unpublished letters to and from Fitzgerald as one could wish for. More, in fact, than one had wished for. This volume has been put together with a reverential scholar's eye: no cable is too insignificant, no postcard too slight, no book dedication too flippant to reproduce in full. It is a disappointing collection, partly because many of the truly interesting letters have been published before and are not reprinted here, but mostly because Scott's was a slim, sterling gift and he knew enough not to tarnish it with overuse.

"I think you'll like a series of sketches I'm starting in *Esquire* next month," he wrote to Beatrice Dance, a married woman with whom he had a brief affair, "they can tell you more about myself than I ever could in a letter because unfortunately, in my profession correspondence has to be sacrificed to the commercial side of being a literary man and I am probably the worst letter writer in the world." But it wasn't simply a matter of good tactics; Fitzgerald was a zealous watch guard of his talent precisely because he sensed that its wellsprings were not all that deep. Although his style was inimitably lovely—indeed, there are sentences in *The Great Gatsby* and *Tender Is the Night* that leave one breathless—he was also one of those writers whose style exceeds their repertoire of perceptions. What he saw he saw, as Marjorie Kinnan Rawlings wrote to him, with "that terrible, clear white light you possess." Even the firmest of admirers must notice, however, that there were startling blind spots in Fitzgerald's gaze, whole realms that failed to interest him or escaped his attention altogether.

Still, there are curious and beguiling things to be found here if one is willing to wade through the picayune details that make up much of the correspondence. It is interesting to see, for instance, how early and completely Fitzgerald developed his myth of desire—the gleaming girl whom everyone wants and who, in her infinite suggestiveness, stoked the fires of his dreamy imagination—that propel his novels. "Her face was sad and lovely with bright things in it," Nick Carraway says of his cousin Daisy in *The Great Gatsby*, "bright eyes and a bright passionate mouth, but there was an excitement in her voice that men who had cared for her found difficult to forget: a singing compulsion, a whispered 'Listen,' a promise that she had done gay, exciting things just a while since and that there were gay, exciting things hovering in the next hour." A nineteen-year-old Scott sent his younger sister, Annabel, a letter that is a short course in the art of seduction as the Jazz Age conceived of it: "You've got the longest eyelashes!" and "I hear you've got a 'line'!" are his examples of how a girl should open conversation with a boy. "Don't be afraid of slang—use it," suggests this older brother who could not spell, "but be careful to use the most modern and sportiest like 'line,' camafluage etc." "In your conversation," her worldly sibling goes on to advise, "always affect a complete frankness but really be only as frank as you wish to be." He gives her some pointers on proper carriage while dancing, then solemnly concludes this paragraph, "And dancing counts as nothing else does."

At twenty-three Fitzgerald would marry the Alabama belle Zelda Sayre. A letter from her, dated two months before their wedding in 1920, contains the following complaint about Frank Norris's *McTeague*, a novel she was reading at Scott's behest: "All authors who want to make things true to life make them *smell bad*—like McTeague's room—and that's my most sensitive sense. I do hope you'll never be a realist—one of those kind that thinks being ugly is being forceful." Small chance. Zelda's letters, by the way—all of them printed here—justify the volume as few of Scott's do.

This Side of Paradise was published March 26, 1920, eight days before the Fitzgeralds took their wedding vows in St. Patrick's Cathedral. Thereafter came the high times—tanning on French beaches, famous friends, partying. Throughout those years Scott worked hard, nudging his editor, Max Perkins, with publicity gimmicks and displaying, as book followed book, the "ungodly facility" that John Peale Bishop called his "worst enemy." In 1930, Zelda had a breakdown and was sent to the first of many psychiatric clinics. She was diagnosed as schizophrenic. As the sunlit world of their first ten years together was cast abruptly into ever-lengthening shadow, Scott sent this terse letter to his mother from Switzerland: "No news. I'm still here waiting. Zelda is better but very slowly. She can't cross the ocean for some time yet + it'll be a year before she can resume her normal life unless there's a change for the better. Address me Paris, care of Guaranty. Actually I'm in Lausanne + migrate to Paris once a fortnight to see Scotty who has a small apartment. So we're all split up."

"Normal life" was never resumed. The Depression was fast approaching; Zelda would get better and then worse; Scott returned to America saddled with the care of "my invalid," as he called Zelda, and with overseeing the education of their daughter. Money wasn't coming in as abundantly as it once had from the popular magazines where Fitzgerald's stories appeared, owing both to his declining literary reputation and to the declining fortunes of the country generally. In 1937 he began writing for Hollywood, and in 1938 Scottie was admitted to Vassar at reduced fees. In a letter to Zelda that same year he described himself as "a pretty broken and prematurely old man who hasn't a penny except what he can bring out of a weary mind and a sick body."

It has been suggested more than once, most recently by Gore Vidal in *The New York Review of Books*, that Fitzgerald was a whiner. I see few traces of the habitual complainer in him; rather, he seems to have lost—and at an unfairly young age—the ebullience, the shiny-eyed habit of response that had once been his trademark. As he wrote to Beatrice Dance, "My capacity for wonder has greatly diminished." In its place were only the specters of ruin. "The possibility of dissipation," he wrote to one of Zelda's psychiatrists in 1940, a little less than a year before he died, "frightens me more than anything else—which I suppose is poetic justice."

What should be remembered is that for all his resentment (call it whining if you want to), Scott never seriously considered the idea of abandoning Zelda—certainly not financially and even less so emotionally. "I loved you," he wrote to his wife in the fall of 1939, "romantically—like your mother, for your beauty + defiant intelligence; but unlike her I wanted to make it useful." He continued to alert Zelda's doctors to her "very extraordinary mind" for as long as he lived. Whether or not he drove her crazy, as her family thought and her biographer, Nancy Milford, seems to think, is not, I believe, an answerable question. Would Zelda have utilized her considerable talents for writing (as evidenced in her novel, *Save Me the Waltz*) and painting more completely if she hadn't married Scott? My guess is that she would not have; her indulgent Southern upbringing and her temperament—even in its sanest form—militated against it. Instead, she served as an erratically compliant muse. "But don't fret—if it hadn't been you," Scott wrote in one of his last letters to Zelda, "perhaps I would have worked with more stable material." They were a lavishly misspent pair.

ON NOT LEARNING TO FLIRT

2010

It begins with your father, the First Man in your life, this primal love affair—not sexual in nature, but with the faintest erotic undertone—that will lead to other, more fleshed-out romances. At some moment in time you start to take in the Otherness of him, the ways in which he is different from you, from the muscles in his arms to the scratchiness of his cheeks. It might be on a day when you are rushing past him in your corduroy overalls to rescue your favorite stuffed panda that has gotten stuck behind a bookcase and he swoops down and picks you up, unable to resist your allure. You in turn giggle happily and throw your arms around his neck, lay your head on his reliable shoulder, the two of you basking in mutual adoration. Or it might be on a summer afternoon when he carries you in your striped bathing suit with the sweet ruffles into the ocean, tall and strong, stronger than the waves, and coaxes you into the water, the first step toward learning how to swim. "Don't be afraid, Princess," he says. "I'm here."

Years later, you begin to realize that the power is more two-way than you had once thought, with his being in the position of knowing how to do everything, from science experiments to driving a car, and you in the position of willing acolyte. You begin to realize, that is, that *you* actually have some power over *him*, can wheedle him into overriding your mother's refusal to let you meet up with some friends on a school night. Somewhere in adolescence or just before, when boys come into your life bearing their weirdness and their desirability, you try out some of your father-proven feminine wiles on them, smile and play with your hair and talk in that soft, slightly unsure-of-itself voice that your father always responds to. And so the pattern is set, encoded early on before you are aware of it, to be called upon later in earnest when the dance of the sexes heats up.

Or so, at least, is how I imagine it happens: how one learns to flirt. Your father sees you through the rapt gaze of paternal love, and you in turn borrow from that gaze, envision yourself as covetable, expecting the males who come in contact with you to share this point of view. Admittedly, I base this developmental scenario on secondary rather than primary sources—on observation and induction rather than my own experience, seeing as how my father never called me Princess, although I conceived a desire to be addressed like a royal when a friend at sleepaway camp received a postcard addressed thusly. Nor do I remember ever catching the moonlight in his eye. My father's interest lay firmly elsewhere, in his work, in the life of the synagogue, in my mother. I recall trying to inveigle him into focusing on me, clambering on his lap when I was little, where I languished; writing him a poem when I was older, which I was the only one to be moved by.

So no, it never clicked for me the way it's supposed to, this first of all love affairs. This maladaption is something I think about from time to time, but especially around this time of year, with Valentine's Day hovering round the corner, wrapped up in red roses and heart-shaped boxes of chocolate, gooey with official sentiment. The holiday itself leaves me cold, but I'm not sure whether this reaction is a critique of consumer culture or merely an ingrained defensive posture on my part because of a lack of "sweetheart" sentiment early on.

I was, for all intents and purposes, a fatherless girl, looking for a male presence that was mostly an absence. And whereas this lack might have caused someone else to redouble her efforts, might have created an ever-stronger wish to coax forth an engagement with or at the very least a minimal awareness of herself, things didn't happen that way for me. By the time I was an adolescent, I had pretty much given up the fight. I decided to ignore my father's relevance to me, if only to minimize the impact of my irrelevance to him. I pretended that we were passing ships in the night, two people who just happened to be related and could be found peering into the same near-bare fridge at the midnight hour only because of proximity.

More important, I refused to woo the attention of my male peers the way I saw other girls doing: playing dumb, playing with their hair, acting all admiring. I told myself that I didn't see the point: What were boys, after all, but posturing members of the opposite sex, unknowable (despite the fact that I had three brothers), unpredictable, insatiable in their need for admiration? Looking back, it would be more truthful to say that I never learned how to stoop to conquer, how to stroke the male ego and get my own stroked in return. And so I decided to preemptively reject before I could be rejected.

Oh, there were the occasional boys who got through my armamentarium beginning in high school, who saw through my defenses and stirred my interest. There was Victor, who was intense and moral to the point of self-righteousness; David, who made me bootlegged tapes of Bob Dylan and tried to get me to enjoy smoking pot as much as he did by rolling me enormous roaches that I, in turn, would let rot in my desk drawer. And then there was Alan, whom I found immensely sexy—sexy enough to kiss in the presence of some ancient stone-carved onlookers in a room at the Met when I was sixteen—even though I didn't agree with his reverent feelings about Ayn Rand. More than thirty years later I still think of all three of them, gone off into the vast recesses of adult life, wonder if they ever think of me.

But those were the exceptions, the boys who might have appreciated my looks—for all my radiating hostility, I had long, straight hair, large breasts, and almond-shaped "bedroom" eyes—and were willing to overlook the tensions that marked my interchanges with the opposite sex in favor of my barbed wit and diverting if melancholic line of thinking. In the main, I remained resistant, refusing to flirt with the gorgeous Israeli who taught us Hebrew and whom all my friends vied for in my junior year of high school, then acting hesitant several years later with the brainy

Shakespeare professor at Columbia who clearly warmed to me. (And I to him, truth be told.) The problem was that, caught up as I was in self-protective measures lest I be made a fool of, imagining myself the apple of an eye that had barely noticed me to begin with, I could never figure out a way to indicate the *attraction* the male sex held for me.

The apotheosis of that attitude—its defining moment, so to speak, after which things began to thaw—came in my early twenties. I was invited one summer to spend a weekend in New Hampshire with the writer Saul Bellow at the behest of his agent, who had recently taken me on as a client. Bellow was his larger-than-life, oxygen-eating self, as charming a host as you could wish for, discoursing on everything from Bach to his secret recipe for tuna fish salad that called for a tablespoon of ketchup. He was solicitous of me, praising what writing of mine he had read, and in general conspiring to make me a happy guest. But his very assumption of masculine irresistibility, which his agent had succumbed to long ago, put my teeth on edge, and I spent a good deal of time taking walks by myself so as not to have to be an audience to his sweltering ego.

Toward the end of the stay, Bellow and I were talking outside, just the two of us, while he tilled his bounteous garden. I could swear he did an imitation of Marlon Brando in *The Godfather* by cutting an opening into a piece of orange skin, sliding it over his teeth, and then smiling at me ghoulishly, but whether I am inventing this in retrospect or it really happened, I know I suddenly felt tenderhearted toward him. As Bellow was seeing us off, I leaned over to give him a hug, and after we had said our good-byes, he added, in a quiet voice, "Be kinder to the male gender." This suggestion, in the simplicity of its appeal and the vulnerability that lay behind that appeal, broke through my already-wobbly defenses, opening up vistas of affection withheld and received that I mostly had shied away from. I cried all the way to the airport and then throughout the plane ride, feeling that I had been seen and understood, that the once-ignored little girl was now an adult woman whose feelings and responses left their mark on the male beholder.

And yet even that is not the whole story. My father may not have known the names of any of my friends or bothered to attend my college graduation, but he did keep copies of almost everything I wrote—the extent of which I only discovered after both my parents had died. Although it was not his style to make encouraging noises, I knew he respected my work—indeed, that he shared my interest in singular words and the construction of shining sentences, notwithstanding (or, perhaps, precisely because of) the fact that English was his third language.

According to psychological findings, one of the most positive effects of a good father-daughter relationship is in the way it equips girls with a sense of mastery, helping to make young women effective in the outside world. Somewhere along the way I must have imbibed from my father that writing was a worthwhile occupation and that my thoughts—at least on books—were not to be sneered at. Indeed, some months ago, a woman doing research for a book about successful women and their fathers came to interview me. In my conversation with her, casting about for memories, I was suddenly reminded of the birthday cards my father used to send me, which always included a little witticism or play on words. (I recall one such card he signed "Enchanté," shortly after my novel *Enchantment* had come out.)

So you might say that if I failed to learn how to flirt in the more obvious, Hugh Hefner–ordained ways, I learned an alternate means of flirting—flirting with my mind, which was the part of me my father honored. And although that is a more rarefied form of seduction, leaving out whole swaths of the male population, for those men to whom it does speak, it tops a glimpse of décolleté or fawning questions about his day at the office each and every time. This approach may not pan out in the conventional way, and it certainly won't bring you roses on Valentine's Day. But you can always look ahead and buy yourself some daffodils in time for spring.

GLASS HOUSE

(J. D. SALINGER AND JOYCE MAYNARD)

I remember the first time I came upon Joyce Maynard. It was a Sunday morning—late morning, no doubt, because I hated getting up. I sat down at my parents' dining-room table, blearily pulled the *Times Magazine* toward me, and there she was: a small-boned young woman with enormous eyes, dark bangs, and a pixie charm that practically tap-danced off the page. She was eighteen years old, not much older than I was, but she looked younger. She looked, in fact, like a nymphet with soul, an Ivy League Lolita, sitting cross-legged on the cover, dressed in blue jeans and sneakers, an oversize watch drooping from her slender wrist. While I'd been sleeping late, Maynard, a Yale freshman, had been busy, summing up her generation in a lengthy essay called, majestically, "An 18-Year-Old Looks Back on Life." She had caught the attention of the world by mouthing off like a Wise Child, a teenager who could explain her less articulate peers to adults, and in a way that would leave them smiling.

Among the many people who noticed Maynard that day— April 23, 1972—was someone who could be considered the reigning authority on precocity, J. D. Salinger. Salinger was, of course, almost as famous for his disappearance from the stage of life as for his fiction; he had moved to Cornish, New Hampshire (population one thousand), in 1953, a year and a half after the publication of *The Catcher in the Rye*. In 1965, after publishing three more books, he appeared in print for the last time. Indeed, it was hard to imagine him picking up something as prosaic as the Sunday *Magazine*; one thought of him as more removed than that, communing with the birds and a favored few, like William Shawn.

I remember hearing sometime later that Maynard and Salinger had become involved: it seemed almost ghastly in its unlikeliness, the venerated hermit of the hills taking up with the cultural pinup girl of the moment. But this coming together of two generational mascots also made a kind of sense—the one forbidding and soured on mankind, the other chirpy and fresh-faced. ("I'm basically an optimist," Maynard had written.) Salinger, it seemed, had been hiding behind a one-way mirror: although he had resolutely cut himself off from his readers, when *he* wanted to communicate he had only to reach out a long arm from his rural hideaway and beckon to whoever caught his fancy. There was, too, the thirty-five-year difference in the couple's ages—that faint whiff of pedophilia. This was a writer whose greatest lyricism was saved for the subject of young girls, whose Seymour Glass, in "A Perfect Day for Bananafish," had given a tender goodbye kiss to the arch of a little girl's foot before going back to his hotel room to kill himself. However you looked at it, though, Joyce Maynard was living out the fantasy of ambitious, neophyte female writers everywhere: to be taken under the wing of a Famous Older Male Writer.

And then, just as precipitously, the affair was rumored to be over. In the years that followed, with rare exceptions, Salinger maintained an unbroken silence, while Maynard went on to clamorously document her life in newspaper columns, magazines, and books. Meanwhile, she championed the rewards of motherhood and domesticity until she got divorced, then wrote about that. She also became an avid self-promoter, setting up a website for her fans before it was de rigeur and marketing a CD of songs she'd listened to while writing one of her novels. I never heard Maynard's name without thinking of her dazzling leap into Salinger's arms. How had it happened? And what had gone wrong between them? Their romance seemed almost mythic, like a vine-covered cottage in a fairy tale.

Now, in a flurry of publishing excitement, including a juicy excerpt in *Vanity Fair*, Maynard has gone public with the details of an affair that has continued to haunt her. In the introduction to her memoir, *At Home in the World*, she says that she remained "desperately in love" with Salinger: "For more than twenty years I revered a man who would have nothing to do with me . . . But I put the experience away, just as I'd put away the packet of letters he'd written me." The obvious question is why Joyce Maynard has unlocked this drawer again after all these years, and the obvious answer is that ours is a culture addicted to exposure, to "outing" ourselves and others. But do we really want to hear that the author of "For Esmé—with Love and Squalor" spent time whipping up arcane homeopathic cures for both people and dogs? Or that his diet consisted of frozen Birds Eye Tender Tiny Peas for breakfast and laboriously prepared organic-lamb patties for dinner?

J. D. Salinger has been the last holdout against guts spilling, and, no matter how fetishistic his position, we've come to respect it. Ian Hamilton suggests in his foiled biography, *In Search of J. D. Salinger*, that there is something disingenuous about his subject's passion for privacy. It is a gauntlet thrown down—an elaborate game of come and get me. "To what extent," Hamilton asks, "was Salinger the victim of America's cultural star system? To what extent its finest flower?" Even so, many of us continue to feel a protectiveness toward Salinger that other writers don't inspire. His real-life aloofness is directly at odds with his literary gift for intimacy: to read him is to be invited into a magic circle in which your unacknowledged aura of specialness—your genius— has finally been recognized. (It is this same effect of inclusive self-regard, this "terrifying narcissus pool," as Mary McCarthy called it, that some critics have questioned.)

Maynard's pretext for breaking a code of silence that she had repeatedly vowed to honor is the usual one offered in such memoirs: the quest for self-knowledge. "All my life," she writes,

"I had been trying to make sense of my experiences without understanding a crucial piece of my history." Thus, after hundreds of pages of autobiographical minutiae (her affair with Salinger actually takes up less than half the book), Maynard arrives at the conclusion that it took a relationship with someone as powerful as the fifty-three-year-old writer to help free her from her parents. "It was a terrible, wrenching way to be taken from my home." Taken from her home? You would think that Maynard was a helpless child, scooped up from playing with her crayons and dragged off to Salinger's cave, when the plain truth is that she had already separated from her parents in the age-appropriate way that many privileged young adults do—by living in a college dorm. But at this point we've grown accustomed to Maynard's habit of glossing over her own extraordinary force of will and to her slightly hysterical, movie-of-the-week sense of drama.

Joyce Maynard conceived of herself as destined for great things from the start. She was the younger of two sisters who grew up in an intellectually vibrant household in Durham, New Hampshire. Her father taught eighteenth-century literature and was a passionate amateur painter. Her mother was Jewish, an intense woman who had a doctorate in English. They were doting, albeit problematic, parents. Joyce's "Daytime Daddy" taught her the crawl and took her on long walks; her "Nighttime Daddy" drank and roamed the house, "red-eyed and ranting." Joyce's mother was highly invested in her daughter: she knit a sweater on toothpicks for her daughter's toy bear and catered to her picky eating habits with special soufflés. But she also cuddled inappropriately: "She may comment on my body," Maynard writes, "check to see if I have any pubic hair yet, make a joke about my pink, childish nipples."

It's all a bit contradictory, depending, at any given moment, on whether Maynard wants to blame her parents for insulating her from grown-up reality (she claims that her mother never discussed menstruation with her) or for failing to keep their dirty grown-up secrets to themselves. "Who else has a mother," she demands, "who taught her the meaning of the word 'cunnilingus'?" Still, her parents' greatest sin was arguably that they led their daughter to believe that she, as well as everything she said or wrote, was of supreme interest. Witness a notation in the eleven-year-old Joyce's journal (which she has preserved, along with every other scrap of paper in her life): "I realize now that even Mummy has flaws! I guess truly no one can come into the 'divine circle' except me. One is always so alone!"

Maynard's affair with Salinger must have seemed like a triumphant end to her loneliness. A few days after her essay appeared in the *Times*, she received a letter from him, in which he warned her about the hazards of visibility. She hadn't read anything he'd written, but "the fact that a famous man has conferred approval on me thrills me." For the next six weeks or so, their correspondence flew fast and furious. "This half-Jewish business" that they share weighs heavily in her favor, as does her non-intellectuality. He told her that they are "landsmen"—from the same place—and that they're both lowbrows. "We share a deep affection for Mary Tyler Moore," Maynard writes, "although we like Carl Reiner a lot, too." She went to visit him in June, wearing a short, sleeveless A-line shift "printed with ABC's in bright primary colors" and "purple Mary Jane–style flats." She and her mother have concocted this fetching "child innocent" outfit, and I assume that its subtext is lost on neither of them.

Salinger had prepared a pristine lunch of bread, cheese, and nuts, which he set on folding TV tray tables, and the two traded banal confidences. She told him that Joyce was actually her middle name, while he said that he hated his own given name, Jerome: "Sounds like a podiatrist." For the Fourth of July weekend, Salinger drove to New York City (Maynard had begun a summer job as an apprentice editorial writer at the *Times*) and brought her back to New Hampshire. They retreated to the bedroom, where Maynard got her first glimpse of a naked man, but then the romantic scenario bogged down. "When we attempt intercourse," Maynard writes, "the muscles of my vagina simply clamp shut." Salinger promised to help her, and Maynard, like a terrorized mail-order bride, felt fatally connected to him: "It is my new, terrible secret . . . The fact that Jerry knows binds me more tightly to him than ever." Their failure to complete intercourse over the next five days didn't curb Salinger's ardor. When he left Maynard off in the city, he told her, "I couldn't have made up a character of a girl I'd love better than you." That fall, she dropped out of Yale to move in with him.

Who was it that Salinger saw in Joyce Maynard? Was she the embodiment of Phoebe Caulfield—Holden's younger sister, a lissome reflection of all he held dear? And what did he see when, less than a year later, he groaned, "How did I let this happen? What have I brought on myself?" It was nine months after their affair began that Salinger abruptly ejected Maynard from his bizarre and exclusive universe, sending her back to snowy New Hampshire to pack up her belongings while he and his two children remained behind on a vacation in Florida. If we are to accept Maynard's account, much of Salinger's behavior during the months they lived together was moody and mean: he left her alone in the house while he wrote or pursued his Eastern meditations and kept track of her food consumption in an alarming fashion, icily noting when she had eaten too much of the cheddar cheese he occasionally bought as a treat. She also claims that he taught her how to induce vomiting by sticking a finger down her throat, though it seems odd that a girl who by her own admission was fanatically obsessed with being thin (she weighed eighty-eight pounds when she left Exeter) wouldn't have resorted to this method before.

In the end, it's impossible to know what to believe. Too much of *At Home in the World* takes the form of reconstructed conversations from more than twenty-five years ago and is narrated in a hazy dream time where past and present blur. Maynard uses this chronological impressionism to plant observations that are clearly meant to lead the jury. She describes how she performed oral sex: "He takes hold of my head then, with surprising firmness, and guides me under the covers . . . I close my eyes. Tears are streaming down my cheeks. Still, I don't stop. So long as I keep doing this, I know he will love me." The subliminal message here is that Maynard was Salinger's nubile sex slave. But elsewhere she portrays the two of them as a legitimate couple, telling us that they hated to be apart and that they discussed having a child together (an idle plan, since Maynard insists he never managed to penetrate her). Similarly, Maynard writes that after she turned nineteen, she worried, "What if I'm getting too old for him?" This feels like a suspiciously neat emotional flashback, but it's useful to Maynard's version (or one of her versions) to imply that a large part of her allure for Salinger was her youth—just in case we've forgotten.

If there is something unsavory about a fifty-three-year-old man's fascination with an unformed girl, there's something equally creepy about an unformed girl's deliberately shaping herself to fit a role, the personification of a recurring motif in Salinger's imagination. She emulates his writing style ("My letters to him are full of . . . parenthetical asides, qualifiers, interior debate with myself") and admits that she presented a tidy version of herself to him—the same eager-to-please version she presented to her parents. She inserts comments that seem designed to appeal to his disdainful, alienated outlook: "There's so much perversion all around me," Maynard writes to him, as though they were two elderly monks.

Maynard appears to suffer from multiple-persona disorder: one minute she is a naïf, lost in the woods, and the next a resilient survivor who rises from the ashes of her affair with Salinger to become a star reporter at *The Times*. Indeed, her writing career is hardly incidental to this story. I had the eerie sense that Maynard is not simply reproaching Salinger but competing with him as well—the pupil who needs to outshine her teacher. She was always a good student, the kind of girl who applied for all the glittering prizes with a zeal worthy of the young Sylvia Plath: *Scholastic* contests, assignments for *Seventeen*, admission to Exeter (where she is a member of the first coed graduating class), the *Mademoiselle* Guest Editor contest. When she was eight or nine, Maynard wrote to the president of CBS, informing him that she was available to replace Angela Cartwright on *Make Room*

for Daddy. It is possible, in fact, to read her *Times Magazine* article as an application—a bid—to be loved by the world. The man
who responded to it had scant use for the world, but inside Salinger's misanthropic recluse, we sense, has always lurked a sentimental pushover.

Now Holden's adoring little sister has gone and sold him
down the river, or at least tried to. *At Home in the World* strikes
me as a bit deluded, as though Maynard thought she could force
Salinger to acknowledge her by blowing his cover. The attempt
seems not only misjudged but grasping, and one understands
why he wearied of her—just as one understands what her sister
means when she tells Joyce at one point, "You . . . take . . . up . . .
so . . . much . . . space." There is something of the stalker in
Maynard, of the oxygen eater. At the end of the book, on the eve
of her forty-fourth birthday, she drives to New Hampshire and
waits on Salinger's doorstep until he comes out. She asks him
what he wanted from her—what was her "purpose" in his life.
It's a question that, even unanswered, is more lonely and true
than any of Maynard's breathless confessions. Perhaps the real
sadness lies not in her betrayal but in the larger, negating absence
that hovers over these pages. After a heated exchange about the
motives behind her memoir, and about who has exploited whom,
Salinger tells her, "I didn't exploit you! *I don't even know you*."
Search as we might in these untranquil recollections, we don't
know him, either.

SO NOT A FAG HAG

2011

I am standing at water's edge on a broiling afternoon in late summer, lost in conversation with my friend David. We are exploring the whys and wherefores, as is our habit: how come we are the way we are, our problems with maintaining intimate relationships, which sleeping pills are effective and which zonk you out for the next day, how hard it is to get our work done. We've had conversations like this many times before and will no doubt have them many times again. It is the song we trill together, mining the inner landscape of the psyche the way other people might discuss their tennis game or the latest sex scandal.

David has never learned to swim, which I find oddly endearing. He also smacks noisily when he eats, which I find less so. We've known each other for what seems like forever and often bicker like an unhappily married couple. We could, in point of fact, never be married, because David is gay, although I sometimes find myself wondering how things might have developed between us if he weren't. What's certain is that we would have had good-looking children.

David is one of a handful of gay men I have been close to over the years, men who provide a different kind of lens on the world than my female friends or straight men. It's impossible, however, for me to think of my dealings with gay men without the term "fag hag" immediately attaching itself to these relationships, making a cruel comedy out of what is a complicated and intriguing phenomenon.

In the popular media, gay men generally feature as bitchy, high-strung confidants to brassy straight women—hairdressers of a sort, the men to whom you tell your more embarrassing secrets and confide trivial concerns. So it goes in TV shows like *Will & Grace* and *Sex and the City* and countless movies, such as *The Next Best Thing*, the dismal Madonna–Rupert Everett vehicle. The idea that a straight woman's friendship with a gay man may serve a function beyond light relief—that it could touch on deeper needs not met by other relationships—is rarely addressed. One recent exception was the Sundance Channel's *Girls Who Like Boys Who Like Boys*, a short-lived docu-series (inspired by a collection of essays with the same name) in which straight women and their queer male companions laughed together—and, at times, cried together—all the while displaying the fortitude and strength of their platonic bonds. Albeit melodramatic at times, the show proved more layered in its depictions than the usual fare.

I've known David for nearly two decades. We are both writers and were drawn together by shared interests as well as a shared mood disorder marked by free-floating anxiety and a tendency toward depression. Like some, but not all, of the other gay men I've known, David is not immediately identifiable as homosexual. This has made it more difficult, if anything, to accept the fact that he is sexually indifferent to women; there's nothing, on the face of it, that should make it so. Although the common wisdom on the origins of gayness has gone in less than a century from viewing it as a pathology in need of correction to viewing it as a completely genetic trait, like a gift for numbers, I find myself wondering whether our relegating it all to one side of the nature-nurture equation is not a matter of studious political correctness rather than scientific truth. Isn't it more likely that homosexuality is a combination of genetics and environment, like so many things?

I first fell in love with gay men through reading novels and essays by writers like Henry James and E. M. Forster, who happened to be gay but seemed to have an astonishing amount of insight into women. Given a choice between macho Ernest Hemingway and spinsterish Forster, for instance, I would have picked Forster every time, both as a man and as a writer. Then, after I discovered the Bloomsbury set and immersed myself in their lives and writings, I became enamored of their freewheeling and somewhat confusing domestic arrangements, in which gay men lived with straight women (Virginia Woolf's sister, Vanessa Bell, and the artist Duncan Grant) and even occasionally believed they were sufficiently in love with one of the women to propose marriage (the writer Lytton Strachey and Virginia Woolf). Strachey, of course, was "out" in a time when being closeted was the norm; he was openly attracted to men yet had close friendships with a number of women. He eventually set up a household with the painter Dora Carrington, with whom he lived until his death. Carrington, who married another man to keep Strachey happy, was so distraught after Strachey's death that she killed herself shortly thereafter. I remember being shocked when I read of her suicide—they weren't lovers, after all—but also feeling a bond with their singular pairing and the unique passion it might have inspired.

Which brings me back to my dislike of the term "fag hag" (or *Haggus fagulous*, as Simon Doonan once coined it) and everything it implies—including an ostensible fear, on the hag's part, of straight men. In a virulently homophobic article I read, "The Fag Hag: How a Girl's Misguided Friendship Choices Can Lead to a Lifetime of Loneliness," the author conjectures that acne (!) is one reason an adolescent girl will seek out gay male friends and asserts the following: "Homosexuals of all ages and young women share many similar obsessions—clothes, gossip and melodramatic TV shows—and this is what draws them together." Although all stereotypes have bits of truth to them, I, for one, have never watched *Glee* or dyed my hair an outrageous color.

"You're so not a fag hag," my daughter says to me when I tell her what I'm writing about. I guess I know what she means, if by "fag hag" one is thinking of Liza Minnelli, but even though I detest the moniker, I find myself brooding at being excluded from the category. The closest I have come to having what could be called a classically fag-hag type of relationship was with a man named John, whom I met in my early thirties. The first time I saw him, he was wearing a wig and very black mascara, the better to highlight his siren-blue eyes. I'd become acquainted with him through his partner, who sang in the chorus of the Met, and discovered that John had a wicked sense of whimsy—early in our friendship, he painted a sky with clouds on the roof of my balcony—and I also loved (there go all my protests to the contrary) his interest in the finer points of skin care and makeup.

It was John who introduced me to the pore-tightening capacities of a certain white lotion by Janet Sartin and the necessity of using an eyelash curler. There was something infinitely pleasurable about sharing my interest in such beautifying concerns with a man. Men usually seemed immune to these sorts of anxieties, after all; they were supposed to be the object at which such obsessive female primping was directed rather than a partner in these very rituals. It felt cozy to be part of a coed team when agitating about what pair of shoes looked better on me as I sat trying them on in a department store—less lonely than being sequestered on the girls' side of the playground. After his partner died, John moved to Florida, and we fell out of touch, but to this day I can't buy a new lipstick without wondering what he'd think of the color.

An article I read recently in a teen magazine took up the subject of the GBF (Gay Best Friend) phenomenon, noting that "being part of a GBF couple has become the new platonic ideal"—as crucial an accessory to *Gossip Girl* tweens as a Mulberry bag on one arm and a preppy jock on the other used to be. But much as it may fill the pages of magazines and style sections to ruminate on gay guys as trendy appendages, it seems to me that the more serious story underlying these relationships is that they allow for an escape from the constriction of gender binariness—from defining oneself along a limited spectrum of acceptably female roles. These friendships speak, that is, to the sexually androgynous aspect that is a part of many women's personalities, distinct from our socialized "feminine" selves. What I have in mind has less to do with a specific trait and more with a kind of brainpower—a penetrating analytic bent, say, or a corrosive wit—that makes straight men feel uneasy or downright threatened. My gay friends, by contrast, seem to enjoy precisely the "strong" or "ornery" sides of me.

Another way of putting it might be to say that such men draw on the inner nonconformists that reside next to our groupthink identities—the ways in which we depart from the norms of our gender and class. To the extent that you don't have to be gay to feel like an outsider—you can feel like an outsider and be a functioning heterosexual—there is a feeling of relief that comes with having a common take on things, which is usually that of the ironic observer. I have aired some of my best renegade thoughts—I can't stand Jon Stewart, I miss typewriters—on my gay friends, safe in the knowledge that they won't immediately regard me as an alien.

These relationships also encourage an experience of intimacy with a male that doesn't balance precariously on an erotic fulcrum, the all-or-nothingness of sex. Although there is always the possibility of a sexual charge hovering in the air even between gay men and straight females, the charge is usually faint by virtue of being ignored or sidestepped. Its absence provides a freedom of sorts; in its stead can be found a more relaxed atmosphere of mutual recognition that manages to draw on the native differences that exist between men and women without being filtered down into the ultimate test of sexual desire. Although friendships with gay men have some of the easy camaraderie of those with women, they're often blissfully free of the competitive edge that marks the latter, the constant impulse to contrast and compare.

In the past year and a half, I've become close friends with a gay man whom I knew in passing while we were both growing up. He got in touch with me after a decades-long relationship with a partner painfully ended, suggesting that we might get to know each other better. We've since spent a lot of time together, going to movies and plays, eating out, having intense conversations about everything under the sun. Through M., I've come to better understand the complexities that define homosexuality, the many varieties of gayness that coexist. Not long ago I went to a dinner party at his apartment, the first gathering he'd hosted since his breakup. The table was beautifully set, the food impeccable, and the talk lively. The company was a mix of straights and gays, and at some point someone asked me what I was working on. I mentioned this piece, which immediately propelled the conversation into an impassioned discussion of whether there existed such a thing as a "gay" sensibility, whether it was all culturally dictated or whether there was an inherent proclivity toward certain traits. At the end of the dinner, an elegantly dressed, good-looking man wearing several bracelets, with whom I had chatted over hors d'oeuvres, walked me partway home. When it came time to say good night, he kissed me on both cheeks and proposed that we meet soon for dinner. "We're going to become the greatest of friends—I'm sure of it," he said in his animated way. To which I can only say, "Bring it on." The world would be a paler, emptier place without my gay friends; that's all I know, fag hag or not.

A MATCHED PAIR

(TED HUGHES AND SYLVIA PLATH)

2003

Them again. Just when you thought there was no more to be said, the ransacked remains of Ted Hughes and Sylvia Plath float to the surface once more. The occasion this time is Diane Middlebrook's *Her Husband*, which offers up yet another look at this much-prodded-at, larger-than-life marriage. Middlebrook, whose most recent book was a biography of the cross-dressing musician Billy Tipton, has also written an excellent biography of Anne Sexton, so she knows from self-destructing poets. And as with the Sexton book, which ignited controversy at the time of its publication because it drew upon confidential psychiatric records that were made available to Middlebrook by Sexton's daughter, she has again benefited from access to previously off-limits material, including letters and manuscripts by Ted Hughes. Still, one would be tempted to groan at this latest exhumation—if only it weren't so transfixing a tale.

He was the "black marauder," as Plath called him, a gorgeous hunk from a working-class Yorkshire background, who dressed in raggedy black and wanted to wrench modern British poetry from its fuddy-duddy moorings. She was the genteelly raised girl from New England, a bottle blonde with long legs and a sterling "bobby-sox" education, as Hughes would later describe it in *Birthday Letters*, the collection of poems about Plath that he published shortly before his death in 1998.

When they met at a Cambridge literary party, he already had

a rep as a magnetic womanizer, and she already had a hair-raising psychiatric history. Their first kiss drew blood, and for the next six years they combusted their way through love, marriage, and the birth of two children. For a while they appeared to have it all, starting with great sex—in bed they behaved, as Plath modestly put it, "like giants"—which seems to have been stoked by their mutually aggressive erotic styles. She brokered his poetry—Plath typed and submitted the manuscript of *The Hawk in the Rain*, Hughes's first, prizewinning collection—and perfected her culinary skills. (She packed the *Joy of Cooking*, which she once described herself poring over "like a rare novel," in her honeymoon luggage, along with her Olivetti portable.) But she was also determined to become a famous writer in her own right. "It is sad," Plath observed in her journals, "only to be able to mouth other poets; I want someone to mouth me." Hughes cheered her on through her despairs—the "blank hell in back of my eyes," as she called it—and despite his complaints to his friends that she never sewed on buttons, divvied up the domestic chores so that each could get a fair share of unencumbered writing hours.

At the time of Plath's suicide, however, there was no contest as to which of the two geniuses (if they agreed completely upon anything, it was that each of them was married to a genius) had triumphed. Hughes was a heralded poet, surrounded by bohemian buddies and infatuated women, including the stunning femme fatale Assia Wevill, whom he had dumped his wife for. Plath, by contrast, had been left to fend for herself and their two young children during a brutal London winter—the coldest in half a century, as we have repeatedly been told. Nearly friendless, she was further isolated by the toxic atmosphere of gossipmongering that surrounded the dissolution of her marriage. Plath was also relatively unknown as a writer—she had published one slim, unearthshaking book of verse, and her novel, *The Bell Jar*, had come out a month earlier, under a pseudonym, to little notice—except for a few, like the critic A. Alvarez, who sniffed her bonfire talent. The last person to see her alive was the grouchy downstairs neighbor, who reluctantly entered into conversation and sold her stamps so she could mail a final letter to her mother.

At a small gathering after the funeral, Hughes blurted, "Everybody hated her."

The trouble with the foregoing, however, is that it is but one cobbled-together narrative among many possible narratives, all of them jockeying for centrality. There are Plath's own accounts, of course; whether in the form of poetry, fiction, or journals, they are imbued with a kind of feverish authority, as much because of the power of their witnessing as the vividness of the prose. Then there is the chirpy, bright-eyed plotline relayed by the dutiful "Sivvy" of *Letters Home*, who sounds, with her incessant busywork and her annoyance at her mother-in-law's "sloppy cupboards," like a gushing precursor of Martha Stewart.

There has also been a trove of Plath biographies, including Anne Stevenson's much-plagued *Bitter Fame* and Ronald Hayman's empathetic and considered *The Death and Life of Sylvia Plath*. The poet Elaine Feinstein weighed in with a judicious biography of Hughes two years ago, and his own moving but also shrewdly self-exculpating version of the story is presented in *Birthday Letters*, where he is featured as a long-suffering husband who was helpless against a doom foretold before he ever arrived on the scene. There are, as well, a growing pile of competing memoirs (the latest of which, *Giving Up*, is by Jillian Becker, the woman whose house Plath retreated to on the weekend before she died); a novel about Plath's last days, called *Wintering*; psychoanalytic studies, such as Jacqueline Rose's *The Haunting of Sylvia Plath*; and Janet Malcolm's cool-eyed telescopic take in *The Silent Woman*.

Given that there is so little agreement on the details—whether, for instance, the headband Plath wore on the night they met was red, as she had it, or blue, as Hughes recalled—it is all the more surprising that Middlebrook's overarching interpretation of the marriage as a partial triumph, rather than a wholesale tragedy, makes as persuasive a case as it does. Instead of ascribing blame or censure, she focuses on the ways in which the union of these two gifted and complicated people was, for a sustained period, a singular creative partnership—a "productive collusion"— that led to an almost magical symbiosis. "They were a matched pair," Middlebrook writes, "as country people used to say of horses . . . Each was the other's best critic of their writing." Despite vastly different upbringings and influences, she suggests, Plath and Hughes connected at the deepest level from the moment they met, recognizing in each other a force—half-demonic and half-angelic—to be harnessed and reckoned with. "The sense of being bonded to each other through their instincts was one element in their compatibility, not only as lovers but as artists."

No matter that he was essentially undomesticatable, and that she was scarred by a furious negativity that had its roots in pathology as much as it had its flowering in her late poems. ("The one factor that nobody but close friends can comprehend," Hughes wrote to his brother, "is Sylvia's particular death-ray quality.") To Middlebrook, what's fascinating is not that the relationship failed but that their "dynamic of agreement and differentiation" lasted as long as it did. In much the same fashion, Hughes's continuing dialogue with Plath, either directly in his work or indirectly—via the statements and letters he wrote over the three and a half decades that he and his sister, Olwyn, hawkishly presided over her literary estate—is a tribute both to the hold Plath had over his imagination and to his wish to break free from its entanglements.

"It is only a story. / Your story. My story," Hughes wrote in "Visit," one of the poems in *Birthday Letters*. Umpteen books later, we have tried to make it our story, a paradigmatic instance of the relations between men and women, art and madness, passion and pain. By giving us a more mediated sense of the two poets' life together than the victim/victimizer model, *Her Husband* enables us to move beyond the stagnant issues of how hopelessly nuts she was or how badly he behaved. (There's no doubt that Plath was high maintenance, while Hughes seems to have tried in his way to make a go of the marriage, given that he was not built along the lines of the self-sacrificing Leonard Woolf.)

Middlebrook casts a skeptical eye on most of the heartening postmortem conjectures that have been broached over the years; she doubts that Hughes was really planning to come back to Plath or that she believed she'd be found before she was dead.

What I feel certain of is that her attentive and clear-eyed account won't be the last. The saga of Ted and Sylvia is like a ballad that goes on and on, stanza after stanza, with no end in sight. Still, even Middlebrook's inspiring slant can't obscure the chill at the heart of this story. The blood-jet was poetry, and at some point it began leaking all over the place. "And everything holds up its arms weeping," Hughes wrote in "Fate Playing." Or, as John Berryman, another poet-suicide, put it, "All the bells say: too late."

THE CONSOLATIONS OF
THREAD COUNT

2005

On a lazy Saturday morning not long ago, I was sitting at a neighborhood coffee shop counter with my fifteen-year-old daughter, enjoying a bonding moment over eggs and toast, when an attractive but slightly distraught-looking woman sitting on my other side started up a conversation. This woman, who had been feverishly underlining phrases in a dog-eared paperback, appeared, in spite of her waist-length hair and teenager-like outfit, to be in her forties or fifties. After commenting favorably on the sophisticated tone of our mother-daughter dialogue, she abruptly segued into a detailed account of her ill-fated romantic history, which had conspired to land her here, seeking salvation in a self-help book on the subject of (what else?) how to stop falling in love with the wrong men. I could sense my daughter, who is an empathic but not always patient soul, listening with rising anxiety to the woman's Miss Lonelyhearts saga, and she soon began unsubtly signaling her wish to leave by pinching my arm. When I had finally extricated us and we were safely outside, my daughter went into a rant about the horrifying (indeed, from the evidence, traumatizing) sight of older women who sit by themselves in coffee shops. "Promise me you won't do that when I'm gone," she begged me. "It's too pathetic for words."

What is it about the specter of a woman on her own, aging on the vine without a husband or lover or child in sight, that strikes fear and self-loathing in the hearts of females of all ages and persuasions—the liberated and enlightened as well as the old-fashioned and clueless? Why is there a mystique to the male loner in all his variegated and uncoupled forms—whether in the guise of the solitary cowboy, the bohemian wanderer, or the intriguing recluse—while the female loner is always a troubling, even freakish apparition, someone who appears to be independent-minded and strong-hearted but turns out to be so desperate for attachment that she is willing, like the Glenn Close character in *Fatal Attraction*, to go to any lengths, including murder, to hold a man? Is it true, as the poet Louise Bogan wrote in "Women," her species-defining poem, that women "have no wilderness in them"? Are we hopeless when wrenched from a context of coupledness and set on our own two feet—despite having come a long way, baby, as the old Virginia Slims advertisement had it? Lacking as we do the friskiness of a Y chromosome, do our attempts at flying solo conjure a sight so inherently forlorn—a bleak image of incipient bag-ladydom rather than dashing Amelia Earhart adventurousness—as to send the spectator running in the other direction?

Ah, but surely everything is different now, you're thinking. Surely women are no longer imprisoned by gender—"Content in the tight hot cell of their hearts," as Bogan wrote in that same poem, "to eat dusty bread"—and my daughter's response is indicative of nothing more than an adolescent's cruel pity for her divorced and unremarried mother. Look at all the empowering strides we've made—from sending female astronauts into space to launching forest-destroying amounts of chick lit into the marketplace, featuring maritally challenged but intrepid twenty- and thirtysomethings who conquer towering professions in a single bound and treat the opposite sex as fungible bedmates in the tried-and-true male manner, all the while dressing in red-carpet-ready ensembles.

Take Bridget Jones, who was among the first—not to mention the funniest, feistiest, and bestsellingest—of the chick-lit heroines to appear on the scene. Bridget has a degree in English, and she's given to consulting her strident inner feminist for guidance ("We are a pioneer generation daring to refuse to compromise in love") when she feels especially faltering. She works in swanky settings, looks to women like Goldie Hawn and Susan Sarandon for inspiration, and has a seductive way with interoffice e-mails. She is also—most crucially—over thirty, and when she's not worrying about her caloric or alcoholic consumption, she's pent up with chronic anxiety about the stark plight of being a Singleton in a world of Smug Marrieds. More specifically, she has terrorized herself with the bone-chilling final act that awaits all who tarry at the marriage threshold: "dying alone and being found three weeks later half-eaten by an Alsatian."

Whether or not young women have substantially changed their views about the prospect of taking on life without the net of a partner, they are marrying later (the average age is twenty-five—higher for college-educated gals) and worrying longer about what their future holds—hearth and home, or death by wild dogs. The sociologist E. Kay Trimberger's *The New Single Woman* is but the latest in a series of efforts to put a positive spin on the "stigma of being single" in a society that continues to promote "the cultural ideal of the couple as the only route to happiness, as the only protection against loneliness." The last book in this vein that I read closely, hoping to glimpse my destiny outlined on its pages, was Marcelle Clements's *The Improvised Woman: Single Women Reinventing Single Life*, in 1998, which dilated upon the many wonders (and the few reluctantly admitted-to trials) of singleness as experienced by roughly a hundred women of all ages. I remember coming away with a new appreciation for the significance of a high thread count in bed linens and an abiding sense that, unlike some of the women interviewed, I didn't make productive enough use of my free time—what Clements calls "creative solitude."

Like that earlier study, Trimberger's book is a mixture of sociological tidbits (statistics and poll data and such), personal reflections, and impressionistic reporting. Notwithstanding a discernible seriousness of purpose, these books share an emphasis on optimistic assertions rather than rigorous data. The twenty-seven women Trimberger talked to range in age from thirty to sixty—the never married, the divorced, the childless, single mothers, heterosexuals, bisexuals, and lesbians. Those who have adapted successfully to an unpartnered life can lay claim to some or all of the "six pillars of support" that Trimberger defines as being crucial to the "new type of single woman, one quite different from the traditional spinster or single girl in her twenties": a nurturing home environment (presumably one outfitted with Egyptian-cotton sheets); satisfying work; involvement with the next generation, through blood ties or volunteer work or mentoring; a network of friends who are there to help in times of trouble; a rewarding role in a community; and an unconflicted sexuality—meaning that one has either found a means of gratifying one's erotic needs or has embraced something Trimberger calls "sensual celibacy." Although she takes pains to distinguish this state from virginity and chastity (or, lest you think she is trading in high-flying euphemisms, masturbation) in its ability to replace the joys of "genital sexuality," the concept struck me not only as vague but as more than a bit oxymoronic. The author has herself been celibate for more than twenty years, and the strongest case she makes for the sublimated pleasures of sensual celibacy rests on one woman's passion for flamenco dancing.

It's with her insistence on the consolations of community—described, in a curiously dated (not to mention sexist) Cheeveresque image, as being the sort of loosely connected realm in which "a friend from church knows your golf buddy"—that Trimberger begins to lose me, just as she did on the issue of sensual celibacy. I'm not convinced, when it comes down to it, that she has figured out the life project of being single all that well, but perhaps the problem lies less with her than with the myth, propagated by Helen Gurley Brown's sex-and-the-single-*Cosmo*-woman on a gullible female public, that it's possible to have it all. The un-American truth is that most of us can't, if only because options are often mutually exclusive, a matter of opening one door and closing another. Trimberger, being a sociologist and not a zeitgeist shaper, allows this piece of sobering realpolitik to appear between the lines, if only for the benefit of those who are paying very close attention. "It may be impossible for most single women," she admits in passing, "to simultaneously maximize autonomy, intimacy, and sensuality." To which I can only add: You can say that again.

All the same, with Trimberger's six building blocks in place, you have at least a hope of flouting your mother's dreams of a doctor husband for you, as well as the conventional female mandates of motherhood and nurturing that prevail in spite of *Roe v. Wade* and the emergence of support groups with names—such as Single Mothers by Choice—that sound as if they were lifted straight from *About a Boy*. (Remember Hugh Grant's frenziedly chanting "Single parents alone together" with a bunch of bedraggled women in his search for a new babe to bed?) In other words, you have a hope of making single life a choice, a road deliberately taken, rather than a default fate or a compensatory strategy.

The most thought-provoking aspect of Trimberger's account— and one I wish she had devoted more space to—is her decoding of the cultural imperative that posits coupled love as the only route to personal happiness, especially "the romantic ideal of finding a soul mate." She points out that this uncompromising (and largely unrealizable) conception holds sway over women who have not yet found a partner, allowing them to present their single lives to others and themselves as a temporary problem awaiting a permanent solution in the form of Mr. Other Half. She quotes the psychologist Stephanie Dowrick on the benefits of freeing oneself from this terrorizing ideal of intimacy: "a life not shadowed by myths and longing for what might never happen, but shaped instead by less ambitious pleasure in what is."

In the years between Clements's and Trimberger's books, we have been hit by any number of new sociocultural developments— some good and some bad—but most of all we have had six seasons of the HBO hit show *Sex and the City*, which probably did more to move forward the idea of female bonding as the new urban family than all the research projects and surveys in the world. The show gets its share of credit in *The New Single Woman* for fostering an affirmative view of the single life.

———

This month, as it happens, Candace Bushnell, whose columns in *The New York Observer* provided the inspiration for the Manolo Blahnik–shod world of Carrie & Co., is out with a new novel. *Lipstick Jungle* features three fast friends who scale their way to the tops of their respective mediagenic Manhattan empires with nary a concern about soul mates or sensual celibacy—or anything, for that matter, that smacks of meaningfulness (how unhip can you get?)—to snag their seamless journey to personal and professional dominance.

In its own profoundly superficial, cosmetically enhanced way, *Lipstick Jungle* depicts the sort of having-it-all world the "new single woman" might have wished into existence if she came equipped with the right sort of plastic organ for a heart: post-coupled, post-intimate, post-maternal, post-nurturing, post-autonomous, and post-sagging. Bushnell's three glossy fortysomething heroines look great, their bodies kept on a tight leash of exercise and nibbling, and they can outsmart any man they meet. Victory is a brilliant fashion designer who dates a Mr. Big–type tycoon whom she improbably charms by treating him like a dirtbag. Wendy, a movie executive, is married to a househusband who has delusions of becoming a screenwriter while she supports their family in the lifestyle to which he has grown accustomed in return for his staying at home and looking after their three kids. And Nico, a magazine editor, is also married to a nonessential man with whom she hasn't had "decent sex" in years (thus providing an excuse for her to hook up with a gorgeous young model–cum–aspiring actor for some trendy rear-entry intercourse) but who tends to their town house and cocktail parties in wifely fashion, leaving her quality time to spend with their ten-year-old horse-riding, preppy daughter.

This is the kind of preposterously posh fictional milieu where all earthly desires have become commodified for instant charge-and-send—a strangely glittering planet on which the only restaurant worth name-dropping is Cipriani; the only champagne is Cristal; the only SUV is a Cadillac Escalade; and freedom's just another word for having enough moxie and cash to buy your own bling at a Sotheby's jewelry auction rather than waiting for

some soul mate with chest hair to come along and do it. I tended
to confuse the three women until their final collectively engineered
triumph, but I trust I'm not casting undue aspersions if I point
out that this is not the kind of novel you read for nuances of
character or perception so much as for the ludicrous but smile-
inducing stiletto-heeled escapism of it.

By chance I recently got a glimpse of how women coped before people talked about their feelings, much less their orgasms,
when I came across *Live Alone and Like It* by Marjorie Hillis.
Billed as "the classic guide for the single woman," it was originally published here in 1936 and has just been reissued in Britain. It speaks to a radically eclipsed moment when doctors still
made house calls and no woman worth knowing would be caught
without a wardrobe of bed jackets and "at least one nice seductive tea gown" to wear when dining alone or entertaining gentle-
men visitors. All the same, you could do worse than borrow some
of its insouciant but vigilant attitude, which merrily endorses lady-
like feints and delicate gestures as long as they don't compromise
one's indubitably high character.

Still, whether the year is 1936 or 2036, it's my guess that
sleeping alone will never become truly fashionable, not because
we can't live without sex or without being part of a couple, but
because there is nothing more consoling at three o'clock in the
morning than body warmth—what one of Clements's interview-
ees calls "the cuddle thing." Another sentient, sensate human
being to rub up against during the night: now, that's hard to do
without over the long stretch of a lifetime, no matter how true-blue
your friends or how downy soft your sheets.

CAN THIS DIVORCE
BE SAVED?

2002

It's late at night, and I'm reading E. Mavis Hetherington and John Kelly's *For Better or for Worse*—billed as "the most comprehensive study of divorce in America"—trying to figure out where and how I fit into the book's madly taxonomic universe. Lost in a sea of nomenclature, infinitely titrated statistics, and "points to remember," I feel my identity slowly slipping away from me. I'm a divorced woman who has not remarried and is the mother of a twelve-year-old daughter. What does that say about me? And, more important, what does my divorced state, this closely studied yet elusive condition, augur for my daughter?

Hetherington, a professor emerita of psychology at the University of Virginia who has conducted interviews and gathered data for the past three decades, clearly knows her material. She launched her research project, called the Virginia Longitudinal Study, in 1972, as a way of exploring "postnuclear family pathways." And she set about answering a basic question: "Was there a unique developmental dynamic—perhaps even a uniquely harmful dynamic—in divorced families?"

To this end, she scrutinized nearly fourteen hundred families, including more than twenty-five hundred children, from every angle possible; her team of investigators used standard tools such as questionnaires and tests, but they also observed the families in their homes "as they solved problems, as they chatted over dinner, and in the hours between the child's arrival at home and bedtime." A designated "target child" in each family was assessed at the playground, in school, and in the eponymous Hethering-ton Laboratory. The parents in the study kept diaries, where they jotted down the intimate details of their daily lives at half-hour intervals three days a week. Finally, Hetherington worked all the data into a paint-by-numbers typology, which is where things get sticky.

For starters, I'm having trouble determining what kind of marriage—there are five models to choose from—I had before I got divorced: Was it the Pursuer-Distancer Marriage? (It's "the most common type," Hetherington observes, and "also the most divorce-prone.") Or was it the Disengaged Marriage? Such mar-riages, which have a high failure rate, may drift along for years before finally ending, "with a whimper rather than a bang." I suppose the description of the Operatic Marriage comes closest, given a certain volatility of temperament that my ex-husband and I shared, but, unlike Hetherington's sample couple, we never smashed shiny new kitchen cabinets with a hammer, screaming, "I'll show you ugly!" and then went on to have explosive sex. ("For Operatics, quarreling often is a trigger for sex. Indeed, passionate lovemaking follows furious fighting . . . routinely.") I glimpse ingredients of my marriage everywhere, not excluding a dash of the Cohesive/Individuated Marriage (the cultural ideal for baby boomers, combining "gender equity" and old-fashioned intimacy) and two level teaspoons of the Traditional Marriage (breadwinner man and homemaker woman—which turns out, disconcertingly, to be the stablest arrangement of them all).

Even worse, I seem unable to locate myself on the continuum of "postdivorce adaptive styles." Once again, there are a number of floor models to choose from. I study Hetherington's six cate-gories closely, hoping to place somewhere not too inglorious between the "divorce winners" (also referred to as "success-ful changers") and the abject losers. Front and center are the Enhancers; members of this group, mostly women, actually thrive after their marriages collapse, taking on a previously unsuspected aura of authority and competence—"a quiet gravitas." Then, there are the Good Enoughs, who are the most typical among the divorced; though "less resilient" than Enhancers, they stumble along as well as they can. Two other categories—the Seekers and the Libertines—are, as you might guess, predominantly male. Seekers are made uneasy by the single life; without a wife to "supply validation," they exhibit sexual problems and signs of depression. (Hetherington intrepidly tails her subjects right up to the bedroom keyhole, noting that, "after divorce, a number of men in the group became vulnerable to erectile dysfunction for the first time.") Seekers nudge everyone they know to fix them up and tend to remarry relatively quickly. Libertines, on the other hand, act like college kids on spring break, turning to drink, drugs, and casual sex to allay their self-doubts, but within a year most of them, too, have begun to look for long-term relationships.

The remaining two styles—the Competent Loner and the Defeated—sound equally dispiriting, but Hetherington insists that the Competent Loner represents a "divorce winner" every bit as much as the Enhancer. Members of this group are generally not interested in remarrying; they have their jobs, friends, and hobbies to keep them warm. (I envision such people as having the admirable but slightly irritating resourcefulness that goes along with compulsively organized CD collections.) Although these self-sufficient folk make up only 10 percent of the study's sample population, their influence should not be underestimated; Hetherington points out that they may be "a harbinger of things to come," given the divorce rate, the general delay in marriage, and the steep rise in cohabitation (a living arrangement that portends badly for an enduring marriage).

Finally, down where no light shines, live the mole people known as the Defeated. This designation might seem self-evident, but Hetherington is determined to provide the grim details, perhaps by way of a cautionary example. She describes the history of a "mild-mannered" college professor named Walter who left his wife to marry a scheming and seductive babysitter and was, in turn, dumped for a SoHo artist: "Alone, he became deeply depressed, ignored his appearance, was unprepared for classes, saw less and less of his children, and spent most of his free time staring at the television set, smoking dope, or drinking." And there he stayed: "At the twenty-year follow-up, Walter was still single, still depressed, and still Defeated."

I'm no Walter, but clearly my postdivorce adaptive style leaves a lot to be desired. I am, if truth be told, looking for a narrative to call my own, something to help me explain why I am lingering on the stage set of life after the curtain has come down and the other players have married or died. Marriage and death have always been the two paradigmatic endings in Western culture, which raises the question of how to make sense of the havoc represented by divorce, as either an end or a beginning. Perhaps divorce is a way of living two lives for the price of one. Surely this is what the social historian Lawrence Stone had in mind when he noted that the remarriage rate in the seventeenth century was similar to that of today, with divorce replacing death as its precondition: "Indeed, it looks very much as if modern divorce is little more than a functional substitute for death. The decline of the adult mortality rate after the late eighteenth century, by prolonging the expected duration of marriage to unprecedented lengths, eventually forced Western society to adopt the institutional escape-hatch of divorce."

The implications of his argument are not entirely consoling: Was divorce my reward for not dying in childbirth? And although the historian does not address the small matter of what to do after one has escaped the institution, it seems almost a foregone conclusion that one will try to decode the experience by referring back to the original script. Marriage, that is, impels one to remarriage, if only because there seems no other way to correct the narrative rupture that is divorce.

On the other hand, it may already be too late for me to get back in the game. "Of all the divorce statistics I read," Wendy Swallow writes in *Breaking Apart: A Memoir of Divorce*, "the one I hated the most stated that if a woman was going to remarry after being divorced, she would do so in the first four years. After that, the odds went way down." Although it may seem obvious that age is a big factor in the social life of women after divorce, given that it is an important factor *before* divorce, Hetherington has put in a lot of research time to reach the same conclusion. Indeed, she pronounces on the issue as though she had just retrieved it from an overlooked file: "Women who were in their late thirties or older at the time of divorce had fewer dating opportunities than younger women or middle-aged men. At the twenty-year follow-up, they were much less likely to have remarried."

Now, in one of those clear-eyed moments that invariably hit after midnight, I see the future rising up before me, bringing loneliness and ruin, and marking me as a divorce loser. At this point, I'll take any postdivorce style that will have me: perhaps I could audition as a Competent Loner by polishing up my cooking skills, improving my Hints from Heloise laundry acumen, and keeping my desk neater. (Competent Loners, both male and female, are good homemakers.) Before falling asleep, I try to imagine myself as Mary McKay, an Enhancer who in six years went from being a "desperate humiliated woman" worried about paying her next bill to being a savvy entrepreneur with her own catering business. In your dreams, as they say.

The prevailing wisdom on divorce—and specifically the nature of its effect on children—has, like other cultural attitudes, changed along with the times. Do divorced but happier parents make for happier children, as was once thought, or is even a contentious but intact marriage better for children, as the more recent line of thinking has it? As the research has piled up over the past several decades, with recantations and modifications following each new finding, one senses that divorce has come to be a leading cultural indicator, the locus for a whole cluster of our anxieties about everything from sex to death.

Or it may be that I am hopelessly dating myself by the intensity with which I approach the subject: perhaps, for the generation coming up, it will be just another rite of passage to be navigated, like getting one's first job. I am referring to the marital micro-trend known as starter marriages. Such blitzkrieg unions are, their enthusiasts tell us, all the rage; they last five years at most, are childless, and are usually over and done with before either partner reaches thirty. In a book called *The Starter Marriage and the Future of Matrimony*, Pamela Paul predicts that these sped-up scenarios are the wavelet of the immediate future. "People will slide wedding bands on and off," she reports, "with the same ease with which they whip out updated résumés." There is no doubt that she is onto something marketable: herself a starter-marriage survivor—in the glittering company of Drew Barrymore, Uma Thurman, and Angelina Jolie—Paul has already appeared on the *Today* show. She insists that this kind of marriage is entered into with expectations of permanence. All the same, a starter marriage sounds suspiciously like a starter apartment: a provisional arrangement, a necessary first step on the road to a more gratifying marital habitation—one with a top-of-the-line kitchen and a river view.

Divorce, then, isn't what it used to be: the exotic condition of the daring and the derelict. There were, for instance, no more than two or three divorced families in my class when I graduated from high school, in 1971; it was a rare enough occurrence to merit, if not quite a cover-up, then a hushed-voice treatment. As an adolescent, I was struck by the domestic setup portrayed in the original version of the movie *The Parent Trap*, which features a divorced couple who live in different states and are the parents of identical-twin daughters (played by Hayley Mills), who meet for the first time at summer camp. When the movie came out, in 1961, it appeared risqué and modern even as it reaffirmed the shimmering ideal of the nuclear family. Of course, the film was really about marriage, not divorce; its fantasy ending of a blissful reunion suggested that, with just a little more understanding and consideration, all marital squabbles could be resolved.

Soon enough, though, this tranquil cinematic image dissolved to a more fractious social landscape. The traditional view of marriage as a social contract based on a civic-minded ethic of duty to others began to loosen its hold sometime during the Swinging Sixties. Whereas for Tennessee Williams's Big Daddy "truth is pain and sweat and paying bills and making love to a woman that you don't love anymore," a younger generation foraged for truth within its overscrutinized psyche. A new ethic stressed an individualistic duty to self, which was encouraged by the growing influence of psychotherapeutic values. People were urged to look to marriage for inner satisfaction—and, naturally, they mostly failed to find it.

The real boost to what Barbara Dafoe Whitehead, in her book *The Divorce Culture*, calls the "sad business of marital dissolution" arrived roughly with the Beatles, when it was discovered that all anyone needed was love and that obligations—including those toward one's children—could go take care of themselves. Any economic and psychological harm to women and children was serenely overlooked, and, with the passage of the first no-fault divorce law, in 1969, in California (a state, fittingly, with a divorced governor), this song of the self grew louder. The imperative to keep a strained marriage afloat "for the sake of the children" morphed into an imperative to end a strained marriage for the sake of the adults—and, it was blithely assumed, for the greater happiness of the offspring involved. This liberating, 1970s view was reflected in books with titles such as *The Courage to Divorce* and *Creative Divorce: A New Opportunity for Personal Growth*. In *The Future of Marriage*, the sociologist Jessie Bernard went so far as to declare that a woman had to be "slightly ill mentally" in order to suffer the indignities of a traditional marriage.

In the 1980s, an inevitable backlash started. We began to hear about the punctured self-esteem of the "maritally challenged" children of divorce. These worries, in turn, meshed with the more conservative climate of the Reagan years to create a revisionist perspective—what might be called the new stoicism—according to which a bad marriage was seen as ultimately less pernicious for children than divorce. Finally, there was the publication, in 1989, of the bestselling *Second Chances*, by the clinical psychologist Judith Wallerstein. After studying sixty families in the Bay Area, she arrived at gloomy and guilt-inducing conclusions about the damage suffered by children of divorce. The book, which is anecdotal and impressionistic in character, offered the most effective challenge to the meliorist view of the previous decade. From these disparate trends, a new consensus was joined together.

In time, it was put asunder as well. Wallerstein was widely

faulted for her failure to use a control group: she interviewed mopey, disgruntled children from divorced homes but didn't compare them with children from intact families, many of whom are, of course, mopey and disgruntled, too. And then there was the question of self-selection. Parents who volunteered for the study may have been drawn by the offer of free clinical treatment. A disproportionate number—around 50 percent—were seriously disturbed; in the first write-up of her research, *Surviving the Breakup* (1980), Wallerstein described them as "chronically depressed, sometimes suicidal individuals, men and women with severe neurotic difficulties." Another 15 to 20 percent had even more extreme problems. As Andrew J. Cherlin, a sociologist at Johns Hopkins, has pointed out, "Troubled parents often raise troubled children."

Given that Wallerstein based her findings on repeated personal interviews, one has to wonder, too, about the way preconceptions shape perceptions. Researchers have found, for instance, that schoolteachers who watch a videotape of an eight-year-old boy are more likely to conclude that he has adjustment problems when they are told his parents are divorced. We see, in short, what we expect to find. In Wallerstein's most recent opus, *The Unexpected Legacy of Divorce: A 25 Year Landmark Study*, co-written with Julia M. Lewis and Sandra Blakeslee, and published in 2000, she shifted her focus to the delayed impact of marital breakup: her somewhat troubled children have become even more troubled adults, who have difficulty entering into and sustaining marriages of their own. Though this time she made an effort to consult a comparison group, one isn't entirely surprised to learn that, say, the statistics about second-generation divorce rates don't fully support her doom-ridden pronouncements. The continuing popularity of her arguments among conservative commentators suggests that, in the Kulturkampf over divorce, children have, willy-nilly, become conscripts—ideological proxies in Pumas and Petit Bateau T-shirts.

It is plainly as an antidote to Wallerstein, who remains the most influential of the divorce theorists, that Hetherington advances a cheerier assessment: that the majority of the children of divorce—75 to 80 percent—do surprisingly well. "Most of the young men and women from my divorced families," she declares, "looked a lot like their contemporaries from non-divorced homes." As in all such wobbly but firmly stated arguments, little weight is given to the countervailing facts she has collected: that a significantly higher percentage of children from divorced families than from non-divorced ones—25 percent, as opposed to 10—had serious adaptive difficulties, and that it took six years for "the cloud of anxiety and depression that hung over children in the first year" to disperse.

From Hetherington's perspective, every bump is a boost. Indeed, she can sound unsettlingly like a Chinese fortune cookie: "Don't focus on the past, focus on the future." As long as you have "competent-caring" children—Hetherington even offers a typology for the children of divorce—your marital breakup will leave them adept at conflict resolution and sensitive to the emotional needs of their peers. "Coping with the challenges of divorce and life in a single-parent family seems actually to enhance the ability of some children to deal with future stresses," she writes. These scenarios may be less slaphappy than those of the 1970s liberationists, but one gets the feeling that for Hetherington, no less than for Wallerstein, empirical research has become something of an Easter-egg hunt, where you find only what you've already planted.

It's hard to sustain the faith that social science will guide us toward any deep wisdom about marriage and divorce. Too often, it seems, the rhetoric of rigor conceals an impassioned agenda. And the acrimonious claims and counterclaims can reproduce the atmosphere of a divorce court as petitioners battle for custody of the truth. Maybe that's why in the past several years the vicissitudes of marriage have been taken up more convincingly by memoirists and essayists, who eschew the realm of mutating statistics and tendentious conclusions for the open acceptance of bewilderment. The only certitude they offer is that one person will feel guilty about leaving and the other person will feel humiliated at being left. The precipitating cause is often, but not always, sexual faithlessness, and betrayed wives still seem more the norm than cuckolded husbands.

Catherine Texier's *Breakup*, an anguished chronicle of the final year in a tumultuous eighteen-year marriage—her husband leaves her for his book editor—is a case in point. The narrator flails about, trying to figure out when and why "our little world of the two of us" fell apart, setting down her feelings of rage and pain, her bemused sense that she has wandered into the wrong movie, the overworked genre of the woman scorned: "I sit down on the bed next to you and ask you the classic question (we are back in the bad screenplay, uttering tired clichés): are you having an affair?" She experiences her suffering as inevitably compromised by the fact that she's seen this picture before: "Some women lacerate the guy's best suits with a razor blade, cut up his boxers to shreds. I visualize pouring bleach all over your Agnès b. shirts. Streaking your Armani and Hugo Boss jackets with Day-Glo paint."

The narrator of John Taylor's memoir, *Falling*, appears, by contrast, too stony, and his side of the story too convenient, by his own admission. All the same, his book offers a rare glimpse into the maelstrom of feelings that divorce elicits in the less emotionally articulate sex, as well as a demystifying look at the time-honored strategy of "compartmentalization" that men purportedly resort to in order to deal with conflict. "As complications branched out in my life, as my approach to my marriage became more dutiful and formal, I decided that the theory of the unified personality was a fiction," Taylor writes. "I subscribed instead to the Japanese theory of the masks of life: the mask of the father, the mask of the husband, the mask of the employee." The book is compelling precisely because Taylor makes no attempt to airbrush out the incriminating details, including the fact that his wife developed Parkinson's disease during the course of their eleven-year marriage. In one scene, set in the office of the therapist of a woman he is having an affair with, he rationalizes his behavior: "I didn't want to leave my wife and child, I said. I felt I had a duty to support them, particularly in light of my wife's condition. On the other hand, I didn't see the point of remaining faithful. In a loveless marriage it seemed an exercise in futility." But only a few pages later, while on a picturesque summer vacation with his wife and daughter, the narrator seems genuinely baffled at finding himself stuck in a deadened marriage, kept alive only by the "excuse" of shared parentship. The dilemma is no doubt an age-old one; what makes this a book of our time is the lack of shame in the recounting.

In Arnold Bennett's 1906 novel *Whom God Hath Joined*, a woman who starts a legal action to divorce her adulterous husband finds him reaching for the moral upper hand:

> "You *must* think of the children," he insisted, with a pathetic air of wisdom and authority [. . .]
> "It will cling to them all their lives," said he.
> "What will cling to them all their lives?"
> "The scandal of the action—if you let it go on."

His wife is undeterred. "People like you are apt to give too much importance to scandal," she tells him. "I've thought a good deal about the scandal, and it seems to me that it will only be like an illness. It will cure itself."

But has the cure—the social acceptability of divorce—given rise to an even graver illness? That's essentially James Q. Wilson's argument in *The Marriage Problem: How Our Culture Has Weakened Families*. As feminists and other misguided sophisticates have given the no-fault divorce cultural as well as legal currency, he maintains, they've only led their less privileged fellow citizens into the mire. What seemed advanced and adventurous in Marin County yields misery and mayhem in South Central L.A. Wilson wants us to consider the civic consequences of our faddish allegiances. "Our society has managed to stigmatize stigma so much so that we are reluctant to blame people for any act that does not appear to inflict an immediate and palpable harm on someone else," he writes. "We wrongly suppose, I think, that shame is the enemy of personal emancipation when in fact an emancipated man or woman is one for whom inner control is sufficiently powerful to produce inner limits on actions that once were controlled by external forces." Except that shame *is* an external force; pretty much by definition, it's a social sanction, not a psychological barrier. The sanctimonious philanderer of Bennett's novel was correct in identifying his wife's petition for a divorce, rather than his own affair with the governess, as the scandal.

Whatever Wilson's overreachings or Wallerstein's methodological weaknesses, though, the new stoics get one thing right. Divorce has very little to recommend it. Aside from the disorienting upheaval in a familiar if not necessarily blissful way of life, a divorce, especially if it involves children, often leaves bloodshed in its wake. The ferocious wranglings that catch the media's attention tend to have mega millions at stake and frequently hinge on surreal demands for child support. But I would guess that few divorces manage to avoid a hostile atmosphere, marked by petty and vengeful impulses: the sums may be smaller, but the bitterness is not.

In the end, I don't think there is any way of getting around the failure that divorce represents; however confused our sense of direction, our children want the old, linear plotline. Despite our wish to suspend narrow judgments of what constitutes a normal family, children are inherently conservative. They love the reassurance to be found in not breaking the mold, and they cling to an idyllic and intransigent image of family life. In this enchanted version, it is always a spring day some time before the divorce revolution, in some suburb where the neighbors are friendly behind their white picket fences and where kids sit down to a home-cooked dinner every night with two parents, one male and one female. Grown-ups, meanwhile, long ago consigned this picture to the dustbin of nostalgia for what probably never was. How sweet, we tell our children. How fake, we tell ourselves.

I imagine that my daughter is fairly typical in her eagerness to divest herself of all traces of credulous innocence. She exhibits a precocious—if somewhat abstract—sophistication about what she refers to as "issues" (having mostly to do with sex), gleaned from her ardent watching of *Dawson's Creek* and *Ally McBeal*. She also likes to watch *Gilmore Girls*, which follows the small-town adventures of a ditzy unwed mother and her sober, goal-oriented daughter. You would think that all this exposure to irregular domestic arrangements would have helped reconcile her to her own situation. And perhaps it has. But she is also a closet fan of *7th Heaven*, in which a large, intact, and over-relating family have their misunderstandings but never forget that they love each other. For that matter, *The Parent Trap* has held up surprisingly well over the years, winning over an entirely new audience with the 1998 remake.

I don't delude myself that the traumatic effect of the divorce on my daughter will ever entirely vanish. Children have long memories, and my daughter seems to have an elephantine retention of the details leading up to the breakup of my marriage. She was not yet four when my ex-husband and I separated, yet she insists that she can vividly recall climbing up on the black chaise in the living room of our old apartment to kiss her father good night during the transitional period when he and I were sleeping under the same roof but not in the same bed. Although the passage of time has weakened her hopes of a magical ending, and for months at a time it seems as though she has accepted the reality of our parting, she can become wistful at a moment's notice.

What is hardest for her is being at family gatherings with my five siblings (none of whom is divorced, in defiance of the statistics) and her multitude of first cousins. A few months ago, on a Sunday night when we had come back from one such gathering, we lay on my bed talking. Somehow or other, she brought the conversation around to her father. He wasn't really the business type, she mused; perhaps he should have remained in California and pursued his artistic calling instead of moving to New York to try his hand at the stock market. I pointed out that if he hadn't moved to New York, he and I would never have met and we wouldn't have had her, but she wasn't buying my logic. Instead came her *j'accuse*: Why, she wanted to know, had I married her father in the first place? It wasn't a demand so much as a plea for coherence. She listened patiently to my jumbled explanation, and I remember thinking that I sounded exactly like the mother on *Gilmore Girls*. Before falling asleep, she clutched at her old fantasy as though it were a stuffed animal she had outgrown but still occasionally needed to hold. Did I think, she inquired just as her eyes were closing, there was any chance that her father and I would get married to each other again?

BRILLIANT MONSTERS

(V. S. NAIPAUL)

2008

It is a truth insufficiently acknowledged that those whom the gods grant special gifts often also get stuck with neurotic difficulties up the kazoo. Behind many great men peek long-suffering wives or abused mistresses, and sometimes both at once. (Great women are generally no picnic, either.) The jagged relations between unusually talented men and the women in their lives are especially intriguing to us—if only because they tend to unspool like an extreme version of the power plays and shady maneuverings that go on in all intimate pairings. The discrepancies and imbalances in the weaknesses and strengths of the partners in these unions are easier to make out because their bond so often exists in a collusive—or, as the tired vernacular has it, codependent—form.

There is, in other words, an enduring symbiosis, a match of pathologies lying just beneath the surface. The uncomfortable truth is that victimizers need willing victims, and serial seducers who happen to be married (their name is legion) require wives or companions who bear up with two-timing or ill-treatment because of their own needs. The list of writers who have killed their wives softly while producing their art includes Charles Dickens, Thomas Carlyle, and Leo Tolstoy. There are many more cases where those came from, and each of them tells us in its own way about the compromises and bartering that go on in most marriages.

The revelations that appear in Patrick French's superb authorized biography, *The World Is What It Is*, concerning the Nobel
Prize–winning writer V. S. Naipaul's often brutal behavior toward his wife and his mistress have aroused fascination and horror. But for anyone who has even sampled Naipaul's prolific work
(twenty-seven books in all) and is familiar with his dispassionate,
witheringly judgmental, and adamantly politically incorrect views,
the cold, hard facts don't come as a total shock. In both his early
fiction (*A House for Mr. Biswas*; *The Mystic Masseur*) and his
innovative historical and global reportage (*The Middle Passage*;
A Turn in the South), there has always been a cruel streak as well
as a great melancholy. One has the sense that Naipaul writes
with a wounded pen, as if his psychic life depends on it, and because the void—the "spiritual emptiness" he refers to in his most
recent book, *A Writer's People*—is never far off.

Naipaul transcends genres and fashions prose that is piercingly
insightful and never effete; he has scant use for borrowed ideas or
the clanking apparatus of theory, whether he is responding pre-
sciently to the rise of Islamic fundamentalism (*Among the Believers*; *Beyond Belief*) or the fate of newly independent African
countries (*A Bend in the River*; *In a Free State*), preferring to rely
instead on a kaleidoscopic approach, a constantly shifting pattern
of finely tuned responses. He has an unparalleled ability to imagine his way into other people's shoes yet has always made a point of
slashing at fools of every stripe without regard for their feelings.
Indeed, his take on the world seems to alternate between bleak
and bleaker, veering off for light relief into rage.

It would be difficult, then, to imagine a man this complex,
intense, and solipsistic leading a happy home life with the wife
and kids, inviting the relatives over for Christmas Eve dinner, or
shoveling the snow. Still, the extent to which Naipaul's existence
has been a tortured and torturing one, per French's account, is
eye-opening, moving us to wonder: Why do artistic gifts seem to
come at such a high relational cost? When does playing the muse,
the hovering and ever-facilitating female presence, mutate into
something more psychologically disturbing? Does the proximity
to fame compensate at all for the pain and humiliation of such

relationships? Would Naipaul's first wife and his mistress have been happier had they never met him, or were they both in their own ways doomed to a downward trajectory? And, perhaps less obviously, does a roller-coaster ride of intimate relations offer a life of excitement that may mask deeper questions and qualms about one's existence?

Brilliant monster that he may be, it is all the more to Naipaul's credit that he consented to sit for this shadow-filled portrait in the first place, providing access to his archives as well as talking openly to his biographer. "Of all the people I spoke to for this book," French notes, "he was outwardly the frankest," adding that he had "no direction or restriction" from his subject. Naipaul in turn read the manuscript and returned it without changes. Most writers go to great lengths to keep their images free from tarnish, either by hand selecting an authorized biographer, as Philip Roth did, or by dismissing a too inquiring or critical investigator, as J. D. Salinger did with Ian Hamilton. It says a lot about Naipaul's passion for truth telling—as distinct from his much-commented-upon passion for self-aggrandizement—that he agreed to this enterprise.

Vidiadhar Surajprasad Naipaul—known as Vido as a boy and Vidia as an adult to those who were close to him, or who wished to be (such as Paul Theroux, who exhumed his long, unrequited romance with Naipaul in *Sir Vidia's Shadow*)—is a pioneer of postcolonial writing. The second of seven children, he was born in 1932 into rural poverty on the polyglot island of Trinidad. His Hindu parents were part of the wave of bonded Indian laborers brought to work on sugar plantations after slavery ended. (Naipaul would later claim to be of Brahman descent, but this point of pride has never been verified.) He grew up in a matriarchy: his powerful grandmother moved her offspring like chess pieces around the family compounds, none of them grand—for a time, his family lived in servants' quarters with a roof of corrugated iron and branches—and his strong, proud mother was determined that her children be properly educated and rise above their beginnings.

Despite the fact that Vido's father, Seepersad, was largely

absent for the first six years of the boy's life, he was the biggest
influence on his son's identity. Having escaped the fate of a rural
laborer in India, Seepersad had taught himself to read and
write—he was an admirer of O. Henry and Somerset Maugham—
and became a reporter for the *Trinidad Guardian*. "Pa and
Vido," French tells us, "positioned themselves in an ordered fantasy world derived from European literature, far from the noise,
squalor and their own powerlessness in Petit Valley." As fragile as
his wife was tough, Seepersad suffered a breakdown when he was
criticized for writing about the superstitions of rural Indians.
Naipaul recalls his mother's explanation of his father's condition:
"He looked in the mirror one day and couldn't see himself. And
he began to scream." Seepersad eventually recovered enough to
write an accomplished story collection, and Naipaul drew on the
memory and literary passion of his father, who died in 1953, to
forge himself into becoming a writer; his breakthrough novel, *A
House for Mr. Biswas*, was a tribute to him.

In 1950, having won a scholarship to Oxford, Naipaul set out
for a country "that had been presented to him as the epicentre of
civilization." Although he did well academically, he suffered from
loneliness, penury, and a palpable sense of the racial prejudice
lurking in the "cliquey, smirking, undergraduate atmosphere."
Adrift and depressed, Naipaul met a slim, pretty undergraduate,
Patricia Hale, who was reading history at a women's college. She,
too, was from a humble background and had reached Oxford on
scholarship. Both of them were ardently literary, manifestly shy,
and sexually repressed. They slept together for the first time seven
months after they met; Naipaul assessed their early sexual encounters as "fumbling and awful for both of us. Pat was very
nervous. I wasn't trained enough or skilled enough or talented
enough to calm her nerves, probably because I didn't want to calm
her nerves. It didn't work."

Sex between them would never work—not through forty
years of a troubled and faithless (on Naipaul's side) union, in
which Pat played nursemaid and amanuensis while he failed to so
much as acknowledge her existence in even his most personal
writings, such as his autobiographical novel *The Enigma of Arrival*.

Although Pat envisioned a shining future before the two twenty-two-year-olds were married in January 1955—"I am convinced that we are going to be a distinguished couple"—the auguries were there before they tied the knot. Within months of their meeting, Naipaul, ever the snob, patronizingly quizzed Pat, who had taken elocution lessons to get rid of her Midlands accent, on her pronunciation of the word "bourgeois" and inquired as to whether she might have it in her to lend her correspondence a touch of eroticism. "I do wish," he wrote, "you could make your letters really 'lurid.'" The chances for bawdiness were next to none, given that Pat referred to a bra as "the garment I dislike mentioning."

The pattern for their marriage was set when Naipaul failed to produce a wedding ring, an oversight Pat piteously protested months later. "I do feel the lack of a ring very acutely," she wrote to him. "You did promise & I will think you don't quite realise how 'odd' it seems to people." (She ended up buying herself a plain gold band, which went mostly unworn.) When he wasn't ignoring her, leaving her with little money as he journeyed alone—or, eventually, with his longtime mistress—Naipaul was irked by Pat's self-abnegating presence. "Don't shout at me," she once told him. "There is no one in the whole world besides me who takes you really seriously." He began visiting prostitutes in 1958, which was one of the few seamy secrets he kept from Pat. Later, he would readily confide in her about his stormy affair with Margaret Gooding, a married Anglo-Argentine woman ten years his junior, seemingly unaware of the pain he was causing his wife. "She was so good: she tried to comfort me," he commented in his journal. "I was so full of grief myself that in a way I expected her to respond to my grief, and she did."

The question that nags as one reads French's biography is why Pat didn't have it in her to leave Naipaul. She had been capable early on of standing up to his demands of "one-sided submission," as she described them. Indeed, it took a great deal of nerve on her part to stick with Vidia, since her father was adamantly against her marrying a "wog." But over the decades, Pat's life turned into one long, heartrendingly servile performance. "Pat treated him with great reverence," noted one of their few mutual friends. "It was almost like appreciating a deity. She was awed by him, and I think it made it difficult for her because she was aware that she had to do her bit to encourage the flowering of his talents . . . She was a very Indian wife in many respects—more Indian than most Indian wives."

Naipaul would go on to bear the aura of the great man Pat had always taken him to be (in her notebooks she called him "the Genius"), becoming ever more "tetchy" and "pompous" in the process. He gained a prize-bedecked reputation in England and then a more international one as his books were translated into Greek, Serbo-Croatian, and Hebrew, culminating in his Nobel Prize in Literature in 2001.

Naipaul's first real carnal pleasure came when he was forty, with Margaret Gooding; their relationship was passionate but rapidly became sadomasochistic. "The cruelty was part of the attraction," French writes, "which had the effect of stepping up the cruelty." At one point, as Naipaul recalled, Margaret "was having a relationship with [a] banker for the means to get to me . . . I was extremely upset . . . I was very violent with her for two days with my hand; my hand began to hurt . . . She didn't mind it at all. She thought of it in terms of my passion for her. Her face was bad. She couldn't appear really in public. My hand was swollen. I was utterly helpless."

The triangle continued for two decades. Naipaul toyed with leaving his wife, but in the end, although Margaret left her husband and children for him, he remained married to Pat. The couple had long since retreated to separate bedrooms, and Pat scrambled to find a place for herself, literally and metaphorically. When they moved in February 1982, Pat "recorded her tentative, shamed efforts to carve out a space for herself in Naipaul's new house. 'He asked: Would I be moving out again soon? . . . I made a bedroom for myself in the little pink room, Vidia settled himself in the red.'"

Pat dabbled in journalism, researched *Love Letters: An Anthology* (irony of ironies) for Antonia Fraser, dutifully took dictation from Naipaul, and accompanied him on trips that he "summoned" her to be on "in imperative terms" to take Margaret's place. Naipaul treated both Pat and Margaret more like schoolgirls than like grown women; they were always being "dismissed" or "sent away" by him when they transgressed or simply got on his delicate nerves. "I have behaved foolishly all day," Pat remarked in her notebook, enthralled by her own abjection, "and have ruined every last relationship I have. I have agreed to go back to London after the weekend. Vidia says he can't stand my eccentricity any more and I will destroy him."

The human wreckage in this judicious and keenly observant biography keeps piling up, with the three damaged people at its center suggesting just how right the poet W. H. Auden was when he described the desires of the heart as being "crooked as corkscrews." In 1994, Naipaul's predilection for engaging with prostitutes when he was younger was revealed in an interview in *The New Yorker*. This having been the one malfeasance he had not discussed cozily with the all-accepting Pat, she—already ill with breast cancer—received this further "insult to her status as his loving wife" very badly. In 1995, Naipaul, leaving a seriously ill Pat behind, flew to South Asia to start *Beyond Belief*, his second look at the rise of Islamist ideology. While in Pakistan, he met a brash forty-two-year-old newspaper columnist who wrote under the byline Nadira. They clicked immediately, and before he left— Pat not yet dead and Margaret crossed off the list without being informed—Naipaul asked Nadira if she would one day consider becoming "Lady Naipaul."

Pat, who had largely disappeared into herself, tranquilized and disconnected, died on February 3, 1996, at age sixty-three, leaving Naipaul at a loss: "Having spent a lifetime shunning friends, he had no network of support." Her cremation was attended by a small group of mourners, with no readings, music, or addresses. Naipaul married Nadira that April in a tiny ceremony; Margaret would learn of her existence from the newspapers. On a Saturday in October 1996, Naipaul and Nadira scattered Pat's ashes in the countryside near their home. Nadira walked into the woods, alone, and said a Muslim prayer for Pat. French's biography closes on a wrenching note, the anguish seeping out between the carefully composed sentences: "Nadira walked back, out of the woods. V. S. Naipaul, the writer, Vidyadhar, the boy, Vidia, the man, was leaning against the car, tears streaming down his face, lost for words."

DO I OWN YOU NOW?

2011

Girls in their summer dresses we all know about, but what about boys in their summer bathing trunks? Him, in particular, his long-legged body, not hideously six-packed in the current style, but elegantly constructed—beautiful even, in an antelope kind of way. His smooth olive-toned skin tanned to an almost non-Caucasian pitch, and my own much lighter skin burnished to a red brown by incessant and patient exposure. He always wore the plainest of suits, black or navy, not a man to take sartorial chances—or risks of any sort, really, except in bed, where he kept leading me forward, closer to the precipice, that moment where you drop off the boundary of your own precarious identity and into someone else's terrain.

"Do I own you now?" he used to ask me breathlessly after some particularly entwined bout of lovemaking. Neither of us tended to speak much during sex, except for his habit of punctuating the silence with cursory yet infinitely flattering statements like "Someone should bottle you" after he rose up from nuzzling me below. So the ownership question came out with the force of a mission statement, one I signed off on. That summer at least, he owned me. What was the point in pretending otherwise?

Who can forget a summer swimming in sex? Even now, far from those days and that sort of abandon, I have only to conjure up that time, more than three decades ago, to feel cramped with longing, something dropping deep inside me. That was also the

summer I was introduced to a kind of sex I hadn't yet let myself
in for, either because it wasn't available or because I wasn't.
Nothing to do with nipple clamps or threesomes or licking honey
off a prone and naked body—none of that would have appealed
to me then, as it doesn't now. No, it had to do with the way he
took forever about gliding himself into me and the way he pushed
me into new positions, and new submissions as well, not overtly
of the S&M kind, but with a subtext that always hovered around
the issue of power, intimating at the unspoken questions *How
much do you want this?* and *What are you willing to do for it?*

I can still recall, as though it happened the day before yesterday, walking out of the ocean that Saturday, aware of his
studiously pretending not to watch me from where he lay on his
towel, conscious of the way the brief dip had made my already
conspicuous nipples stand out and the way my wet, slicked-back
hair brought out the angles of my face. That was the summer my
body was ripe for the taking in a black one-piece; I've always preferred the subtle eroticism of a one-piece to the soft porn of a
bikini, but sometimes I wonder if these were the kinds of prefer-
ences that drew us apart in the first place. That, and his wish to
torture me—not in a good, tantalizing way (although he did that
well too), but in a steely, withholding style that made me feel
madly in need of sustenance, like a hungry baby groping for a
nipple. For a while, I was willing to do anything. Bend over with
my head on the bed and my ass high in the air so that he could
stick his finger way up and enter me from underneath, like a ship
coming into its berth, filling me out perfectly.

I liked that part of my body paid attention to, stroked, warmed
in preparation for what would come next. I also liked that neither
of us saw the other's face, which is often taken to be intrinsically
demeaning and developmentally arrested but which I found to
be the best way of getting past the endlessly scrutinizing aspect
of sex. For a while after we parted (the final time we parted, I
should say, because by then parting itself had become a kind of
coming together), I would lie on my bed and try to reenact this
particular position in my mind—a monologue pretending to be a

dialogue, bent over on my bed and envisioning him entering me from behind.

He took up all the available space in my head that summer, even though I was supposed to be busy pursuing my higher literary calling. To which end I had gone off at the beginning of July to spend a month at Yaddo, the artists' colony in Saratoga Springs, New York. You had to jump through various bureaucratic hoops in order to be accepted to the place, which prided itself on its pedigreed history of guests, and I guess I should have been flattered that it took me, someone in her early twenties with only a sheaf of book reviews and two published short stories under her belt. But what hope did Yaddo have, with its mosquitoes and its self-conscious poets and networking novelists, of holding my attention when he (I'll resort to the slightly French affectation of using initials and call him JC) was back in New York City? I wanted his fingers on my breasts, his hands sliding down my body as though he were just discovering my contours all over again. I wanted him inside me or lying, exhausted by exertion, next to me as we slept.

For ten days, I went dutifully to my studio in the woods with my notes and tried to write. I think in all that time, when I wasn't lying by the pool or talking with other Yaddo residents at dinner about suitably bookish things, I managed to finish the second half of a book review I had started back in the city. Mostly, I was lost in visions of JC's playing with his rubber duckie in the bath, JC's tracing and retracing his long fingers around first one of my nipples and then the other, JC's putting his mouth on mine as if he were planning to suck the air out of me, kissing me with consuming but unslobby ardor. What was it about the tip of his penis that so moved me when he began to put it between my legs, that soft, velvety tip? This seemed far more important for me to parse than why—for the sole purpose of improving my standing in the colony's tacit but very obvious hierarchy of talent—X was so inexplicably overrated as a novelist when Y was so clearly the one with the better prose style.

On the second Friday, I gave up on the charade. I first booked a round-trip train ticket, so as not to lose my blinding sense of intention, and then explained to the writer who ran the colony with his much older (and more famous) wife that a dire family emergency had suddenly burst over the horizon and required my immediate but short-lived attendance back home. I was torn, I assured the director, about whether to go and interrupt this extraordinary opportunity to convene with the woods à la Thoreau, but I would make it as quick a stay as I could. He bought into my bald excuses with utmost grace. How was he to know that under my serious-seeming writerly self was a creature deranged by sexual longing, an updated and less provincial version of Madame Bovary, dying to escape her small-town existence and have another fling with the callous Rodolphe?

I was back in the city and in JC's low, not particularly comfortable bed by Friday evening, basking in an almost bovine sense of sexual well-being. Yet by the next day something had gone wrong: I might have said something mocking but affectionate that he took to be merely snide during the trip to Fire Island, I can't remember anymore. I only know that by the time I walked out of the ocean, we were no longer on speaking terms. JC ignored me as I settled myself back on the beach towel he had brought, and he continued to lie silently on his side of the towel, his arms folded behind his head and his eyes closed as he gave himself up to the peak rays. I lay on my stomach, staring out onto the crowded beach that seemed to shimmer in the heat, wondering why I had ever succumbed to a man who must have disliked me as much as he lusted after me right from the start.

For the next hour or two, as the afternoon grew cooler and my skin took on the crunchy texture of sand mixed with tanning cream, we continued to coexist without a word passing between us. As I wildly scrambled to find a foothold in the chaotic intermittency of JC's affections, I made several firm decisions in my head. The only one worth noting here was the decision to bring this day to a close without getting teary or angry—and then, calling on whatever lingering strength of character I had, to put JC and his bedroom skills behind me forever.

Somewhere between leaving the beach and getting on the

ferry, we started talking again. JC's relational style was to act as if nothing had ever gone awry—no icy walls put up between us— once he decided he had been punitive or distancing enough. By this point, I was so reduced by his ability to leave me behind like a used tissue that I leaped at the chance to be part of a couple again, my girlfriend to his boyfriend.

It was in this abject state that I went back to his apartment. He warmed up some uninspired leftovers, and we sat at the small half circle of a table in his minimalist studio apartment and made desultory conversation. At some point I gathered up my few remaining shreds of dignity and murmured unconvincingly that I had to make the last train back to Saratoga Springs. As if on cue, JC got up and sauntered over to his bed, which was all of a few feet away, and lay down on it. "Come over here," he said. "You don't really want to go now, do you? I bet I know what you want."

You bet he did. What's the point of fighting the insinuating nature of desire when it won't leave you alone, won't shut up until you attend to it? I walked over to the far side of JC's bed and stood there shyly, like a girl fresh off a Nebraska farm. I was wearing a long, flimsy skirt, circa the late 1970s, wondering how to move the scene forward without completely selling myself out. And then, in his deft, wordless way, he put his hand under my skirt and pulled down my underpants—not all the way, but somewhere in the vicinity of my ankles—as he continued to watch me closely.

The frenzied feeling of being hundreds of miles away from him, followed by the thwarted day at the beach, followed now by the way he seemed to coax me into my own need for him, all worked in desire's favor. "You feel so milky," he said, as he continued to keep his finger inside me. When he came inside me, smelling of Old Spice and the faintest whiff of something musky coming off his skin—he was the most excretion-less man I've ever been with, and I don't think I ever saw him sweat—it all made sense again. "Do I own you now?" he asked, as though the whole point of our tortuous dance were to corral me like some undomesticated beast and lead me on a rope into the tent he had pitched against the encroaching darkness. "Yes," I whispered, as I always did.

I returned to Yaddo the next day, but by then it was already too late to pretend I was serious about becoming part of a writerly community. I was a carnal creature at heart, looking to be taken up by someone who understood that, under my barricaded demeanor, I was bursting to open my gates to the next proprietary male. It couldn't last, of course, that kind of is-this-love-or-is-this-hate entanglement, but I swear it makes my brain smoke just to consider it all these years later.

ACKNOWLEDGMENTS

I am grateful to all the editors who've encouraged me, tweaked my prose, and tolerated my perfectionist predilections about everything from word choices to whether an em dash might make more sense than a comma. These include Tina Brown, David Remnick, Henry Finder, and Deborah Garrison at *The New Yorker*; Gerry Marzorati, Katherine Bouton, Megan Liberman, and Vera Titunik at *The New York Times Magazine*; and Stefano Tonchi at *T Magazine*. Andy Port went above and beyond the editor's role at *T*, providing laughs and comfort as well as her unerring literary instincts. Chip McGrath gave me space to write my mind at *The New York Times Book Review*. Alana Newhouse provided a receptive ear at *Tablet*, as did Lucas Whitman at *The Daily Beast* and Abigail Walch at *Vogue*. I'd also like to express my deep appreciation to Robbie Myers, Laurie Abraham, Ben Dickinson, and Anne Slowey at *Elle*.

Infinite thanks to Susan Squire, for decades of acute reading and inspired friendship. To Elaine Pfefferblit, for her discerning eye and unconditional encouragement. To Deborah Solomon, a witty co-conspirator lo these many years. To the friends who've offered various sorts of tea and sympathy: Anne Roiphe; Honor Moore; Brenda Wineapple; Dina Recanati and Michael Recanati. To Jorie Graham, for her generous advocacy; to Lev Mendes, for his intellectual enthusiasm; and to Ewa Cohen, for her nurturing presence.

This book took a long time to pound into shape and would not exist without the input of some crucial first readers—including Alice Truax and Amy Hertz—and the ministrations of a bevy of assistants over the years, including Lila Feinberg, James Williams, Aniella Perold, and Sophia Harvey. My current assistant, Kristin Steele, has been invaluable in getting the book off my desk and to my publisher. Dan Simon of Seven Stories Press was the first supporter of this collection.

I am also indebted to Markus Hoffman, my exemplary agent; to Ileene Smith, my steadfast and sage editor at Farrar, Straus and Giroux; to Lottchen Shivers, for helping to spread the word; to John Knight, for all his assistance; and to Jonathan Galassi, for putting a writer's roof over my head.

Last but very much not least, this book would not have come into being without the support and encouragement of my daughter, Zoë, and of M.P.—both of whom, in their different ways, keep me going.